(Marks noted @
the Center Rfs. mcy
4/5/17)

ELTON

ELTON
Made in England

JUDY PARKINSON

MICHAEL O'MARA BOOKS LIMITED

For RMP

First published in Great Britain in 2003 by
Michael O'Mara Books Limited
9 Lion Yard, Tremadoc Road
London sw4 7nq

A CIP catalogue record for this book is available from the British Library

ISBN 1-85479-314-4

1 3 5 7 9 10 8 6 4 2

www.mombooks.com

Designed and typeset by Martin Bristow

Printed and bound in England by The Bath Press, Bath

Photograph Acknowledgments:

Page 1: Richard Young/Rex Features; pages 2–3: Pictures supplied by and copyright of Edna
Dwight. (A donation was made to the British Heart Foundation for the use of these images);
page 4 (top): Mitchell Gerber/Corbis UK Ltd; page 4 (bottom): Rex Features; page 5 (top):
Richard Young/Rex Features; page 5 (bottom): Dennis Stone/Rex Features; page 6 (top):
Rex Features; page 6 (bottom): Sygma/Corbis UK Ltd; page 7 (top): Press Association; page 7
(bottom): Bettmann/Corbis UK Ltd; page 8 (both): Rex Features; page 9: Bettmann/Corbis
UK Ltd; page 10 (top): David Dagley/Rex Features; page 10 (bottom): Neal Preston/Corbis UK
Ltd; page 11 (top): Neal Preston/Corbis UK Ltd; page 11 (bottom): Rex Features; page 12 (top):
Richard Young/Rex Features; page 12 (bottom): Bettmann/Corbis UK Ltd; page 13 (top):
Ray Tang/Rex Features; page 13 (bottom): Richard Young/Rex Features; page 14 (top): Richard
Young/Rex Features; page 14 (bottom): Sygma/Corbis UK Ltd; page 15 (top): John McCoy/
Los Angeles Daily News/Sygma/Corbis UK Ltd; page 15 (bottom): Sygma/Corbis UK Ltd;
page 16 (top): Sygma/Corbis UK Ltd; page 16 (bottom): Brendan Beirne/Sygma/Corbis UK Ltd

With grateful thanks to ZOOID Pictures Limited and the individual agencies listed above.

Contents

Author's Acknowledgments

My thanks are due to the following, with whom I spoke during the course of my research into the many aspects of Elton's life: Edna Dwight (Elton's stepmother), Geoff Dyson (early band member of Bluesology), David Furnish, Lin Watson (Elton's former housekeeper in Holland Park, 1992–7), Gabrielle Hardy (former Rocket employee), Nicola Greening (former Rocket receptionist), Andrew Twort (photographer for *Elton John's Flower Fantasies* book), Barry Mason (songwriter who knew Elton at Mills Music), Xavier Russell (film editor), Stuart Windsor (photographer), John Coldstream, Felix Tod and Jason Saks.

I would also like to thank all at Michael O'Mara Books for their support and hard work, especially Michael O'Mara, Toby Buchan, Helen Cumberbatch, Gabrielle Mander, Diana Briscoe, Martin Bristow and Clare Lattin.

Lastly, thank you to my daughter, Tara, and my friends for listening to many Elton anecdotes.

chapter one

·

Sir Elton John

ELTON JOHN is the ultimate rock superstar. He is a larger-than-life English
eccentric, a living metaphor for excess, a born entertainer. He is a record-
breaking, Grammy and Oscar-winning singer-songwriter – the original
Captain Fantastic. He is also the chairman of his own international charity
and the Old Vic Theatre. He was honoured with a CBE in 1996 for services to
music and knighted in 1998, and was awarded an honorary doctorate by the
Royal Academy of Music in 2002. He enjoys the freedom of the cities of
Atlanta, Nice and Watford.

Elton's story is a journey through triumph and trauma to tranquillity. It
begins with a spectacular rise to fame and fortune, followed by an equally
extravagant fall before the renaissance that established him as the much-loved
international treasure he is today. It is a saga of emotional and material excess
with enough plot turns to have kept him in the public consciousness for more
than thirty years. It encompasses suicide attempts, drug addiction, marriage,
gay sex scandals, divorce, libel cases, rehabilitation and redemption.

Over-achievement has coloured every aspect of Elton John's life – his
prodigious talent, his prolific song-writing, his profligate shopping habits, his
prodigal affairs, his precipitous platforms, and his pre-eminence on the music
scene and in society. For all but three of the last thirty-four years, he has
released at least one album a year. He has sold more records than Elvis Presley
and The Beatles. At his peak it was estimated that his records accounted for 3
per cent of total record sales worldwide. He has written or recorded more than
500 songs, and enjoyed almost continual global success throughout the last
three decades, with at least sixty Top Forty hit singles and forty-three best-
selling albums. He has achieved sixty-three platinum awards in Britain alone.
His elegy to Diana, Princess of Wales, 'Candle In The Wind '97', is the highest-
selling single of all time, raising over $30 million (£20 million) for her
memorial fund. His own charity, the Elton John AIDS Foundation (EJAF), has
raised more than £20 million since 1992.

Slice through the superlatives, and his personality is revealed as a high-
calorie *millefeuille*, a rich confection of shyness, a tendency to hero worship, a

highly original sense of humour, competitiveness, generosity, acquisitiveness, an obsession with detail and an encyclopaedic knowledge of music and football.

The enigma of Elton John lies in the multitude of contradictions that co-exist within the man. How does he manage to be simultaneously extreme and mainstream; a shy extrovert; a self-effacing egotist; a modest show-off; overwhelmingly generous, yet greedily acquisitive; elegantly controlled, yet infuriatingly capricious; a narcissist who recoils from his own reflection; a gay man who wanted a straight marriage; an exhibitionist who hates being photographed; a frisky party animal and a four-eyed wallflower? He claims to be unable to write his own lyrics, yet is an eloquent interviewee. 'I had to communicate through my melodies,' he pleads. 'I could never do it in conversation.'

In many ways he remains a small boy who sometimes behaves like an attention-seeking little madam, locking himself in his dressing room just before he is due on stage, flouncing off the tennis court in a fit of pique, or throwing objects across the room (as long as they are cheap). He is meticulously tidy, insisting that the pile on his carpets and the fringes on his rugs all lie in the same direction; each precious possession has its own special place, each cushion must be perfectly plumped. He cannot sleep peacefully unless the television remote control is in its place. How, in the 1980s, could this ordered perfectionist and self-proclaimed 'housewife of the year' have allowed his life to descend into chaos?

Elton John is an addict. He has addictions that lift his spirits and shape his life – music, football, tennis, work, shopping, flowers. He has had and overcome addictions – alcohol, food, drugs, sex – in quantities that might have killed a lesser man. Then he became hooked on the therapy which helped to save him and in 1990 finally woke up to reality. This prompted Elton's biggest reinvention – not of the public or stage persona, but of the inner man whose spirit, despite all his achievements, had reached rock bottom and had nowhere to go but up. The turning point was the death of a haemophiliac teenage boy from an AIDS-related disease.

Elton was a lonely only child living in the shadow of his parents' unhappy marriage, the effects of which would torment him for much of his adult life. He sought father figures, yet he had a devoted father of his own. He found surrogate brothers in Bernie Taupin (his lyricist), Graham Taylor (former manager of Watford Football Club) and the late Gianni Versace, yet he has four half-brothers of his own. Since childhood, when he dreamed about being in a band, he has been dedicated to working in the music business. 'If I hadn't been a performer,' he says, 'I would have been happy working in a small CD store sharing a flat with David.' On closer examination, his life has been a spectacular rise up the social scale, from humble beginnings as a clever suburban boy to friend of the royal family and many of his heroes from the music, stage, screen and sports worlds.

From the moment he amazed his fellow students at a school dance, as the fat boy at the piano overtaken by the spirit of Jerry Lee Lewis, he courted the adoration of his virtual lover, the audience. With sheer determination he rose from pub pianist to royal elegist. He could never have been the archetypal pop star, all slim-hipped and long-haired, so he threw dignity to the winds and disguised his shortcomings – his receding hairline, his shortness, his plumpness, his myopia – through self-mockery. He over-compensated for his shyness and physical flaws wrapped in the comfort blanket of his outlandish persona both on and off stage. He laughed at himself before anyone else could, dressing up in a ludicrous armoury of feathers, furs, lamé, Lurex, quilting, sequins, pom-poms, fairy lights, rhinestones, vertiginous footwear, wild spectacles, wacky wigs and assorted millinery, all of which provided an ironic counterpoint to the mastery of his music.

Despite the ever-changing fads and fashions of popular music, Elton remains at the top, still fresh today. This showman has always seemed closer to his fans than his peers, never failing to give audiences more than their money's worth, striving for musical perfection with unrivalled stagecraft. 'I've seen Elton John doing two or three-hour shows all over Europe,' his friend Graham Taylor said. 'Consider the sheer logistics, and I've seen the state he's been in after a tour. He's done forty-nine concerts in fifty-six days and made every audience feel that he was only ever going to do one show and it was the one they were watching.'

He endeared himself to the public not only with his vaudevillian stage antics, but with his down-to-earth manner and plain speaking. He heralded an age of the public confessional, sharing his problems with the world, in the hope that he could help others.

His image sells newspapers and magazines, but he is the most unlikely cover girl. He is not some silver spoon-fed aristocrat, squandering his inheritance, or a fat-cat capitalist living off the toil of the workers – he is lower middle-class Reg from Pinner, made good. He is proud to be British, a home-grown megastar who takes Marks and Spencer's muffins and HP sauce abroad with him. He is a classic impulse buyer who loves the ephemeral – the flowers fade and the clothes are recycled at his charity sales. An energetic collector since childhood, his possessions are his friends. He told Oprah Winfrey in 1997: 'I'd rather go to a porcelain exhibition than a rock concert.' He owns one of the most important collections of twentieth-century photography in the world and has been appointed a trustee of the Wallace Collection, the London museum famous for its rococo fripperies and Sèvres porcelain.

He achieved a spectacular rise to international fame in 1970, and within three years was the biggest pop star in the world. He became a victim of the superstar lifestyle, virtually imprisoned by life on the road, protected and pampered by his support mechanisms – his manager, his minders, his sycophants. The pampered man-child never had to burden himself with responsibility, coming to depend on others for his every need; for him it was twenty-four hours a day, all year-round room service. His fall from the top, and from grace, was equally sensational, and he was lucky to survive the vortex of sex, drugs and rock and roll. He credits his association with Watford Football Club for keeping his platformed feet on the ground. By his own efforts he has risen again to favour, honoured with a knighthood for his charity work and services to music, his name at the top of any society guest list.

In the modern age we have celebrity icons instead of classical heroes. Celebrities play a strange and new kind of role as the characters in real-life soap operas acted out in public for a population to whom God and the Queen mean less and less. Contemporary celebrities are often distinguished by particular failings or special needs, traits that make them seem closer to us, and Elton is the great aunt of them all. We may all aspire to success and the spoils that come with it, but we also derive a certain amount of pleasure from other people's misfortunes – especially famous people – and Elton has obligingly invaded his own privacy and laid bare his soul. Private pain became part of his public persona.

His fame rests on his natural talent not only as a musician and entertainer, but for self-promotion. For a story to run and run the hungry media need events that change and develop, and the narrative flow of Elton's life has provided it all. Nothing has ever stayed the same with Elton – his weight, his hair, his clothes. He buys, then he sells. He proclaims himself bisexual and then he gets married. He becomes an addict, then he sobers up. He announces he is never going to make another record, then he changes his mind. At the time of writing he is planning to relinquish his trademark specs after laser eye surgery. It is a measure of his achievement as a public figure that, like the royal family, his very presence is newsworthy.

Who is he? Two theories exist, the first of which is the compensation theory, which suggests that an attention-seeking adult compensates for lack of parental attention in childhood. According to psychologist Dr Glenn Wilson: 'Deprived of love at some critical time in babyhood, the individual is stuck in a groove of neurotic neediness for attention that pushes them to the permanent pursuit of praise and applause.' Did Elton feel deprived by his father's absences abroad with the RAF? Second, the reinforcement theory, which suggests that he was nourished by being the focus of attention and receiving his mother's praise for performing his piano pieces as a child. Put simply, if he plays the piano like a good boy, he gets the attention and praise he craves. Elton has supreme levels of energy and competitiveness, arguably more common in men than in women due to the male sex hormone, testosterone. Glenn Wilson suggests that homosexual men have an advantage over heterosexual men and women – they have the drive to create and to succeed without the traditional family responsibilities to absorb their energies. Perhaps Elton has the best of both worlds, piling his psychological goody bag to the full.

His lifetime of conspicuous consumption started with his boyhood collections of Dinky Toys, graduating to pop records as a teenager. He knew every A- and B-side title, every performer, writer and publisher, every catalogue number and every record-company logo of his immaculate collection. Once he began to make millions, he never felt the need to exercise control over his spending, collecting real cars, jewellery, jukeboxes, Tiffany lamps, paintings, porcelain, flowers, shoes and clothes. And still more records.

He is a pop mastermind who still memorizes the charts every week so that he can check off the names of new musicians and champion their work – Diana Krall, Anastacia, Ryan Adams, Mary J. Blige, Moby, Shea Seger, Nelly Furtado, Rufus Wainwright, Air, Groove Armada, Basement Jaxx, Coldplay. He is enthusiastic and generous in his support for younger musicians. 'If there is a better singer in Britain than Craig David,' he said, 'then I'm Margaret Thatcher.' He has promoted the careers of many of his heroes and friends, among them John Lennon, Cliff Richard, Neil Sedaka, Kiki Dee, Rod Stewart and George Michael. Much has changed since the early 1970s and Elton is now a venerable figure in the rock aristocracy, yet he still retains a certain cool quotient; his self-deprecating sense of humour is undimmed, and he is admired and respected across generations.

He is one of the first pop stars to have performed for charity; early in his career he supported the National Youth Theatre and Goaldiggers, a charity to provide football facilities for deprived children. He has also supported the Sports Aid Foundation, the Invalid Aid Association, Live Aid, the Princess of Wales Memorial Fund, and many others. In 1992 he established his own charity, the Elton John AIDS Foundation, to help fund the fight against the disease. It is a cause dear to his heart because the virus has affected many people who are – or were – close to him. He is also a patron of many AIDS-related organizations, including UNAIDS and Amnesty International.

Honesty is the key to Elton's life now. He has beaten the demons of addiction and sexual confusion, and now lives happily with David Furnish, the partner with whom he wishes to spend the rest of his life. 'As a gay man I am perfectly happy with my sexuality and my life. I can honestly say that the deepest longings of my heart are satisfied.'

But can Elton claim to be honest when he always sings someone else's words? For most of his thirty-six years as a performer, he has sung Bernie Taupin's lyrics, but Elton paints in emotion through his melodies as he sings the words of the man who has been his soulmate, his alter ego, his platonic lover. Their relationship is the root of the work's integrity. 'There have been things that have pulled us apart, marriages, distance, fame,' said Elton. 'There have been difficult passages when we've disagreed – lifestyles, drugs – but our friendship is much stronger than that. I could never dream of not having him in my life. It's a kind of love affair between two people who have never slept with each other.'

When Elton married Renate Blauel in 1984 he was living a lie. He had already come halfway out of the closet when he admitted to *Rolling Stone* magazine in 1976 that he was bisexual; he thought everyone knew anyway. In a haze of confusion he thought a conventional marriage would change things, since none of his other relationships had worked, but he could not control his addictions. 'I am very lucky,' he said. 'I should be dead, if not through the amount of drugs I have taken, then from the amount of unsafe sex I've had.' It is one of his proudest achievements that he has remained sober for more than twelve years, allowed himself to be honest about his sexuality and gained a balance between his all-consuming career and his personal happiness. 'His life is so much better since he got sober. You only have to look at what he's achieved in the last decade,' said David Furnish.

In the television documentary, *Tantrums and Tiaras*, made by David Furnish and broadcast in 1996, Elton was filmed for a year. The project became another form of therapy for him. It taught him about aspects of himself – his appalling behaviour, how pampered he is, how difficult he can make life for those around him. 'I looked at myself and thought, "She's an absolute cow",' he said. 'I had to laugh. I was just impossible.'

While researching this book I received no cooperation from Elton's inner circle, his AIDS Foundation nor Elton himself. Graham Taylor would only speak to me with Elton's blessing, as would members of staff. Following my request to speak to Elton, his management replied: 'We have decided as a matter of policy not to collaborate. Neither Elton nor myself will assist you.' This policy represents a tightly controlled grip on the release of information, exclusive nuggets of which I understand are being held back for Elton's no-holds-barred autobiography which has been planned since 1997. Robert Key, Executive Director of EJAF, told me that Elton's cautious attitude towards biographers goes back to 1991, when he spoke to a previous biographer who published more detail than Elton thought he had agreed to. Elton loves talking about himself to the media when he wants to, and there is an overwhelming wealth of detail to be found in what he has said and the way he has said it. However, others who were willing to speak have been mostly enthusiastic and affectionate in their commendations of the man and his work. A chance meeting with David Furnish, who has his own life as a film-maker and does not care to join Elton on the road, revealed one half of a very happy and grounded couple. Elton could not have stood the gentle assertion of David's independence in the days when he used to consume his lovers' personalities and place them on the 'Elton conveyor belt', from which they would emerge with the standard Cartier watch and Versace suit.

The note I received in response to a request to interview former manager John Reid about his side of the story, was from his company – appropriately named Short Fuse Limited – and characteristically curt: 'Mr Reid would definitely not in any circumstances wish to speak about his involvement with Sir Elton.' Weeks later, Reid announced that he would be writing his memoirs.

With his forty-second album, *Songs From The West Coast*, Elton declared that he wanted to remind his fans that he made his name through his music, not by the distractions of his colourful lifestyle. Since 1976, however, he has single-handedly undermined his profile as a serious musician, not only by producing a string of mediocre albums, but by regularly exercising his knack of making headlines for reasons unconnected to his musical ability. That leaves a younger generation ignorant of his remarkable musical contribution to the 1970s – they know him only as a high-profile charity worker and voracious party animal who wears funny suits. Elton admits that he thinks *Blue Moves* in 1976 was his last decent album, after which his increasingly fabulous, and sometimes grotesque, lifestyle got in the way of his music. 'Things became less innocent, less instinctive and less fun,' he remembers. However, in *Songs From The West Coast* he has produced an album that comes close to his mid-1970s form – a time when he had six consecutive American number ones, and he and Bernie were considered major talents to equal The Beatles. In 2001 he proved that he is no kitsch period piece, and once again his peers and fans are taking him seriously. Here he avoids the bloated middle-of-the-road muzak, which in many ways was the hallmark of most of his albums in the intervening years. He promises never to make another sloppy album.

The up-to-the-minute pop fan took inspiration from a twenty-four-year-old American singer-songwriter, Ryan Adams, who made his album *Heartbreaker* in just twelve days. Elton and Bernie used to make simple, pure and honest albums in a matter of days in their golden era; *Goodbye Yellow Brick Road* was written and recorded in less than three weeks. This time he was determined to make an album that sounded like Elton John, and he produced twelve utterly convincing songs.

Bernie stayed with Elton in the South of France for a week to work with him on the album. As in the early days, when they shared a bedroom in Elton's mother's small flat in Pinner, the two soulmates worked together under the same roof. Words poured from Bernie's pen – enough for eighty-five songs – which Elton took to a recording studio in Los Angeles. He felt the fear, which he says spurs him on. 'The fear factor should always be there,' he said. 'It's like being a great sportsman in a final.' He works fast. 'If I haven't got anywhere in twenty, twenty-five minutes, I'll go on to something else,' he explains.

A musical magpie, he has always found it easy to slip into dance, R&B, Tamla Motown, Philadelphia strings, or any other style rather than his own. The classic John-Taupin style is almost a genre in itself, with piano and voice stripped down to basics, and Bernie's densely perceptive words set to haunting melodies and rhythms; sweet words set to minor chords, *double entendres* sung with choirboy innocence; sad words that become brain-teasingly hummable. The themes of this album are political, dark and sobering, addressing gay rights, AIDS and romantic disillusion. According to Bernie: 'The album is both a baptism and an exorcism. It is a statement befitting our years. I love its truth and honesty.' In its first week the album entered the British charts at number two and went platinum with sales reaching more than 300,000.

Just two months after the release of *Songs From The West Coast* in 2001, Elton made headlines and prompted career obituaries all over the world when he announced that it would be the last record he would ever make. 'I'm fed up with it,' he told his audience in Manchester, New Hampshire. 'I like playing to you guys, but I hate the music industry.' It would have been out of character for 'Mr All Mouth and No Trousers', as he has described himself, not to retract his statement next day, saying, 'I was just having a bad day.'

Elton now conducts a love-hate relationship with the camera. His wide, gap-toothed grin (without lipstick) was the centrepiece to his pose between singers Shirley Manson and Mary J. Blige to advertise a special edition MAC lipstick in support of AIDS charities. He also appeared in an American campaign to advertise milk, sporting a white milk moustache, and donated his fee to EJAF. Conversely, Elton fought shy of appearing as himself in his video for 'I Want Love'. Video director, photographer and friend, Sam Taylor-Wood's creative solution was to cast actor Robert Downey Jr speaking over the heartbroken lyrics as he wanders through an empty mansion. The video for 'This Train Don't Stop There Any More' stars singer, Justin Timberlake, dressed in a wig and big suit as an early 1970s Elton miming to the song.

Despite shunning the camera for his own music videos and declaring 'I hate doing videos', he appeared in Ryan Adams's video for his single, 'Answering Bell', as a bespectacled Wizard of Oz, enveloped in a purple cape waving a magic wand. He also jumped at the chance to play himself in a television commercial for the Royal Mail. Was it the Royal connection, the male pun or the opportunity to promote his new album? The script called for a character who was famous for shopping – Elton was the natural choice and top of the casting wish-list. After much negotiation and for a small fee of less than $150,000 (£100,000), filming took place over two days in Atlanta. The album cover appears on his computer screen and his single 'I Want Love' plays on the soundtrack as Elton indulges in a spot of online shopping, only to be inundated with parcels delivered by a host of Royal Mail delivery boys and girls. Sometimes when non-acting celebrities are cast in commercials, they freeze in front of the camera because they do not possess the necessary acting skills – Elton needed no direction, however, he simply played himself. According to the art director from the Royal Mail's advertising agency, Bates UK: 'He came across as camp and as brilliant as we wanted him to be.' At the end of filming his parting comment to an executive of the Royal Mail was a minor complaint about British postage stamps: 'It's a shame there's only room for one queen.'

chapter two

Lonely Boy

METROLAND STRETCHES THROUGH the cosy counties of Middlesex, Hertfordshire and Buckinghamshire. Pinner lies on the Metropolitan line, on the north-western branch of the London Underground, which meanders through desirable meadows and grassy uplands embroidered with a patchwork of cricket pitches, tennis courts and golf courses, just twenty minutes from central London, and a few stops south of Watford.

The end of the Second World War marked a time of renewal. Houses were built by the thousand, identical nesting boxes replacing the pastures and orchards that had once surrounded London. The new suburbs offered idyllic countryside, village-style communities and large, comfortable houses set in quiet courts, crescents and cul-de-sacs. They were home to millions, who marked out their territory with manicured lawns, guarded by garden gnomes and bordered by flowerbeds full of roses and dahlias, and meticulously trimmed hedges. The suburbs were burgeoning enclaves of quiet snobbery, and families worked hard to keep up appearances. Children deferred to their elders and betters. Manners and careful accents were beacons of respectability that demonstrated a sense of social place.

Women gave up work when they married, and sons obeyed their authoritarian fathers. Wives stayed at home, cleaned, cooked and chatted to the neighbours over the garden fence, while their husbands brought home the bacon. Consumption was never conspicuous in these austere post-war years and thrift was next to cleanliness in its godliness.

Men had spent years in uniform obeying orders and hiding their emotions on the battlefield, so when they came home they were not used to overt displays of sentiment. Their sons grew up mistaking discipline for lack of affection. It was expected that bright suburban boys would set their sights on a safe job in a bank or the armed services, just like dad, with his stiff upper lip, short back and sides, and sensible shoes. The pattern of life in the post-war suburbs was rather dull, with little to inspire the imagination, at least, little of which parents would approve. The concept of the teenager had not yet been invented, but the generation gap was widening. Kids were discovering new idols. The clean-cut, wholesome heroes of the war, such as Kenneth More and James Stewart, were being replaced with dangerous rebels like James Dean and Marlon Brando. And Elvis was making a new kind of music with a new kind of attitude.

Flight Lieutenant Stanley Dwight of the Royal Air Force and office girl Sheila Harris were married in 1945, five months before the end of the war. Their son was conceived in the early summer of 1946.

Music has been central to the Dwight family for at least three generations. Edwin Dwight, Stanley's father, was a soprano cornet player, a talent that was his entrée to a job at Callander's, a cable-making firm in Kent that prided itself on its brass band. Edwin, a slim, moustachioed, Edwardian gent, and his wife, Ellen, a not insubstantial dowager figure, had six children, and Stanley, the youngest, was born in 1925. Edwin and Ellen considered family responsibilities to be paramount and took in two of their grandchildren after the death of their son Ted's wife in childbirth. Ted himself died of tuberculosis aged thirty-four and the two orphaned grandsons, Roy and Dave, grew up looking upon their Uncle Stanley as a brother.

Stanley grew up to be a sturdy young man with a round face, a wide smile and a determined chin. He had a quick wit and modest manner. His father taught him to play the trumpet and he was good enough to play in a number of amateur swing bands. Stanley was a diligent student at Dartford Grammar School and anxious to get on in life. His first job was as an apprentice to a small boatbuilding company in Rickmansworth. Anxious to play his part in the war effort, seventeen-year-old Stanley left his job in 1942, and signed up for active service. He volunteered for the Royal Air Force Naval Reserve and was accepted for air-crew training. A well-organized, well-mannered and assiduously tidy recruit, he was soon recognized as officer material. He was charming company with a lively sense of fun and while he was stationed in London, formed an RAF band under the name of Stan Wight. This was strictly against the rules – hence the stage name – and he had fond memories of convincing the duty sergeant to allow him back into base in the morning after a night's playing in the West End.

Stanley was still only seventeen when he met sixteen-year-old Sheila Harris one evening, when he was playing the trumpet in the Eric Beaumont Band at the Headstone Hotel, North Harrow. Sheila was helping the war effort by standing in for her brother, delivering milk for United Dairies in the Pinner and Eastcote areas. Stanley and Sheila's courtship lasted three years. They wrote fond letters to each other, and met when work allowed. While he was rising up the ranks in the RAF, she gave up the milk round and joined the ATS as a clerk, at Coastal Command Centre in Northwood, in January 1945. The couple got married at Pinner Parish Church and moved in with Sheila's parents, Ivy and Fred Harris, at their modest, semi-detached council house. It was not easy for young newly-weds to find a home of their own at that time, and as Stanley was often away on duty, Sheila preferred to stay with her parents, sister Win and brother Reginald. When Sheila became pregnant, Stanley considered returning to his old job at the boatbuilders so he would not be away from home so much. But he had had a good war, impressing his superiors and making steady progress, and decided to stay in the RAF. He set his hopes on climbing the career ladder and giving his family a more secure financial future. He was promoted to flight lieutenant and was stationed in nearby Ruislip when, in 1947, Sheila gave birth to a son.

Reginald Kenneth Dwight was born on 25 March at his grandparents' home at 55 Pinner Hill Road. Sheila insisted on naming the child after her brother, a name Stanley disliked as much as his son would as he got older. 'How can you name a baby Reginald?' the future superstar would later whine.

At the time of his son's birth, Stanley was commuting to the RAF base in nearby Ruislip, and continued there until 1949 when he was posted to Basra in Iraq, where he could have also taken his young family. Sheila, still only in her early twenties, insisted on staying in Pinner to be near her friends and parents with the fifteen-month-old baby. Stanley was distraught that he should have to spend so much time away from his son. For his first Christmas away from Reggie he ordered a top-of-the-range pedal car from Hamley's, London's biggest toy shop, and arranged for it to be delivered to Pinner Hill Road on Christmas Eve. Sheila, and her mother and sister, were devoted to the pampered and protected little prince, tending to his every whim. The late 1940s was a dreary time of food rationing and shortages, but Sheila ensured there were plenty of bonnets, romper suits and bootees for baby Reggie, who was a beautiful child with a mass of cherubic golden curls.

Aged only three, Reggie is said to have shown prodigious talent for playing the piano, fostered by his grandmother who would sit him on her knee so that he could reach the keys. He showed an early talent for mimicry and could listen to a piece of music and then play it by ear almost immediately.

Reggie lived in a mainly female household until he was four. His grandfather died when he was five and his nan, Ivy, married an ex-serviceman from the First World War called Horace Sewell. Despite having lost a leg, he was a keen gardener and made sure the small garden was always full of colourful flowers, especially dahlias and roses. Horace worked at a local gardening firm and shared his enthusiasm with Reg, encouraging him to help him mow the lawn.

When Reggie was six, his father was promoted to squadron leader, and this time the three of them moved to his new posting at RAF Lynam in Wiltshire, to a spacious, four-bedroomed house, courtesy of the RAF. Away from familiar surroundings, and despite the apparent luxury of her new home, however, Sheila was uncomfortable in the role of officer's wife. She disliked what she perceived as the social climbing and snobbery of the military lifestyle; not for her pink gins, stuffed olives and small talk before dinner. Stanley and Sheila were growing apart, and soon she and Reggie moved back to Pinner.

In spite of their marital difficulties, their son was not neglected, and they made sure that he had regular music lessons. He was a diligent pupil and, although shy and reserved, would always be picked out to play the piano at family gatherings, school concerts and assemblies. He made his first public appearance at the age of twelve at the Ruislip-Northwood Music Festival playing 'Les Petites Litanies de Dieu' by Groylez. A snapshot of him at the piano shows him sitting at the keyboard looking over his shoulder, as all piano showmen do, smiling at the camera with his gap-toothed grin, round face and neat hairstyle with perfect parting – a picture of a very earnest boy.

While practising the classics for his music exams, Reggie listened to the popular piano stars of the time. He loved extrovert pianists such as the rumbustious Winifred Atwell, who had come to Britain from Trinidad in 1946. She was classically trained and played hard, thumping, honky-tonk piano on the music hall circuit. She was extremely popular in Britain, playing at Royal Variety performances and on television.

Another keyboard hero was Russ Conway, who began his showbiz career playing the piano for Gracie Fields and Joan Regan. His sing-along, toe-tapping style endeared him to a wide audience through his regular spot on the *Billy Cotton Band Show*, one of the top television programmes of the late 1950s, and later, on his own television series.

Liberace was top dog among the show-off pianists, and his flamboyant, camp style at his candelabra-decked piano had no small influence on the impressionable Reggie. In the austerity years of the 1950s, *The Liberace Show* lit up black-and-white television screens like Cartier's Christmas window display. Watching his high-speed playing and cheesy grin, Reggie became fascinated by his camp extravagance and luminosity.

The future star would later look back on his early childhood and unreservedly describe himself as a mummy's boy. Reggie grew up with his doting mother, Sheila, his beloved grandmother, Ivy, and his Aunt Win, the women to whom Reg turned for support and love. He spent many happy hours with Ivy, who was a pivotal influence. She was always there to welcome him home from school and make his tea, while his parents were working.

At home he would stamp his foot to try and get his own way, and sometimes throw minor temper tantrums, but at school Reggie was a conscientious and exemplary pupil. He kept his desk extremely tidy, was polite in class, had a faultless memory and was no mean tennis player. He liked to keep busy and he took a paper round, spending every penny of his earnings buying records for himself or presents for his mother.

Reggie shared his father's passion for football and Stanley took him to see Watford play on Saturday afternoons whenever he could. When Stanley was at home he brought order, good manners and discipline with him, possibly in an attempt to counteract the overwhelmingly feminine influence on his son. In later years, Elton would describe his relationship with his father in less than flattering terms, revealing that Stanley's very presence seemed to make him feel awkward and clumsy; his fear would make him nervous and he would drop things, which would anger his father, so he never felt able to bond with him. The future star would paint a sad picture of his home life, which must have baffled his father as much as it hurt him. He would reflect that Stanley argued with Sheila, but seemed to take all his frustrations out on Reggie by constantly scolding him for any minor misdemeanour, such as slurping his soup, eating celery too loudly or kicking a football too near the house in case he damaged the roses. He even disapproved of his son wearing Hush Puppies. These may have been only passing criticisms, but they took on huge significance in Reggie's, and later Elton's, mind.

When Stanley was abroad he kept a photo of Sheila and Reggie by his bed and wrote every day. He spent months away from home on postings, mostly in the Middle East. The fact that other officers had their families with them would have made Stanley's existence all the more lonely. To alleviate his solitude he organized football matches and swimming lessons for the children on the base. Without regular contact with Reggie, Stanley was worried about him being over-protected in an entirely female household, for he was discouraged from playing with local children. He was also unhappy about Sheila's insistence on working in a grocer's shop when she did not need the money.

On one posting to Aden, Stanley suffered a severe electric shock and spent months in hospital. During his final three-month convalescence in Britain, his loneliness must have been intensified by the fact that he was not visited once by Sheila or Reggie. When he recovered, he returned to Pinner and took a long-term posting at Marlow in Buckinghamshire, which meant he could settle permanently in England. He could now afford to buy a detached family house in Northwood Hills, near enough to Pinner for Sheila to visit her parents while Stanley commuted to Marlow. However, he could not ignore the gossip. It soon became clear that Sheila had resumed a friendship with a man named Fred Farebrother, a painter, decorator and general handyman, whom she had known since the war. When Stanley went to call on Farebrother at his council house in nearby Carpender's Park, the door was answered by a harassed Mrs Farebrother, surrounded by children, who told Stanley that she also wished she knew where her husband was because she had no money. Stanley felt so sorry for her that he generously gave her some cash.

While the Dwights battled to keep up appearances, tensions between Stanley and Sheila were growing in the house at 111 Potter Street, creating a turbulent atmosphere for their shy young son.

In the late 1950s, the children of the lower middle classes could improve their social status via grammar school and university. Reggie was a clever boy and, aged eleven, won a scholarship to one of the country's top private schools, the academic John Lyon School in Harrow. Its Dickensian atmosphere did not appeal to him, however, and he insisted on attending the local grammar school, Pinner County, one of the best state schools in the area with a fine academic and sporting record. It was run on public school lines, boasting a crest embellished with a rearing stag and a motto, 'Honour before Honours'. Reggie's old, brown blazer badge is now a glass paperweight which takes pride of place on the desk of the Pinner County old boy.

At eleven he also won a junior exhibition scholarship to the Royal Academy of Music in Central London as a piano student of special interest. He attended Saturday morning piano classes for five years, where his talent for playing complex melodies by ear was nurtured. Although he claims not to have liked playing classical music and did not practise very hard, he sailed through all his grade exams, yearning to be pounding out rock-and-roll tunes by Jerry Lee Lewis rather than Chopin études.

In the drab late 1940s and early 1950s, home entertainment consisted of the wireless and the record player, and many families had an upright piano in the living room. There was always music in the Dwight household because both Sheila and Stanley were avid collectors of the big, brittle 78 rpm discs by pre-rock-and-roll era stars like Guy Mitchell, Frankie Lane and Rosemary Clooney. Sheila used to treat herself to a record every Friday so Reg's early years may have been lonely, but they were accompanied by a lively, middle-of-the-road soundtrack. As a small boy, he was enthralled by rock and roll, thanks to his mother's increasingly daring choice of records – for example, Bill Haley's 'ABC Boogie' and Elvis Presley's 'Hound Dog'. Elton later remembered: 'One was on Brunswick and the other on HMV. I really freaked when I heard them, and I went on from there.' But even Sheila disapproved of Little Richard's 'The Girl Can't Help It'. His passion was indulged by his grandmother, mother and father, all of whom bought him records.

Reg was shy of other children, so he immersed himself in his music lessons. He had a full schedule with after-school piano practice and his Saturday mornings at the Royal Academy. His schooldays were not the happiest of his life and Reg was often on his own. Although not a recluse, he was never part of a gang, and always felt on the fringes. 'Going out to the cinema with mates, I was always the last one to be asked,' he has said. 'I've been picked on more than anybody else because I'm an easy target, I'm open. I was Fat Reg to start with.'

In his neat, brown school uniform, he never really stood out from the crowd until he was about thirteen, when he started wearing dark-rimmed glasses in homage to Buddy Holly, an early rock-and-roll hero who had died in a plane crash in 1959. The glasses affected his sight and made him myopic, however, and while putting on weight, with his round face and snub nose he looked more like Billy Bunter than Buddy Holly. He recalled: 'I was always spotlessly clean as a child. I was wheeled out at every occasion to play the piano. It was a way of getting attention and approval. It was what I turned to for safety – music and food.'

Apart from music, Reg's best subjects were English and languages, but despite his obvious ability he never excelled. He was criticized for being too casual with his music homework, just because it came naturally to him. He was an average and conventional student; his quick wit and excellent memory made little impact on his academic progress. 'Satisfactory' was a common remark in many of his school reports. Reg got all the education he needed from his growing record collection: history and geography – jazz and blues from America; science – 78, 33 and 45 revolutions per minute; and maths – totting up the cost of an afternoon in the record shop.

Reg seemed older than his years, more grown up, more refined than the other boys. He always stood up when a lady entered the room and addressed older men as 'Sir'. Out of school he wore a tweed sports jacket, collar and tie, and grey flannel trousers. With his horn-rimmed spectacles, he was a boy dressed as a little man. He may not have been in with the in-crowd but Reg was popular with the girls. He was the perfect companion – funny, interested in all sorts of subjects, polite, and he never made a pass. He would later admit that he found the notion of sex utterly frightening while he was at school, with everyone boasting about it. He would not have sex with anyone, male or female, until he was twenty-three.

A gift for entertaining was emerging – he turned wordplay into an art form and his schoolfriends would make up hilarious languages and have their own catchphrases. A consummate impressionist, he could recite whole sequences from his favourite radio programmes, such as *The Goon Show*, *Round the Horne* and *Hancock's Half Hour*, mimicking all the voices, male and female. His favourite television programme was *Steptoe and Son*, which featured a horse called Hercules. Years later, in 1981, Elton John paid $21,000 (£14,000) at a Christie's auction for the original scripts of BBC Radio's *The Goon Show*. This purchase consisted of 6,000 pages with handwritten annotations by Spike Milligan and Peter Sellers. Elton instructed his spokesperson to tell the press in Bluebottle's voice: 'I have boughted dem because I loved dem.'

Towards the end of his time at Pinner County School Reg learned how to work an audience. His early showmanship was clear for all to see when he played the piano during lunch breaks and at dances in the assembly hall. Schoolmates loved dancing to Reg's high-energy renditions of rock-and-roll numbers. The spirit of Jerry Lee Lewis took over and Reg would pound the keyboard with his feet, kicking the stool away for a finale. The classical music student was no longer the self-conscious, podgy, four-eyed loner; at the keyboard he was a rock-and-roller, an entertainer with an audience that wanted more, not least because the transformation was so unexpected. For a reserved boy who wanted love and approval from his peers, this was heaven.

Stanley encouraged Reg to study classical music, but, as in the case of most adolescents, his father's attitude made Reg determined to do the opposite. He was far more taken with the new music craze from America – the full-blooded kind of rock and roll; not for Reg the anodyne Adam Faith or the poor man's Elvis, Cliff Richard, who were all the rage in Britain. When Reg saw the larger-than-life pianists such as Little Richard, Fats Domino and Ray Charles, or the pyrotechnic antics of Jerry Lee Lewis, abusing their instruments in the name of rock and roll, he knew exactly what he wanted to do. It was different, dangerous and suggestive – everything classical music was not. Even the language was incomprehensible to the older generation with songs like 'Tutti Frutti' and 'Be Bop A Lula'. The music and the culture that went with it were alien to the older generation, who hoped it would be a passing fad. Elton, perhaps unfairly, would say that his father thought he should, 'get all this pop nonsense out of his head, otherwise he's going to turn into a wild boy'. On one occasion Reg went to see Little Richard at the Harrow Granada Cinema. When he jumped up on the piano Reg thought, I wish that was me.

Reg's childhood and early teens were sheltered, mostly spent in the company of his *Boy's Own* comics, pop and football heroes, and his classical sheet music. His first collectibles were Dinky Toys and Matchbox cars, which were kept in perfect order in his bedroom. Tension at home was palpable and Reg was all too aware of the cracks appearing in the harmonious façade. He recalled: 'I would lock myself in my bedroom. My father would come home and there would be a row. I expected it and lived in fear of it.' His bedroom became a refuge from the frosty atmosphere downstairs, a place where he could impose his own sense of order. In his room, Reg lived in a world of his own, immersed in his two pet subjects, football and pop music. In this safe haven, he learned how to love his possessions, developing a tendency to hoard, and sharpening his obsessive eye for detail. He would listen to the radio and meticulously note down all the football results and chart positions of the latest records, updating them weekly. He followed the triumphs and disasters of Watford Football Club, and the pop hits and misses which became the main events in his own uneventful life.

Reg's room was a shrine to both Watford FC and rock and roll. Here he painstakingly catalogued his growing record collection and placed his LPs, EPs and 45s in alphabetical order. At an early age he was an aficionado of a range of musical genres from folk, jazz, country and western, and rhythm and blues to rock and roll. He studied the labels and logos, the emblems of rock and roll, passwords to another world – EMI, RCA Victor, Capitol, Blue Note, Riviera, Gardena, Mercury. He knew the name of every A- and B-side, every artist, every writer, every publisher; he memorized and filed the catalogue numbers, and carefully wrapped each precious record in a protective brown-paper cover so that the sleeve designs would not be damaged. On each package he inscribed in neat writing, 'The property of Reg Dwight'. He never lent his records to anyone and he looked on the discs as his friends. He would later say in a fit of peevishness: 'I look back on my old 45s and remember when they gave me a bit of happiness. Which is more than human beings have ever done.'

He studied the pictures on the record sleeves and fantasized about the lives of the musicians on the covers, who became his imaginary friends. Everyone was hip and glamorous. He yearned to join in the camaraderie of the groups and in his dreams was one of the lads, going on the road, bonding, joining in the banter and best of all, playing rock and roll full-time.

As a plump, starstruck teenager, Reg did not embody a pelvis-thrusting rock star, but he dreamed of stardom all the same. He would stand in front of the mirror miming to Jerry Lee Lewis, practising his stagecraft. The fabulous reflection that shimmied back at him was not fat Reg, but a star with an adoring audience calling for more. Elton later recalled: 'I always thought I'd be a star since the age of four or five . . . anybody can be a star if they put their minds to it. I don't look like a star at all, but that's what fascinates me about it. I've always looked like a bank clerk who freaked out. That's what makes rock and roll so great, that someone like me can actually be a star.'

With long periods apart, and constant rows, the Dwights could no longer sustain their union and it was clear that the fifteen-year marriage was over. Stanley filed for divorce when Reg was thirteen, and he moved back to Kent to lodge with his sister, Ivy. As an RAF liaison officer, he spent his time commuting between the Air Ministry in London and Harrogate. By now he was in line for promotion to wing commander.

Socially, divorce was still unacceptable. Legally, divorce was possible only if one side had committed a 'matrimonial offence', such as adultery. There had to be a guilty party, so Stanley accused his wife of adultery with Fred Farebrother, whom she later married in 1972. At the time Reg was too young to understand the intricacies of adultery and the pain of an unfulfilled marriage, but he came to blame his father for portraying his beloved mother as a scarlet woman in court. He would say in 1988, after his own divorce: 'When my own parents got divorced it was so uncommon in those days. My mother took the can for it. It split the family. Nobody talked about it. It was such a disgrace.'

Many children suffer guilt over the break-up of their parents' marriage, believing they are to blame in some way, but for teenaged Reg, it seemed he had emerged unscathed. While Stanley was waiting for the divorce to be finalized he first met his future wife, Edna, in Harrogate, and they were married at the end of 1962. He made great efforts to ensure that Reg did not feel rejected. Although granted custody of his son, Stanley asked Reg which of his parents he would prefer to stay with. Understandably, Reg chose to stay with Sheila in Pinner. Stanley opened a charge account at Horne Brothers in the Strand, so that Reg could buy whatever clothes he wanted, which rather disproves the myth that he objected to Reg's fashion sense. Stanley also made a clandestine arrangement with one of Horne Brothers' staff, whom he paid to accompany Reg to football matches when he was unable to go himself. Though he was not well off, shortly after his second marriage Stanley bought a Collingwood upright piano for $102 (£68) for Reg to play in his new home.

Stanley left the RAF and settled in Essex with Edna, to be near Reg and see him regularly. They opened a general store selling toys, travel tickets, stationery and tobacco in Chadwell Heath. Reg wrote to his father in January 1963, thanking him for his postcard from the honeymoon in Spain, giving the marriage his blessing and asking about Edna. 'Thank you very much for your letter and the enclosed ten shillings. I'm glad that you had a nice honeymoon, but you didn't mention anything about your new wife. I was rather hurt,' he wrote. 'You know I do not mind you getting married again. So please don't be scared to mention her.' He said how much he was looking forward to visiting the shop and meeting his new stepmother. Reg also asked his father if he would attend his school to meet the employment officer to discuss his career options, and described his ambitions. 'I want to entertain . . . to sing and play the piano. I know it is not easy and I appreciate that it takes a lot of hard work, and of course luck. I hope you don't think I'm foolish, but I thought I would tell you anyway. I hope your new shop will thrive so that you can set me up in a record shop when I am out of work,' he joked.

Reg, with his new piano and record collection, Sheila, with her divorce settlement of half the proceeds of the old house, all the furniture and the car, and her new partner, Fred Farebrother, moved into a first-floor maisonette in Frome Court, Northwood Hills, yards from the old family house. Fred's wife was a Catholic and would not divorce him, so he did not marry Sheila for another nine years. He was a tall rough diamond with thick-rimmed glasses and a tattoo on his forearm, a generous character who made a big effort to make friends with Reg. The boy appreciated Fred's enthusiasm for pop music and, in return, gave him an affectionate nickname, Derf (Fred spelled backwards), which he still uses, and referred to him as Dad. He settled into his smaller bedroom, carefully arranging his records, his pop and football charts, music magazines and posters. Dusty Springfield joined his football heroes on the walls. When he inducted her into the Rock and Roll Hall of Fame many years later, he would say: 'I fell in love with the beehive hair, the pink top, the purple skirt . . . it had no effect on me whatsoever.'

Reg was also intrigued by the American singer Bob Dylan who, in the early sixties, was writing serious songs about his own life. From a folk background, he was no sexually-charged Elvis but he was cool, and he was laying the ground for a new kind of pop music. In 1963, sixteen-year-old Reg was also buying records by some new British heroes who did not just sing cover versions of American hits, but wrote their own – The Beatles were the hottest new group in the hit parade.

However unsettling the divorce may have been for Reg, he seemed as comfortable with Edna as he did with Fred. He would visit Chadwell Heath regularly and in the flat over the shop he would chat to Edna and make her laugh. He would entertain on her piano, and in the kitchen, on one occasion successfully baked her a Victoria sponge cake.

Reg was thrilled when the first of his four half-brothers, Stanley, was born, and told Edna that he had always wanted a brother or sister. He sent affectionate congratulations cards when each of the boys was born. Stanley took his extra parental duties seriously, but still continued to provide for his firstborn. He paid Sheila maintenance for Reg until he started work and, through the Horne Brothers account, he supplied him with trendy clothes.

Concerning careers matters, Reg perhaps respected his father's opinion over his mother's because Stanley took the day off specially to discuss his son's options with the school. According to Edna, it was the careers adviser, not his father as Elton would later imply, who thought he should get a sensible job with BEA airlines, or Barclays Bank. Stanley never actually told his son that he did not want him to be a musician – he was mainly concerned that he had a good education and paid enough attention to his schoolwork.

Stanley might have been more worried about Reg's academic progress had he known that his son had taken a job in the local pub as resident pianist while still at school. Fred Farebrother arranged Reg's first job in showbiz, at the Northwood Hills Hotel, a short walk from Frome Court. It was a typical early 1960s pub opposite the tube station, with an old piano in the bay window. The carpets were caked in dried spilt beer and the atmosphere was musty and smoky. The impression Reg gave behind the ancient upright was not exactly that of a budding Liberace. The plain, podgy, bespectacled entertainer wearing his collar and tie, with his ginger tweed jacket and neat short back and sides lacked a certain stage presence. His mother and Fred acted as road crew to assist him with a basic microphone and loud speaker. He played every Friday, Saturday and Sunday, and never once missed a gig. He performed bar-room standards such as 'My Old Man Said Follow The Van', 'Roll Out The Barrel', and old favourites by Jim Reeves and Ray Charles.

From these early beginnings Reg fully appreciated earning a few pounds, plus tips, remembering how he 'packed the place out and earned a fortune – enough to buy a car, a radiogram, a television set, an electric piano and an amplifier.' The pub job lasted for nearly two years, despite the behaviour of the rowdy drinkers who would sometimes show their appreciation by throwing ash-trays, empty chip bags and beer into the piano.

As his local reputation spread Reg was invited to join a couple of mates, Stuart Brown and Geoff Dyson, in a band called the Corvettes. Reg was a far better musician than any of the others and with his skill for mimicry he could not only play anything, but keep the boys amused with his Goon and Kenneth Williams impressions. Even with the protection of the keyboards shy Reg immediately upstaged lead singer Brown, kicking away the piano stool as they belted out a few rocking Jerry Lee Lewis numbers. At best they earned $3 (£2) a night for gigs at local church halls and youth clubs. Dyson said of Reg: 'I remember how dapper and conventional-looking he always was. While the rest of us would be in jeans, he'd be in grey flannels. Reggie played any available piano which would always be out of tune, leaving the rest of the band to tune their guitars to it.' Sometimes there would be more people in the band than in the audience and so after a few months the Corvettes split up.

In 1962 the ex-Corvettes reinvented themselves as Bluesology, inspired by the record *Djangology* by the three-fingered jazz guitarist Django Rheinhardt. They described themselves as 'a snobbish soul band' and aspired to be cool and sophisticated, playing songs by Jimmy Witherspoon, Memphis Slim and Muddy Waters, which were all suggested by Reg, who took great pride in his superior musical knowledge. Bluesology's musical sophistication did not appeal to all, however, as one night a fracas developed at the South Harrow British Legion hall when a group of rockers drove up on their motorbikes and threatened to smash up the gear if the band did not play rock and roll. 'I was into that,' said Elton. 'Because all the time all I really wanted to do was play like Jerry Lee Lewis or Little Richard.'

Reg's cousin, Roy Dwight, who had been a gifted footballer since childhood, and who turned professional with Fulham in 1950, would have a key role in deciding Reg's future. In 1958 he helped to take Fulham to the FA Cup semi-final, after which he signed for First Division Nottingham Forest for a then huge transfer fee of $23,250 (£15,500). The following year, Nottingham Forest reached the FA Cup Final against Luton at Wembley Stadium. In the thirty-third minute of the match, however, Roy's promising career on the pitch came to a premature end when he broke his leg after blocking a heavy tackle. He would spend the rest of his career as a coach. Roy kept in touch with Sheila after her divorce from Stanley and promised to help Reg if he could, through his numerous contacts in sports and show business. Knowing that Reg was desperate to get into the music industry, he set him up with an interview for an office-boy job at the song publishers, Mills Music, and accompanied him to the office in Denmark Street in central London. The well-mannered Reg was successful and taken on at $7.50 (£5) a week.

Consequently, Reg chose to leave school aged seventeen, just a term before he was due to sit his A levels. The decision caused outrage. He was the school's only music A-level student and he had a flair for English when he made the effort. 'The sixth form was just a waste of time because I wanted to do music as a full-time thing,' he recalls. His tutor at the Royal Academy was dismayed by Reg's decision because, in her opinion, his academic and musical potential should have been explored at university. Stanley was particularly unhappy that Roy had not consulted him before arranging the job interview for his son.

Reg's new job may have been a milestone in his career, but it was a turning point in his relationship with his father. Stanley felt a great sense of rejection, not only to discover that Reg called Fred Farebrother 'Dad', but to find that his son had been working in a pub for two years, and had left school without consulting or informing him. As the provider of pocket money and clothes, Stanley felt he could not keep up with the indulgence and lenience of his ex-wife and Fred. With Reg at work in London and, inevitably, fewer visits from him, there was now nothing to keep Stanley and Edna and their new family in Chadwell Heath. They sold the shop and moved to Cheshire to live near Edna's elderly father.

Reg's Pinner County schoolmasters were more philosophical about his decision. His history teacher, Bill Johnson, said to him, with prescience:

'When you're forty you'll either be a glorified office boy or you'll be a millionaire.'

Reg started his first full-time job in March 1965 in Denmark Street. At ground level were small musical instrument shops where young pop hopefuls could buy their first guitars, drum kits and amplifiers. Between the shops, tiny doorways were portals to another world. Narrow stairs led to pop nirvana in a warren of offices and makeshift recording rooms, where songwriters had tunes published as sheet music and wannabe musicians recorded demos. This was where Brian Epstein had met publisher Dick James in his shabby two-room suite in 1962, with a clutch of future Lennon-McCartney hits.

Swapping his brown school blazer for brown office boy's overalls, Reg never met the big stars on Mills Music's books, such as Fats Waller, Duke Ellington, Cliff Richard and Russ Conway, but he did serve tea to hopeful singer-songwriters Terry Venables and George Graham, then junior footballers at Chelsea. Venables remembers Reg as a funny kid who would regale visitors with his Kenneth Williams impressions, and songwriter Barry Mason remembers Reg as a polite, shy lad. Under the roof of Mills Music, pop met football in other ways – Eric Hall, who later became a successful football agent, also worked in the warehouse with Reg, packing orders for sheet music, making tea and taking parcels to the Post Office.

While it was an inauspicious start to a glittering career, working in the West End did mean that Reg could spend his lunch hours sifting through American imports in the Musicland record shop in Berwick Street, where he became a regular customer, or occasionally buying a coat or way-out T-shirt from trendy Carnaby Street nearby. Otherwise, he would ask permission to play one of the arrangers' pianos in the office during his breaks. As a result, he was persuaded to play his old pub favourites for the Christmas party, which was attended by all the Chelsea football players.

Tea boy and gofer would do as the day job, but Reg was moonlighting in Bluesology. The band were determined to be successful and began to enter amateur talent contests, practising at the Northwood Hills Hotel when it was closed to the public on Sunday afternoons. Bluesology were ambitious and keen to move on, and they added a saxophone player to the line-up. With an early eye on his stage presence and having a keyboard that stayed in tune, Reg was inspired by Alan Price, keyboard player with The Animals, to buy himself a red Vox Continental organ, which became his trademark. In July 1965 the band made their recording debut on the Fontana label with 'Come Back, Baby', which credited Reg Dwight as writer. Against strong competition from the Rolling Stones, The Byrds, The Animals and The Who, however, it failed to make an impression on the charts.

One Saturday morning in late 1965, the band auditioned at the Kilburn State Cinema and turned professional with the Roy Tempest Agency, which booked them to back American R&B solo performers who were touring in Britain. He handed in his notice at Mills Music and gave up his $7.50(£5)-a-week job for the precariousness of life on the road as one of the boys in the band, to join in the camaraderie, and, most importantly, to play rock and roll.

Their first audition was with the American soul singer, Wilson Pickett, but his guitarist was so unimpressed that Pickett pulled out of the deal and they did not even get to meet their hero, let alone play for him. Before the next audition they practised solidly for two weeks and were chosen to go on tour with American jazz and soul singer Major Lance, who recommended them to other American R&B artists. This was their first break, and so significant that, twenty-five years later, Elton would remember: 'Backing Major Lance was probably the biggest thing that had ever happened to me.'

The lonely fantasies of the shy hero-worshipper were coming true. He had managed to find a way of getting closer than ever to his musical heroes. The catalogue of stars with whom Bluesology were working was becoming impressive. Among them were The Ink Spots, Doris Troy, Patti LaBelle and the Blue Belles with Cindy Birdsong, the future Supreme. They were paid $22.50 (£15) a week, but they worked hard for every penny, sometimes performing two or three gigs a night. A typical Saturday night might start early at a London venue, followed by a mad dash up the motorway to Birmingham, then an end-of-evening line-up in a dank bar back in London just as dawn was breaking. There were no luxuries on the road, no roadies to lug the equipment in and out of the venues and up the stairs to Reg's first-floor maisonette. The boys in the band had to do it all themselves, and soon Bluesology were touring all over Britain and Europe.

A second single composed by Reg, 'Mr Frantic', was released in February 1966, but it received very little air play and made no impact on the charts.

In September 1966 Reg met the respected blues singer Long John Baldry in the Cromwellian club in South Kensington, London. Often described as the father of British rhythm and blues, he was extremely tall, with a taste for Savile Row suits with LJB-monogrammed silk linings. Bluesology were playing in the basement when Baldry discovered them one evening. Although he thought Reg's red Vox Continental looked 'rather hideous', Baldry asked the band to back him. He never thought Reg looked prepossessing, describing him as shy and introverted on stage.

After a tour of Sweden, Bluesology reformed in December with Baldry as lead singer. 'They drove off the ferry, straight to Birmingham University where I had a show booked,' he remembered. 'We did the show without any kind of rehearsal, we just winged it and it worked out very well.' Baldry arranged for his management to pay them a weekly wage, and expanded the group into a nine-piece, adding Elton Dean on saxophone, and on guitar, Caleb Quaye, son of the bandleader Cab Quaye, whom Elton had first met in his office-boy days when Caleb Quaye worked for a rival music firm. When the band restyled themselves for the hippy crowd, Baldry described Reg as, 'Quite porky. In a kaftan he looked like a myopic nun'.

Life in the band was not all that Reg had dreamed of and he retreated from the front line, allowing Baldry to take the limelight as lead singer. Of the six, Reg was the odd one out, drinking little alcohol and smoking neither cigarettes nor marijuana. He was self-conscious about his weight, for which he was taking amphetamine slimming pills that he claimed to have taken from his mother, as well as his thinning hair, which he often disguised under a wide-brimmed cowboy hat. He was, however, the clown of the band, and during the many long road journeys, he kept everyone amused with his Goon impressions and wordplay. The others observed Reg's occasional unpredictable mood swings – one minute he would be doing sublime impressions of Colonel Bloodnok, the next stamping his foot like a spoilt little madam. He would sometimes flounce off after a gig with the words, 'Forget you lot – I'm going places.' Baldry referred to these outbursts as Reg's 'screaming fits', the others called them 'Reggie's Little Moments'.

Former front man, Stuart Brown, was relegated to back-up vocals, with Reg a rung below him in the vocal pecking order, feeling distinctly marginalized. The band did not even play on Baldry's big 1967 hit, 'Let The Heartaches Begin'. A pre-recorded backing tape was used instead, although Reg's name did appear as co-writer on the label of the B-side for, 'Hey Lord, You Made The Night Too Long'.

As time passed, Bluesology merely became Baldry's backing band on the cabaret circuit, performing soft ballads to people more interested in playing bingo, which depressed Reg. 'It's the graveyard of musicians,' Elton would say later. 'I'd rather be dead than playing cabaret.'

Baldry restyled the band to complement his foppish Beau Brummel look and took the lead. The others had to wear yellow frilly shirts and green double-breasted suits from Carnaby Street tailor John Stephen.

Although not entirely happy with the new arrangements, Reg stayed with Bluesology to maintain an income. However, he looks back on them now as 'a second-rate band, trudging up and down the motorway playing "Knock On Wood" for the 115th time.' He was bored, in a rut and could not face such a miserable prospect for the rest of his life.

chapter three

I'm Going To Be A Teenage Idol

IT WAS 1967, the summer of love, and the post-war generation of babies was coming of age. Psychedelia, peace and love were omnipresent and London was swinging. *Sgt. Pepper's Lonely Hearts Club Band* was released by The Beatles in June and all summer long flower power blossomed. The air was thick with the scent of marijuana, joss sticks and patchouli oil. It was cool to wear antique military jackets, fur coats, ruffled shirts, floral kipper ties, cow bells and beads. Hippy culture was a way-out concoction of drug taking, transcendental meditation, radical politics, pacifism and a desire to get back to nature. Everything was changing: personal relationships, sexual permissiveness, attitudes towards authority, self-expression, civil rights, feminism, art and music. In short, the idealistic youth of the late 1960s would not be like their parents – they aspired to make the world a better and more peaceful place.

Meanwhile Reg Dwight hardly had time to go window-shopping at the psychedelic department store. He was still serving his apprenticeship in the music business, spending hours on the road with Bluesology. He was beginning to despair of getting anywhere as a performer in his own right with Long John Baldry constantly sidelining him. This was the reality of his lonely bedroom fantasies of being one of the boys in the band – playing in gloomy venues that were anything but psychedelic. 'We were the night-club entertainment, helping the food go down nicely,' he remembered. 'I began looking through the papers to try and find a job. I didn't care what it was, working in a record shop – anything.'

On the road with the band in June, in Newcastle upon Tyne, he spotted an advertisement in the *New Musical Express*: LIBERTY RECORDS WANTS TALENT. ARTISTES / COMPOSERS / SINGERS / MUSICIANS. TO FORM NEW GROUP. It was to be a turning point in the lives of two young men.

Liberty Records, one of the legendary labels from Reg's record collection, was looking for European talent to add to its American roster, which included

Bobby Vee and The Chipmunks. Confidence waning, Reg turned to his mother, who persuaded him to persevere and helped him write to Liberty Records.

In the spirit of the times, most people in the music industry were young and hip, and groovy eighteen-year-old, man-about-town Ray Williams was no exception. Reg went to meet him at his Liberty Records office in Albemarle Street, Mayfair. 'He was a bit fat, a bit forlorn looking,' Williams has said, 'dressed in blue denim, with all his stuff in a carrier bag, like Tiny Tim.' Reg told Williams that he could not write lyrics or sing very well, but thought he might be able to write songs. Williams warmed to the polite, well-spoken Reg who opened up his heart, confiding in him about not being allowed to sing in Bluesology, and feeling lost and unloved. Too nervous to play his own compositions, Reg sang two Jim Reeves' songs, 'I Love You Because' and 'He'll Have To Go', on the office piano for Williams, and behind the keyboard the little boy blue was transformed into a relaxed and controlled performer. But however much Williams liked this engaging fellow, he could not offer him an immediate escape from Bluesology.

From the sackful of replies to the advertisement, Williams had also pulled out a collection of lyrics sent by an aspiring poet called Bernie Taupin, and he suggested that Reg might put them to music. Reg took the lyrics home to read in his bedroom and was inspired. Elton recalled: 'I found it easy to write melodies to these songs. They were naïve and pretentious at the same time, but then that was the year for pretentiousness.' He set about writing melodies for twenty of Bernie's poems.

Through Williams's connections Reg spent his time off from Bluesology in a two-track studio owned by music publisher Dick James, and run by his son Stephen. Stephen James had set up This Record Company ('This' is an anagram of 'hits' and 'shit') to handle the output of the studio, which song-writers and musicians associated with Dick James Music, such as Roger Greenaway and Roger Cook (David and Jonathan), Spencer Davis, Graham Nash and Allan Clarke (The Hollies), used to record demos. The engineer was Caleb Quaye. Along with two songwriters who had also answered Williams's ad, Nicky James and Kirk Duncan, the shy pianist Reg Dwight joined the team who were allowed to use the studio. With Quaye's cooperation, he stayed on late into the night, recording demos of songs he had written for Bernie's lyrics.

Bernie Taupin's background could not have been more different from Reg's. He was born on 22 May 1950 into a happy household in the Lincolnshire countryside. His French father, Robert, was a farmer and worked for the Ministry of Agriculture. Bernie grew up in a cultured Catholic family, with French as a second language. His maternal grandfather was a classics teacher who passed on his love of literature to his grandsons, reading them the great English poems, such as Coleridge's 'The Rime of the Ancient Mariner' and Tennyson's 'The Charge of the Light Brigade'. Bernie loved reading stories – anything from *The Wind in the Willows, Winnie-the-Pooh* and the Narnia stories, to Wild West adventures. Like Reg, Bernie lived in an imaginary world of his own, not with football results and pop charts, but immersed in Sir Walter Scott's 'Lochinvar', and stories about Jesse James or Billy the Kid. Bernie spent his hours reading narrative poetry rather than working on the farm. 'I always loved stories,' he said. 'So to write a story and to put it to music – I thought that would be wonderful.'

Using his father's transistor radio at night he listened to Radio Luxembourg or the American Forces Network, which broadcast to the many US air bases in East Anglia. He was obsessed with Americana and loved songs with Western narrative themes. He was inspired to start writing lyrics and poems by country and folk music, and by Woody Guthrie in particular, but it was Bob Dylan who really unlocked the door to the power of words and song for Bernie.

Bernie left school at sixteen and had no interest in following his father into a farming career. He worked briefly as a journalist, a printer and a fruit-machine mechanic, and even indulged in petty burglary. At seventeen, he had just lost his job as a chicken farm labourer when he happened to see Ray Williams's advertisement in *New Musical Express*. He crafted a carefully worded letter and collected a handful of poems to send with it, then put the envelope on the mantelpiece, forgetting to post it. The story goes that his mother spotted it and posted it for him.

A week or so after Reg's visit, Bernie was invited to London for an interview with Williams, who arranged for the two to meet the next day at Dick James's demo studio. Elton remembered: 'I was sitting in the studio and Bernie appeared one day and said, "I'm the man who writes lyrics." He was extremely shy and so was I, so we went and had a cup of coffee round the corner in Charing Cross Road.' They discovered that although they were very different, they had plenty in common. Bernie recalled: 'We were both mad about pop music and both desperate to write songs.' They shared a love of Tamla Motown, The Beatles and Bob Dylan, and were both fantasists living in make-believe worlds of music and words. Music was a link between their different backgrounds: suburban maisonette – idyllic farmhouse, distant father – loving father, lonely only child – carefree child with two brothers, pub pianist – chicken farmer. Bernie observed later: 'We were complete opposites, town mouse and country mouse'.

When Bernie met Reg he thought he was urbane, pleasant and jolly. He thought, 'We'll have fun for a couple of years, then I'll go back to Lincolnshire and drive a tractor,' when in fact, they would become one of the most successful songwriting partnerships in the history of popular music.

In the recording studio, Reg and Bernie found they could work together at speed. The melodies, chords and compositions flowed quickly to Reg's piano keyboard, often in as little as ten minutes. Their first song was 'Scarecrow' and within a week they had produced more than a dozen. Reg was still committed to tour dates with Bluesology, so Bernie would either return to Putney, where he was staying with his Uncle Henry, or home to the farm in Owmby-by-Spital, sending lyrics to Reg by post. This would become their working method for years to come, whether they were miles apart or in the next room. And with the support of Caleb Quaye, Reg would record demos late into the night at James's studio.

Sgt. Pepper had an overwhelming influence on musicians of the time, and according to Bernie: 'Everybody was trying to get on the "Lucy In The Sky With Diamonds" bandwagon.' In his naïvety, he used every psychedelic cliché in the book. He remembers coming up with an unending stream of awful abstract notions, 'Marshmallow melodies in my mind, the sky is bleeding, rainbow slide city' and so on. But nothing was too rococo or too weird for Reg when composing his increasingly assured melodies. The words always came before the music and Bernie was never prescriptive about what sort of tune might suit, beyond an occasional hint that this might be a slow ballad, or that an up-tempo number. It was more than likely that Reg, with his finely honed sense of the absurd, would put a melancholy tune to jolly words, and upbeat rock and roll to sad words.

Dick James was born in 1919 in East London as Richard Leon Isaac Vapnick, the son of a kosher butcher of Polish extraction. Aged fourteen he was inspired by a Bing Crosby movie and left school to become a singer. He changed his name to Lee Sheridan and later Dick James, crooning with a variety of dance bands. In the late 1950s, as a session singer, he sang the theme tune to the television series *The Adventures of Robin Hood*. The song became an international hit, but James only received his session fee of $25.50 (£17). At the age of thirty-two he decided that his prospects might be rosier if he published songs rather than sang them.

Since 1962, Dick James had done rather well publishing Lennon-McCartney songs. For this purpose he had set up Northern Songs, which in 1965 became a public company, reaping vast dividends for himself as managing director. He also had shares in a glittering line-up of other artistes' publishing companies, including Cilla Black, Billy J. Kramer, The Hollies, the Spencer Davis Group, Gerry and the Pacemakers, and The Troggs.

To Reg, James was the living embodiment of his dreams and pop-hero worship. As well as his association with The Beatles and other gods of his record collection, the sound of his voice reminded him of home, bringing back memories of the crooners and swing bands on his mother's wireless, not to mention the Robin Hood theme tune. For advice and support Reg would turn to the avuncular James who, with his balding head, thick-rimmed specs and kindly voice, seemed to fill an emotional void. 'Dick is a straight, right-down-the-middle Jewish publisher,' said Elton. 'To me he's been like a father. If there's any problem, Dick will sort it out for me.'

James gave his twenty-year-old son, Stephen, responsibility for running the office. In the era of the singer-songwriter, The Beatles, and many who followed them, wanted to sing their own songs, and it was becoming increasingly difficult to persuade pop stars to sing songs by other people. Stephen convinced his father that DJM should have in-house recording facilities where singer-songwriters could be nurtured to produce marketable records. Of course, for some time there had been plenty of singer-songwriting activity in the studios after hours. Stephen was not worried by the illicit use of the studio and its facilities, providing he could hear the results. He listened to the tapes that Reg and Quaye had produced, and liked them enough to play them to his father.

In November 1967 Dick summoned Reg and Bernie for a meeting. Elton recalled how nervous they both were: 'It was like waiting for O-level results.' They were ushered into the executive office, its walls lined with gold discs and photographs of their heroes, The Beatles. To their astonishment, Dick offered the young songwriting partnership a formal contract. Dick and Stephen were impressed by these well brought up, polite young men, especially the witty and diffident Reg. Dick decided that they had enough talent to offer them a contract with his publishing company, Dick James Music. On 7 November they signed the deal. They were both under twenty-one, so their signatures had to be witnessed by a parent. Reg's mother remembered: 'It was like a dream come true. I was very green behind the ears and I never thought about going to a solicitor, I just trusted Mr James.' But she admitted in court, in 1985, that she had not understood what she was signing. Under the terms of the agreement, DJM owned world copyright of their songs, which should be no less than eighteen titles, over a renewable three-year period. In return Dick paid them a joint advance of $150 (£100) against royalties (10 per cent of the marked selling price of each copy after the first 250 copies, and 50 per cent of proceeds from recording, live performance, radio and television broadcasting and sub-licensing abroad). They would also receive a weekly wage – $22.50 (£15) for Reg and $15 (£10) for Bernie.

Stephen set about playing demo tapes of Reg and Bernie's songs to his Artist and Repertoire (A&R) contacts at all the record companies, in order to sell their talents as songwriters for other artists. Unexpectedly, he was told the songs were too quirky for the likes of Dusty Springfield, Sandie Shaw or Lulu, and that Reg's own voice was interesting enough to perform them himself. Reg had lost confidence in himself as a performer but, bolstered by the DJM deal, he decided to get into shape for appearing as a front man. He raided his mother's bathroom cabinet for slimming pills and succeeded in losing twenty-eight pounds. He replaced his Buddy Holly specs with rimless 'granny' glasses like those worn by John Lennon, and he was ready to face an audience.

It was the longed-for way out of Bluesology and, on 10 January 1968, Reg signed a recording deal with This Record Company, again witnessed by his mother, because he was still ten weeks short of his twenty-first birthday. He agreed to record at least two albums a year. For this he would get a royalty of 20 per cent of all net monies received by the company, after all expenses, which meant that he would receive about 2 per cent of each record's retail price.

Reg had never had much luck with girls, which he may have put down to his shyness and fear of rejection. He had enjoyed numerous platonic friendships with girls from school, but these liaisons were never at all serious. At the end of 1967, after one of his last gigs with Bluesology at the Cavendish Club in Sheffield, Reg embarked on a very unlikely relationship. He fell for a woman accompanied by a midget disc jockey called the Mighty Atom. To Reg, Linda Woodrow – heiress to the Epicure pickle and chutney empire – was glamorous and attractive, and nearly as tall as Long John Baldry.

Reg and Linda decided to find a flat together. The pair soon became a threesome in a rented basement flat at 29 Furlong Road, Islington, when Bernie moved in too. He was not alone in wondering what attracted Reg to a girl three years older, six inches taller, who looked – thanks to her hairpieces, false nails and false eyelashes – twenty years older. Reg was not the ideal flatmate. He was used to being looked after by his mother, aunt and grandmother, and had a lot to learn about domestic chores such as washing, ironing and cooking. He frequently phoned home for housekeeping advice from his mother. Bernie and Reg spent their days in Dick James's studio and Linda would sometimes visit at the end of her nine-to-five day job as a secretary. She had strong views – not only about how the flat should be run, but how she envisaged Reg's future. She wanted him to be a sophisticated cabaret star like Buddy Greco, not a pop singer.

When it came to sex, Reg was shy, nervous and not particularly interested, from what Linda remembers. He was confused about his sexual identity and would later admit that he had fancied Bernie, although it was never a sexual relationship. 'I would never leap on him, I just adored him, like a brother,' he said. Reg and Bernie spent most of their time in each other's company and formed a close bond. Whether they were whipping up instant meals in the flat, visiting the laundrette or writing songs, Bernie became the brother Reg had always longed for. 'He was the first love of my life,' Elton would say later. 'Physically never, but emotionally. That love never really died.' They shared everything that was most important to Reg: heroes, ambition and LPs.

Reg was allowing himself to drift into a domestic situation with Linda. Despite feeling uncomfortable with the circumstances, he simply did not have the nerve to end their relationship. Shy and conventional, he had been brought up to do the right thing at all times and on his twenty-first birthday on 25 March 1968, Reg and Linda announced their engagement. According to Linda: 'He didn't exactly go down on his knees. He just mumbled something about "We may as well get married". I had to pay out £5 for my own engage-ment ring – it had a small diamond – as Reg didn't have any money.'

Reg's father sent him a birthday present and Reg's thank-you letter shows that, despite the ructions over his having left school to work in the music industry, he was still on the fondest terms with both his father and stepmother. He first thanked them for the briefcase they had sent him, which would be useful for carrying around his song lyrics, and told them that his birthday had been quiet but relaxing. Reg then revealed his engagement to Linda: 'We do not intend to get married yet, or at any rate not until my career takes shape. She is a very understanding girl and realizes that at the moment my work must come first.'

As the months rolled on, Bernie and Reg were frustrated that their first record together, 'I've Been Loving You', a routine ballad with both words and music by Reg (although Bernie was given a writer's credit), failed to make it into the charts. Despondency set in as they continued to write and compose commercial songs for other artists.

At the same time, things were not going well for Reg and Linda either. Physically, their relationship was without fulfilment, and he could not face getting married and settling down with her. Consequently Reg decided to take drastic action. No one had understood the depth of his depression and confusion until Bernie and Linda found him with his head in the gas oven in the flat. He had taken a few safety precautions, however, ensuring the gas was on a low setting, opening the window and taking a cushion for his head. Bernie pulled him away from the oven while Linda moaned about wasting the gas. He would later describe it as a 'very Woody Allen-type suicide'.

The wedding arrangements were all but finalized. The register office in Highbury was booked, the invitations were in the post and the cake was iced. Reg phoned his father and invited him but, according to his stepmother, Stanley did not believe there would be a wedding. Edna recalled Stanley saying: 'His mother will see to it that he won't get married.'

Three weeks before the wedding, Long John Baldry, who was to be best man, decided to have words with Reg. 'Bernie, Reg and I started out the evening in The Shazz, a drinking club above the Marquee Club in Soho,' Baldry recalled. We ended up in the Bag O'Nails and he was obviously in a despondent mood. Reg said, "This woman, she's trapped me into marrying her and I don't want to."' Baldry advised him to pack his bags and go home to his mother, which is exactly what he did. Or, rather, he phoned home and Fred Farebrother came to Furlong Road in his van to pick up Reg, his belongings and his soulmate Bernie, to take them home to the Frome Court maisonette. A distraught Linda was left to pick up the pieces in Islington. Reg would later claim that the song 'Someone Saved My Life Tonight' was written about Baldry, although some credit must go to Bernie who had actually pulled him from the oven, and who was not one to ignore a half-hearted suicide attempt as a good subject for a song.

Frome Court would suffice until the dust had settled, but in fact, they ended up staying for another year and a half, sharing Reg's bedroom, the haven of his lonely boyhood dreams and home to his precious record collection. They bought bunkbeds, a record player and a television, and were tidy enough to share the tiny space. It was here that their songwriting started to blossom. Bernie would sit on the lower bunk in their bedroom writing the words and shuttle his lyrics along the narrow passage to Elton, sitting at the piano in the lounge.

Reg had been worried for some time that his name didn't exactly scream rock god, and felt that 'Reginald Dwight' was a name more suited to a librarian or accounts clerk. He wanted to be taken seriously in the music business, and decided it was time to reinvent himself. According to Baldry: 'It actually happened on an aeroplane from Edinburgh to London on May 12 1968. Elton John was born on that flight.' Reg took the forename of Bluesology's saxophonist, Elton Dean, and his new surname from Long John Baldry. Reginald Kenneth Dwight flew out of Edinburgh but it was Elton John who landed at Heathrow. Some years later, Elton would add an ironic middle name – Hercules, after the carthorse on his favourite television programme, *Steptoe and Son*. 'It was like slipping into a Superman costume,' he remembered.

'Suddenly I was no longer Reg Dwight from Pinner, and I believed that anything was possible.'

Elton and Bernie's efforts for DJM, inoffensive pieces which showed little of the originality to follow, were beginning to picked up by other performers. 'Turn To Me' was recorded by Plastic Penny, 'When The First Tear Shows' was sung by Brian Keith, and 'The Tide Will Turn For Rebecca' was sung by the actor Edward Woodward. The most notable record was picked up by Roger Cook, soon-to-be lead singer of Blue Mink: 'Skyline Pigeon' was a reflective song about a caged bird set free by a prisoner, and hinted at the quirky narratives that would become the hallmark of much of Bernie's future work.

Elton was never afraid of hard work, and took the opportunity to earn some extra cash when he began freelancing as a session pianist and back-up vocalist. In 1968 he was an uncredited contributor on hits by The Barron Knights and Scaffold, sang on Tom Jones's enduring belter, 'Delilah', and played piano on The Hollies' hit, 'He Ain't Heavy, He's My Brother'.

Steve Brown joined DJM in September 1968. He had been a plugger at EMI Records and was ambitious to advance his career as a record producer. His sole responsibility at DJM was to nurture Elton and Bernie. Brown came straight to the point and told them how awful their efforts were, but persuaded them to concentrate on less commercial material, contrary to what Dick James wanted. Elton said later: 'It was a very brave thing for Steve to do, telling us "Don't take any notice of the boss."' Brown inspired Elton and Bernie, and the significance of his creative direction cannot be underestimated; he opened Elton's eyes to other kinds of music, including the experimental electronics of Pink Floyd. 'I used to be very bigoted in my musical opinion; it was Steve Brown who played a very important role in my musical career,' said Elton.

'Lady Samantha' was Elton and Bernie's first record under Brown's regime, which was released on 10 January 1969. It failed to enter the Top Fifty, but received good reviews in the music press, and through the efforts of Brown and Stephen James, 'Lady Samantha' was accepted onto the Radio One play-list. With sales of 4,000 copies, the BBC called Elton in for an audition to sing live on radio. He scored a three-all draw with the six-man panel, with reviews such as, 'Thin, piercing voice with no emotional appeal. Don't think this singer doing his own weird material is right for radio at present.' Elton was given a chance, however, and appeared as a solo artist on the *Brian Matthew Show*, performing three songs and giving his first radio interview. In his unassuming way, Elton said: 'I've got a partner who writes the lyrics to my songs. I haven't had a hit yet, but I've been lucky.' Even though 'Lady Samantha' had not been a commercial hit, its radio success meant that Brown could persuade Dick James to let Elton and Bernie go ahead and make an album of their own. This was a bold leap of faith on James's part, as most pop acts only recorded singles. Long-playing albums were for stars in the league of The Beatles and the Rolling Stones.

Thanks to the decline of Dick James's relationship with The Beatles, Elton and Bernie were given the chance to make their first album. The fifty-fifty deal for publication of songs through Northern Songs that had seemed so generous to Lennon and McCartney in 1963 seemed, six years later, unfairly burdensome to the most successful songwriters in history. James's 23 per cent share in Northern Songs made them feel exploited by 'the men in suits'. Kindly Dick James suddenly seemed old-fashioned and out-of-step with the chaotic aspirations of The Beatles and their business venture, Apple Corps, the conceptual *White Album*, and John and Yoko's calls for world peace. With share prices in Northern Songs taking a downturn, James sold his 23 per cent to Lew Grade's ATV organization for more than $1.5 million (£1 million) in early 1969. DJM looked after Northern Songs for three more years, but a burden had been lifted from James's shoulders, and he began to focus his thoughts on his in-house talent.

Consequently he was easily persuaded by Steve Brown to offer Elton and Bernie a chance in the studio to record an album's worth of the many songs they had written together in Northwood Hills. *Empty Sky* was to be their first album, recorded in a few days in February 1969, in the DJM studio, at a bargain cost of $225 (£150) per track, and produced by Steve Brown. It showed an early glimpse of future potential, with a hotchpotch of folksy songs about literary myths and the Wild West such as, 'Val-Hala' and 'Western Ford Gateway'. Answering Brown's calls to be experimental, a haunting guitar sound was achieved by putting the guitarist out on the fire escape. The album featured the debut of Nigel Olsson and Roger Pope on drums who would both become close, long-term collaborators. Although Elton's voice was described as reedy and high-pitched, it was evident that he was a talented musician and thoughtful singer.

The album was released in June 1969 and, despite all the hype and publicity dreamed up by DJM, sold less than 4,000 copies. Its eclectic mix of poetic, fanciful songs did not thrill the record-buying public who were still tuned into themed albums like *Sgt. Pepper*.

The early days were like a fairytale, according to Bernie. He has vivid memories of the two of them recording *Empty Sky* late into the night, then wandering off into the dark West End streets. Elton remembers: 'Making *Empty Sky* still holds the nicest memories for me because it was the first, I suppose. When we finished work on the title track it just floored me. I thought it was the best thing I'd ever heard in my life.'

Elton was frustrated by his lack of chart success, but he still lived for music and continued doing session work. He sang on the popular soundalike compilations, cheap imitations of real hits, that sold on the Marble Arch, Avenue, Ace of Clubs and Music for Pleasure labels. His talent for mimicry meant that he could impersonate Stevie Wonder on 'Signed, Sealed, Delivered' or Mungo Jerry on 'In the Summertime'. It was a way to make ends meet, but he began to wonder if he would ever have a hit of his own.

DJM did not give up on Elton and, despite his reticence, launched him as a live performer. He appeared as a backing singer on BBC television's *Top of the Pops*, supporting The Ladybirds, Brotherhood of Man and Pickettywitch. Elton and the line-up on *Empty Sky* did a few gigs in and around London. In this mood of despondency, the spirit of Jerry Lee Lewis was eerily absent and Elton could not summon up the dynamic stage presence he had displayed as Reg Dwight at school dances. His spirits were so low that he made no effort to dress up, coming on stage in his square, old, tweed jacket and corduroys.

Elton wanted action and seriously considered leaving DJM to find a new manager. He was courted by Chris Blackwell of Island Records who offered him a $15,000 (£10,000) advance, as long as he could be released from his DJM contracts without legal difficulties. Blackwell read the small print and ominously told Elton that he thought there were holes in them.

It was make or break time for DJM and the John-Taupin team. In nearly two years, DJM had spent nearly $105,000 (£70,000) on developing Elton John (equivalent to about $750,000 (£500,000) today), on recording, publicity and promotion. Against all the odds, Steve Brown persuaded Dick James to give Elton and Bernie one more chance to capitalize on the creative progress they had made on *Empty Sky*.

They booked an upmarket production team and a proper studio, Trident, in London's West End. Orchestral arranger Paul Buckmaster, whom Elton had already met at a Miles Davis concert in 1969, was impressed with two demo tracks, 'The King Must Die' and 'Your Song'. Buckmaster had recently had a hit with David Bowie's 'Space Oddity' and brought in his producer, Gus Dudgeon, who would become to Elton what George Martin was to The Beatles, in creating the Elton John signature sound. The atmosphere at Trident was worlds away from the small DJM studio. Buckmaster brought in a full symphony orchestra, complete with harp, and all the scores were written in meticulous detail. The album took eighteen days from December 1969 into January 1970. The themes and songs were similar to those on *Empty Sky*, poetic and bawdy, manic and moody. But the grandeur and scale of the recording sessions and the talent of the producers combined to deliver a prodigious performance from Elton.

Buckmaster's arrangements were revolutionary for the time and his sweeping strings were said to be inspired by Dvorak. Elton's classical training was obvious, his intricate percussive piano lending drama to each song. In an interview with television presenter David Frost in 1991, Elton recalled how he would write his songs: 'In those days it took me about fifteen to twenty minutes to write a song, and half an hour to an hour to memorize it because I didn't put it on tape. I didn't put any of the songs on tape. So at one point, I had about thirty or forty songs stock-piled in my head that I'd written by memory.'

Elton John was released to rave reviews in April 1970, with an article in *New Musical Express* headlined: IS THIS THE YEAR OF ELTON JOHN? He was described in *NME* as 'a big talent . . . who sounds as if he has lived in Nashville all his life'. The album sold 10,000 copies, which kept it in the charts for fourteen weeks during the summer, holding its own in the company of *Let It Be* by The Beatles and *Bridge Over Troubled Water* by Simon and Garfunkel. The only thing missing in Dick James's strategy was a big-selling single. Elton John would not be destined to remain a mere cult name in the record collections of discerning music fans.

James was so impressed with his investment that he reviewed the recording agreement he had made with Elton in 1967. A new deal, superseding the previous one, stated that Elton was bound to DJM for five years, and he should make three instead of two albums a year. His percentage of This Record Company's receipts from Philips was doubled to 40 per cent, so that he would receive about 4 per cent of the retail price. Two years later the figure would rise to 60 per cent, that is 6 per cent for him.

The first single to be released from *Elton John* was 'Border Song'. It did not enter the charts, but made enough of an impression for Elton to be asked to sing it on *Top of the Pops*. The occasion meant more to Elton than appearing solo on the programme for the first time because backstage he came face to face with his ultimate pin-up, Dusty Springfield.

The only way to sell records and become a household name was to go on the road. This meant taking centre stage, which to the shy, unassuming and self-conscious Elton, was wholly unappealing. He was paralysed with stage fright and resisted as long as he could, but said: 'I suddenly decided it was the only way if the records were going to sell.' They needed a new manager, and chose Ray Williams, who had originally introduced Elton to Bernie. A band was hastily assembled with Dee Murray on bass guitar, Nigel Olsson on drums, and Elton in front on the piano. The group gelled almost immediately. Murray said: 'It was just like magic. Elton was great to play with because he gave you complete freedom.' All three were dedicated musicians; Olsson

practised his drums for four hours every day and was constantly experi-
menting and trying to broaden his range of instruments. His association with
Elton John would redefine production standards for ever.

Bob Stacey, from the Spencer Davis Group, joined the team as road
manager and would remain with Elton for years, eventually taking charge of
his wardrobe. The band were paid $75 (£50) a night for their first gigs at
various regional universities. They had one van and a few pieces of essential
equipment, but Elton had to make do with whatever piano was available,
often out of tune or without foot pedals. In the beginning, Elton's stage act
was hardly dynamic and when performing their first international gig in
Paris, they were booed off stage and bombarded with hot-dogs. Gradually,
Elton shook off his shyness and started to engage with the audience. The
trio were booked to perform as a warm-up act with the Pretty Things,
Heavy Jelly and T. Rex at the Roundhouse in Camden at the Pop Proms in
June 1970, which was hosted by John Peel. On stage a breakthrough
occurred; mid-song, Elton accidentally knocked the piano stool over – the
crowd adored it. Memories of his flamboyant performances at Pinner
County came flooding back. He also demonstrated a natural ability to
connect with the audience at a festival in Yorkshire when, in atrocious
weather, he passed bottles of brandy into the audience to keep them warm,
making him the star turn of the day.

Thanks to DJM's close contacts in the United States, 'Border Song' was
released as a single there, but only reached ninety-two on the Billboard chart.
The album *Empty Sky* was deemed too unhip and introspective by the music
business and, apparently, the record-buying public. The current flavours of
the month were post-Woodstock rockers Buffalo Springfield and Crosby,
Stills, Nash and Young. However, Russ Regan, head of Uni Records in
America, loved the eponymous *Elton John*, and said he would release it if
Elton went over to promote it. Dick James would have to pay for the trip, so if
the boys were going to go, they would need to play some concerts to make it
worthwhile. Elton reluctantly agreed, although he thought a transatlantic tour
was premature given that the band had only been together for five months.
Nevertheless, it was a chance for him and Bernie to play tourist and visit the
country where cowboys, film legends and rock-and-roll heroes originated.
And, as Bernie remembers: 'We thought we might as well go over, just to check
out the record shops.'

Persuading venue owners to accept an unknown singer and his small band
was far from easy, but eventually they were offered a week at a well-known
folk club in Los Angeles, the 350-seat Troubadour, for the princely fee of $500
(£333). Elton John would top the bill with the late folk singer David Ackles,

another of his early heroes. The Troubadour was a famous showcase and social mecca for the industry on the west coast, and was celebrating its twentieth anniversary in August 1970.

Ray Williams brought in an American publicist, Norm Winter, to whip up some headlines and create a buzz in town. Winter was known in the American industry as a man of endless zeal and unbounded energy, to whom generating hype and publicity stunts came as second nature. He hired a red London Transport double-decker bus, plastered with a banner reading 'Elton John Has Arrived', to drive Elton and his entourage from the airport to the hotel. After a long economy-class flight the last thing the boys wanted was to get on a bus. It was so unglamorous – where were the record-company limos? Elton found the stunt tasteless and embarrassing, but the polite Pinner boy told *Rolling Stone*: 'You can't be rude to people. I'd rather go through with things, suffer inside, and grin and bear it, than be really nasty to people.'

In the three days scheduled for recovery before the concerts, Ray Williams organized a day trip to Palm Springs to meet a friend of an old girlfriend; they hoped to borrow a hairdryer since no one had packed one. It was on this occasion that Bernie met his future wife, Maxine. Elton decided he did not want to go, so they all set off for Palm Springs and left him behind on his own. Williams should have perhaps realized he was dealing with a sensitive personality, having observed Reg's diffidence three years earlier. Left alone for a whole day in an anonymous hotel room, 5,000 miles from home, had clearly upset Elton. His dreams had seemed to be coming true but now he felt abandoned – this was his hour of need and he was not the centre of attention. By the time the boys had returned to the hotel, Elton had suffered a panic attack. He was nervous and absolutely petrified. He was the one who was going to be out in front, singing the songs; he was the one who had to overcome his stage fright, his shyness, his lack of self-esteem. Elton had phoned Dick James in London and told Williams that he was going to take the next plane home, regardless of the damage it could do to his career. This was more than a tantrum; it was a serious threat. After a few tense phone calls and some delicate diplomacy by Williams, Elton calmed down and prepared himself for Tuesday night at the Troubadour. This outburst was a prime example of one of Reggie's Little Moments and was the first time he had suffered one prior to a performance. It would not be the last.

Publicist Norm Winter had dedicated himself to hyping the concert. Every record shop in town displayed the sombre black cover of the *Elton John* album, and every DJ had a free copy. The Troubadour's owner, Doug Weston, invited a star-studded audience including Beach Boy Mike Love, Gordon Lightfoot, David Gates of Bread, Don Black, Quincy Jones and a long list of influential rock journalists. Many of the industry people had come based on the understanding that Neil Diamond was performing, but the singer had merely been persuaded to introduce the unknown Elton John.

Elton's sensational debut at the Troubadour would be a life-changing moment for him and a key event in pop history. In 1990 *Rolling Stone* magazine rated it among the twenty concerts that changed the course of rock and roll. In one night, Elton was transformed from a struggling unknown from Pinner, into the industry's most talked-about newcomer.

Elton made his debut on Tuesday 25 August 1970, at 10 p.m., sporting a beard, bell-bottomed jeans and a red T-shirt emblazoned with the legend 'Rock 'n' Roll'. The one-hour set got off to a slow start, reminiscent of the band's recent underwhelming gigs back home. From the staid portrait on the album cover and posters, the audience may have expected laidback, lounge-type entertainment, so continued to chat and order drinks, ignoring the music. After three or four songs Elton had had enough and something snapped. Producer Don Black recalls: 'He stood up, kicked away his piano stool and shouted, "Right. If you won't listen, perhaps you'll bloody well listen to this!"' He started beating the piano, using it as an acrobatic prop for 'Burn Down The Mission'. Everyone stopped talking. 'It was electrifying. It was a charged evening,' Russ Regan said. 'We knew within forty-five minutes that we had a superstar.' By the end Elton was kneeling on the floor, playing, singing and telling the audience to join in the choruses. America had never seen anything like it – a rock-and-roll knees-up. Everyone wanted to meet Elton after the show, but backstage he reverted to the tongue-tied, humble pop fan as he greeted many of his heroes face to face.

Elton packed out the Troubadour each night until 30 August, and word spread like wildfire. A Los Angeles radio station, KPPC, took a full-page advertisement in the *LA Free Press* to thank him for coming over. On the second night, Leon Russell, one of Elton's favourite singer-pianists turned up. Luckily, Elton did not spot him until the final number: 'Thank God, I didn't. Because at that time I slept and drank Leon Russell. When I saw him I just stopped and he said, "Keep on." There he was sitting in the front row. My legs turned to jelly.' During this incredible week Leon Russell invited Elton and Bernie to visit him at home to jam with him. Elton and Bernie visited Beach Boy Brian Wilson's house and were fêted wherever they went. They were special guests at Disneyland where Elton bought a pair of Mickey Mouse ears, which he wore on stage that night. A week later, promoter Bill Graham offered Elton an unprecedented $5,000 (£3,300) to appear at the much bigger venues of Fillmore East and West. Nearly two weeks after his first Troubadour performance, the *Elton John* album had sold 30,000 copies.

The band's low-budget city-break had turned into a fully-fledged tour, with bookings at the San Francisco Troubadour, in Boston, Philadelphia and New York.

Returning to England in September 1970 to renew his visa, Elton experienced a welcome that was decidedly low-key. He was booked as a warm-up act for a band called Fotheringay at the Royal Albert Hall, and arranged to meet his mother and Fred Farebrother by the main entrance, where no one recognized him. Few people in the British music business knew what Elton had achieved in just three weeks in America. An interview he gave to Richard Williams for *Melody Maker* was relegated to the inside pages, and therefore Elton's feet were still firmly on the ground: 'You simply can't sit back and believe everything people say about you, or you'd get terrible ego problems,' he said. 'I do believe we write good songs, but I get very embarrassed when people say so.' He also revealed his developing taste for eye-catching stagewear, having brought back a few souvenir items including a gold lamé tailcoat from a Busby Berkeley musical, which he was going to wear for the Albert Hall gig. Naturally he stole the show, upstaging the folksy Fotheringay every night.

Elton's and Bernie's lifestyles were slow to change and they carried on living in their shared bedroom at Sheila and Fred's. Their third album *Tumbleweed Connection*, was released on 30 October 1970, hot on the heels of *Elton John*, and contained a collection of songs full of references to firearms, bank robberies and stagecoaches. They had all been written in the flat the previous summer and were recorded without the lush orchestral arrangements, allowing the sound of Elton's voice and piano to dominate. The songs were described by Q magazine as 'a slightly eccentric excursion into the imagery of American hicksville'. The British public were not yet aware of Elton's dynamic stage antics, and the songs were appreciated only by a small, discerning constituency of record buyers – pop purists, listeners to John Peel's nightly Radio One show and fans of J. R. R. Tolkien's *Lord of the Rings*. But in America, everyone was talking about Elton John and *Tumbleweed Connection* went to number five in the Billboard chart.

By Hallowe'en, he was back in America opening his first proper tour, the record-breaking pace of which would set the tone for future tours. Swiftly organized by Elton's British booking agent at DJM, ex-jazz band leader Vic Lewis, it covered the major US cities, and in Los Angeles alone he gave five auditorium concerts. In Chicago he was hoisted into the air by police to be whisked over the crowds. On 17 November he appeared on WABC radio in New York in a live studio concert, backed by Murray and Olsson. The 125 studio tickets went to fans, press, friends, record executives and contest winners. The session was recorded on the live album *11-17-70*, although Elton said later that he was not aware that the session was being taped. Three days later at Fillmore East club in New York, Elton made his East Coast debut when he shared the bill with Leon Russell. Then he and Bernie were introduced to even bigger heroes, Bob Dylan and The Band, who were in the audience. Not only did they get to meet their heroes, they were also fêted by them. Elton was the focus of attention on stage, but Bernie's lyrics were admired by Bob Dylan and Robbie Robertson of The Band; in fact, they asked Elton and Bernie to write a song for them. 'I think Bernie was a bit embarrassed,' recalled Elton, 'because Robbie was his current idol.'

To Elton's tight and professional band the music came first. To the press Elton was a refreshing change from the usual pretentious rock star. He was, and still is, a genuine pop fan; knowing his subject and dedicated to his music. He was also polite, friendly, straightforward, unassuming and down to earth. He was always at pains to make sure that Bernie's role in the partnership was acknowledged: 'Without Bernie, there'd be no songs. I get very annoyed when people ignore him.' And he was keener to talk about his many musical heroes than himself.

Elton seemed to hit the right note in America. All his British understated-ness and shyness could be disguised with garish, wacky clothes. He could send himself up before anyone else did, satirizing what he saw as his physical limitations. The short, tubby, balding Elton could be an antidote to the serious, early 1970s rock star with his phallocentric electric guitar, slim hips, hollow cheeks and long mop. Elton sat behind nine feet of solid wood, a solitary rock-and-roll choirboy singing his sad songs with the involuntary movement of a bushy eyebrow. It worked beautifully – American audiences lapped up his spectacular showmanship and couldn't get enough of his music.

On this tour, Elton's first outrageous performance in top gear was in the 6,000-seat Santa Monica Civic Auditorium. He was third on the bill after Ry Cooder and Odetta, and wore a jump suit beneath a blue velvet cloak, a brown leather top hat, and high silver boots adorned with stars. He was clean shaven and had a pair of huge Afrika Korps-style specs perched on his nose. As he ran through his set of songs from the two albums, he embarked on a cheeky striptease: he peeled down to a souvenir Fillmore West T-shirt, and a pair of purple tights. At each show, he would build up through the slow moody numbers, via some soul and gospel, to unleashing the spirit of Jerry Lee Lewis for the finale, when he would kick away the piano stool. He would never miss a note, whether playing with his hands or his feet, whether squatting, high bunny-kicking or lying prostrate under the piano. The crowd loved his antics and exaggerated clowning at the keyboard, and 'went mental', according to Elton.

Several pundits noticed an extraordinary change in Elton backstage, as he reverted to the shrinking violet from Pinner. On stage he soaked up the unconditional love of the audience, feeling he belonged. But backstage, while everyone else consumed champagne and anything else on offer, Elton would stand silently on the sidelines alone, still the odd one out. Fame made Elton more self-conscious than ever. When fans approached to ask for autographs it meant a lot to him, but he would always blush and say a quiet thank-you to them.

He was excruciatingly conscious of his body image and seemed to hate having his photograph taken. Stuart Windsor, a photographer on *Disc and Music Echo*, remembers him as surly and uncooperative sitting in Dick James's office in London, lolling in the maestro's chair with his feet on the desk, unwilling to pose for publicity photographs for *Tumbleweed Connection*.

Between gigs in America, Elton would hit the record shops to add to his collection. He told *Rolling Stone* that he had amassed a staggering '5,000 albums, 2,500 45s, 100 EPs, 60 78s, 500 eight-track cartridges and 300 cassettes'. Elton continually surprised his American interviewers with his extensive knowledge of every style of music. The minutiae of the tours fascinated Elton, and he scrupulously noted in his diary the statistics of the day – an estimate of audience numbers and the box-office takings, not forgetting the chart performance of his own records.

By late 1970, the American album-orientated stations were playing several tracks a day from *Elton John*, which aroused huge public interest. The album contained classics that remain peerless to this day. Elton John had provided the soundtrack of 1970. He would play to ever-growing audiences and all his insecurities, his sexual identity and his stage fright dissolved into the background. He said: 'For the first five years of my career I just loved every minute of it. I was having a ball.'

chapter four

Who Wears
These Shoes?

$\mathbb{E}$LTON AND BERNIE had begun 1970 as two struggling session musicians and jobbing songwriters, and ended the year as the toast of America. They were the only British pop act to break through in America before doing so at home. When Elton and Bernie returned home for Christmas they had two American top-five albums, and *Elton John* was about to go gold for sales worth $1 million (£666,600). While elfin Bernie still looked like a country mouse, Elton turned up at the DJM Christmas party dolled up like Greta Garbo. But was it too much too soon? Elton was already being warned by his doctors to cool off and relax more, and there were reports that he was close to a nervous breakdown; his solution was a strict diet of vitamin pills.

The time had come for the boys to move out of Frome Court. Bernie had fallen in love with Maxine Feibelman, the woman he had met in Palm Springs on his first day in America. They were married in early 1971 in Lincolnshire, with Elton as best man. As a world-class singer and entertainer, it was also time for Elton to fly the nest. He bought a luxury apartment in central London – 384 The Water Garden, near Marble Arch, and decided to trade in his humble Ford Escort for something a little more upmarket. His new car, a second-hand mauve Aston Martin, was previously owned by the late Bee Gee Maurice Gibb. Describing it as 'his first great car' it sparked a new passion. He would continue to buy 'great cars' just as he had collected Dinky toy cars as a boy.

In his pursuit of a chart hit in his home country, Elton began his long quest for a British number one. 'Your Song' was released as a single on 8 January 1971. Stephen James had been reluctant to select it as a single because of its pensiveness, which was out of tune with the fashion for driving guitar rock by artists such as Dave Edmunds and Hawkwind, or quirky songs by Mungo Jerry and David Bowie. The decision was inadvertently made by Radio One DJ Tony Blackburn, who heard it with a selection of songs sent out to DJs by

Stephen. Blackburn, who presided over the all-important breakfast show, promised to make it his record of the week if it was released as a single. 'Your Song' would become one of Elton and Bernie's greatest successes. It hit exactly the right note and marked the end of the psychedelic era of the 1960s, reaching number seven in Britain and number eight in the American singles charts.

Bernie Taupin remembers exactly how their first big hit was written: 'I wrote this song after having bacon and eggs in his mother's flat in Pinner, while he was having a bath in the other room.' The original lyric sheet is still stained with egg and coffee. Was it a poem from Bernie to his best friend and room-mate? Elton wrote the melody in ten minutes on 27 October 1969, and noted in his diary: 'In the end I did nothing today . . . wrote a new song called "Your Song".'

It introduced a new fashion for the lone voice with piano, followed by stars such as Gilbert O'Sullivan, and John Lennon with 'Imagine' later that year. Lennon complimented Elton on 'Your Song': 'There was something about his vocals that was an improvement on all the English vocals till then,' he said. Lennon, the bard of the 1960s, handed the baton to Elton, the witty and soon-to-be wildly eccentric new superstar.

As early as January 1971 the strain of his new working lifestyle was beginning to show. Elton had to cancel three British concerts on doctor's orders because of exhaustion after the pressure of his gruelling American tours. A disastrous trip to Cannes for the annual music industry festival, MIDEM, in January, prompted a furious hissy fit from Elton when his appearance on stage was delayed by Eric Burdon, ex-vocalist with The Animals. Scheduled for a fourteen-minute set, Burdon hogged the limelight with his new band, War, for over an hour, even after Elton and his band had been introduced. Elton was said to have left the theatre in a rage, vowing never to play in France again. In the event, Elton was persuaded to perform a short set the next evening, despite catcalls from the audience and the curtain falling down. After that he told the French what he thought, storming back on stage shouting, 'Whoever organized this fucking thing is a fucking idiot!' to a round of applause, before walking out. After one of his Little Moments he would always be full of remorse and eager to explain himself to journalists. He told *Melody Maker*: 'I've been feeling so rough, and I can only think it's been the strain of all the work.'

The lack of direction in Elton's life was mainly the result of not yet having a full-time manager, but it must have troubled the inveterate list-maker with the immaculate record collection and innate sense of order. He had a perfect writing partner, the best music publisher in the land, a team of the finest producers and musicians, but no single person to co-ordinate it all. Elton had been working his fingers to the bone, touring Britain and Europe before embarking on two more American tours. There was no proper strategy to planning his career, promoting him or controlling bookings. His image was unfocused to the point that he might be appearing at the Royal Festival Hall with a symphony orchestra one night, and camping it up on the *Andy Williams Show* on television the next. Neither was there a marketing strategy or a considered schedule for album releases, resulting in a glut of Elton John products with four albums in the shops at the same time. *Elton John* preceded *Tumbleweed Connection* by only six months, then a mere five months later came an ill-conceived movie soundtrack *Friends*, for a long-forgotten film directed by Lewis Gilbert. It might also have been wiser not to release the live album, *11.17.70*.

As a consequence Elton and Bernie became seriously concerned about overkill. Elton recalled later: 'I was getting more and more unhappy about it. I thought, "we've worked so bloody hard to get this far, and now we're blowing it". It was Elton himself, with a little encouragement from his mother, who suggested that his new friend and flatmate, John Reid, should be considered as his manager.

Elton's West Coast city-break had taken in some more stopovers on the heels of his sensational debut in Los Angeles. In San Francisco he met the man who would become his partner, his manager and the person with whom he would share the fabulous rewards the music business had to offer. In Bernie Taupin he had found a brother, his creative confidant. In John Reid he found his other self, someone who could take care of business, be his public face, fight his fights, defend his corner.

John Reid was born on 9 September 1949. His father was a thread-reeler at a cloth mill in Paisley. He grew up on the tough streets of the town in western Scotland, with a brief interlude when he, his parents and older brother emigrated to New Zealand in 1959. His father's company decided to transfer the whole operation, including the workforce, down under. After two years his mother, Betty, grew homesick and they all returned to Paisley when his father got a job as a welder at Chrysler's Linwood plant. John and his brother were bright enough to win places at St Mirin's Academy, the local Catholic grammar school, where John was a diligent student and a good all-rounder. He also took an interest in school social life and acted in school plays. He was a well-behaved teenager, typically going to youth-club dances, listening to music and going out with girls. He left school at sixteen to study marine engineering at Glasgow's Stow College. At this time, he took more of an interest in show business, joining an amateur dramatic society, appearing in several musicals and singing cover versions of pop hits with the house band at the Locarno ballroom. He dropped out of college after two years to find fame and fortune in London.

The city was still swinging in the late 1960s and Reid's ambition to get into the music business led him to the doors of EMI Records, the largest record company in Britain at the time. He started off by lying about his age and eventually got a job with Ardmore and Beechwood, then EMI's sole music publishing subsidiary. He became a plugger, persuading Radio Luxembourg and BBC radio to play the company's records. Still a teenager, he must have cut a distinctive style in comparison with his hairy, bell-bottomed peers, endearing himself to the middle-aged management types with his short hair, sharp suits and urbane style. EMI Records was to become John Reid's alma mater. He used his time there to educate himself with a crash course in music business methodology, publishing, accounting and contracts.

In a very short time he got his first big break and was promoted as label manager of EMI's operation of Detroit's legendary soul label, Tamla Motown. He was still only nineteen but seemed sophisticated, knowledgeable about art, literature and the theatre; he enjoyed good food and wine, and dined at expensive restaurants. His job was to select Motown tracks for release in Britain, to arrange publicity and promotion, and to look after the stars when they were in London. One of his astute choices was 'Tears Of A Clown' by Smokey Robinson and the Miracles, which was a number-one hit in the British singles chart before its American release.

Reid had already encountered Elton on the London music scene. Elton was well known at EMI Records as a session musician and composer of songs covered by their own aspiring artists, and notorious as an avid record collector, who would grasp any opportunity to acquire American imports from label managers as soon as they came into the country. He would often appear at Reid's office hoping to procure the latest Tamla Motown records from the cupboard. Until August 1970 Reid thought of Elton John only as 'a dumpy, balding little guy in a funny jump suit, who used to go around cadging records'.

Just before his twenty-first birthday, Reid was in San Francisco for a tenth-anniversary party for Tamla Motown. He received an invitation to attend the newly opened San Francisco Troubadour club where Elton would be performing on one of his extra dates in America, fresh from his sensational gig in Los Angeles. Reid recalled later: 'He rang me up, he was bubbling over with what the critics had said and dying to tell someone about it. I was the nearest Englishman – or nearest thing to an Englishman.' At the time Reid did not realize Elton's potential. A few days later, Elton asked Sue Ayton at DJM in London to send a birthday telegram to a 'John Reid'.

Weeks later the pair were living together in the Water Garden apartment. This move was a significant step up both the social and lifestyle ladder for Elton. He fitted effortlessly into a new life with Reid. Elton's mother and Fred warmed to the personable Reid and he developed a close rapport with Sheila, who did not fear that he threatened her relationship with her son. Sheila saw immediately that his evident qualities could benefit Elton and it was she who first tried to persuade Reid to be his manager, although Reid himself was not enthusiastic. Fred painstakingly redecorated the flat, and Reid furnished it in contemporary bachelor-pad style. It soon became a repository for the souvenirs and trinkets that caught Elton's eye on his travels. Reid was careful not to offend Elton's long-time room-mate and best friend, Bernie, and Elton was also concerned that Bernie should not feel rejected or replaced. 'I think Elton was more concerned than I was about us not being as close as before,' Bernie said.

To the outside world Elton and Reid were conventional flatmates, and in the innocent days of the early 1970s, that is exactly how they seemed. They were close companions and it was probably assumed that they had scores of girlfriends.

His youth apart, Reid fitted the template of the older, smarter manager like the cultured and urbane Larry Parnes, who was behind Billy Fury and Georgie Fame, and the impeccably tailored Brian Epstein, manager of The Beatles. Temperamentally, Elton and Reid complemented each other from the start. Reid's confidence and outward aggression were a perfect foil for Elton's shyness and lack of self-esteem. Elton was the plump vaudevillian and Reid his counterpart, the diminutive, dapper businessman. Reid was meticulously tidy and well organized. He was not only a fellow music devotee, friend and lover – most importantly, he was a father figure. John Reid would come to know Elton's every whim and he became the ultimate personal manager. It was said that he would 'kill for Elton'.

Always arguing, but ferociously loyal, they were more like a married couple than a successful business partnership. When Elton nominated Reid as his new manager, DJM staff were amazed to find the two were already living together. They formed a deep personal bond and their partnership would become not only the most profitable in pop history, but also the most competitive, turbulent and tempestuous.

Reid worked out his notice at EMI and joined the DJM team on a salary of $6,000 (£4,000) a year, on the understanding that when the DJM management contract expired in 1973, Reid could manage Elton exclusively. On the publishing side, Elton and Bernie extended the period of agreement with DJM for two years with a rise in composer's royalties from 50 per cent to 70 per cent, and in a decision that would have serious repercussions in the future, Dick James retained the copyright to all Elton and Bernie's songs for the full term of copyright; that is, for the lifetime of the writers, plus seventy years after their death. Dick felt that he owned enough of Elton so happily handed over 20 per cent in the form of the management contract to Reid.

Between April and June 1971, Elton undertook another frenetic American tour. His fourth in just eight months, it would last ten weeks and take in fifty-five high-energy stopovers, putting Elton into the dollar millionaire league. For the first time the esteemed *Rolling Stone* magazine featured him on its front cover. Top photographer Annie Leibovitz took his portrait, although he hardly appreciated her status and still disliked having his picture taken even after a year of success in America.

If Reid's time at EMI Records had been an apprenticeship in the music business, joining DJM was a degree course where he could learn from a master. Reid made sure he spent as much time as possible attending personal tutorials in Dick James's office, soaking up stories from the great man's thirty years in the business. He pored over every detail of Elton and Bernie's recording contracts, publishing agreements, worldwide sub-publishing agreements, spreadsheets, accounts and audits. 'Because things were happening so fast, most of the work I did in the first couple of years was on the business level: arranging tours and looking into his contracts,' Reid has said.

On one hand Dick James was relieved that Elton had a full-time chaperone, but the relationship between Elton and James entered a new phase as a result. Until Reid had arrived on the scene Elton had looked to James as his father figure. The two had spent many hours together, Elton, no doubt confiding private thoughts and fears about his confidence and his sexuality. Reid's presence affected the relationship. Everything concerning Elton had to go through Reid, and even band members Dee Murray and Nigel Olsson felt awkward. Before Reid, the band had been like brothers, all equals together. Now Elton was the star and, just as he had been as a small boy, he was pampered, protected and provided for, not by a bevy of women, but by his ferocious sidekick and guardian.

They set themselves a gruelling work schedule just as the critics were beginning to turn against Elton. In a twelve-month period from 1971 to 1972 Elton recorded two albums, made two concert tours of America, and one each in Britain, Europe, Scandinavia, Japan, Australia and New Zealand, but less than six months after he had been hailed as a new superstar, the music press were already preparing to write off Elton's career. Serious critics had trouble with the yellow jump suits, Mr Freedom boots with wings, top hats and acrobatic handstands at the keyboard. *Melody Maker*'s Los Angeles correspondent reported that the concerts were not selling out and that he appeared to be having a problem with middle America, observing: 'He's dead in New York. And everyone knows New York is the centre of popular opinion.' The owner of the New York Fillmore East, Bill Graham, defended Elton's reputation as a sell-out act when he said, 'Elton John was alive and well at the Fillmore East. I consider Elton one of the truly great entertainers working today.' He effortlessly upstaged other acts, treating the piano like Jimi Hendrix treated his guitar – leaping on it and kicking it.

During the tour Elton John seemed less and less like an archetypal rock star. He had spent a few days in Maui, Hawaii, and his forehead was sunburned and peeling, his knees were bruised from stage antics, and his fingers sometimes actually bled after pounding the piano night after night. Much as Elton loved performing, he found the tours to be tough on his body and his mind. 'They just kill you. They physically kill you,' he said.

Elton was probably the first rock-and-roll star to invite his mother on tour. Sheila and Fred were in the audience in New York when he played at Carnegie Hall, when he made an appearance on the Dick Cavett television show and when he was presented with his third gold disc for the *Friends* soundtrack. Sheila was thrilled. She was also delighted when she returned home – Elton had bought a three-bedroomed house for her and Fred in leafy Ickenham, Middlesex, not far from Pinner. He also persuaded her to give up her job as a government clerk.

It had taken three years for Elton and Bernie to achieve some success, with two gold discs under their belts, but it would take another big effort to reinforce it. Failure seemed imminent.

Rolling Stone magazine's first feature on Elton examined this endearingly frivolous British export who had torn up the rock-star job description. He didn't have the right face, he didn't have right physique, he didn't wear the right clothes. He used the piano as a piece of gymnastic equipment. He was more Pierrot than pop star. In less than six months after being welcomed as rock's new superstar, articles snappily announced 'the death of a clown'. British critics turned on Elton too, writing him off for touring too much, releasing too many albums, enjoying too much praise in America. He was now hailed as a nine-day wonder, over there today, gone tomorrow. In the summer of 1971 he topped the bill at the Garden Party Show at Crystal Palace in London, but critics slammed him for performing the entire, yet to be released, *Madman Across The Water* album.

Elton went back to Trident Studio in August to record *Madman Across The Water*, his sixth album in nineteen months, hoping to show the critics that he and Bernie could match the innovation of their first successful album, *Elton John*. *Madman* has since been described as a quintessential Elton John piano album. The collection reverted to the powerful orchestral arrangements by Paul Buckmaster, mixed with strong piano introductions for Bernie's words, which took the form of lyrical American postcards. These were based on first-hand experiences of actually visiting the country, not wistful imaginings from a bunkbed in Pinner. It took a mere six days to record and one week to mix. This album revealed Elton and Bernie's abilities to create pop standards, but at around six minutes per song, all the tracks were considered too lengthy to be released as singles. Elton insisted that none should be cut, however, with the result that no tracks from the album were released as singles in Britain. The album reached a disappointing number forty-one in Britain, and number eight in the American charts.

Major critical setbacks and continued lack of British chart success – what he yearned for most of all – did not sap Elton's energy for work. He was determined to consolidate a year of unprecedented success. In September 1971 he embarked on another mini world tour of Japan and Australia. John Reid had now taken over as his manager, dedicated to Elton's wellbeing and round-the-clock schedule. On paper Reid was an employee of This Record Company, but it soon became clear that all his loyalties lay with Elton and not his employers. Reid widened the chasm between Elton and the rest of the band, and on this Far-East tour Elton was projected as the star of the show; everyone else was merely support. The others found Elton moodier and sulkier; and his close relationship with Reid seemed to bring on more of his Little Moments.

Possibly inspired by the neon lights of Tokyo, when Elton arrived in Australia he had dyed his hair orange, with green behind the ears. Unfortunately he managed to offend the Dean of Perth by declining to attend a reception on arrival in the country because he felt exhausted after the flight. He returned from Australia saying the trip had been a nightmare, marred by bad press about the controversial snub as well as bad weather, but he remained upbeat and said he would probably return.

Elton had achieved fame and success beyond his wildest dreams, but he was exhausted with recording and touring, and disappointed with the performance of *Madman Across The Water*. He was still concerned about the perils of over-exposure and insisted that he would be touring less, to spend more time recording and writing. 'When I think about it, it's a wonder I've survived the last few months,' he told Bob Randall of *NME*.

By January 1972 he had changed his name by deed poll and formally become Elton Hercules John. His middle name would come to represent not only Elton's quirky sense of humour, but also the labours he would perform in the coming years. Reginald Kenneth Dwight was no more, and that was official.

Rod Stewart had become one of Elton's longstanding friends. As a schoolboy, Elton had seen him perform with one of Long John Baldry's bands, Steampacket, and plucked up the courage to ask him for an autograph. After that their paths crossed on a number of occasions. The two became friends not least because of their love of football, and in typical Brit-bloke style they hid their affection for each other behind tirades of fake insults, banter and camp bitchery. They called each other by girls' names: Elton was Sharon Cavendish, after the Cavendish Club in Sheffield where the band also played, and Rod was Phyllis Stewart. John Reid was known as Beryl, after the actress Beryl Reid.

Their mentor, Long John Baldry, had not enjoyed much success since his big hit 'Let The Heartaches Begin' in 1967, and he was now managed by Rod's manager, Billy Gaff, who persuaded Elton and Rod to co-produce a new album for Baldry. Despite any bad feeling after his break with Bluesology, Elton was keen for some respite from the limelight and seized the opportunity to help an old mate and spend time in the studio. 'I hadn't done any producing and the idea gave me the horrors,' said Elton, 'but nevertheless I said yes, because I like John.' Together they produced *It Ain't Easy*, with Elton working on one side and Rod on the other.

After a brief tour of Germany and America, Elton wanted to return to the studio to produce another album for himself. A number of successful groups, notably the Rolling Stones, had become tax exiles and taken to recording in style in France. Elton was also advised to record outside Britain for tax reasons, so he too looked to the continent. His producer, Gus Dudgeon, found a studio at the seventeenth-century Château d'Hierouville in idyllic countryside just north of Paris. It had a swimming pool, tennis court and a studio called Strawberry. After the rigours of the previous year and the seriousness of *Madman Across The Water* it was time to enjoy himself, and Strawberry, in its aristocratic château in the early French spring, could not have been a more perfect setting. Elton later described *Honky Château* as one of his happiest albums. The band bonded as a team again, along with newcomer Davey Johnstone, ex-Magna Carta guitarist, who added a new, delicate, acoustic dimension to the existing electric guitar sound. He would become one of Elton's most enduring associates.

As soon as Bernie had finished writing the lyrics in his bedroom, they would be despatched directly to Elton at the piano, and he would begin composing. Usually within two hours the song would not only be written, but recorded as a demo, and all the tracks were recorded within three weeks. The songs were pure pop craftsmanship, with Bernie's bittersweet lyrics in perfect counterpoint to Elton's musical themes; frivolous and serious, light and dark, biblical themes and blasphemous rhythms, with more than a touch of black humour. Many of the songs achieved wide radio play, not least the one that would forever be associated with Elton, 'Rocket Man (I Think It's Going To Be A Long, Long Time)' and the first track 'Honky Cat', a rousing New Orleans style R&B piece, both of which were top-ten singles. The album itself shot to number one in the American album charts, and a respectable number two in Britain. The critics loved it, *Rolling Stone* wrote, '. . . a rich, warm, satisfying album that stands head and shoulders above the morass of current releases . . . his best work to date.'

Elton had thought that 'Rocket Man' was too slow to release as a single, but he bowed to Dudgeon's better judgement. 'Rocket Man' almost achieved Elton's longed for number one in Britain, but it only reached the second spot, and number six in America. It happened to strike a chord with space travel in the news, following the launch of the three-man Apollo 16 flight.

The serious British critics liked *Honky Château* and excused Elton's glut of product by praising him as an artist. *The Times* hoped that he would now get the recognition he deserved in his home country, saying that 'such over-release of material could have killed off lesser artists'. The press called him an 'electric Liberace' which, naturally, he took as a compliment. Elton, an entertainer at heart, said to *NME*'s Julie Webb: 'I've never regarded pop music as an art form. I think it is just entertainment and I think that is why pop groups are coming back because people are fed up with moodies and they'd rather go out and have a good time.'

Spring 1972 was a creative, joyful time for Elton, and he had money to spend. For the first time he could enjoy the fruits of his success. Elton and John Reid had moved out of London and acquired a pad in the pastures where stockbroker belt meets rock-star ghetto – Weybridge in Surrey. The split-level bungalow on an exclusive estate next to Wentworth golf course, with a large garden, a swimming pool and a mini football pitch, was snapped up for $75,000 (£50,000). They threw a housewarming party for 250 celebrities, with drag acts and strippers. They changed its name from 14 Abbots Drive to 'Hercules' and it became the first depository for Elton's burgeoning shopping sprees and growing record collection. Elton was not restrained by a lack of money anymore, and saw no need to control himself as he filled Hercules with a profusion of Victorian, Art Deco and Art Nouveau clutter that was considered desirable at the time. He purchased on an epic scale and gathered whole collections rather than one-off pieces. There were Tiffany lamps, ornate coffee tables, gilded mirrors, mirrored chessboards, huge Victorian posters and stuffed animals including a bear, a cheetah and a warthog. Two stuffed leopards stood guard by three Rembrandt etchings. It was not quite wall-to-wall kitsch; his collection of Pop Art included an important Andy Warhol 'Electric Chair' screen print. All his music industry trophies lined the walls and a huge neon sign spelled out 'Hercules'. Thousands of impulse buys and gadgets filled every corner. The games room was equipped with a fruit machine, ping-pong, table football, indoor golf and naturally, the true mark of a 1970s groover, a jukebox permanently stacked with Elton's up-to-the-minute listening choices.

The driveway at Hercules reflected his passion for cars. He began to collect Aston Martins, soon joined by a Bentley, a Rolls-Royce Corniche hardtop, a Ferrari Boxer, a Mini GT and a Rolls-Royce Phantom VI. He generously bought his mother a white MGB which was parked proudly outside her new Ickenham home.

Elton was beginning to find happiness through objects, things he could touch and place in order, just as he had as a lonely boy in his bedroom. Among all his precisely positioned possessions, which represented some kind of gilded autism, Elton revealed himself as meticulously houseproud. He still refers to himself as 'Housewife of the Year' to his staff, and told the *Sunday Mirror* in 1972: 'I live on my own, without servants. I do my own housework, ironing, cooking and the rest of it. I like doing these chores. And that way I know they've been done to my satisfaction. I can't stand tattiness and dirt.'

Fred Farebrother became his stepfather when he married Sheila in May 1972. They used Hercules as their address on the marriage certificate, and Reid's mother, Betty, and Elton Hercules John were recorded as witnesses. Fred took charge of the redecoration of Hercules, and would stay at the house with Sheila whenever Elton and Reid were away and, among other duties, look after the dogs – Brian the spaniel and Bruce the Alsatian. Elton was as close to his mother as he had been as a child and still relied upon Sheila's common sense. He would spend time with her whenever he could. Sheila remembers that sometimes he would ring and say, 'I've got the day to myself, Mum – come on over and spend it with me.'

Elton wanted everyone to see what he had achieved. He opened his doors to the rock and roll nobility who lived nearby and was more than happy to talk about his contentment to passing rock journalists. Keith Moon, the madcap drummer of The Who, and Rod Stewart were frequent guests. Marc Bolan of T. Rex became a special friend. Elton made a guest appearance in Bolan's film, *Born To Boogie*, singing 'Children of the Revolution' with Bolan and Ringo Starr. At the grand age of twenty-four he now saw himself as an elder statesman, full of admiration for the work of younger artists. He not only hero-worshipped the established stars of screen, stage and vinyl, but also the pop newcomers.

The 1970s is remembered as the decade taste forgot, and Elton played a key role in dragging bad taste to its nadir. He was busy building up a wardrobe to match his status as a seventies superstar in his own unique style. Gaudy suits, shirts, jackets and platformed shoes began to fill the wardrobes at Hercules. Most notably, he was acquiring a vast collection of spectacles. A Hollywood shop made them for him in ever more elaborate designs, in all shapes and sizes and in every possible colour, sometimes even fitted with Venetian blinds or windscreen wipers. No design or accessory was too ludicrous. Elton was at the heart of the glitter-rock style already adopted by artists such as David Bowie, Marc Bolan and Slade. However Elton could not hide his magpie nature and his eye for kitsch; while the elegant Bowie styled himself as high-concept fashion icon, Elton was stout, high-street pantomime dame.

As early as 1971 David Bowie was exploiting the fashion for gender-bending with his flamboyant stage personas and his lyrics. When he first announced his bisexuality, a tabloid headline proclaimed 'OH YOU PRETTY THING', based on a song from his 1971 album *Hunky Dory*. Throughout this time, when the words homosexuality and androgyny entered everyday vocabulary, Elton kept his sexuality resolutely hidden beneath his over-the-top pantomime costumes, specs, shoes and wigs, even though his homosexuality was an open secret in his own circle.

Elton's stage costumes were the armour under which he could hide, and the more elaborate they became, the more he could conceal his real self, and the more fun he had with his audience. He was like an actor putting on his costume for a role. He said: 'I don't really feel the part until I'm into what I'm going to wear.' It no longer mattered that he had short legs and short sight.

Following his American success, Elton put extra effort into his 1972 British tour to appeal to his home audience. He drafted in Steve Brown's sister-in-law, freelance designer Annie Reavey, to maximize his visual impact. Her first design for him was for his twenty-fifth birthday party, an outfit consisting of a fur cloak decorated with embroidered palm trees and a tall, quilted hat from which an EJ monogram was suspended. He was so thrilled with her unique creation that she worked on his costumes for the next three years. Quilted satin suits were particular favourites, with embroidered picture-book scenes of seascapes, sunshine, musical notes and spectacles festooned on their backs. Her brief was simple – keep it as ostentatious as possible. Reavey remembered a Valentine's Day costume which she thought he would never go for: 'It was pink and gold Lurex brocade, trimmed with gold lace; it had a pink and gold heart embroidered on it. And short pants. But he loved it.' Reavey skilfully designed the costumes to underplay Elton's physical shortcomings, broadening his shoulders and camouflaging his squat legs. And the eight-inch rainbow-platformed shoes gave him much needed extra height when he made his majestic entrance on stage. Elton gave his designers complete artistic freedom and never rejected any of their increasingly wild ideas. 'I'll do anything,' he said. 'If anyone's prepared to make it and make it work, I'll get into anything.' And he did.

Self-mockery and dressing up masked his vulnerability and got him out on stage. He played to the gallery like a caricature of a pop star, full of mock seriousness and bombast. The audiences loved him – he let them in on the joke. His demented costumes and crazy glasses became as much a trademark as his gymnastics at the piano at the end of the show. Meanwhile, the critics praised him as a composer and took him seriously as a musician. According to *The Times*, 'It is not all fun with Elton John, his songs have a way of purveying the sadness of life as well. Therein lies his strength.'

At last Elton was gaining fame in his own country, but pundits were curious about the pop star who broke the mould. This was no long-haired rebel but a balding, articulate entertainer. He told the *Sunday Mirror*, 'Can't grow my hair long, it's too thin. The dark glasses I started to wear when I was thirteen, trying to copy Buddy Holly. Now my eyes are weak, with or without them. So if fans are thinking about copying me, I advise them to forget it.' The writer also observed that Elton could not be not rock-and-roll superstar material because there weren't any groupies hanging around outside Hercules.

In 1972 Elton performed one of his first benefit concerts for the National Youth Theatre, in which John Reid took a great interest. Attending a perform-ance of *Good Lads At Heart*, a play about Borstal boys, awoke Elton's enthusiasm and he was keen to help raise funds for youth theatre. He gave four concerts, one of which was attended by Princess Margaret. This was a winning social move which enabled him to step up the social ladder by several rungs. Through the NYT he also consolidated his friendship with fellow Weybridge resident, the actor, film director and writer, Bryan Forbes.

For the upwardly mobile socialite and fan, Bryan Forbes was the perfect neighbour. He had appeared in such film classics as *The Quatermass Experiment* (1955) and *The Guns of Navarone* (1961), and directed *I Was Monty's Double* (1958), *Whistle Down The Wind* (1961) and *The L-Shaped Room* (1962). At the end of his film career he had opened a bookshop in Virginia Water before embarking on a career as a novelist some years later. He lived in a house called Seven Pines, a few minutes' walk from Hercules, with his wife, the actress Nanette Newman and their two daughters. Elton was becoming a regular visitor and was spellbound by Forbes's endless stories from the world of movies and his famous friends, especially the former Goon Peter Sellers. He also used to visit Forbes in his shop and would often buy every book in the window display. Elton was a diligent collector, however, and the books were not just for show, according to Newman: 'When you talked to him you realized how amazingly well read he was.' He was so impressed by the style of the interiors at Seven Pines, which was full of tasteful artworks and furniture, that he asked for Forbes's advice: 'Can you help me? How do I acquire taste?'

Through the couple, Elton met several West End art and antique dealers, and they also introduced him to Bryan Organ, the painter, who had recently painted Newman's portrait. Elton immediately commissioned Organ to paint his own portrait, and for once the self-conscious Pinner boy forgot himself under the gaze of the artist. Newman was responsible for introducing him to Cartier, the jewellers. On his first visit he found the jewellery vulgar, yet irresistible. He scuttled round the shop scooping up presents for everyone.

Elton was living at breakneck speed and the strain was beginning to tell. In summer 1972 he had to cancel an Italian concert at the last minute, and was due to return to the château to record his next album, *Don't Shoot Me, I'm Only The Piano Player*. He thought about postponing the sessions until after a longed-for holiday in Malibu, in July, but changed his mind again and decided to go ahead with the recording. Suffering from stress and exhaustion, he contracted glandular fever, but through sheer willpower wrote twelve new songs in two days, seven on the first day and five the next. The maverick musical magpie paid tribute to a whole range of pop genres: 'Crocodile Rock' was a bubble-gum rock-and-roll parody, on which he brought together snippets and strains from a multiplicity of sources reminiscent of his childhood, including Bill Haley, Bobby Vee and Eddie Cochrane; 'Daniel' was a grown-up ballad about a disillusioned Vietnam veteran. This classic was one of the speediest productions in his repertoire. After writing the lyrics in about thirty minutes one morning, Bernie took them down to Elton at the breakfast table. Elton stepped over to the piano and the song was written in fifteen or so minutes, then recorded. The track was complete by the end of the day. Bernie's lyric style was developing and on this album he was less contemplative and more pop orientated, with tracks such as 'I'm Gonna Be A Teenage Idol', in homage to Marc Bolan. The album would be Elton's second American number one and his first at home. It would take less than a year before this outstanding success was eclipsed by the next John-Taupin offering.

The much-needed holiday in a palatial Malibu beach house had been planned for some time and was Elton's first proper break since the start of his professional career. He and John Reid played host to Bernie, Maxine and the

Forbes family. Elton's exhaustion and illness caused a few moments of friction initially, but by the time the Forbeses had arrived he was back on jovial form, especially as there was a galaxy of stars to meet in the shape of Bryan's friends and associates.

Elton and Bernie went to meet Mae West in her white apartment with white carpets and white piano, and were served carrot cake by two beefcakes. 'Miss West came in dressed up to the nines in white,' Elton remembered. 'And said, "Ah, wall-to-wall men!"' On another occasion they went to a friend's house and watched a private screening of a Marx Brothers movie, only to find that Groucho himself was in the audience. Marx was intrigued by Elton John's name, which he thought was back to front, and he insisted on calling him John Elton. During the banter Elton put up his hands in mock surrender and said to Marx: 'Don't shoot me, I'm only the piano player,' thus naming his new album.

Bryan Forbes also celebrated his birthday during that holiday, which led Elton to make a particularly outrageous gesture. Forbes was born under the sign of Leo, and on looking out of his window on the morning of his birthday, found an adult lion in the courtyard. Elton had arranged with a local zoo for a lion and trainer to appear as Bryan's surprise.

Elton could not resist the pleasures of shopping while in Malibu. He began to call it 'looting' and he binged on bulk purchases every day. Forbes and Bernie would go to bookshops and Elton would be straight round to the tablecloth shop. Elton commented: 'I go back to England every time from a tour with at least eight more suitcases than I started with. And I never know where to put the bloody stuff when I get home anyway!'

John Reid had taken over Elton John the product, and started to control the timing of album releases to avoid swamping the shops like the previous year. After *Honky Château* had run its course in the market place, *Don't Shoot Me, I'm Only The Piano Player* was released in February 1973. This time, against Elton's gut feeling, 'Crocodile Rock' was released to trail the album in October 1972. Elton's preferred choice had been 'Daniel', but both Dick and Stephen James felt that it was too slow and quiet to be a success. The Jameses thought the upbeat 'Crocodile Rock' was a perfect contrast to the thoughtful 'Rocket Man', Elton's last single. The Jameses' were proved right, and 'Crocodile Rock' went straight to number one in America and number five at home.

'Legs' Larry Smith of the Bonzo Dog Doo Dah Band, who had stepped in on *Honky Château* playing the spoons, became a close friend and perfect stage foil for Elton. He joined him on his autumn forty-eight-date tour of America. With his long legs, apache-style hair and military moustache, the sight of 'Legs' Larry tap-dancing in American football gear and a silver helmet with a miniature bride-and-groom wedding cake decoration on top was always in ridiculous contrast to Elton's extravagance.

Halfway through the tour Elton was summoned to return to England to perform in front of the Queen at the Royal Command Variety Performance. In spite of the upheaval it would cause, Elton would never have declined such an invitation. He flew to Britain overnight and, with very little sleep, rehearsed, performed and flew straight back to resume the tour in Tulsa, Oklahoma. During the rehearsals Elton had been tired and fractious. Bernard Delfont, the show's producer, and Dick James wanted him to sing 'Rocket Man' and 'Your Song', nice, safe numbers to present to the Queen. Elton wanted to do 'Crocodile Rock' and 'I Think I'm Going To Kill Myself' with 'Legs' Larry on spoons and tap-dancing duty. Surprisingly, Elton got his way and it can only be imagined what the Queen and the Duke of Edinburgh thought as Elton, in his shiny suit and platform shoes, playing a piano draped in pink satin and a twinkling fairy, sang a song about suicide, while a tall dancer in a crash helmet set off balloons. Afterwards Elton told the press that although his appearance at the Variety Performance had cost him a lot of money, he had wanted to do it anyway, adding arrogantly, 'Because 25 million people will be able to listen to my latest record, and this is the only chance I've got to plug it.'

Apart from the opportunity to promote his new single, Elton got the chance to meet one of his all-time heroes and influences, Liberace. He was fortunate enough to share a dressing room with the great pianist, and watched in awe as Liberace's countless costume cases were squeezed into the room. Liberace's bejewelled outfits made Elton's look like thriftshop bargains. The snooty British press were not impressed with Elton, and described him as a 'musical dwarf' compared to Liberace. Elton was nonplussed – to him Liberace was the only decent thing on the bill that night. In a right royal strop he told *Melody Maker*: 'Those two days were the most harrowing experience of my life. Only Liberace kept me sane.'

Returning to pound the keys on the rest of his sell-out tour, all Elton's albums were being snapped up in America and by the end of 1972 they had all gone platinum – over a million copies each had been bought by an eager American public. Elton had become Britain's most successful rock-and-roll export.

chapter five

High Flying Bird

I N THE SUMMER OF 1972, John Reid, aged only twenty-three, resigned from DJM and set up his own company, John Reid Enterprises, with a bank loan of $7,500 (£5,000) and his management contract with Elton as security. It marked the beginning of the end of Elton's relationship with his original patron and father confessor, Dick James. Reid was unhappy about the small proportion of royalties from the foreign sub-publishing arrangements, especially the American agreement under which DJM companies took 70 per cent of the sale of proceeds leaving 15 per cent each for Elton and Bernie. However, the agreements were due to expire the following November and Elton would continue to issue his product through This Record Company until 1975, under the five-year recording agreement signed in 1970.

Although DJM had made the right decision about releasing 'Crocodile Rock', it still upset Elton that he had been overruled on 'Daniel'; indeed the Jameses were not keen on releasing it as a single at all. They could not imagine that people would buy a single about a blind war veteran in the sequinned climate of 1973, especially after the upbeat 'Crocodile Rock'. Elton was furious, and did not hold back on his criticism of the Jameses' decision. He talked to the music press and the row became public. Eventually Elton got his way and the single was released on 12 January 1973, although Dick James refused to spend any money on publicity unless it reached the Top Ten. 'Daniel' had its first public outing when Elton appeared on BBC television's *Parkinson* chat show, dressed in a one-piece silver creation. He tottered down the staircase in high platforms, like a club-footed mermaid, to an affectionate welcome from the audience. 'Daniel' was set to be an enormous hit, reaching number two in America and number four in Britain.

DJM had been an extremely supportive record company, allowing him to record where he wanted, with the musicians he wanted and the graphic design he wanted on the albums, but Elton was still annoyed about the 'Daniel' incident. Further adding to his irritation, his US company, the small Uni label at MCA, which had been releasing his albums, transferred *Don't Shoot Me* to the main MCA label, resulting in a clumsy, incongruous marketing campaign for the album.

Like The Beatles, the Rolling Stones, Deep Purple and the Moody Blues, Elton sought to use his money and influence to launch other artists as well as to have more control over his own output. His encyclopaedic knowledge of pop, and admiration for his peers and younger artists, made him an ideal talent scout. He wanted to give something back to the world that had made him a star. Whether it was supporting an old friend in the recording studio, as he had with Long John Baldry, or helping an old hero like David Ackles who had fallen out of chart favour, or investing in new talent, he was as zealous an A&R man as he was a pop star.

The decision to form Rocket Records was made while Elton was recording at Château d'Hierouville. His guitarist, Davey Johnstone, wanted to make a solo album but could not find a label to support him, so a decision was made to form Rocket Records, with Elton, John Reid, Bernie Taupin, Steve Brown and Gus Dudgeon in control. The aims were honest and altruistic. Elton declared: 'We want to start a company that's for the artist, both creatively and money-wise. We want to be a friendly record company. We'll pay a decent advance, a decent royalty and when we sign anybody we'll work our bollocks off for them. It'll be like a family.' Rocket Records would exist for the benefit of new artists, while Elton himself would continue to release records through DJM until 1975.

Offices were set up in Wardour Street, central London. Their logo was a Thomas the Tank Engine-style locomotive with a jolly face and a friendly wink. The first signing was Davey Johnstone; another was a band called Longdancer, which included a young Sunderland guitarist called Dave Stewart who, with Annie Lennox, would later form the successful 1980s band, Eurythmics.

Reid's relations with the Jameses took a final blow when he persuaded their personal assistant, Maureen, to join him at Rocket. Elton himself made a thinly veiled reference to Dick James in an interview with *NME* when he referred to himself as 'the star who hates those men in the music industry with big fat cigars' – and he was starting his own record company to prove it.

Among other Rocket signings were the pub band Stackridge and Elton's friend Kiki Dee. A Sheffield-born singer originally named Pauline Matthews, Dee had been signed to Tamla Motown as its first white female singer, which was where she had met John Reid, but had yet to achieve the success of the likes of Diana Ross and Gladys Knight. Elton was a fan of her strong, dusky, soul voice and distinctly unvampish asexual style.

On 30 April 1973, Rocket Records was launched with a *Listen With Mother*-themed party on a chartered Thomas the Tank Engine-style train. No expense was spared as 200 invited passengers, including the music press, Rocket's directors and various new signings to the label, boarded at Paddington and chugged along to the pretty Cotswold village of Moreton-in-Marsh. Accompanied by a brass band, they trooped into the village hall for a fabulous party and entertainment by the signed artistes, with Elton, Bernie and Reid as backing singers.

However secure Elton may have felt with his live-in partner, his multitude of material possessions and his international success, he still needed his mother. A year after they had gone to live in Ickenham, Elton moved his mother and stepfather into a house next to Hercules. He still yearned for the security he had craved as a child, and as well as wanting his mother next door, he needed Fred's skills as a handyman, especially for hanging his growing collection of art. He developed passions for the work of certain artists from various periods, starting with Bryan Organ who had painted his portrait; he favoured Lowry and Rembrandt as well. He also bought his grandmother, Ivy, a house in Ruislip near her daughter, his Aunt Win.

Elton was equally generous to his employees at Rocket whom he looked on as extended family. They were presented with gifts ranging from Fortnum and Mason hampers to Cartier jewellery. At Christmas he would play Santa Claus, whirling round the office with a cardboard box, handing out Cartier watches and pens to everyone. The Rocket boys and girls, in turn, gave Elton the affection and approval he craved, especially on his birthday, a very important day for any kid. If he was abroad on the day, they would all crowd round the phone and sing 'Happy Birthday'.

Stanley Dwight had taken a job as a supplies controller at Unilever in Cheshire, and had proudly followed his son's transformation from podgy teenage dreamer to the biggest pop star in the world. Everyone at work was talking about Elton John without knowing that he was Stanley's son. Although Elton's busy schedule kept him from seeing Stanley, Edna and their four sons, he still found time to send affectionate postcards from his travels with jolly descriptions of life on the road, celebrities he had met and how thrilled he was to be 'mobbed' by fans. He always sent Christmas cards and one year his gift to them revealed his weakness in arithmetic, something he might have cause to consider in later years. Accompanying a cheque for $375 (£250), he had written in his Christmas letter, 'a hundred pounds for you and Aunt Edna, and £25 each for the boys.'

When the Dwights discovered that he was playing at the Liverpool Empire, they bought tickets. They sent a message to Elton through the box office that they were in the audience and in the interval John Reid came to look for them, recognizing Stanley immediately because of the strong family resemblance.

They met a delighted Elton in his dressing room after the show, who promised to organize tickets for the whole family the next time he performed in Liverpool. This promise was fulfilled in early 1973, and the day after the concert, Elton and Reid went to visit them for Sunday lunch.

Elton arrived in his white chauffeur-driven Rolls-Royce, and Reid followed in his Jensen Interceptor. After lunch, Elton led a singsong with his four half-brothers playing 'Crocodile Rock' on the piano, then he and the boys played football in the garden. Edna joked: 'My boys must have been better footballers than him because they missed the roses.'

Elton and his father shared a love of cars and together looked through some motor magazines. A Mini driver at the time, Stanley pointed out his favourite family car, a Peugeot Estate, so Elton immediately wrote out a cheque for $3,000 (£2,000) to buy the Peugeot. But Stanley refused to accept it. John Reid tried to persuade him to keep it. 'It's nothing to him,' he said, 'it's only a drop in the ocean.' Elton told his father that he was looking forward to seeing the photographs when he bought the car, but Stanley handed back the cheque.

When it was time to leave, the boys wanted a ride in their big brother's Rolls-Royce, and as Elton's driver was not sure of the way to the motorway, Stanley led a convoy in his Mini, with Edna and her four sons in Elton's Rolls and Reid in the Jensen behind. At the motorway they said their goodbyes and Elton slipped a piece of paper into Edna's pocket. 'Give this to Dad,' he said. 'He knows what it is. Tell him he's to have it.' Stanley was furious and, to her lasting regret, Edna persuaded him that it would be right to buy the car so as not to offend Elton. They bought the Peugeot Estate and sent Elton photographs of it, and of the boys on family picnics, but because it was too expensive to run, they eventually had to sell it.

Elton was enjoying unprecedented success with his fans, especially with the teenyboppers who thought they had found a new sex symbol to rival the likes of Marc Bolan and David Cassidy. Despite his somewhat asexual persona on stage, or perhaps because of it, Elton was becoming an object of public fascination. His face appeared on the covers of heart-throb magazines as the bespectacled boy-next-door, albeit one who liked dressing up as the Queen of Sheba. Still painfully aware of how he looked, he told Bob Harris on the *Old Grey Whistle Test*: 'I know I haven't got the best image for rock and roll, and that probably gets in the way of my music sometimes. But most of my clothes are just for a laugh.'

He was mobbed by fans in spring 1973, when he embarked on his first major British tour. 'I find touring rather boring,' Elton admitted. 'Not the gigs, but driving to Bolton isn't quite as glamorous as driving to Santiago. But we really have got to get our finger out and do it.' In Glasgow he and the band were barricaded inside the venue for an hour when fans stormed the exits, while his promoter broke his ankle struggling to keep the fans at bay.

Elton allowed his trusted friend Bryan Forbes into his innermost circle to film a documentary of his life during the summer of 1973, as a well-observed and affectionate portrait of an established star and popular public figure, on the threshold of even greater fame. Forbes acted as narrator, while images of Elton's on-stage antics were intercut with shots of a charity cricket match, scenes of Elton jogging along country lanes, punting along a river in backlit innocence, mixing classical and honky-tonk music at the piano, and playing up to the camera with Goon impersonations and slapstick stunts.

Listing the contradictions in Elton's character, Forbes described him thus: 'A child with every toy in the shop and not a key to wind them with . . . as much an enigma to himself as to his friends . . . now possessing no inhibitions, now totally inhibited . . . seeking fame one minute, determined to reject it the next . . . jealous of his privacy, hating to be private . . . arrogant, contrite . . . gifted, lonely . . . the superstar who does his own hoovering.'

The documentary showed an upbeat Elton, but Forbes included interviews with John Reid and Sheila that hinted at a darker side. Reid described Elton's character as unpredictable, with a Jekyll-and-Hyde quality, and his mother perhaps revealed too much. 'He's had darker moods since he made it in the pop world than he ever did before,' she said. 'He's always been a very quiet boy, never the sort of boy to have the gay life. I know when he's in a mood, but I never expect him to be over the moon any time. He's just not [got] that nature.'

With his next album, Elton would produce a collection of songs to eclipse any existing or future work, though the project started amid some major setbacks. Elton's favourite studio, the idyllic Château d'Hierouville, which had been used to great success on his previous two albums, had closed because of a legal dispute. Instead the team went to the Dynamic Sounds studio in Kingston, Jamaica, chosen because the Rolling Stones had recently been there to record *Goat's Head Soup*. Elton and his entourage arrived at the height of political turmoil and near public hysteria surrounding the world heavyweight boxing championship between Joe Frazier and George Foreman. The streets were teeming with people and the hotels were almost fully booked. Elton and Bernie ended up in the Pink Flamingo Hotel in Kingston, miles from the rest of the band and the production team. Whatever black moods he might have suffered, he set out to beat his own record for songwriting. Holed up with Bernie and an electric piano, Elton composed twenty-one songs in three days, enough for a double album. Elton's only respite from the four walls of his hotel room was the bar at night, listening to one of his jazz heroes, pianist Les

McCann, who happened to be the resident entertainer. The studio was hardly conducive to either a creative atmosphere or a happy Elton, surrounded as it was by barbed wire, with armed guards at the doors and an alarming absence of recording equipment, from microphones to Elton's grand piano. 'There wasn't a single positive vibe in the place,' observed Bernie. Elton's mood was only lifted by news that *Don't Shoot Me* had reached number one in America.

A decision was made to decamp to New York, where they heard the great news that the dispute at the Château d'Hierouville had been partially resolved and the venue would now be at Elton's disposal. As before, Bernie would deliver lyrics to Elton, and the band would learn the songs over the breakfast table in the kitchen, equipped with an electric piano and small drum kit. Because they were familiar with the bones of the songs from Jamaica, they worked at a phenomenal rate, with four songs written and recorded every day, in an idyllic atmosphere.

The scope of the new album was wide-ranging. Bernie's collection of cameos alluded to American culture and its dark side, to Roy Rogers and Marilyn Monroe, and to his own English heritage – harking back to the streets of Lincoln and drinking too much beer on 'Saturday Night's Alright (For Fighting)', which would become a blistering finale for concerts. Other tracks 'Dirty Little Girl', 'Sweet Painted Lady', 'Jamaica Jerk Off' and 'All The Girls Love Alice' hinted at the seamier side of life. The instrumental and melancholic 'Funeral For A Friend' could not have been more of a contrast. 'Candle In The Wind', used as a track title, was not an original phrase, having previously described the singer Janis Joplin, who had died in 1970 after a heroin overdose, aged twenty-seven. Marilyn Monroe had become a sex symbol to a new generation since her death in 1962, but to Bernie her story was a parable of fame, beauty and youth cut short in its prime and about how people are elevated to iconic status. The title track, 'Goodbye Yellow Brick Road', encapsulated Bernie's experience on the road to fame, on which he had literally found a pot of gold at the end of the rainbow, but to him the rest was spiritually meaningless.

At first Elton was reluctant for *Goodbye Yellow Brick Road* to be released as a double album, in case it was too expensive for his teenage fans. His record companies, DJM in Britain and MCA in America, both insisted that it would count only as a single release under the terms of his contract whether it was a double or not. However, he acknowledged the quantity and quality of all seventeen tracks and, like The Beatles had done with the *White Album*, decided to go for the double. Released on 8 October, *Goodbye Yellow Brick Road* was hailed as a masterpiece and remains a classic, still high up in most pollsters' 100 greatest albums listings. Public reaction was rapturous and nearly all the songs were played on the radio. Elton knew this album had to be good; he desperately wanted to win back fans who had deserted him after his two previous 'pop' albums. 'It's an important album for me in my career at this point,' he said. Within days of its release it stormed to number two in America and number six in Britain, and was soon at number one on both sides of the Atlantic, staying at the top in the American charts for eight weeks and spending forty-three weeks among the forty best-selling albums. Elton would end the year as the undisputed biggest rock star in the world.

During his forty-three-date, August-to-October US tour, Elton was booked at the two main venues, Madison Square Garden in New York and the Hollywood Bowl in Los Angeles, to launch *Goodbye Yellow Brick Road*, for what would come to be described as his finest hour. Just three years after his momentous breakthrough at the Troubadour in Los Angeles, on 7 September 1973, Elton was back in LA to take his extravagant showmanship to new heights in front of 16,000 fans at the Hollywood Bowl. The sell-out concerts were advertised on huge billboards on Sunset Boulevard, displaying a black-and-white cut-out Elton in black top hat, cane and white bow-tie, flanked by high-kicking dancers, towering over Hollywood. It may have been called the Yellow Brick Road Tour, but the imagery harked back to every classic Hollywood spectacular, and brought Busby Berkeley style into the glitter-rock era. The stage set, with spotlights on the Hollywood Hills, was a backdrop of Elton in his Fred Astaire-meets-Aubrey Beardsley costume, which lowered to reveal a forest of potted palms and a glittering staircase sweeping down to five multi-coloured grand pianos on stage.

The infamous porn star, Linda Lovelace, who was compere, began her introduction with, 'Ladies and Gentlemen, let me introduce you to . . . the Queen of England.' Her Majesty stepped down the sparkling staircase, followed by a multitude of other celebrity lookalikes, including many of Elton's idols and acquaintances. The assembled crowd was reminiscent of the cover of the *Sgt. Pepper* album, with Groucho Marx, Mae West, Elvis Presley, Marilyn Monroe, John Wayne, Batman and Robin, Frankenstein's monster, the Pope and The Beatles. Elton was dressed like an owlish bird of paradise, wearing white feather breeches, a white feathered bonnet and huge white-framed specs. This vision imperiously acknowledged his famous stage 'friends', to the deafening sound of the Twentieth-Century Fox fanfare booming from the PA system. As he stomped over an artificial privet hedge, he took his place at his piano and the lids of the other pianos lifted to reveal in silver letters, ELTON, underneath. Then 400 white doves were released, with a little help from Bernie hiding in one of the pianos, which fluttered into the night sky. The audience went wild.

Elton never lost his finely tuned sense of the absurd, and the costumes never got in the way of the rock and roll. During the show Elton belted out his hits, and during 'Crocodile Rock', his sound engineer, Clive Franks, pounded the electric organ dressed in a huge crocodile outfit. In the middle of the concert Elton changed into a purple jump suit covered in large musical notes, wearing specs with frames that glowed like the huge rings on an electric cooker.

The concert reviews were ecstatic. Later Elton spoke to Bryan Forbes for the documentary, describing his feelings on stage and the dynamic between himself and the vast audience. Elton said it had felt close to having a sexual experience with the fans. 'It's like fucking for two hours and then suddenly finding out there's nothing you can do after that. It's so emotional and so physical, you don't ever want to do anything else.'

At this time in his life, Elton was the cleanest-living pop star around. He was up with the lark playing tennis or down at the shops looting, the kind of star who preferred to buy and cherish objects than smash them up in hotel rooms. On really special occasions he would allow himself a bottle of Double Diamond beer, but generally his strongest after-show tipple was a refreshing bottle of Perrier water. Between concerts he would keep his diary up-to-date, meticulously noting his daily worldwide chart positions, audience numbers, record sales and football results from home.

MCA Records had laid on a Boeing 707 aeroplane for the tour, which relieved the team of gruelling overnight bus journeys. But the luxury travel arrangements did not seem to keep Elton's outbursts and mood swings at bay. He would frequently snap at his entourage, often in public. It was as if he could not balance the enormous highs he felt on stage with the comparative lows of doing normal things like having breakfast with his mates. It seemed as though he wanted to be the centre of attention all the time; he needed people to listen to him, to laugh at his jokes; he hated being ignored. He was beginning to feel lost when his virtual lover, the audience, was absent.

On one occasion Elton was in a particularly black mood when he boarded the Boeing for a short flight from New York to Boston, possibly because he had not received his chart placings that morning. His tour organizer, Sharon Lawrence, laid on a big surprise for him. As Elton entered the plane, Stevie Wonder, one of his all-time Motown heroes, was at the end of the cabin at the electric piano singing 'Crocodile Rock', still in convalescence following a serious car accident that had left him in a coma for short time. Elton, utterly consumed by his mood, stormed on to the plane and sat in the front cabin without noticing Wonder, until Lawrence pointed him out. That night, however, Wonder joined Elton on stage for his encore, and they played

'Superstition', and 'You Are The Sunshine Of My Life' together. Afterwards Wonder spoke of that concert as the start of his recovery.

While Elton was in America he was very upset to hear that his Aunt Ivy, Stanley's sister, had died. He had often visited her as a child and knew her children well. He requested that his mother attended the funeral on his behalf. The occasion was the one and only time that Sheila met Stanley's second wife, Edna. After the funeral service, Sheila proudly told everyone about Elton's triumph at the Hollywood Bowl and naturally all the family were extremely interested. Attention also turned to Edna because some of the family had not yet met her, so Stanley introduced her to everyone, and they proudly showed photographs of their four sons. Sheila observed how happy they were together, in contrast to her own period of marriage to Stanley. Sheila may have suspected that they had met before the divorce, and wondered whether the humiliation she suffered when pleading guilty to adultery in court could have been avoided. No doubt Sheila considered the evidence: a happy ex-husband after eleven years of marriage, and four children in rapid succession. Had she been tricked into admitting adultery? Had her ex-husband been guilty all along? She must certainly have considered the possibility, and may well have shared her thoughts with her son.

Soon afterwards Elton's letters and postcards to his father and Aunt Edna stopped, and their letters to him remained unanswered. It would be another two years before Elton made a public outburst against his father.

Elton ended his superlative year, in 1973, by recording a Christmas single, 'Step Into Christmas', but it only reached twenty-four in Britain. He also began a tradition of Christmas concerts at Hammersmith Odeon, naturally dressed as an over-the-top Santa Claus, showered with fake snow.

On the crest of the wave of his success as the biggest pop star in the world, Elton embarked on an association which would keep him grounded and occupy his thoughts when he was not on the frenetic tour treadmill. Since his childhood visits to Watford Football Club matches with his father, Elton had always been a devoted fan of the Hornets in their black-and-yellow colours, following their progress or lack of it, wherever he was in the world. Watford was not the most attractive team in the league. It was mediocre at best, nestling in the far reaches of the suburbs and at the lower end of the third division. A young journalist and football enthusiast, Julie Webb, from *New Musical Express*, mentioned to Elton, during an interview in late 1973, that Watford was seeking new sources of funding and suggested that he might perform a benefit concert. He responded with great enthusiasm at the opportunity to help his favourite team, and the board of directors welcomed both him and the publicity that would be generated by his involvement. As a reward for his purchase of a block of shares in the club and the promised concert, Elton was duly made honorary vice-president. He now had the chance to step out on to the hallowed turf at Vicarage Road, kicking a ball around the pitch with a few of the team players, something he had dreamed of since his youth. Elton took his title very seriously indeed, attending as many home and away matches as his schedule would allow. His vice-presidency was one of his proudest achievements. The name WATFORD would henceforth appear in lights behind Elton on stage.

As a follow-up to *Goodbye Yellow Brick Road* Elton was always going to face a difficult task. He and the team decided to revert back to the more relaxed mood of *Honky Château*. At one stage Elton thought of calling it 'Ol' Pink Eyes Is Back', with a cover shot of himself as Frank Sinatra, sporting a fedora, cigarette in his mouth and jacket flung over his shoulder. He dropped that idea when Ringo Starr suggested that he should name the album after Caribou, the new recording studio Elton had found in Colorado when he was touring, which was situated on a ranch 9,000 feet up in the Colorado mountains, and just as idyllic as his beloved Château d'Hierouville.

The album was made under huge stress in February 1974. The band were exhausted and fractious from touring, while Elton and producer Gus Dudgeon argued frequently. It was the first time they had recorded in America and the unfamiliar technical methods added to the tension. The two men had never had a serious quarrel before and, as perfectionists, they found the time constraints almost impossible. There were just ten days to go before a tour of Japan, Australia and New Zealand. Elton and Bernie had almost no time for creative thinking, and they wrote the songs at breakneck speed, in just two days, then recorded them in under a week. Elton added a new member to the band's line-up, percussionist Ray Cooper, a former member of Blue Mink. Cooper contributed a lot of fun to the Elton soundscape, with a menu of zany, circus sound effects.

The two big hits from the album were 'The Bitch Is Back', inspired by a verbatim comment made by Maxine Taupin about Elton when he was in a bad mood at Hercules one day, and 'Don't Let The Sun Go Down On Me'. The latter was extremely difficult to record. It took so many unsatisfactory takes that Elton wanted to drop it from the album altogether, and told Dudgeon in no uncertain terms to discard the song, or give it to Lulu or Engelbert Humperdinck. Elton would later name the song as one of his top three favourites, and admitted that it was his tribute to the Beach Boys.

Everyone in Elton's circle knew *Caribou* was a mediocre album, especially as a follow-up to *Goodbye Yellow Brick Road*, but when the band went on tour, Dudgeon was able to polish the songs. His post-production turned an all too hasty effort into a transatlantic hit, and earned him a nomination as producer of the best album of the year. Every track received airplay owing to Elton's enormous popularity and, despite the conflicts in the studio, the album achieved the number-one spot on both sides of the Atlantic.

The tensions of the *Caribou* recording session spilled over into the Far-East tour, one of the last tours set up by Vic Lewis, Elton's contact from the NEMS agency, under the expiring agreements with Dick James. Reid could not wait to break the ties with James, and looked upon Lewis as a throwback to a past era. Elton had always been fond of Lewis, another semi-paternal figure, who had been instrumental in setting up the Troubadour breakthrough. They shared a love of football – particularly Watford – cricket and the Goons. To Reid, however, Lewis was soon to be yesterday's man, and the Scot was aggressive to him throughout the tour. Lewis observed that Elton's moods and tantrums seemed to be brought on whenever Reid was around, otherwise Elton would be the polite, enthusiastic and humorous man Lewis had first encountered only a few years ago.

Australia loved Elton and he returned the compliment. He became its biggest-selling artist and for some time would call Australia his second home. Elton performed at sell-out concerts there, and the entourage then flew to New Zealand for a concert in the 34,000-seat Western Springs Stadium near Auckland. It was decided that the whole team would take a week's holiday in Tahiti afterwards, before Reid and Elton flew on to Los Angeles to negotiate a new deal with MCA Records.

Unfortunately, all did not go according to plan. The band were booked to attend an extravagant press reception at Auckland Park before the concert, with a Maori welcome committee performing a ceremonial war dance. Reid had mysteriously gone missing, however, and Elton refused to go to the reception without his manager. Reid finally appeared, but during the delay, the war dance had almost become a real battle. Elton diffused the tense atmosphere by playing the fool, joining in with the Maoris, prancing about and pulling faces at their spears and chants. The long wait had meant that the press had plundered the bar, so when Reid arrived and ordered a glass of whisky, only to be told they had run out, he was not pleased. When the organizer offered him a glass of champagne instead, Reid threw it back at him and stormed out. Shortly afterwards he returned and sat at the bar with a reporter, Judith Baragwanath, who mentioned that his behaviour might have been a little over the top and, allegedly, called him a 'poof'. For that, he hit her and she fell to the floor. The whole of Elton's party were advised to get into their Rolls-Royces and take refuge in the hotel for their own safety.

Later that evening Elton and Reid attended a concert by David Cassidy, and dropped in on the after-show party. Tensions were riding high and when one of the reporters there mentioned that the whole entourage were 'marked men', Elton grabbed him by the collar. Reid soon took over and knocked the scribe to the floor.

The next day, despite Reid's apologies to both reporters and an offer of out-of-court settlements, he was arrested, along with Elton, for alleged assault. Reid's application for bail was refused and he spent the night in Mount Eden prison. Elton stamped his foot and refused to go on stage while his manager was in prison. Much frantic legal activity and arm-twisting took place, resulting in a meeting at the judge's house an hour and a half before the concert. In the event, Reid was granted bail on condition that he surrendered his passport, so the show went ahead.

Instead of going to Tahiti the following day, Elton and Reid appeared in court. Elton, who had committed the more minor offence of pulling a reporter's lapels, produced a letter from Princess Margaret as a character reference, in which she thanked him for his work on behalf of her charity, the Invalid Aid Association. The treasured royal letter proved invaluable and he was let off without conviction, and paid NZ$ 50 costs. Reid's case was less straightforward. Despite profuse apologies to both reporters, and the mitigating factors of stress and exhaustion, Reid was sentenced to a month in prison. The rest of the band went on holiday to Tahiti, leaving Elton and Reid in New Zealand. For the first time Elton was left to stand by his manager. The staff at Rocket Records in London had done an almost perfect job of keeping the story out of the British newspapers, and so were amazed when Reid returned to request his press cuttings.

The letter that had saved Elton in the New Zealand court also served to show how high up the social ladder he had climbed. Princess Margaret had been guest of honour at the Invalid Aid Association concert, which Elton performed at the Royal Festival Hall, and was so taken with him that she asked her friends Bryan Forbes and Nanette Newman if they could arrange for him to give a private command performance. According to Newman, Princess Margaret had spoken to her mother about Elton, who was also 'terribly keen to see him as well'. And so the first of Elton's many private recitals at Royal Lodge, the Queen Mother's out-of-town residence at Windsor, was arranged. The Queen Mother was enchanted by Elton's cheeky charm and wit. During 'Your Song' he changed the line, 'I'd buy a big house where we both could live,' to, 'I'd buy Windsor Castle, Your Majesty.' After the performance, the Queen Mother announced that there would be dancing, and selected her own favourite to play on the gramophone, a rousing military ditty called, 'Slattery's Mounted Foot'. She seized Elton and they worked the dance floor.

Elton's achievements reached new heights in the spring of 1974 when he became a director of Watford Football Club, superseding his honorary title. Knowing that the club was in need of more cash and more publicity, Vic Lewis contacted the chairman of Watford, Jim Bonser, with an appealing proposal. The board jumped at the idea and both Lewis and Elton were made directors. He meant it when he told Lewis: 'This has to be the happiest day of my life.'

After the heavy touring and recording schedule, his directorship at Watford was a chance to be normal again and meet ordinary people. He would say about Watford: 'I love it as much as music itself. It's like erasing five or six years of my life and I'm here as if nothing had happened.' Elton would arrive at the ground in his Rolls-Royce wearing a black and yellow scarf like any other fan. Mixing with the rough and tumble of the football crowd rather than the adoring concert audience also exposed Elton to the word on the street. As he took his seat in the director's box in full club regalia the crowd cheered, but there was one ominous cat call: 'Yer great poof!'

The promised benefit concert for Watford FC took place on 5 May 1974 and a crowd of 40,000 attended the ground, more than any match had attracted. Elton topped the bill looking like a demented bumble bee, in a black and yellow jacket with yellow pom-poms and black satin trousers with a yellow stripe. He was joined by his friend, verbal sparring partner and fellow football fan, Rod Stewart. A great time was had by all, despite an almighty downpour.

Elton's planned British and European tour was postponed two weeks after it was announced, due to the 'severe strain' that Elton and the band were suffering – an extension of the tensions that had blighted the *Caribou* sessions, and so his British fans would not see him again until the end of the year.

The recently chastised Reid was on his best behaviour when he and Elton went to New York to sign a new recording contract with MCA, in what was hailed as the 'best deal anyone ever got', at $8 million (£5.3 million) for five albums, (later rumoured to be much more) plus a large increase in royalties, from 15 per cent to 17.5 per cent on records already released and 20 per cent on all future records. After the lukewarm reviews of *Caribou*, the only stipulation was that Elton should reduce his frenzied work-rate to one album a year, which didn't please the hardworking artist.

The combination of *Caribou*'s rushed recording and the tempestuous Far-East tour had turned Elton into 'a physical wreck'. He had started drinking heavily and had put on weight, so he went on a crash diet and decided that exercise was the only cure. His relationship with Reid was showing the strain and in a rare gesture of independence, Elton booked himself on a tennis holiday in Scottsdale, Arizona – on his own. In between matches he spent his time writing songs for his friends, including 'Let Me Be Your Car' for Rod Stewart and 'Snookeroo' for Ringo Starr.

While Reid's stay in New Zealand was temporarily prolonged, Steve Brown had run the office in his absence. On Reid's return, however, arguments between the two men ensued, resulting in Brown's departure. It was a blow to Elton, who would miss the inspired creative direction he had offered over the past five years. To replace Brown, David Croker, ex-boss of EMI's Harvest label, came to Rocket. Clive Banks, DJM's promotions manager, also defected to Rocket.

Rocket had signed eight acts, solo singers and bands, but despite everyone's best endeavours none had achieved much success, though Kiki Dee had enjoyed some chart success with her first single, a torch song called 'Amoureuse'. Instead the label found better fortune through the re-launches of the ailing careers of two more mature crooners, Cliff Richard and Neil Sedaka.

One of the biggest heroes to the still unabashed hero-worshipper was John Lennon. Elton and Lennon had met through Tony King, a former DJM plugger who progressed to work with The Beatles' label, Apple, when Lennon was recording with Phil Spector in Los Angeles in 1973. Elton remembered: 'He's probably the first big star who I instantly fell in love with.' During their infrequent encounters Elton reverted to the tongue-tied fan, too shy to forge much of a bond. Lennon was suffering after the break-up of his marriage to Yoko Ono, and because the US Immigration Department, with a little help from the CIA, was trying to deport him as an undesirable alien. Lennon left his wife in 1973 and went to Los Angeles for the year he came to call his 'lost weekend'. During these months he got to know Elton, and a strong friendship developed.

While Elton unquestionably worshipped the Beatle, Lennon certainly looked up to the younger musician and admired his stamina. Elton recorded 'Lucy In The Sky With Diamonds' as his next single, as a tribute, and as encouragement to a hero who had lost his confidence. He returned to the Caribou ranch for the recording in the summer, and Lennon joined him in the studio – his input was credited as 'the Reggae guitars of Dr Winston O'Boogie'. To return the compliment Elton joined Lennon to sing some back-up vocals on his new album *Walls and Bridges*, recording a track entitled 'Whatever Gets You Through The Night'. Elton asked Lennon if he would sing the track live on stage with him, and in the headiness of the moment Lennon agreed, only if the record got to number one. 'I said sure,' said Lennon, 'not thinking in a million years it was a hit.' This was an enormous commitment from Lennon who, apart from one charity appearance in 1972, had not sung live since The Beatles' farewell gig on the roof of the Apple building in 1970.

His stage fright had developed into a phobia since his self-imposed seclusion in the US.

The 'severe strain' of the early months of 1974 seemed to have lifted by June, and Elton could not wait to get back to work, despite the slow-down clause in his new deal with MCA. His next record was a compilation of greatest hits, which became the best-selling album in the Elton John catalogue, and in America it became the first 'Best Of' album to reach number one. However, that did not stop Elton going back to the Caribou studio for the second time in six months. After the criticism of *Caribou* Bernie produced lyrics for a concept album rather than a multi-faceted collection of pastiches. It was to be an autobiography of their childhoods – *Boy's Own* comic superhero meets down-home country boy, otherwise known as *Captain Fantastic And The Brown Dirt Cowboy*. For the first time Bernie did not write the lyrics at high-speed. He reflected on and recalled events: his first meeting with Elton, their all-night songwriting sessions, their disappointments, their first pay cheque from the music publishers and their flat-sharing days when the Brown Dirt Cowboy saved Captain Fantastic from death by gas. He produced a collection of introspective and nostalgic masterpieces.

On receipt of the lyrics Elton took a slow boat from Southampton to New York, booking himself and a few of his entourage on to the luxury liner SS *France*, on her final voyage. He tried to book the music room, but an opera singer beat him to it and took up residence for the entire five-day trip. In the middle of the day she took a two-hour break. 'So every lunchtime,' remembered Elton, 'I'd nip in there and grab the piano just for those two hours.' He might finish a song in an hour and play it to the band who were accompanying him. During the cruise he played squash with Apple's Tony King, always attracting an ogling crowd. Elton, sporting green hair, relaxed by playing competitive bingo and backgammon. He diligently kept in touch with the progress of the sales of *Caribou* by ship-to-shore telephone to discover that the album had gone platinum during the voyage.

He arrived in New York with the completed score for the album. His first booking on American soil was on a tennis court in Philadelphia for a friendly match with his new friend Billie Jean King, en route to the studio. The recording session took much longer this time, however, as he completed each song in order, but in the opinion of Gus Dudgeon, the time was well spent. 'The whole thing is perfect,' he said. 'It's the best the band have ever played, it's the best Elton has ever played and it's the best collection of songs.'

It equalled *Goodbye Yellow Brick Road* in quality and re-established Elton's and Bernie's reputations as consummate pop composers. '*Captain Fantastic* was for me one of the best albums we ever recorded,' Elton said in a radio interview in 1990. 'I felt more involved in the lyrics. They were all about Bernie and me.'

There was no let-up in the touring schedule, and Elton and his entourage embarked on another US tour, this time using the newly refurbished private Boeing aircraft, renamed Starship One. The tour was organized with military precision: when the plane landed on private airstrips, there would be a line of limos to whisk the band to the venues and whisk them back afterwards for the next flight on to the next city. Elton's outfits entered science-fiction territory when he donned a black Lurex body-stocking adorned with masses of coloured balls bouncing on strands of piano-wire. In a subsequent concert Elton wore a pink-and-silver sequinned catsuit topped off with an Edwardian hat draped in gigantic ostrich-feather boas. On stage, Elton's name, and that of each band member, was depicted in neon letters above them, a sight that surpassed the excesses of any previous stage sets. But once Elton got down to business at the keyboard, he would shed his fluff and feathers, and let the spirit of Jerry Lee Lewis take over for a finger-shredding two-and-a-half hours. He told *LA Times* reporter Robert Hilburn, who accompanied him on the tour: 'Forget about the costumes and staging – it's the music that counts. If you don't keep on improving you're wasting your time.' Elton's love affair with his audience was as passionate as ever and he has always said that performing is his *raison d'être*. He told Hilburn: 'It's the greatest thing in the world to stand on a stage and see people smiling, and know they came to see you.' It was not unknown for him to yell out to the crowd, 'I'll play for you even if I have one finger left!'

Because he was in Los Angeles for about four months a year, Elton and his team rented a Tudor-style, six-bedroomed house high up in Beverly Hills, for $50,000 (£33,300) a year. It was furnished in museum deco style with lots of theatrical drapery that Elton hated, so he accessorized it with his own things, such as a Rockola jukebox in the entrance hall stocked with his favourite records of the moment. In 1974 Elton opened the house to *Rolling Stone*, whose reporter observed a television and videocassette unit blocking the fireplace, a Victorian desk covered with trade magazines, and records neatly arranged on the floor stacked against the bookshelf. *Rolling Stone* also noted a distinctly all-male bias in the house – assistants, friends and Elton's manager, John Reid. The article described Elton in his white-and-blue terry towelling bathrobe and rose-tinted specs with tiny, red palm trees on the frames. Reid would be sitting on the sofa in his bright red robe briefing the road manager. The all-boys-together theme was merely suggested, but it was also noted that Elton and Reid shared a house in Surrey. Elton deftly danced round any insinuations. 'No,' said Elton. 'He's just my manager. I have a close circle of friends who just aren't in the public, sort of like Elvis. It's very much a family – that's why it's so incestuous sometimes.'

Back in England, Elton made a major addition to his record collection when he paid $8,000 (£5,300) to a former BBC producer for 30,000 singles, reputedly every single released in Britain in the previous fifteen years. He knew he had no space for it, but for this avid filing clerk, the priority was to get each disc catalogued, and he thought he might ask his mother to do it for him once he acquired a new house. He told *Rolling Stone* that he felt particularly uneasy when his things were out of order. 'I feel that inanimate things have feelings,' he said. 'I hate having my records strewn around the floor.'

The whole of America buzzed with the news of Elton's tour of 1974. The three dates in Los Angeles had sold out after almost six hours and so another show was quickly added. His opening night was star-studded with Elizabeth Taylor, David Cassidy and Barbra Streisand in the audience. Elton shopped, the fans kept buying Elton records and the radio played almost nothing but Elton music. His collaborations hit the high spots too – Kiki Dee's single, 'I've Got The Music In Me' charted in the American Top Twenty. Her jaunty singing owed much to Elton's humour, for during an uninspired recording session, Elton sneaked into the studio through a back door, hid behind a screen, and according to Gus Dudgeon, 'he took off all his clothes and suddenly streaked across the studio, stark naked.' Despite the shock, Dee managed to keep her composure and produce an excellent vocal.

The high point of the year came when John Lennon's record 'Whatever Gets You Through The Night' went straight to number one in America in November. It was the cue for Elton to contact Lennon to remind him of their bargain, and the ideal time would be the climax of Elton's current tour at Madison Square Garden on Thanksgiving night. In spite of his massive success with The Beatles during the 1960s, Lennon was now stricken with fear at the thought of performing in front of an audience. Reluctantly he attended a rehearsal, but it was by no means certain whether he would have the nerve to perform after such a long absence.

The rumours were flying and soon New York was abuzz with the news that John Lennon would appear with Elton John as the crowning glory to an exceptional tour. In anticipation Rocket Records had flown Elton's mother and stepfather, plus a large British media contingent to New York.

Along with the rest of New York, Yoko Ono wanted to be there to see the spectacle, and she requested a seat where she could clearly see the stage, but where her husband could not see her. On the night she was shown to her seat after the lights went down in the Garden.

In the build-up to the concert Lennon was physically sick with stage fright. He forgot how to tune his guitar and had to ask Elton's guitarist Davey Johnstone to help him. Minutes before the start of the show, two gift boxes were delivered backstage, one for Elton and one for Lennon. They contained white gardenias and a note in each from Ono, wishing them both luck. 'Thank God Yoko's not here tonight,' Lennon said, 'otherwise I know I'd never be able to go out there.'

He was due to come on stage towards the end of Elton's act, but as the concert progressed it was still uncertain whether he would make it. Elton, dressed in an ensemble of pink hot pants covered in hearts set off with a red boa, perhaps did little to settle Lennon's nerves.

When he got his cue to join Elton, Lennon asked Bernie to accompany him on stage. Bernie walked the first few steps, and then Lennon was on his way. As he appeared in a black suit with his gardenia pinned to the lapel, the 22,000-strong audience gave him a spectacular standing ovation, illuminated by a blinding white light sweeping across the whole stadium. The noise was breathtaking. The rousing show of appreciation continued for ten minutes as Lennon tried to stop it, and out of sight in her seat Yoko was in tears, thinking how lonely he looked on the stage, bowing over and over again to his fans. Elton was elated. 'It was the warmth and love. It was incredible,' he remembered. 'For anybody to play on stage with any one of The Beatles is like a dream come true.'

Eventually they sang three numbers. First, 'Lucy In The Sky With Diamonds' and 'Whatever Gets You Through The Night' to fulfil the bargain. Then Lennon referred to his old partner, 'We thought we'd do a number of an old estranged fiancé of mine called Paul ...' to a conspiratorial wave of laughter from the audience, and they sang, 'I Saw Her Standing There'. It was the first track on the first Beatles album, *Please Please Me*, released in January 1963, and until that night Lennon had never sung the lead before.

Emotions were running high on the first occasion a concert audience held up lit candles and cigarette lighters, but after Lennon's departure from the stage, Elton was still able to give a perfectly controlled rendition of 'Candle In The Wind'. Afterwards Yoko asked Tony King to take her backstage to surprise Lennon. It was a meeting that marked the beginning of their reconciliation. They started to see each other again, John promised to clean up his lifestyle and they settled down, back at home in the Dakota Building to have a child and spend the rest of their lives together. A year later, the couple would ask Elton to be godfather to their son, Sean.

The event would remain in Elton's mind as one of his most moving and memorable shows. Blessed by a Beatle, in front of 22,000 people, it was as much as he could do to sign off: 'This has been a very emotional night for me . . .'

☆

By the end of 1974, Elton had reached the zenith of his career, the pinnacle of his climb to the top. It would be another twenty-three years before he would experience anything near the same level of emotion.

What set Elton apart from his peers was that his appeal knew no demographic or generational limits. His act was based in music hall, with a touch of vaudeville and more than a dash of pantomime. His audiences were a mixture of serious musos, hippies, celebrities and ordinary people of all ages from teenyboppers to their parents and grandparents. Elton knew his appeal was high street, not high brow, mainstream not extreme. 'I've always thought rock and roll was people's music,' he said. 'It's always been a thing everyone should enjoy.' In his opinion people buy records for their sound, their melody and, most importantly, for their singalong quality.

One of Elton and Bernie's strengths was that neither of them took themselves too seriously, against the prevailing fashion in rock. Bernie always denied that he wanted to influence people. 'We don't know enough about the world to preach to people,' said Bernie. The songwriting method had not changed. Elton never interfered with Bernie's often dense and allusive words, while Bernie's part of the fantasy was to hear his poems become songs. The unique blend of musical sophistication and optimism that became their signature sound, is as apparent as that of the Beach Boys or The Beatles. All their albums featured some good, old-fashioned rock and roll, some gospel and some country and western, with which they created a canon of outstanding versatility.

chapter six

Desperation Train

URING HIS TENNIS SABBATICAL IN 1974, Elton, passionate sports groupie as well as fanatical pop fan, met Jimmy Connors and Billie Jean King, and was considered good enough to play against the champion herself. Having become a big fan of King's World Tennis League team, the Philadelphia Freedoms, he asked Bernie to produce lyrics for a song, inspired by King, to capture the idea of winning despite all odds. When writing the music Elton included the distinctive Philadelphia orchestral sound made famous by artists such as the O'Jays and Hall and Oates. In February 1975 'Philadelphia Freedom', the first single from the forthcoming album, *Captain Fantastic And The Brown Dirt Cowboy*, was released.

Billie Jean King has remained one of his closest friends, and during Wimbledon fortnight he would take her out to dinner in London. 'She's lots of fun,' said Elton. 'I draw a parallel with her and Lennon. It's that their public image has nothing to do with what they're really like.' Elton had much in common with King, including her sense of humour, determination to win and hatred of losing. 'She's very like me, because if I play any sport I always talk to myself and hit myself,' he said.

'Philadelphia Freedom' achieved a number one in America, but only made it to number twelve in Britain, possibly due to a minor spat Elton had had with the BBC. He had refused to appear on *Top of the Pops* because of a new ruling by the British Musicians' Union that orchestral tracks had to be specially pre-recorded by British musicians for inclusion on the programme. As a perfectionist Elton insisted that the Philadelphia sound could not be reproduced by British session musicians so he refused to make an appearance on the show, missing the one essential opportunity to promote the single in Britain.

On the back of his phenomenal success in America, *Empty Sky* was re-released and reached number six on the Billboard chart. Early 1975 was a relaxed time for the Elton John Band, with nothing in the calendar until May, when *Captain Fantastic* was to be released. The team took an extended and much needed break; everyone, that is, except Elton.

Without a tour, a recording session or a concert to engage him, Elton had time on his hands, which did not suit him at all. He suffered a kind of lack-of-motion sickness, finding it impossible to calm down. When the juggernaut that was his career suddenly stopped, Elton found himself in a vacuum, and he spun around looking for ways to fill it. In March he swept up to Broadcasting House in central London in his Rolls-Royce with a boot full of cardboard boxes containing a selection of his records. He appeared on BBC Radio One as EJ the DJ, in a special programme called *Don't Shoot Me, I'm Only The Disc Jockey,* playing current hits and golden oldies with lots of typical Eltonian banter in between, including football jokes and Goon imitations.

He appeared as the Pinball Wizard in Ken Russell's feature film of The Who's rock opera, *Tommy,* singing Pete Townshend's song of the same name. The outstanding feature of his costume was a pair of giant Doc Martens boots designed by Ken's wife, the costume designer Shirley Russell. They stood 5 feet high and were built out of glass fibre, with calliper-like contraptions to hold Elton's legs in position. They were so tall and unwieldy that he could hardly walk, and he had to hold on to the props to stop himself from falling over during his scene. However uncomfortable, the rapacious souvenir hunter wanted to take them home, and stood them among the stuffed furry animals next to his Picassos.

At last he was able to get back on the work treadmill in May when he returned to America to launch *Captain Fantastic.* Before a single track had been broadcast it was already known to be his most successful album yet – advance orders had exceeded a million copies and it went gold just two days after its US release.

The appearance of the album in the shops laid bare the tensions behind the scenes at his record company. DJM priced it as a double LP instead of a single because of its elaborate packaging. *Captain Fantastic* was the penultimate studio album under Elton's recording agreement with DJM; he still owed them two albums under the original agreement – one studio album plus a compilation. Relations between John Reid and the Jameses were little better than hostile, with Stephen convinced that Reid had betrayed his father to spirit away DJM's most precious asset.

The concept for the cover design had been dreamed up by Bernie, who commissioned pop art illustrator Alan Aldridge to create an elaborate and whimsical illustration. Aldridge presented DJM with a bill that was far beyond their expectations. In the past the Jameses might have indulged Elton and paid the artist's fee, but this time they refused because Stephen thought it was 'too introverted and indulgent'. If Elton wanted to use it then he would have to pay for it. It was eventually agreed that the copyright of the illustration would remain with Rocket and they would lease it to DJM to use on the album cover. Once in the shops, the packaging was an added complication to the marketing of the album, which came with two intricate booklets and a sleeve design that did not even include a list of tracks. Elton was furious that DJM had increased the cover price, telling *Melody Maker*, 'It's their decision, not mine. There's only one album left to do in the DJM contract. After that I'm free.'

Elton's mood swings were becoming increasingly obvious to the public, thanks to his bitter comments to the press, but they were also starting to affect the band. It came as a shock, not only to the musicians themselves but to the whole team, when out of the blue and while the band were on holiday, Elton fired bassist Dee Murray and drummer Nigel Olsson over the phone. It was an act of sheer capriciousness. After sharing success for five years, his band had seemed solid and strong. They had just created their best work and each had their names in neon lights on stage. Looking back on his career, Elton would say in a radio interview in 1990: 'I knew that they were going to be extremely hurt because they had been with me from the word go. I told them over the phone which was an extremely awful way of doing it, and I regret that immensely.'

Elton later said that he made the decision after the 1974 American tour when he came back home and felt low. 'I don't know why I get depressed. I can be very happy and then all of a sudden I'm on a comedown . . . I thought I was just unhappy,' Elton said. 'Then I realized – I had to change the band.' He kept guitarist Davey Johnstone and percussionist Ray Cooper. Roger Pope, a session musician from *Empty Sky*, became the drummer; Caleb Quaye, his old friend and DJM studio engineer from the early days, played guitar. To replace Murray, Elton took on an American bass player, Kenny Passarelli. He also added another keyboard player, James Newton Howard, the highly regarded session man and noted Moog synthesizer player, to give him more freedom to move around the stage and not be stuck behind his piano.

There was no major summer tour on the agenda in 1975, and instead there was to be an Elton John concert at Wembley Stadium on 21 June, with the Beach Boys as a support act. Wembley was Elton's only appearance of the year in Britain, and it had to be spectacular. He decided to play the whole of the *Captain Fantastic* album, in order. To help his new band get to know each other, and to rehearse his repertoire intensively, Elton took his line-up, including three backing singers, to Amsterdam for a week. Elton was obsessed with keeping fit; constantly on the go, he did not even allow his band to relax. He had them all jogging alongside the canals in oppressive heat during breaks, rather than giving them the chance to wind down in the shade with a few cold drinks.

Elton welcomed journalist Caroline Coon from *Melody Maker* to the band's getting-to-know-you week in Amsterdam. He showed no remorse for his unceremonious dumping of Murray and Olsson, and talked instead about his string of unstoppable hits in America, and his need to keep his attitude under control and maintain high standards of work by 'being 'very, very self-critical.'

Elton chatted openly, revealing more about himself than ever before, offering many clues for those prepared to read between the lines. He said that he did not want to settle down for a while yet, having seen the marriages of so many fellow musicians fail, due to the nature of life on the road. Of his close relationship with Bernie, he said: 'He loved me. We hit rock bottom together so many times and at that point in my life he was the only person I could really call a friend. We found a spark together and a way of writing that's still with us.' He discussed his inferiority complex in more detail, particularly dwelling on his belief that his father didn't love him, and his feelings of rejection when Stanley had remarried and had four children. He explained that humour was always the most effective way to lift him out of a sulk, especially a camp phone call from one of his friends.

The Wembley concert was sold out – 72,000 fans came to bask in the midsummer sunshine in front of a dream line-up, all the acts selected by Elton himself. Stackridge, the Pinner pub band and one of Rocket's signings, was first on stage, followed by Rufus, a black funk group, then Joe Walsh, the country-rock singer, and later The Eagles, at the time a little-known band from the west coast of America. The warm-up act for Elton was the Beach Boys, the choristers of pop, whom Elton had hero-worshipped since his teenage years, and whose close harmonies and melodies had influenced his music. The high point of the show was due to be Elton's appearance at sunset for a two-and-a-half-hour *Captain Fantastic* set.

The laidback Californian sound of The Eagles almost stole the show a good four hours before Elton was due on stage. Then, after the Beach Boys' surfing hymns had provided near perfect accompaniment to a perfect summer afternoon, there was an interlude while, as the sun went down, the stage was reorganized with equipment, fairy lights, potted palms and a neon sign spelling out FANTASTIC. Elton came on to a roaring welcome and whipped up the crowd with 'Saturday Night's Alright For Fighting'. By the time dusk fell, however, hundreds of people were leaving the stadium. The audience had done 'fantastic', they were not in the mood for a pretentious, over-elaborate set. They did not want a sober-suited Elton sitting at the piano singing long, unfamiliar, introspective songs about his life. He had completely misjudged the dynamic of the evening, after the afternoon's upbeat mood of surfing and sunshine, later recalling: 'People were hurtling into the hot dog stands after the fourth song.'

The music press did not hesitate to criticize, as *Melody Maker*'s headline screamed: BEACH BOYS' CUP RUNNETH OVER. ELTON LEFT TO PICK UP THE EMPTIES. Was this to be the beginning of the end for Elton?

The Wembley flop was just the start. His single from *Captain Fantastic*, 'Someone Saved My Life Tonight' peaked at only twenty-two in the British charts, although it made number four in America. After five extraordinary years it seemed incredible that Elton had not achieved the top honour in his own country – a number-one single. But despite the setbacks at home, he was still America's favourite artist, and several radio stations advertised themselves as the number-one Elton John station.

After the unsettling first half of 1975, Elton wanted to get back to work; he missed doing what he loved best, touring and recording. He went back to Caribou with his new line-up to record *Rock Of The Westies*, the last studio album to complete his contract with DJM.

He was also booked at the Troubadour Club in Los Angeles in late August for a fifth-anniversary, three-night charity appearance at the venue where he had achieved his breakthrough. Demand for tickets was so great that they could only be allocated by prize draw. At the opening night, with tickets priced at $250 (£165), Tony Curtis and Cher were among the celebrity-packed audience. Elton's six shows raised $150,000 (£100,000) for the Jules Stein Eye Institute at UCLA. Anyone expecting a re-run of his first-night triumph in 1970 would have been disappointed. The feeling of anti-climax was palpable with Elton's big, laid back, rock-and-roll band making too much noise for such a small venue – the magic had gone.

He took up residence in America for a few months, not as his British fans thought, in a sulk after his Wembley fiasco, but due to complications with the US tax authorities over his vast earnings. A condition of a convoluted plan negotiated by John Reid was that Elton should become an American resident for a few months. Rather than renting a property, Elton paid $1 million (£666,600) for a Moorish-style residence in Benedict Canyon, Beverly Hills, once owned by film producer David O. Selznick and his wife Jennifer Jones, as well as Greta Garbo. It was a dark, spooky house, rumoured to be haunted, with overbearing Gothic interiors that were unlikely to raise Elton's spirits. With ghoulish rocker Alice Cooper as his new neighbour, he moved in with his teddy bears, records and two pinball machines illuminated with the names of his last two albums.

Essentially Elton was on his own. The personal side of his partnership with Reid had gradually diminished, and the two now had virtually independent lives outside their working relationship. However, he boosted his morale with a constant flow of old friends, especially Bernie, who lived in Los Angeles with his wife, and music-business associates. He welcomed a crowd of new friends, sycophants and hangers-on who would be at his beck and call, guaranteed to laugh at his jokes and supply his every need.

The mind and body of this formerly robust and health-conscious pop star, who normally got up early every morning to play tennis before breakfast, were at serious risk while he was holed up in this never-never land of film sets and fantasies. He felt alienated and missed his mother and his football club. It was plain for all to see that Elton's black moods and unpredictability were brought on not just by the pint of whisky he was drinking per day, but by the drugs he had begun taking. After a few months an old Rocket associate, Sharon Lawrence, visited him and she said, 'I remembered this person who was mildly temperamental, but basically happy and organized. Now he was incredibly strung-up, anxious and panicky.'

Elton was exhausted after five frenetic years on the road, but he felt disorientated without a concert tour to look forward to, or the affirmation he craved from his adoring audience. When not writing, recording, performing or travelling, the cracks started to show, and the empty days stretched ahead with nothing to do but to shop, party, eat, drink and admire his fabulous possessions. Another diverting indulgence was to give expansive interviews to passing journalists, perhaps because he felt he could not confide in anyone around him. He gave a particularly articulate and revealing interview to *Playboy* magazine.

The conversation was wide-ranging. He talked of how he was flabbergasted that the American tabloid newspapers, the *National Star* and *National Enquirer,* could make up bizarre and sensational stories about celebrities and pass them off as news – a theme he might come to reflect upon in later years. He discussed his thinning hair, and remarked how unfair it was that no one else in his family had suffered from baldness. He spoke of his concerns about being seen as a failure and losing the love of his fans: 'I think how suddenly, overnight, my records could stop selling. In this business nothing's for certain.' But if his popularity was to waver, he was prepared for a fight: 'I like the struggle to stay at the top. It's what keeps me going.' He side-stepped the question of his sexuality, and was coy when the drugs issue came up. 'I'd like to take LSD to find out what it's like,' he said, 'but it's like going into the unknown with a paranoid attitude. One half of me would love to do it, but the other half owns up to the fact that it might be a bit of a disaster.'

Elton, unexpectedly, began to talk much more frankly when asked about his childhood. He harked back to his lonely years as Reggie Dwight in the unhappy house in Northwood Hills, pouring out his heart about his introversion, his inferiority complex on account of his physical appearance and, in a flood of unreserved and unchecked emotion, he lost all his self-control in a tirade of bitter and untrue words against his father. He spoke of how when he was born, his father was on an RAF posting abroad and did not see him for two years. Then, later in his boyhood, how his father had made life hell for him: 'My father was so stupid with me, it was ridiculous. I couldn't eat celery without making a noise . . . it was just pure hate.'

Depression and solitude in his Hollywood house had allowed him to dwell on the many hours he had spent on his own in his bedroom as a boy, cataloguing his records and checking football results. 'I grew up with inanimate objects as my friends, and I still believe they have feelings,' he said. 'That's why I keep hold of all my possessions.'

He fired another broadside at his father for making his mother pay all the divorce costs and forcing her to admit to adultery, while all the time his father had been doing the same. In fact it was Stanley who had paid all the costs and, although he did remarry soon after the divorce, he had not met his new wife until the decree nisi was through, whatever theories Sheila might have put to her son. And, referring to the birth of his four half-brothers, Elton said: 'My pride was really snipped because he was supposed to hate kids. I guess I was just a mistake in the first place.'

This outburst caused his father's family, with whom he seemed to be on good, although distant, terms, considerable pain. In his stepmother's opinion, only one person could have planted such inaccuracies in Elton's mind – his mother. But other accusations that must have been just as hurtful to his father were Elton's insinuations that, not only that he had never approved of his music, but that he 'didn't say no to the odd Cortina or two'. His father had tried to refuse the cheque to buy a Peugeot on Elton's last visit, but in one cruel breath Elton had managed to make him appear both greedy and lacking in taste. Stanley's brother owned a Cortina and felt obliged to put a notice in the back window saying: 'Elton did not pay for this car'.

Stanley was astonished at his son's harsh accusations and gave a brief interview to the *Daily Mail* in which he put the record straight about his divorce, his second marriage and subsequent family. He strongly denied that Reggie had been a mistake or that he had missed either his son's birth or the first two years of Reggie's life. When he was advised to sue *Playboy*, or even Elton, he steadfastly refused, stating that although he had no idea why Elton had made up such hurtful accusations, he did not want to say or do anything to create further distance between them. He believed his son was extremely unhappy, and was anxious not to add to Elton's problems.

Stanley's concerns were well-founded. Elton was not happy, and by the time he recorded *Rock Of The Westies* he was taking cocaine. The wallflower at parties was using cocaine because he thought it would loosen him up. 'I thought that by doing coke I would finally be in with everybody else,' he said. 'And then I got the taste for it.' At the age of twenty-eight, he discovered he was blessed, or rather cursed, with an iron constitution perfect for a rock-and-roll lifestyle. He could stay up five or six days in a row and then attend a tour rehearsal. Eventually it would take its toll, the fallout of a cocaine come-down affecting everyone in its wake. His intemperance would reveal itself in displays of bizarre behaviour and tantrums. 'On drugs I was divine, lovely and fabulous,' he said, 'coming off drugs I was a nightmare. I used to fly over anger and land in rage.'

Rock Of The Westies was Elton's first cocaine album. At one point during the recording in July, Elton found himself standing in a garden trying to teach the guitarist his chords because he was so stoned. The album title was a feeble play. on the name of the forthcoming autumn tour of US and Canadian towns and cities, which were all to the west of the Rocky Mountains. It also referred to the band's West Coast sound, influenced by Little Feat, The Doobie Brothers and The Eagles, but its mediocrity reflected the exhaustion and level of burn-out Elton and Bernie had both reached, not least because it contains more one-take recordings than any other of their albums to date. Only the Hawaiian pastiche, 'Island Girl', stood out from the list of tired titles, like 'Dan Dare (Pilot Of The Future)' and 'Billy Bones And The White Bird'. The Elton John brand name was still riding high in America where the album reached number one, and 'Island Girl' stayed at number one in the US singles chart for three weeks. The album only reached number five in Britain, and the single peaked at fourteen. In later years Elton would rarely perform material from *Rock Of The Westies*.

Autumn 1975 brought another milestone, when Elton joined the constellation of star names on Hollywood Boulevard, on the pavement outside Graumann's Chinese Theater. The whole street had to be closed off for the first time in history for the ceremony because of the vast crowd of fans. To coincide with the grand finale to his tour, it was declared Elton John Week in Los Angeles.

Although he was delighted with the new band, the effects of his lifestyle were beginning to show. He would be overcome with fits of tiredness when he had to play, and would go to rehearsals only to storm out in a savage mood, then return a few hours later with no recollection of his histrionics. He remembered this tour as a time of being continuously unwell, and he lost a lot of weight. Consequently, people in his closest circle were growing increasingly concerned – even John Lennon had spoken to him about the worrying course his life was taking.

For Elton John Week, Rocket Records specially chartered a Boeing 707 at a cost of $100,000 (£66,600) to fly over a dozen of his close friends and family from England: Sheila and Fred, his grandmother Ivy, neighbours from Pinner, Bryan Forbes and Nanette Newman, TV presenter Russell Harty, who was recording his trip on film, footballer Rodney Marsh, and a handful of journalists. Elton met them at LA airport, and sent them off on a tour of Disneyland, Universal Studios and the boutiques of Beverly Hills. They were all invited to a party on *Madman*, a 65-foot boat belonging to John Reid, which was a gift from Elton on Reid's last birthday.

One afternoon during their stay, his group of house guests were gathered round the pool at Benedict Canyon, when Elton suddenly appeared in his white, towelling bathrobe and screamed: 'Well, that's it then. I'm going to end it all. I've just taken eighty-five Valium!' With that, he clambered on to the diving board, waddled to the end, held his nose and jumped. On his way down he must have had a change of heart. He tore off his sodden bathrobe and bobbed up to the surface, spluttering and choking. Everyone was dumbstruck. His seventy-five-year-old grandmother Ivy, who was on her first trip outside the UK, broke the stunned silence when she said, 'Oh, I suppose we've all got to go home now.' She was one of the few people who could bring him down to earth, reminding him who he really was. He said later: 'I was an immature little schoolboy craving attention on a totally different level to that I was getting as Elton John.' His nosedive resulted in a three-day coma. The incident upset his mother so much that he promised never to think about taking his life again.

The West of the Rockies Tour came to a spectacular climax at the LA Dodgers' baseball stadium on 25 and 26 November, with all 100,000 tickets for both concerts sold out in half an hour. At one of the lowest points in his life he found the energy to give two of his best ever shows decked out in a tight, sequinned, baseball outfit with a cap in Dodgers' colours, for three-and-a-half hours each night. Billie Jean King came on to sing the chorus of 'The Bitch is Back', and Bernie Taupin, Kiki Dee and the forty-five-member Rev James Cleveland Choir joined him on stage. By the end of the shows his fingers were raw and bleeding, but no one in the audience at the Dodgers' Stadium could have guessed that the superstar had been close to death just days before.

By the end of 1975 Elton John was still a dominant figure the music world, but in spite of his achievements he was still shy, lonely, unloved, overweight Reg from Pinner, and there was nothing anyone could say or do to convince him otherwise.

chapter seven

Shine On Through

AT THE BEGINNING OF 1976, Elton left La-La Land for home – and the almighty upheaval that was about to change the British music scene. Elton would later say that if he had stayed in the United States he would either be dead, or he would have ended up 'a complete fruitcake, like Michael Jackson or Prince'.

For financial reasons it would have been prudent for Elton to take up full-time residence in the US. His box-office receipts since 1973, totalling more than $3 million (£2 million), had been frozen by the Internal Revenue Service until he decided whether he was to stay in the US. He had also just netted $1.1 million (£733,300) for the two concerts at the LA Dodgers' baseball stadium. As a temporary resident, his tax affairs were caught between British and US liabilities. Coming home, he could be subject to taxation at the then top rate of nearly 90 per cent, but the lonely and confused party animal desperately missed his mother and his home comforts.

Touring away from Britain had become an emotional and physical drain. For a rock-and-roll tour to be successful, it needed to be run like a military operation, with meticulous planning and paperwork; call sheets, movement orders, equipment lists, wardrobe lists, crew lists, song lists, visas, carnets, venue bookings, hotel bookings, flights, insurances. Vast quantities of equipment would be scheduled to arrive at venues in advance, usually transported in customized juggernauts, and supervised by a large and experienced road crew. If treacherous weather precluded road travel then private planes had to be chartered. Hundreds of costumes would arrive at the hotel to be laid out in a separate room across the bed, the floor and any other flat surface, to enable Elton to make his selection more easily. When he arrived at the venue, he would heave himself into his costume and visit the band for a few jokes and some banter before the show, to create a friendly vibe on stage. Everything was organized so that the only thing Elton had to think about was his performance. If any detail, especially relating to the sound, was not to his satisfaction, heads would roll – and he might lock himself in his dressing room until the problem was fixed.

Consequently he was glad to be back home, and tried to inject some British humour into his spring tour of the UK, the first in more than two years. He played Earls Court, but also low-key regional venues, where he posed for photographs at Scottish castles, drank in pubs, and bought ice cream in village shops.

Elton had acquired several warehouses' worth of possessions and outgrown Hercules – by now more repository than residence – which was eventually sold for the knock-down price of $120,000 (£80,000). John Reid had already moved out of the home he had previously shared with Elton, and moved to an elegant townhouse in Montpelier Square in London.

Before leaving California, Elton had asked his mother to help him look for a stately home of his own. Sheila found Woodside, a three-storey house on the outskirts of Old Windsor, surrounded by thirty-seven acres of rolling Berkshire countryside stocked with deer, pheasant and the odd donkey, and containing three lakes. Parts of the house date back to the sixteenth century when it was the residence of King Henry VIII's physician. As Windsor Castle is clearly visible from the top of the house, the king would order the flag to be hoisted, or have bonfires lit to signal that his gout was playing up, at which the physician would jump on his horse and ride over to attend to the king. According to Elton: 'The Queen Mother says I've easily got the best view of Windsor Castle in the whole of Berkshire.' The house is best described as 'Queen Anne-style mansion meets Barratt executive home' and had every facility the biggest pop star in the world could need: private cinema, disco, squash courts, swimming pool, stables, staff cottage and an orangery. The kitchen had a walk-in freezer, huge pantry and a jukebox in one corner. The library was lined with Elton's favourite reading matter, biographies, and included a pub-style bar and a pool table. The basement contained a well-stocked wine cellar, and the controls to an elaborate alarm system connected to a walk-in safe.

A corridor lined with gold and platinum discs led to a large room set aside for his record collection, which his mother had scrupulously catalogued. The house would become another vast vault and many of the rooms had the air of a museum rather than a home. The squash court, which Elton used for many a competitive match when he first moved to Woodside, soon became a store too. There were suites of rooms for guests, an office for Sheila and a self-contained flat in the Orangery for his housekeeper. But no matter how many rooms Woodside had, they were soon filled to capacity with Elton's collections.

The staff cottage in the grounds was occupied by Elton's chauffeur, Bob Halley, and his wife, Pearl. Halley has remained one of Elton's closest friends and currently works as his full-time personal assistant. They first met when

Halley joined the team as a temporary driver for John Reid in 1974. He first set eyes on Elton when he flew into Heathrow Airport like an exotic tropical bird in a feather costume and six-inch platform heels. On the motorway Halley drove extra carefully, mindful of his precious cargo. Suddenly he heard Elton whisper to Reid in the back, 'Can't she go any faster?' They soon hit it off and Halley was offered a full-time job with Reid. When Elton needed a housekeeper, he asked Halley and Pearl to move to Windsor where they could live in the cottage. When his wife ran off with the landscape gardener, Halley moved into the main house as Elton's general factotum, confidant and best mate. They shared a penchant for indulging in mock insults and blokey banter. Sometimes they would wear His and His earrings. 'I think Elton liked me because I didn't suck up to him,' said Halley. 'I was always honest and we shared the same sense of humour.' Elton would become dependent on Halley over the next few years; he would organize spur-of-the-moment parties and keep Elton company, and even, on one occasion, save his life after a drugs binge.

In spring 1976, Elton succeeded Jim Bonser as chairman of Watford Football Club. It was one of his proudest moments. His fundraising concerts had helped the club considerably, despite the team's ineffectual performance on the pitch. As Elton took up his chairmanship at the end of the 1975–6 season, the club had fallen to eighth in the fourth division.

Elton was anxious to secure John Reid's directorship at the club for the following season, and needed to create a vacant post. Vic Lewis was the man singled out, and unceremoniously, he was asked to resign his position. This was an especially harsh decision by Elton, as it was Lewis who, early in his career, had originally encouraged him to go on the road with a band, and who had played a vital role in setting up Elton's own directorship at Watford. To be treated so thoughtlessly came as a tremendous shock to Lewis.

Not only was Watford FC performing poorly in the bottom division, but the club's bank account was badly overdrawn. Elton soon explained that he was not prepared to become the club's sugar daddy, by spending a fortune on new players. He believed that the club could make money for itself with the creation of new schemes to make the most of its existing assets, and he was even prepared to reduce his tour schedules if the board needed more of his time to help resolve its financial crisis. Elton took heartfelt pride in his work with Watford, explaining how it had brought him 'back down to earth': 'I love it as much as music itself. It's like erasing five or six years of my life and here I am as if nothing had happened.'

Elton's 1976 British tour, Louder Than Concorde, was named after the supersonic plane that had recently made its first commercial flight and was

Elton poses with his proud mother, Sheila, after receiving his knighthood for services to music and charity work on behalf of AIDS victims, in February 1998.

Top left: A babe in arms: Reggie Dwight with his paternal grandmother, Ellen, and grandfather, Edwin.

Top right: Musical roots: an early picture of Edwin Dwight, a soprano cornet-player in the Callander Cables works band.

Left: Elton's father, Stanley Dwight, played the trumpet in an RAF band he had formed under the name Stan Wight.

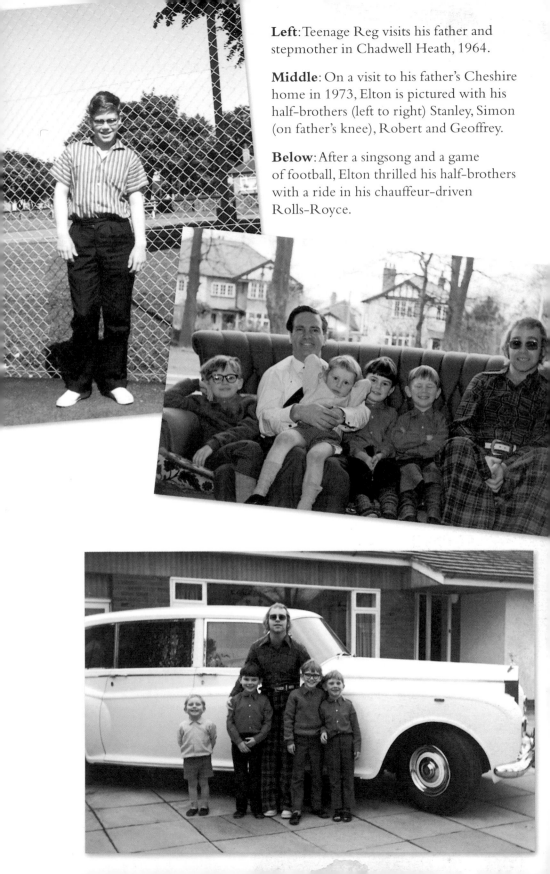

Left: Teenage Reg visits his father and stepmother in Chadwell Heath, 1964.

Middle: On a visit to his father's Cheshire home in 1973, Elton is pictured with his half-brothers (left to right) Stanley, Simon (on father's knee), Robert and Geoffrey.

Below: After a singsong and a game of football, Elton thrilled his half-brothers with a ride in his chauffeur-driven Rolls-Royce.

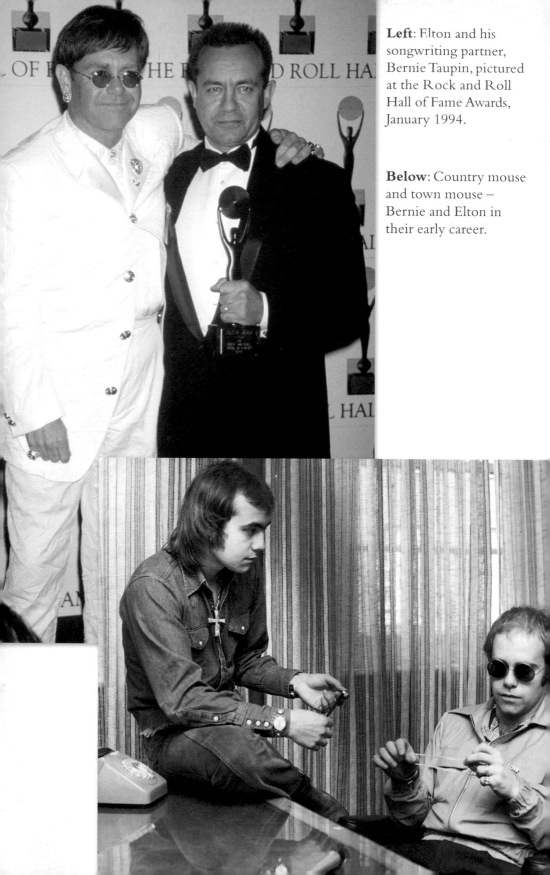

Left: Elton and his songwriting partner, Bernie Taupin, pictured at the Rock and Roll Hall of Fame Awards, January 1994.

Below: Country mouse and town mouse – Bernie and Elton in their early career.

Elton and his former manager and protector, John Reid, pictured in 1979 (**left**) and 1998 (**below**).

Top: Elton has been an enthusiastic tennis player for many years. Tennis champion and close friend, Billie Jean King, is pictured here in a doubles match with Elton.

Right: Elton takes part in a tennis tournament organized by Andre Agassi in Orlando, Florida, in September 1997.

In 1976, Elton accepted the honour of becoming chairman of Watford Football Club, the team he has supported since childhood.

Elton plays football with George Best, dressed in the Los Angeles Aztecs strip, in 1976.

Elton married German sound engineer, Renate Blauel, on Valentine's Day 1984. Always under pressure from Elton's sexual identity crisis, the marriage lasted less than five years.

Elton with his partner, David Furnish, whom he met at a dinner party in October 1993.

dominating the news. The slogan was inspired by a quip made by Princess Margaret after one of Elton's private royal recitals when she told him, 'This tour of yours sounds as if it'll be louder than Concorde.' The tour, which included some charity performances in support of the Sports Aid Foundation, established by the government to raise money for British athletes, reaffirmed Elton's place in the hearts of his fellow countrymen. It also helped to erase the bad memories of his last concert at Wembley the previous year. Throughout the land his concerts sold out as fans clamoured to marvel at his outlandish costumes and his antics on stage, as well as his music.

By 1976 a number-one chart hit in Britain continued to elude him, but more worrying was the fact that his popularity in America was falling, as new bands and new fashions emerged to challenge his formerly unassailable position. His music was beginning to sound old-fashioned compared to the new age of bands like Queen, 10cc and Roxy Music, and country rockers like The Eagles and The Doobie Brothers. Elton's audience was getting older and the younger audience wanted bands, rather than solo performers, whose new songs were harder and weirder.

At the age of twenty-nine Elton spent hours agonizing over his future; he was not yet ready to become a has-been. He decided the best plan of action was to release a single from *Rock Of The Westies*, the distinctly uncatchily titled, 'I Feel Like A Bullet (In The Gun Of Robert Ford)', with 'Grow Some Funk Of Your Own' on the B-side. The single was hardly played on the radio and the WABC station in New York did not even include it on its playlist. Not to be defeated, Elton decided to pull a promotional stunt of his own. He sent an enormous cake to WABC's programme director, decorated with a gun and inscribed in icing, 'Give Robert Ford a shot'. When this did not work, a week later he sent another bigger cake, with the sugar-encrusted message: 'Disregard previous cake. Grow Some Funk is the A-side.' The re-labelled single did manage to reach number fourteen in America, but could not make its mark on the Top Fifty in Britain.

DJM released *Here And There*, an album of live performances from 1974 with the Royal Festival Hall concert on one side, and the Madison Square Garden Thanksgiving concert on the other. The album had fulfilled Elton's contractual obligations with DJM, which meant he was free to sign with any record company. Although they were queuing up for his name on the dotted line, he did what he had vowed he would never do, and opted to record on his own label, though not solely on his own behalf.

'Don't Go Breaking My Heart' gave Elton his first, longed-for number-one hit in Britain in July 1976. It had started out as a song for Elton alone, but because it was lacking in certain respects, Kiki Dee was brought in for a duet, which resulted in media speculation over the true nature of their relationship. Elton had come up with the title and melody, and sung it over the phone to Bernie in Barbados. The writer's credit was not the usual John-Taupin, but attributed to their pseudonyms, 'Ann Orson and Carte Blanche'.

Although his presence in the American charts was in decline, his music was still played non-stop on mainstream radio stations, and on his transatlantic Louder Than Concorde Tour, he was as much in demand as ever, with twenty-nine sold-out shows. But Elton was jaded after six years on the road, and the whole tour seemed like an action replay, with city-to-city shuttles on Starship One, luxury hotel suites and stretch limos. His love affair with the audience was past the first throes of passion, however, and the people who had bought the tickets weren't always affectionate. His warm-up act, the comedian Billy Connolly (another John Reid client), took the brunt of the jeers and catcalls before Elton came on stage. In Detroit Elton was nearly hit by a bottle lobbed from the audience, which fuelled his paranoia. As the tour rolled into each town 'Elton John Day' would be decreed by the mayor, and he would be given the freedom of each city he visited.

Offstage, it was obvious that Elton would rather have been at Vicarage Road; at one point in the tour he even returned to Watford to attend the club's annual general meeting. Onstage, his heart was not in it. Gone was the glamour from his performances – instead of feathers and frippery he wore a tracksuit and trainers, jazzed up with a minimum of dressing-up box accessories. Only in New York did he make an effort – during his seven-day residence at Madison Square Garden in August, he dressed as the Statue of Liberty. He performed encores with the likes of Alice Cooper, Billie Jean King, Kiki Dee and the portly transvestite Divine. On this occasion he broke the box-office record for a rock act, playing to a total of 137,900 people.

Bernie had also had enough of touring, which had made him 30 per cent deaf in one ear. He was as inconspicuous as Elton was famous, unrecognizable as Elton was unmistakeable. Like Elton he had been on the road for most of six years, watching from the wings, taking his half of the credit for the music, living in luxury hotels, flying in private planes, eating, drinking and snorting everything on the rock-and-roll menu. His wife, Maxine, had left him, and the marriage appeared beyond saving after her affair with Elton's bass player, Kenny Passarelli, previously one of Bernie's closest friends.

In the summer of 1976, Elton, the dedicated hero worshipper, finally got to meet the greatest pop idol of them all, Elvis Presley, when he and Bernie went to see Elvis' concert in Maryland. At this stage in his career, however, the king of rock and roll was incontinent, grossly overweight and barely able to see. They were shocked both by his appearance and his performance. 'He was so drugged he could hardly sing,' Bernie recalled. With an invitation to see Elvis backstage, they witnessed his tragic state up close, as he sat in the middle of his dressing room, draped in towels, like a living corpse, sweating profusely, and surrounded by a gang of minders. He was barely aware of Elton and Bernie's presence, and the sad demise of such a remarkable man had a tremendous impact on them both.

Elton granted only two interviews to the music press during his American tour in 1976. He announced to Chris Charlesworth, of *Melody Maker,* that he was giving up touring for a while because he was tired of all the pressure: 'I've done six years and I'm fed up ... with having no base and constantly roaming around. I'm not retiring, just laying off for a while.' Instead, he wanted to devote more time to his role as chairman of Watford FC, to fulfil his dreams of promotion from the fourth division: 'I have to do something positive, and getting involved with a soccer club is my way of doing it. It won't be quite as insane as the music business.'

The other interview he gave while touring was to *Rolling Stone* magazine, which had been his American mouthpiece from the beginning. This articulate and forthright interviewee held a revealing and lengthy audience with journalist Cliff Jahr, in which he revealed the one last detail that everyone in his inner circle had known about for years, which was an open secret to most of the media – his sexuality. It came as no great revelation to observant fans who had read between the lines, and seemed hardly relevant at the tail-end of the gender-bending, glam-rock era.

As Elton's manager, John Reid was firmly against him coming out of the closet in case the revelations damaged his reputation and affected record sales. Elton supported many charities and mixed in top social circles, especially with royalty, and Reid thought he should continue to come across as a positive role model for the young people who bought his records, without disclosing his sexual preferences. Reid and his English publicists, two former rock journalists, had always kept a tight rein on the way interviews were conducted and had a fair idea of the subjects to be discussed beforehand, that is, until the Cliff Jahr interview.

Elton held court with Jahr in his palatial six-room suite in the Sherry-Netherland Hotel, pondering his future and his retirement plans. Still upset by the apparition of Elvis he wondered out loud, 'Who wants to be a forty-five-year-old entertainer in Las Vegas like Elvis?' When the conversation moved on to his homelife and his passions, Elton said: 'I go home and fall in love with my vinyl. I haven't really met anyone I'd want to have big scenes with. I crave to be loved. I want to have a person in my life. I haven't met anyone I would like to settle down with – of either sex.'

In response to Elton's intriguing remark, Jahr asked if he was bisexual. 'There's nothing wrong with going to bed with someone of your own sex,' Elton replied. 'I think everyone's bisexual to a certain degree. I don't think it's just me.' Jahr pressed him on the subject, asking whether he and Bernie had ever been lovers. Elton denied it outright. 'Everybody thinks we were, but if we had been I don't think we would have lasted so long. We're more like brothers than anything else. The press probably thought John Reid and I were an affair, but there's never been a serious person the whole time.'

At the end of the interview, Jahr was so astounded by the scoop he had on his tape machine that he asked Elton whether he would like to edit any of it. Elton declined, he was just relieved that he had been so honest.

The British press repeated the story with surprising lenience and sympathy – the *Sun*, in particular, thought so little of the revelations that they did not even believe they warranted any comment. Perhaps this was because Elton's appeal was never primarily sexual; as an entertainer he was Madame de Pompadour as fairy godmother, not Adonis in drag. The frills and flamboyance hid an ordinary football-loving bloke with a streak of compulsive showmanship.

Elton would remember on Michael Parkinson's show in 2001 that he was in Edinburgh when the news hit the headlines in Britain. His mother had come into his room, and he mimicked her: 'Seen the headlines, Elton? This will be an interesting afternoon.' So he was forewarned when the Sunday tabloid, the *News of the World*, spoke to him at a Watford match in Rochdale. It printed a mild article which featured a number of quotes by Elton on the subject: 'I don't see why people should be so surprised. The only reason I hadn't spoken about it before was that no one asked me.'

Football fans on the terraces were not quite as sympathetic as the tabloids. Watford was now known as a club led by a bisexual, and consequently the players were subjected to verbal abuse themselves, being called 'poofs' by opposing crowds. When Elton took his seat in the directors' box at Rochdale he became the focus of taunts by the rival supporters, who shouted 'Queer!' and 'Poof!'. Various unpleasant chants would also resonate around the ground whenever Elton was present, and he admitted that being the subject of such jeers was unsettling: 'It's been very hard for me, but I've sat there and grinned and borne it, and it's taught me a lot about dignity.'

Later Elton would acknowledge that it would have been better if he had come straight out and admitted that he was homosexual. He told *Q* magazine in 1996 that he was probably scared: 'I suppose it was a cop-out, but at the time I thought I'd be diplomatic about it.' He had thought everyone had known anyway.

His mother confessed that the public revelations had upset her at first, but she conceded that his honesty had been most courageous: 'I think it was a brave thing for him to do. I would still like to think he can find happiness with a male or female, I don't care.'

The news did not go down quite as well in parts of America, where some radio stations stopped playing his music, and some people burned records in the streets. Predictably there was a rush to re-examine Elton's earlier work for clues to his sexuality. 'Daniel' was suspected to be about a gay lover, when the lyrics actually referred to a blind Vietnam veteran. A 'To David' dedication on the cover of *Tumbleweed Connection* was analysed, but found to be a simple tribute to singer-songwriter David Ackles who had headlined with Elton on his first gig at the Troubadour Club.

Elton would admit in 1986 to Paula Yates that after his revelations to *Rolling Stone* he considered suicide, something he had promised his beloved mother he would never try again. He said he was saved by the friendship he found at Watford FC. 'I'd stopped touring and had nothing else to do,' he said. Watford gave him something to focus on and, although he might turn up with bright pink hair and huge high heels, the club indulged him with good humour. Elton has always touched a tolerant nerve in the British temperament.

Following Elton's disclosures about his sexuality, his choice of cover artwork for the next album, *Blue Moves*, came under scrutiny. He selected a Patrick Procktor painting, *The Guardian Readers*, which depicted a group of young men. The *Sun* had been due to give out fifty copies of the album as prizes for a reader's competition, but withdrew the offer at the last minute for the flimsy reason that the cover 'did not feature any women'.

Concentrating on his music once again, Elton produced *Blue Moves*, his first album on the Rocket label. He had great hopes for it, but it represented a blue period for both him and Bernie, who was battling with alcohol addiction. The lyrics reflected Bernie's negative emotions, emanating from his sadness at splitting with Maxine, and as a result the whole album had a gloomy tone. 'Sorry Seems To Be The Hardest Word', which Bernie remembers as one of their best songs from the period, was the first single from the album, and peaked at six in America and eleven in Britain. *Blue Moves* marked a decline in Elton's popularity in America, possibly because it coincided with his sexual revelations, although it reached a reasonable number three in both the American and British album charts. The press considered the album vacuous, but in Elton's opinion it would be another twenty-five years before he made an album to compare with *Blue Moves*.

For anyone with a love of glam rock and a taste for the baroque, 1977 was a grim year. It saw the birth of a completely new kind of music, as discordant as rock and roll had been to the previous generation, and as incomprehensible as rap would be to the next. American and British teenagers left school in the late 1970s to very different prospects from the flower children a decade before. Pompous, overblown, indulgent rock music was the wrong kind of soundtrack for an era of unemployment, terrorism fears, rising inflation and urban decay.

As the punk revolution spread round the world, safety pins replaced feather boas, torn tartan replaced taffeta and tulle, and spiky youths, without a note of musical competence, sneered, swore and spat at their audience. The music was aggressive and cacophonous, the mantra was 'Anarchy in the UK'. Punk's trailblazers were the Sex Pistols, whose feral discords reverberated through the streets and emerged to coincide with Queen Elizabeth II's Silver Jubilee celebrations, only to pour cold water on them. It was not necessary to be able to play an instrument, sing in tune, or be particularly pretty. Elton realized that this was the point – the cheap punk bands were contemptuous of the overblown rockers with their stadium concerts, entourages, outrageous costumes and terminal vanity. As a dedicated student of pop and its influences, Elton has always been open to music trends, and still is, so that when he saw the Sex Pistols slagging him off on television he thought to himself, 'Yes, you *are* a lazy fat sod.'

Overnight he became a dinosaur, the glory days of the early 1970s were over. At thirty he suddenly looked middle-aged and was labelled a 'boring old fart' by the new generation, yet he agreed with them. He recognized that he had become complacent with his big houses, big cars and big lifestyle, saying, 'I think it's very healthy to be kicked in the teeth.' To him punk rock was no more than a passing fashion. 'Five years ago it was high-heeled shoes,' he said. 'Now it's safety pins through the nose. The funny thing is, they have all the same things as we have. There's no way they can avoid having their Rolls-Royces, their accountants. They'll end up the same as we do.'

Under the circumstances, Elton's decision to retire from touring while he was just ahead, was spot on. He devoted his time to working on the careers of others, including producing a second album for Kiki Dee. John Reid, also with more time on his hands, was working hard to extend his company's client base. In addition to Elton, his principal concern, he had taken on the management duties for Queen, and supervised the release of their phenomenally successful single, 'Bohemian Rhapsody'. Elton thought it was a crazy choice as a single, which proves that he was not always right. Its success was promoted by a seminal video showing close-ups of Freddie Mercury and the band performing the song, their images enhanced by innovative special effects, a precursor to the age of the music video and the MTV generation.

There were also glimpses of the darker, contrary side of Elton. When Capital Radio photographer Stuart Windsor was booked to take his picture at the Inter Continental Park Hotel in Park Lane, he arrived with DJ Roger Scott for an 'EJ the DJ' planning meeting. Elton, surrounded by flowers, ignored the photographer and continually complained about every singer and band playing on the radio during his conversation with Scott. He was especially bitchy about his own protégé, Neil Sedaka, whom he called an 'old queen'.

At this time, Reid had begun to delve deeper into proving that Elton's original DJM contracts were more beneficial to DJM than they were to the songwriting partnership. Though the contracts had expired, DJM still controlled the publishing and recording incomes up to 1973 and 1975 respectively. Reid argued that since 1967, the publishing royalties that the duo had received was far less than the sum they were due. In 1975 DJM had altered the network of sub-publishers who collected royalties on their behalf throughout Europe, which they would not reveal to Reid's accountants. Elton and Bernie had a 'privileged form of agreement' with DJM's This Record Company, which guaranteed them a fixed percentage of its income, and would not alter their royalties. Eventually Reid's accountants obtained copies of the new agreement and interpreted it in an entirely different way; that is, that Elton and Bernie's income had been cut by up to 50 per cent.

During the spring of 1977 Elton had football chairman's duties on his mind and he had some tough decisions to make. In his opinion, manager Mike Keen lacked the necessary capabilities to guide his beloved team away from the murky depths of the fourth division. In April he made a formal approach to Lincoln City Football Club for their manager, Graham Taylor. He had already achieved promotion for Lincoln from a similarly poor position in the fourth division the previous year, and at first he was not interested, citing the fact that he did not want to 'go back into the fourth division managing some southern club, with an outrageous popstar messing around as chairman'. Although he declined the offer initially, Taylor was intrigued by Elton's charisma. After a few months Elton approached him again, and changed his mind with his earnest dreams for Watford to rise to the top, and achieve success in Europe. Taylor was equally honest with Elton and told him it would cost $1.5 million (£1 million) to even think of fulfilling such desires. Elton offered Taylor the unusually high annual salary of $187,500 (£125,000), which was especially generous for a fourth division club.

Elton and Taylor were to have much in common: strength of character, their vilification by the tabloid press and a love of football. They liked and respected each other enormously, and Elton knew he could never dominate Taylor, because Taylor would never be dazzled by his status as the biggest pop star in the world. The hallmark of Elton and Taylor's relationship would be their mutual frankness, however tough life at Watford might get. The Watford board decided Taylor was the best young manager in the game and he signed a five-year contract.

From the beginning, Taylor quickly made his mark as manager by introducing a level of respect and decorum to the club, however much Elton was teased from the terraces, and insisted that the players address Elton as Mr Chairman. He was as strict with Elton as he was with the players, and put an end to his habit of posing for wacky photographs and kicking a ball around with the team. Taylor had taken a serious look at Watford's general situation, and come to the candid conclusion that with or without Elton's financial input, they could only achieve success through a combination of hard work and complete dedication. He believed that they should concentrate on boosting support in the local community before money was invested in new players. The Watford stadium would be modernized, with special importance given to facilities for families and children. Graham Taylor would pioneer the concept of family football.

In the first weeks of his tenure at Watford, Taylor's new regime was soon on course. Support was growing on the terraces, judging by the increase in gate receipts, and the club could realistically look forward to promotion, as well as ending the season as Division Four champions. In an incredible four-year run of success, Taylor would take the Hornets from the purgatory of the lower divisions to the paradise of the first division.

In Elton's circle everyone would benefit from his generosity. He made sure he knew each person associated with the Watford team by name, including their wives and children. The pop evangelist would spread the word about the latest albums and buy them for the players to lift their spirits and broaden their taste in music, and he gave them seats in the royal box at his concerts. Highlights of the summer were his garden parties at Woodside for all Watford employees and their families, complete with games and sports events. In Watford FC he had found a new family, whom he nurtured.

It was obvious to all that Elton had been fighting a losing battle with his receding hairline, often disguising it with an array of imaginative head gear, ranging from cloth caps to berets, Stetsons, bowlers, turbans and wigs. Seven years of dying his hair all the colours of the rainbow cannot have helped, and it was doubtless galling to have had more hair on his chest than on his head. In September 1977 reports filtered through that he had consulted a plastic surgeon and trichologist, Dr Pierre Pouteaux, a pioneer in the then experimental techniques of hair transplantation. Hairs on the back of the neck, those with healthy follicles, are removed and inserted one at a time into holes pierced in the scalp. Only a limited number of hairs can be taken from the neck area because the procedure leaves scars. Pouteaux had advised against the operation, because the donor hair on the back of Elton's neck was so weak and fine, but he was persuaded otherwise. Elton was confident that the new tresses would take root successfully, but he would have to wait six months to discover whether the operation was a triumph. In the days that followed he had to apply a cocktail of exotic lotions and hormones, known as topical solutions, to prevent further hair loss.

Away from his duties at Watford, Elton resisted the temptation to perform, write, record or give interviews. Except, that is, by royal command. The news of his bisexuality seemed not to have tarnished his reputation in the eyes of the monarchy, and he was invited to perform in the Royal Windsor Big Top Show, a combination of variety show and circus, which was an event of the calendar of the Queen's Silver Jubilee celebrations. He also appeared at a charity concert in front of Princess Alexandra at the Rainbow Theatre in Finsbury Park, London, at which he performed an acoustic set with his favourite percussionist, Ray Cooper. Elton was in high spirits on this occasion and, as he often does during a show, made a dedication: 'This one's for Charlie – he's doing well tonight.' As a consequence, in conversation with Elton at the after-show party, Princess Alexandra, aware that he was not referring to her cousin, Prince Charles, asked how Elton managed to keep going for two-and-a-half hours on stage. 'Do you take some sort of drug?' she enquired. 'Do you take cocaine?' Elton's indiscretion was compounded when he related the conversation to the press afterwards. He was forced to issue an apology for revealing private royal remarks, and he said: 'I hope I have not embarrassed the princess. I thought it was very amusing, and that's why I repeated it.' He assured reporters that he did not take cocaine and had only intended the reference to 'Charlie' as a 'light-hearted comment'.

Within a year of his number-one single on both sides of the Atlantic, Elton was lucky even to make a mark on the Top Forty thanks to the new wave of punk rock. His single, 'Crazy Water', peaked at number twenty-seven in Britain, while in June, 'Bite Your Lip (Get Up And Dance!)' had a similar fate, reaching only twenty-eight. A second compilation of greatest hits produced by DJM was Elton's only album release of 1977. To boost their original selection, Elton leased them 'Don't Go Breaking My Heart' and 'Sorry Seems To Be The Hardest Word.' The album only reached number six in Britain and a poor twenty-one in America, thereby proving the fact that, for now, he had passed his 'best by' date.

His support for various charities was undiminished, and in November 1977 he topped the bill at Wembley Arena at a gala concert on behalf of the Variety

Club of Great Britain and Goaldiggers, a charity that organized the provision of football facilities for disadvantaged children. Not having played to a stadium audience like it for over a year, his expectations were high, but backstage he felt tense, lonely, misunderstood and unwanted, desperately needing the affirmation and attention of all around him. He began tossing flowers around, and declaring: 'I'm not bloody well going on!'

To a thunderous welcome from 8,000 fans, he came out alone, sat at the piano and appeared visibly downcast. His spirits were lifted when Ray Cooper, Davey Johnstone and the Rocket band, China, joined him onstage for an upbeat rendition of Marvin Gaye's 'I Heard It Through The Grapevine'. The old Elton once again summoned up the spirit of Jerry Lee Lewis with some Olympian acrobatics at the keyboard, and gave yet another audience more than their money's worth. The crowd were ecstatic. Then he made what seemed an off-the-cuff announcement, which came as a complete surprise to everyone, especially to those closest to him.

'I haven't been touring for a while,' he proclaimed. 'It's been a painful decision for me, whether to carry on touring or not. But this is going to be the last show.' While the audience screamed out in protest, he regaled them with 'Sorry Seems To Be The Hardest Word'. Thus the shy showman, the introverted extrovert, won the audience over by blending his strongest points, part tragedienne and part pop tart, all rolled into one.

Elton had an overpowering desire for change. The signs were there in his weight loss and his hair transplant; he had even started wearing contact lenses. He had had an overdose of life at the top, and stood back and seen it in a new light. He said later: 'I can't go back to being Elton John as it was.' He also felt profoundly ambivalent about the music business. On one hand he might announce that he was revolted by the whole business of rock and roll, while on the other he would say: 'I love it so much. I hate it, but I'm so passionately interested in it.'

chapter eight

Sartorial Eloquence

AFTER SIX MONTHS, in early 1978, it was time to revisit his Parisian hair doctor, Dr Pierre Pouteaux. The first operation was followed up with a new improved technique called 'square grafting', which involved a series of painful operations in which selected areas of hair-covered scalp, up to 6 mm deep, are removed from the back of the neck, cut into small squares and forcefully inserted into the bald areas in a chequer-board pattern. In theory the hair should grow more quickly and intermesh to form a thick mop, but if the donor hair is characteristically weak and wispy, this will not change once transplanted. Once again, Elton had to wait patiently for the results of his surgery to develop.

But Elton was still game for some fun at his own expense. He and Bernie were already credited as Ann Orson and Carte Blanche on 'Don't Go Breaking My Heart', and had also worked as Tripe and Onions, and Reggae Dwight and Toots Taupin. Now, in an effort to be anonymous when travelling, he booked himself on to flights as Mr Cheveux. It did not always work to his advantage, however, for on one occasion the first-class cabin was overbooked, and Mr Cheveux and his entourage were relegated to economy class. After a few choice words the situation was, of course, resolved.

During this period offstage, Elton spent many weeks on the move, partying and playing tennis in Hawaii, Florida, Los Angeles and Seattle. Grand tour met grand slam in a round of hedonism, cocaine, black moods and practical jokes. He would only perform three times during the whole of 1978, and he would not have another British top-ten album for five years, and fourteen years in America. He later attempted to chart the development of his cocaine habit and its uninhibiting effect on his sex life. 'It would get to the point where I'd stay up for three or four nights,' he admitted. 'Of course it was fun for a while. It enabled me to be very promiscuous. But the after-effects got worse and worse.' Elton later admitted that the drink and drugs made him unstable, and that he became a nightmare to live and work with.

Elton did not miss one Watford game during the 1977–8 season, and would fly to distant away games by helicopter if necessary. As predicted at the beginning of the season, Watford finished at the top of the fourth division and won promotion to Division Three. Under Graham Taylor's leadership, they earned a club record of seventy-one League points, and after a 2–1 victory in the deciding match away at Bournemouth, Elton remarked that it was 'better than having a record at number one'. With spirits so high at Watford, Elton could not resist the temptation to splash out on some top players. The purchase of Ray Train for $75,000 (£50,000) and Steve Sims for $255,000 (£170,000) were both record transfer fees for the club.

Taylor had also fulfilled his promise to make Watford the first club to install a family area. The greyhound track had gone, the terraces had a fresh coat of yellow paint, a 500-seat family enclosure had been built in front of the director's box, complete with canteen and toilets.

Elton's life had changed beyond recognition – it wasn't just rock and roll now, but sex and drugs as well. Despite his recent denial to the press about 'Charlie', cocaine was the drug of choice. According to Bob Halley: 'Everyone was doing it. In those days, it was almost the accepted thing. People used to have their little boxes, and when you went to parties there was this little ritual.'

Although Elton's sexuality was now common knowledge, he was painstakingly careful in public. When he stepped out with John Reid, he looked every inch the rock star with his protective manager. When his presence was required at a formal Watford reception, Elton, as chairman, would always be accompanied by a female member of the Rocket staff. But in private a stream of blond surfer boys would visit the master's boudoir, none of whom stayed around for more than a few days. Longer-lasting new friends might be given a Cartier watch or a Ferrari before being sent on their way.

At the same time, following Bernie's bitter lyrics in the gloomy *Blue Moves*, the golden songwriting partnership had dried up. As a creative team, Bernie felt they were finished. He remembered: 'At that point, it felt like there was no way we could go any further. There was only one way to go from here.' And it was not onwards and upwards. There was never a formal split. Drink, drugs and bad behaviour intervened – while Elton partied at Woodside, Bernie was on the other side of the world in Los Angeles at his own 24/7 party. He was living on a strict regime of vodka for breakfast, and cocaine, magic mushrooms or LSD for lunch and dinner. The Lincolnshire country mouse had become Toots Taupin; he described himself as 'a nicely tanned drunk' in 'Tonight' on *Blue Moves*, although he failed to add 'bloated bluebeard' to the description. He would later admit that, 'There's nothing heroic in being a fall-down drunk, it's absolutely pathetic.' Luckily, a new girlfriend inspired him to head for a rehab clinic and he checked in to dry out and get back in shape. When Elton was ready to go back into the studio, Bernie was gazing serenely at the sunset in Acapulco, contemplating challenges for his writing talent. Bernie would later describe his relationship with Elton as much like a modern marriage, with rocky patches caused by the various affairs. Unlike Lennon and McCartney, neither could flourish without the other. Their careers languished until their exclusive partnership resumed in 1983.

Elton also ended his working relationship with Gus Dudgeon who had produced his last fourteen albums. Although a director of Rocket, Dudgeon was slightly distanced from the inner circle and its politics – he worked mainly with the artists in the recording studio. He became frustrated with the way the Rocket board operated, creatively and financially, and said he would leave unless things changed. No one tried to persuade him to stay, so he sold his shares and furthered his fruitful career with other artists. Like the callous treatment of Vic Lewis, another stalwart of the original Elton John team was dropped with a glaring lack of ceremony.

In the meantime Elton was excited by a project that did not need the talents of either Bernie or Dudgeon. He had discovered Thom Bell, the producer who had perfected the Philadelphia – 'Philly' – sound of soft soul ballads that had been popular in the late 1970s. He had not only produced but written songs and arrangements for The Spinners, The Stylistics, The O'Jays and The Three Degrees. One of Elton's favourite albums was *Rockin' Roll Baby*, The Stylistics' 1973 hit, and after the success of 'Philadelphia Freedom' he had wanted to record an R&B album.

Elton joined Bell in his Sigma Sound Studios in Philadelphia, his first time in the studio for over a year. Elton provided two songs, while Bell and others produced the rest. After the sessions Elton was less than pleased to discover that Bell and The Spinners had removed almost half his vocals on 'Are You Ready For Love?' and replaced them with their own. He was disappointed with the final album, believing it to be overproduced. Following the drama over the re-recording and re-mixing of three tracks from the original Thom Bell sessions, 'Mama Can't Buy You Love' by The Spinners was released in April in America, and became a big hit, and won Elton a Grammy award in 1979. *The Complete Thom Bell Sessions* was deferred and not released as an album until 1989. It is significant for the fact that Bell persuaded Elton to sing in a lower register, which he later used to perfection on 'Blue Eyes'.

A new generation of singer-songwriters had emerged from the punk revolution – Elvis Costello, Sting, Paul Weller and Bob Geldof. The gritty realities of life and death reflected in their songs were light years away from the gaudiness of *Goodbye Yellow Brick Road*. Elton had to change his style. 'Ego' was a non-album single released in March 1978. It was written originally as an instrumental for the *Blue Moves* sessions and later embellished with lyrics. He wanted to rejoin the contemporary rock-and-roll scene and persuaded MCA to splash out a then massive $60,000 (£40,000) on a promotional video – it was the dawn of the mega-budget, pop video golden age.

A new-look Elton appeared; out went the pantomime-dame costumes, the zany spectacles, the manic gap-toothed grin and fancy head gear. In came a serious, stark Elton, in tune with the severity of the post-punk era; he sported contact lenses and a full head of young, dark hair shoots – not too thick yet, but showing promise. The 'Ego' video displayed this re-styled Elton seated in an elaborately decorated room as a large group of deferential courtiers filed in. He intended the video to be a satire on the type of unpleasant people one could meet in the music business who were full of 'over-inflated ideas and big talk', whom Elton despised. Unfortunately, it was Elton who came across as the man with the ego, as he lorded it up like a self-obsessed, balding fat cat.

The cinema première in London's West End was attended by a tweed-capped Elton. It wasn't the single or the video that attracted press attention though, it was his new thatch. Radio stations showed little interest in the record, which only peaked at thirty-four in the charts, and the expensive video was turned down by *Top of the Pops* because the programme would only broadcast Top Thirty material. Elton might have given up his boas, but feathers flew when he unsportingly attacked the British Market Research Bureau, which supplied charts to the BBC, when a chart in *NME* showed the record had reached the Top Twenty. In his fury, he announced that he would be forced to consider removing Rocket's advertising from any publication that printed the lists produced by the BMRB. The *Daily Mail* announced ROCKETS FLY AS ELTON'S EGO FLOPS, and John Reid telephoned the Rocket office from Australia, and threatened to sack both managing director David Croker and promotions manager Arthur Sherriff if they failed to get the video screened. 'It was all done in a fit of anger,' said Reid later. 'I have apologized for screaming so loudly.'

For his new album, Elton collaborated with Gary Osborne, a writer who had been producing lyrics for Kiki Dee since 1973, and who was also a well-known television commercials jingles writer. He became friends with Elton over ultra-competitive games of poker and backgammon, after which they would fool around on the piano; Elton had promised that one day they would work together. The day came in 1978, when Osborne was called in to write lyrics for several melodies Elton had written during the 'Ego' session; Elton also contributed ideas and one-liners.

Out of this method of writing came the album *A Single Man*, a poignant title reflecting Elton's general loneliness, and the absence of his soulmate and favourite wordsmith. Osborne was no substitute. 'I was only known as the poor man's Bernie Taupin,' remembers Osborne. 'The guy who wrote some of the lighter things for Elton.' Elton defended his new partner, however, and complimented him on fulfilling a creative need.

Perhaps the most memorable song from this period was a sombre instrumental, 'Song For Guy', which ends with the barely perceptible mumble, 'Life isn't everything'. At the time that Elton was working on the album, a seventeen-year-old Rocket messenger, Guy Burchett, died in a motorbike accident. On the day of the tragedy, Elton happened to be writing one of the melancholic dirges of which he was so fond. The next day, when he heard about the boy's death, he contacted Burchett's mother to offer his condolences, and asked if he could use her son's name as a title.

Pop music was changing every season, and in 1978 disco music dominated the charts. Once again Elton was out of fashion. MCA was particularly unenthusiastic about releasing 'Song For Guy' as a single in America, which frustrated Elton, although it eventually became a big European hit. Although critics panned the album with comments such as, 'a single man without any fans', Elton promoted it energetically. In one day in October he conducted twenty press interviews in seven hours in Los Angeles, and he surprised 250 MCA executives at their national convention when he turned up and performed solo for two hours for the first time in a year, including most of the songs from *A Single Man*. Otherwise, he had slowed down a little. 'I've gotten into the routine of doing albums,' he said. 'You can't maintain huge-selling albums. There must be a break sometime.'

When *A Single Man* was released, critics and fans had only one question: what had happened to Bernie Taupin? The mystery deepened when, only two months after the release of *A Single Man*, Bernie's name appeared as co-writer on an Alice Cooper album *From The Inside*, an album reflecting on their shared alcoholism. Elton and Bernie have since downplayed their separation, but there was no doubt that they needed to work individually at the time. Not only were they miles apart geographically, Elton was consuming more and more drugs while Bernie was drying out. Contrary to popular perception, however, Bernie's work appears on all but two of Elton's releases.

In Britain, 'Part Time Love' was a catchily inoffensive number which made it to number fifteen in the charts, qualifying Elton for an appearance on *Top of the Pops*. As a follow-up, 'Song For Guy' was released at the beginning of November, just as Elton collapsed with severe chest pains and breathing difficulties. The initial concern was that he had suffered a heart attack, and he was rushed to the coronary unit at the Harley Street Clinic. The scare turned out to be nothing more than the symptoms of exhaustion caused by a month of intensive promotional antics for the album and taking part in a charity football match for Goaldiggers. The resulting publicity surrounding Elton's health alarm had an unexpectedly positive effect on record sales, with the upshot that 'Song For Guy' reached a healthy number four in Britain. The album itself reached number eight in Britain and fifteen in America.

Prior to Elton's heart scare, his father Stanley had suffered a heart attack. Edna Dwight was certain that her husband's worsening health had not been helped by Elton's cruel condemnation in the *Playboy* article, published in January 1976, and subsequent press harassment whenever Elton made headline news. Convinced that Elton was not receiving letters she had sent to his Windsor house, Edna contacted Graham Taylor at Watford to ask him to tell Elton that his father was not well. Elton heard the news while on tour in Europe, and sent his father some flowers with a message that he would visit on his return, although he never did.

Notwithstanding the clinic's advice to avoid stress, just three weeks after Elton's health scare, Rocket made an announcement declaring that his retirement was over, and that at the beginning of 1979 he would be back on the concert circuit. Elton had changed his mind about retiring in December 1978, when accepting an invitation to perform at the annual British music industry's award ceremony, a forerunner to the BRIT Awards. He received a big welcome, which was enough to convince him that his love affair with the audience was not over just yet.

His initial plans were small-scale and low-key – intimate British venues, no band, just Elton on the piano and Ray Cooper on percussion. That was the original idea, but in the event he embarked on an eleven-country, fifty-six-date tour of Scandinavia, Europe, Israel and Britain between February and April 1979. He performed in France, although he had vowed never to do so again in 1971, and to thank his fans for their warm support of *Blue Moves* he sang 'Iles Amore' in French and 'I Love Paris In The Springtime'. Known as The Single Man Tour, Elton played solo for an hour, after which he was joined by Ray Cooper for another hour and a half. Over a particularly fine lunch with tour promoter Harvey Goldsmith, fortified by the food, wine and company, Elton suggested adding another, more easterly, territory to his tour schedule – Russia.

Russia and Britain have always shared cultural exchanges with ballet companies visiting the UK, and British opera and theatre groups reciprocating, but rock and roll was regarded as decadent and depraved. However, young Russians knew what they wanted to hear and kept up with pop music by tuning in to the BBC World Service and America Today. They paid small fortunes to buy records on the black market, yet only acts considered harmless enough had been allowed to perform in Russia, including Cliff Richard, Boney M and B. B. King.

Goldsmith applied for permission for a series of Elton John concerts through official channels, via the Foreign Office to the Russian Ministry of Culture. His application happened to coincide with Russian preparations to open itself up to the eyes of the world with the 1980 Olympic Games in Moscow. The country needed positive international public relations before the Games. The Russian establishment was also attempting to throw off its dour image, and the authorities felt they could now consider welcoming a suitable western pop star. While on an official visit to Britain, the Soviet Minster of Culture, Vladimir Kokonin, was present at one of Elton's low-key gigs in Oxford, and following the performance, he gave his nod of approval for Elton's visit.

After two years off the road Elton wanted a fresh experience. 'I could not keep on playing in Britain and the United States,' he said. 'It is safe there, but it drains you, and I needed a challenge.' Money was not a motive for this tour – the fee was a nominal $6,000 (£4,000). His Russian hosts would pay all the expenses for up to twelve people, so Elton took his nearest and dearest – his mother and stepfather, John Reid, Ray Cooper, Clive Franks, Harvey Goldsmith, and a small road crew, as well as a film crew that was making a documentary of the trip.

On the eve of his departure for Moscow, Elton received some last-minute good news from Watford. The team had been promoted to Division Two and had reached the semi-final of the Football League Cup. Elton was so thrilled that he gave Graham Taylor the gold disc with which he had just been presented to reward him for sales of *A Single Man*.

Elton arrived in Moscow on 20 May, not a sequin or a zany pair of specs in sight. He was dressed appropriately in a cloth cap, and wrapped up in a striped Watford scarf, to keep out the cold, only to walk into a Russian heat wave, as Moscow basked in temperatures in the high eighties. The party boarded the midnight Red Arrow sleeper-express to Leningrad, a 500-mile rail journey at a cost of $28.50 (£19) a head. Elton performed four concerts at the Bolshoi Concert Hall, all sell-outs, which resulted in tickets changing hands for up to twenty times their value on the black market. People travelled hundreds of miles to see Elton, some without any hope of obtaining a ticket. On the first night, 90 per cent of the tickets had been distributed to the communist elite – party officials and their families, local bureaucrats and members of youth leagues – who filled the front rows, leaving space for a few genuine fans at the back. Prior to the show there was a bleak introduction, including potted biographies of Elton and Ray Cooper.

After this far from scintillating warm-up, Comrade Elton appeared in his proletarian cloth cap, blue satin anorak and matching pantaloons tucked into black patent high-heeled boots. The first hour was an uphill struggle for him, as he was unsettled by the restrained response to his performance. At the end of each song, including 'Your Song', 'Daniel' and 'Candle In The Wind', the attentively stolid audience would politely applaud. Only the kids in the back rows were spontaneously cheering and singing along. When Ray Cooper came on, however, the atmosphere transformed. The fans at the back moved forward along the aisles and danced, sang, whistled and threw flowers onto the stage, and were free to do so without any restraining measures inflicted by the numerous guards in attendance. When he sang 'Goodbye Yellow Brick Road' the stage was spotlit in the red and yellow Watford colours.

The finale included the usual crowd pleasers, 'Saturday Night's Alright For Fighting' and 'Crocodile Rock'. Then, on the spur of the moment, he broke into the refrain of The Beatles' 'Back in the USSR'. He said later, 'I didn't plan to sing that song, it just came to me. I didn't know any of the words, so I just sang "Back in the USSR" over and over again.' The applause was deafening as Elton and Ray threw carnations and tulips back into the audience, who roared and cheered in a magnificent standing ovation. Outside the concert hall, hundreds of ticketless fans stormed through police barriers to plead with people emerging from the theatre for snippets of information about the concert. The British and American press rejoiced that a western pop star had melted the cold hearts of the Russians. ELTON JOHN, SUPER CZAR, ROCKS THEM BACK IN THE USSR proclaimed the *Daily Mail*. After the first overwhelming concert the Russians set down a few ground rules for the remaining three performances: Elton should not kick his stool back, he should be a bit more gentle on the Steinway keys, and he should not sing 'Back in the USSR'. He obeyed the first two but ignored the last.

After the concert everyone was in high spirits, fuelled by vast quantities of vodka, and champagne and mandarin juice cocktails. The resulting hangover the next day meant that Elton was two hours late for a tour of the Winter Palace and Hermitage museums, where he could have marvelled at the collection of a fellow shopaholic, Catherine the Great, Empress of Russia. But he arrived only to storm off in a black mood. Consequently, his film crew had nothing to film, and his hosts were left feeling snubbed.

In Moscow Elton and his mother posed for photographs at the Kremlin, watched Swan Lake in the Bolshoi Theatre, and had a viewing of the plans for the Olympic Games. So thrilled was he by his Russian experience that he offered to write a theme tune for the Games. Elton also watched Moscow Dynamo beat the Red Army team 2–1, and afterwards agreed to try and organize some friendly matches between Watford and the Red Army team.

The four Moscow concerts followed the same pattern as Leningrad; restrained audience for the first half, then a tumultuous finale with fans surging towards the stage with presents, flowers and handwritten notes. Worryingly though, Elton's voice had begun to cause him problems. 'It was dodgy in the sound check,' he said, 'but somehow I shouted and screamed and gargled my way through.' BBC Radio One had a live broadcast link with the second concert, which was picked up on radios throughout Europe. It was the first time that a rock star had ever reached such a huge audience simultaneously.

The trip was hailed as a breakthrough in diplomatic relations. The characteristically inscrutable British embassy in Moscow described it as the greatest progress made in East-West understanding since Hollywood welcomed Nikita Khrushchev on a visit. Elton believed his time in Russia to be the greatest accomplishment of his career, describing the tour as, 'one of the most memorable and happy I've been on'.

The song he wrote for the 1980 Olympics was never sent to his new friends in Moscow – Elton was advised by the Foreign Office not to submit it after Russia invaded Afghanistan and the West boycotted the games.

Elton had succeeded in reinventing himself as a singer and could take great satisfaction in his achievements. Now that he was back in the headlines all over the world, he embarked – again with Ray Cooper – on an American tour, Back In The USSA, widely regarded as one of his best. He spent the autumn of 1979 performing forty-one shows between Tempe, Arizona and Houston, Texas. A decade before the word 'unplugged' was coined, he chose intimate venues to showcase his musical talent – worlds away from the juggernaut stuffed with costumes and crew. The same format was repeated for his tour of Australia at the end of 1979.

The new re-branded Elton was also on loquacious form when it came to talking to journalists. Personal questions, especially about his sexuality, were answered openly and honestly. Away from the media, Elton had received many letters from people who lived in small communities who found it difficult to come out of the closet, and in an effort to prove that they were not alone, he wrote back to every agonized correspondent, encouraging them to keep in touch if ever they felt the need.

The tabloids were full of respect and sympathy towards Elton, so much so that his mother, Sheila, spoke to the *Daily Express* and the *Daily Mail* about how Elton had broken the news to her. When he had first told her of his propensity for men, she was shocked, but she had accepted it some time ago. In Sheila's opinion, a nine-to-five job would have kept him straight. 'Dealing with the rock scene created his homosexuality,' she said, although she would always be proud of her boy. 'In an industry where image is all important and the biggest queens never come out of the closet, my son at least possessed the character to go public,' she added. She was the person who knew him best, although she had always been more worried about his spirit. 'He's got all the possessions you could wish for, but that doesn't make him happy,' she told David Wigg of the *Daily Express*. 'He hasn't anyone to share it with and that's what he needs. I feel that he's got everything – but nothing.'

In between his tours of Europe, Israel and Russia, and then the US, he returned to the recording studio, using facilities at the Musicland studios in Munich and at Rusk Sound studios in Hollywood. The new album, *Victim Of Love* was heavily influenced by yet another musical genre. As soul mutated into disco, the dance craze of the late 1970s swept the clubs in the wake of the film *Saturday Night Fever*, and a soundtrack album produced by the Bee Gees. Elton left the songwriting to producer Pete Bellotte, whom he had met in his Bluesology days. The hawk-eyed record collector had seen Bellotte's name on the sleeve credits of a Donna Summer album, and contacted him. Elton agreed to supply vocals and left Bellotte and others to write the songs. The album became notorious among Elton aficionados for its questionable disco version of Chuck Berry's 'Johnny B. Goode'.

Victim Of Love was another flop, only peaking at thirty-five in America and forty-one in Britain, and is now widely regarded as his worst album. John Reid showed his displeasure by sacking all the staff at Rocket, turfing them out on to the street in the middle of Mayfair. A further example of Reid's unpredictable furies occurred during the tour of America, when Reid was arrested for allegedly hitting a hotel doorman with a walking stick, when he was asked to close his car door because it was blocking the way.

At the end of the 1970s there was an ominous change of tone brewing in the tabloids, particularly those which supported the new prime minister, Margaret Thatcher, and her call for the implementation of Victorian values. In November 1979 Elton was treated well by the press when he talked about his sexuality as if he were reclining on the psychiatrist's couch. But when a snide little article appeared in William Hickey's *Express* column only nine months later, reporting that Elton's mother had left him to go and live in Brighton, leaving mummy's boy to launder his own underwear, it was a harbinger of things to come. The next decade would be an era of xenophobia and prejudice, and develop into the most uncomfortable phase of Elton's life.

chapter nine

Choc Ice Goes Mental

THE 1980S BROUGHT THE YUPPIE, the shoulder pad and the power suit. Love, peace and punk gave way to enterprise, excess and greed. Britain's first female Prime Minister, Margaret Thatcher, told the public that there was no such thing as society – it was every man and woman for themselves and 'I'm all right, Jack' was the prevailing ethos. In pop, the New Romantics celebrated glamour and extravagance in a backlash against the austerity of punk and the Winter of Discontent in 1979. The boys had big hair and wore frilly shirts and mascara, inspired by David Bowie, Marc Bolan and Elton himself. The New Romantics did not really create a new musical genre – they were more about style. But the music encompassed a whole range of sounds, from Duran Duran's classic pop hooks and Spandau Ballet's melodramatic ballads, to the German band, Kraftwerk, who pioneered European electro-pop. The middle of the road was occupied by international singer-pianists Billy Joel and Barry Manilow.

Elton's first album of the 1980s, *21 At 33*, alluded to his age and that this was to be his twenty-first album. It was, in fact, his nineteenth (including two *Greatest Hits* albums), but he counted double albums as two – twenty-one just sounded better than nineteen. For *21 At 33*, Elton resumed his partnership with Bernie who eloquently explained their separation in 'Two Rooms At The End Of The World', in honour of his exile in Acapulco. He also offered a description of what they had been doing in those two metaphorical rooms in the song, 'White Lady, White Powder'. Together with Clive Franks, Elton produced a contemporary electronic sound with synthesizers and electric pianos. The critics were underwhelmed but it still managed to reach a respectable number twelve in the British charts and thirteen in America.

Bernie Taupin had come through the 1970s intact, just. His new wife, Toni Russo, had helped him salvage his mind, body and finances, all of which had spiralled out of control. While Elton was recording *21 At 33* at Superbear Studios in Nice, in 1979, he contacted Bernie again, inviting him and his wife to stay with him in his rented house in Grasse, where Bernie would write three songs. It was a simple reunion that needed no apologies and no excuses. Elton also brought back Nigel Olsson and Dee Murray, and James Newton Howard collaborated on some of the tracks, which took everyone back to the days of recording at the Château d'Hierouville. Collaboration and reunion were the order of the day and Gary Osborne penned the words for 'Little Jeannie', which became a hit single in the US. Elton also recorded tracks by singer-songwriter Tom Robinson, and Rocket signing Judie Tzuke.

However lacklustre, *21 At 33* was Elton's best album since *Blue Moves*, four years before, and 'Little Jeannie' reached number three in the US singles charts. Regaining support for his work in the US was crucial to Elton, after the damaging effect his revelations of bisexuality in 1976 had had on his reputation in the States. Though negative attitudes towards him still remained in some parts of the US, he renewed his love affair with his American fans in the autumn of 1980 with the launch of his first large-venue tour for four years, with forty-four shows from Wisconsin to Hawaii. Here was Elton the entertainer back on centre stage for a sell-out tour. Flattered by the compliments and gestures of the New Romantics, his costumes were as extravagant as anything he had worn at the peak of his mid-1970s success. He borrowed inspiration from the gay band, Village People, dressing up as a sequinned cowboy and a musical chauffeur, while his publicity photograph portrayed him as a butch New York cop.

During the concerts he revisited *Goodbye Yellow Brick Road*, his best-known album, and paid tribute to Nigel Olsson's solo career by allowing the drummer to perform two solos in the middle of the set. In September the high point of the tour was a free concert in Central Park, New York, where his biggest ever audience had gathered, estimated to be almost half a million fans. People camped out in the park for two days in advance to make sure they got a good pitch. The star flew in by helicopter, and once in front of his adoring crowd, he was in his element, as hundreds of red, white and blue balloons were released on the majestic opening bars of 'Funeral For A Friend'. He gave a memorably undignified rendition of 'Your Song' dressed as Donald Duck with bulbous beak and bottom. Bob Halley helped him get into what was more contraption than costume between numbers, and Elton remembered: 'I got my arms in the leg holes and my legs in the arms. Bob has a wonderful sense of humour. We were crying with laughter, I said, "They'll all go away!" and he said, "There are 500,000 people out there, dear – they will not go away!"' He waddled on with yellow bill, pert yellow tail and yellow flippers. As he flapped about the stage, his legs would not fit under the piano. 'When I tried to walk around, I tripped arse over elbow,' he recalled. 'I think at that time I should have retired the costumes.' Among the highlights of the show was his tribute to John Lennon, an affectionate recital of 'Imagine', sung as he gazed upon the nearby Dakota Building where the former Beatle lived.

His position as an elder statesman of pop and much-loved national figure seemed assured when he appeared in a television series, *Best of British*. The show's presenter, Paul Gambaccini, was invited to Woodside to film Elton in off-duty mode. Sitting at the piano, sleeves rolled up, saplings of hair growing healthily, he seemed to have put on weight. His honesty endeared him all the more to his fans, and he was as candid as ever in his conclusions about the previous decade. 'Great from a career point of view, but from a personal point of view, terrible,' he revealed. 'A lot of the time I was a complete mess. There are parts of it I can't even remember.' He also discussed the extent of his dependence on his mother. At thirty-three he still needed Sheila to pamper him and he craved her approval. He would phone her wherever he might be in the world, to tell her about the smallest things, even arriving at a hotel and unpacking his suitcase. He needed her constant reassurance, to hear her telling him he was her good boy. His involvement with Watford was equally important to him. There he was not treated as if he was special – he could take a break from his mollycoddled world, with its chauffeur, personal assistant, minders and gofers, who would never say no. At Watford he could not hide behind his possessions, his staff or his drugs.

The decade dawned with John Reid casting his eagle eye over Elton's accounts. Reid was certain that, in addition to all the millions he had made in the 1970s, Elton should have earned many more. Reid had been in tense negotiation with Elton's former management company, DJM, for nearly six years, firm in his belief that their complicated network of foreign sub-publishing agreements swallowed up far too much of the royalties that Elton and Bernie were due whenever their songs were played throughout the world. After repeated investigation of the business arrangements, Reid decided that the financial interests of Rocket, John Reid Enterprises and Elton John should be dealt with by accountants Arthur Andersen and Company.

With his accounts matters under new management, Elton was told to control his spending, purely because there was more money being spent than being earned. The days of spending a fortune at Cartier and buying Rembrandts as birthday presents were over.

In 1974 the $5 million (£3.3 million), five-year deal Reid had struck with MCA in America had been the biggest ever for a recording star, and it was now time to renegotiate. Although Elton was no longer such hot property, he still made a valuable contribution to MCA's turnover, so Reid wanted superstar treatment from them. He had already dined out on the fact that he was going to secure an advance of $25 million (£16.6 million) for five albums, and so when MCA informed him that they would only consider it for the worldwide rights, he stormed out of the meeting. In a fury, he tried and failed to wrench gold discs off the walls outside the boardroom. Owing to his reaction, and the fact he had called the MCA board 'arseholes', Reid was in a difficult spot. He could not approach EMI or RCA, with whom he had fallen out over previous deals, nor could he go to Polygram, Rocket's European distributor, because that would mean giving world rights to one company, which would take away all powers from himself and Elton.

The only alternative was Geffen Records, set up by David Geffen, whose Asylum Records had dominated the 1970s with Linda Ronstadt, Jackson Brown and The Eagles. Geffen had also secured John Lennon after he had emerged from semi-retirement in New York, with his album *Double Fantasy*. Reid and Geffen were already acquainted with each other, sharing the same gay social circle, and in a last-minute face-saving deal, Reid signed Elton up – not for the bragged about $25 million (£16.6 million), but for $1 million (£666,600) per album, which was much the same as the earlier deal with MCA. Elton was just pleased to be sharing a label with John Lennon, his biggest living idol and now close friend, whom he often visited at his New York apartment. However, Elton would say later that the relationship with Geffen was six years of pure hell, indeed it coincided with a series of albums that the star himself would consider less than excellent.

After a recording session at New York's Hit Factory on the evening of 8 December 1980, Lennon returned to the Dakota building, carrying the tapes of 'Walking On Thin Ice'. As he walked from his car to the door of the building, a deranged fan, Mark Chapman, shot him five times at point-blank range. Lennon stumbled into the Dakota security office and collapsed. He died while being rushed to the Roosevelt Hospital. It was a shocking death of a much-loved star in his prime, and the event resonated round the world in much the same way as the death of John F. Kennedy in 1963. Many people remember exactly where they were when they heard the news – Elton certainly does. 'Would Elton John's party please remain on board while the other passengers disembark,' the pilot announced on a flight carrying the star and his entourage to Melbourne. Reid came on board to break the devastating news.

Next day, he and Bernie wrote 'Empty Garden' as a tribute. Elton was inconsolable and locked himself in his office, refusing to watch the news or read the papers. In a rare moment of indecision, and in his grief, he was unsure about writing a musical tribute in case he was thought to be cashing in on the tragedy. 'But then I realized it was the only thing to do,' he said. 'I couldn't cry because that comes later.'

By the end of 1980, Elton had indulged in another make-over, keeping his chequer-board of sapling hair plugs under a multitude of fetching hats. He was a willing victim of New Romantic fashion and chucked out his contact lenses and 'proletarian' gear in favour of a debonair preppy-schoolboy-meets-W. C. Fields look. He took to wearing pinstripe suits with wing collars and bow ties, often with a jaunty straw boater.

By 1981 Elton had become, de facto, minstrel laureate, and by royal command he provided the cabaret for Prince Andrew's twenty-first birthday in June. In addition to 600 guests, Elton's fifty-strong entourage of musicians, roadies and technicians piled out of a juggernaut at Windsor Castle. When Elton arrived to set up he found himself alone, but for his crew, the dance band and Prince Charles' beautiful fiancée, Lady Diana Spencer. Elton and Diana took to the dance floor for twenty minutes, and danced the Charleston on their own. Then Princess Anne asked him to dance, an offer he could hardly refuse. The party atmosphere had still not yet warmed up and the disco music was playing low. While still dancing with Princess Anne, the Queen and an equerry approached and she asked, 'Do you mind if we join you?' Suddenly the music mixed into Bill Haley's 'Rock Around The Clock', so Elton took the hand of the Queen of England and jived for his country. The next day a thank-you letter arrived at Rocket from 'Diana Spencer' – another royal missive to add to Elton's treasures.

His recent collaborations with Bernie, Gary Osborne and Tom Robinson resulted in nearly an album's worth of extra material, which became *The Fox*, released in 1981. MCA had sued Geffen Records for costs associated with all the songs from sessions recorded while Elton was still signed to them, but had lost the case. The first album for his new record company, it was produced by Chris Thomas, whom Elton had known since the 1960s, and whose track record included Paul McCartney and the Sex Pistols. However, Elton's unhappy association with Geffen began with the new company rejecting six of the songs, which meant he had to return to the studio to write and record new tracks. One of them, axed perhaps unwisely from the album, was 'The Man Who Never Died', an instrumental tribute to Lennon. *The Fox* sold well in Britain, reaching number twelve, but in America it could only manage a lowly chart position of twenty-one, and because the album lacked a big hit single, it received little airplay. The album was critically acclaimed but reflected the emotional turmoil Elton was suffering at the time, and was referred to as 'The Languishing Giant'.

With director Russell Mulcahy, Elton performed in an album-length video of *The Fox*, including a clip for each of the eleven songs. Elton, who detested being kept waiting as much as having his picture taken, earned himself another nickname with the film crew, Elton Gone, after walking off the set following a six-hour delay.

Elton was no longer a lonely party animal; he was surrounded by stars such as members of Spandau Ballet and Def Leppard, and old friends, especially Rod Stewart and Freddie Mercury. Parties would last for three or four days at a time, fuelled by cocaine, Scotch, Martinis, endless joints, fabulous repartee and hilarious impressions. Elton would later admit that cocaine enabled him to open up and talk to people, 'Even if it meant talking complete bullshit all night. Of course it was fun for a while,' he said.

As a consequence of such over-indulgence, Elton was spinning into a vortex of loneliness, black moods and attention-seeking. His behaviour was becoming more and more volatile, except when it came to giving live concerts, which was what he lived for. He felt comfortable showing off onstage but could not cope offstage, so cocaine became his prop. He would often leave cars, aeroplanes or executives in the lurch, cancelling trips and meetings at the last minute, saying he was not feeling well. In fact, he was suffering periods of pain and deep distress. The first stages of bulimia, which involves a persistent preoccupation with eating and an irresistible craving for food, were setting in, joining drug addiction and alcoholism on the list of his problems. Either he would be overeating or on a crash diet, drinking just water or starving himself. After a couple of days of cocaine-fuelled partying he would sleep for two days, wake up ravenous and binge on several pots of cockles, and up to three bacon sandwiches followed by ice cream. Then he would make himself vomit and start all over again. He had no shame. 'I became angry and disdainful,' he said, 'spiteful and irritable.' Eventually, he would feel emotionally dead. Elton himself admitted that he could be a 'vicious, nasty' drunk, and Bernie described him as, 'Santa Claus one minute and the devil incarnate the next'.

Bob Halley had by now become Elton's round-the-clock companion, protector, manservant and nurse. His bedroom was opposite Elton's (which bore his name in neon letters) in case he needed him in the night, and he was always on hand to attend to Elton's moods and ever more tempestuous relationship with John Reid. Elton now admits that he would probably be dead if not for Halley – more than once Elton suffered a fit after a drugs binge and Halley resuscitated him. However frightening these seizures might have been, Elton would still have another line of coke ten minutes later.

When Halley first started working for Elton and Reid, he would go to parties with them and wonder why everyone was still awake and chatting into the early hours. As a newcomer to the rock-and-roll lifestyle, he eventually worked out that they were all taking cocaine. Before long, he discovered for himself that the effect of cocaine is to make people frenetic when they take it, and frenetic when they don't. 'On tour you think you need it to keep going,' said Halley, 'but you don't.' But if Elton's consumption of cocaine and alcohol was remarkable, Reid matched him line for line, magnum for magnum.

Elton's over-emotional outbursts were not just reserved for Reid. On one occasion in the Ritz Hotel in Paris just before a concert, Elton was in a bad mood after some problem had arisen. He stamped his foot and refused to go on stage. It fell to Halley to persuade him, and in response Elton threw a Coca-Cola bottle at him. Halley ducked and the bottle missed his head, hitting a painting, which broke in half. Elton screamed: 'Why did you fucking well duck?' To which Halley replied: 'Because you would have killed me.' Elton was duly presented with a large bill for restoring the painting.

Elton has always had ten times the energy of most of his associates, and hates to sit around. 'The thing that saved my life was that I worked,' he said. 'No matter what shape I was in, I still managed to perform and make records.' He simply would not accept that he had addiction problems. He thought he had everything under control, when in fact he was on the path to self-destruction.

He even deluded himself concerning his beloved Watford. 'I never did coke when I went to the football,' said Elton, as if that made up for being drunk. 'That was the rule.' Graham Taylor, his greatest friend, and one of the few people Elton would listen to, was concerned about his drinking habits and always trying to bring him to his senses. Elton took little heed and arrived for a Boxing Day match against Luton looking scruffy, despite wearing an expensive coat, and very much the worse for drink. The next day Taylor asked him round to his house and greeted him with a bottle of brandy. 'Here you are! Are you going to drink that? What the hell's wrong with you?' shouted Taylor, as he slammed the brandy down in front of Elton. 'Look at the state of you. Get yourself together.' Taylor's anger made a deep impression on Elton, causing him to reflect on the damage he was doing to himself.

While Elton's health situation had grown worse through excess and neglect, his father's health had seriously deteriorated since his heart attack in 1978. In late 1981 Stanley Dwight lost the sight in one eye after a haemorrhage, he had neck and joint problems due to osteoarthritis, and he was on the waiting list for a quadruple heart bypass operation. One of his sons, Geoffrey, made contact with Elton back stage, after performing with Freddie Mercury in Manchester in October. 'We had a great time talking about our memories,' Geoff remembered. 'And he promised to stay in touch.' It transpired that Elton was aware of his father's forthcoming operation, and he promised to give him a call, which he did. He rang before his father arrived home from the office one evening, and chatted affectionately to his stepmother, Edna, telling her that he thought blood was thicker than water, and that he needed to re-establish contact with his four brothers whom he had not seen for a long time. Elton called again an hour later, but Stanley had been delayed by bad weather. He told Edna he would ring back. 'It's all right,' he said, 'I'm only having dinner on my own.' Just as he rang a third time, Stanley arrived home; Edna remembers the tears of joy in her husband's eyes as he spoke to his son. Elton offered to pay for private hospital treatment, which Stanley refused, but he did accept Elton's offer of joining him at Watford's next away match in Liverpool in December. Elton and John Reid took Stanley for lunch in the directors' dining room and Elton proudly introduced him to everyone. While Elton helped his father up the stairs to their seats, the Liverpool and Watford fans chanted, 'Elton! Elton!' It was one of the happiest days of Stanley's life.

Elton was in Australia when his father underwent major surgery in January 1983, but he sent a large basket of red carnations with the message, 'Tell Dad I have been thinking of him all day. I think he is very brave. I am very proud of him and love him very much.' Stanley made a quick recovery, profoundly happy to have reconnected with his son. Elton made many phone calls to check up on his father after the operation and arranged a date to come to the family home in Ruthin for a visit. The spare room was ready, but he cancelled and suddenly the phone calls stopped. Elton would never see his father again.

From the very beginning of the 1981–2 football season, Watford's fortunes were on the way up. Following a highly successful season, and supported by growing crowds, Watford won promotion to Division One for the first time in its ninety-year history in May 1982. The youth team also excelled, winning the FA Youth Cup. The 1982 accounts showed that Elton had boosted the club with $1.8 million (£1.2 million) in interest-free loans. He was also championing a scheme to turn Watford into a tourist spot: for $30 (£20) per person, he was promoting a weekend package that included a VIP seat at a home game, hotel accommodation and the best the town could offer.

Ever since Elton left Dick James Music in 1975, John Reid and his accountants had been regularly pestering Stephen and Dick James for details of the small print or the accounts. According to the agreement Elton and Bernie had signed in 1967, DJM owned the copyright to all their songs to 1973, and although this may have been considered the norm in the industry, Reid argued that it had been unreasonable to let two naive teenagers give away the rights to songs they had written and composed. Similarly, although Elton's records had earned $300 million (£200 million) worldwide, the recording agreement that he had signed in 1968 and 1970 ensured that his share of the revenue was considerably less than he deserved. This was in addition to the ongoing investigation into the foreign sub-publishing agreements. He also claimed that Elton should own the master recordings of all his albums and singles that had sold in their millions, and furthermore, he should be paid in retrospect – the difference between his past income and that due under a fairer contract. Elton remained fond of Dick, however, and only wanted Reid to sue if the figures were large enough. All DJM could do was remind Reid of the risk investment that they had made between 1967 and 1970, before Elton's overnight success, the scale of which had never been imagined.

In 1981 Dick James, like Elton's father, had to go through a quadruple heart bypass operation, and was advised to rest, so he left the day-to-day business to Stephen. He planned to recuperate in the comfort of his penthouse in St Johns Wood and his apartment in Cannes, protected with the knowledge that he had followed standard industry practice to the letter when he had signed Elton and Bernie all those years ago. But the industry standard was about to be redefined. The singer Gilbert O'Sullivan took legal action against Gordon Mills, his former manager and publisher, for the same reasons that Reid wanted to sue DJM. Like Elton, O'Sullivan joined Mills's company on $15 (£10) a week as a songwriter and gofer. His string of huge hits grossed $21.75 million (£14.5 million), but O'Sullivan claimed to have received a mere $600,000 (£400,000) before tax. In May 1982, the judge decreed that Mills had taken unfair advantage of O'Sullivan's inexperience, ruling that the agreement was a 'restraint of trade'. All of O'Sullivan's copyrights had to be given back, master recordings returned and vast back-dated royalties, plus interest, were to be paid to O'Sullivan.

Dick and Stephen James knew that Reid would take similar action against DJM sooner or later, and so Stephen James tried to take steps to negotiate a deal out of court, inviting Reid to discuss the matter over lunch. Reid refused, however, and advised his solicitors to inform the Jameses that he was taking them to court with a claim that was virtually identical to the writ issued by O'Sullivan.

Elton's next album, *Jump Up!* was his second for Geffen, and again he mixed and matched old and new collaborators. Bernie Taupin, Gary Osborne and an old friend, Tim Rice, supplied lyrics, and his old band members, Davey Johnstone, Dee Murray and Nigel Olsson joined his stage band. The only single to have chart success was 'Blue Eyes', a pensive Osborne love song that reached number eight in Britain and twelve in America. Although *Rolling Stone* called it a 'tour de force album', Elton was dissatisfied with the performance of *Jump Up!* which reached number thirteen in Britain and seventeen in America. His disappointment was compounded when 'Empty Garden', his elegy for John Lennon, in which Bernie had adapted the line, 'Won't you come out to play', from The Beatles' 'Dear Prudence', failed to make the Top Fifty in Britain.

The third single, 'Princess', in honour of Princess Diana, was only released in Britain, and also failed to chart. Elton still sent a copy of the album to the Princess of Wales, however, who, in her thank-you letter, informed him that, intriguingly, her favourite track was 'Ball and Chain'.

The Jump Up! Tour was a series of forty-one summer shows across North America, from Denver to New York, followed by a forty-date British tour. It was the first time in seven years that Johnstone, Murray and Olsson had toured with him. Elton finished off his mammoth tour at Hammersmith for the pantomime gig. This festive season did not see him in the mood for cheer and goodwill, however, as Olsson called in sick at the last minute, which put Elton in a bad frame of mind. Furthermore, his party trick of kicking the piano stool backfired when, as he aimed it at the orchestra pit as usual, it flew down a slope in front of the stage and hit a member of the audience on the face and shoulder. Elton was extremely upset and asked the young woman to come back stage where he gave her a bottle of champagne and a leather jacket to apologize. He also sent her shopping with one of his staff to buy her a dress, in an effort to keep the incident off the front pages. He even sent a limousine to collect her for the end-of-show party at Xenon in Piccadilly, but he was incandescent when she arrived in the new dress, a fetching off-the-shoulder number that revealed her trophy bruises. He allegedly snapped at the unfortunate girl, snubbed all his friends and left after fifteen minutes. He was allegedly seen outside banging his head on the bonnet of his Rolls-Royce, screaming at his minders, firing them indiscriminately. This voracious party animal could just as easily turn into the most peevish party pooper.

When the Queen visited America in 1983 Elton was, by royal association, top of the guest list for a gala reception hosted by President and Mrs Reagan in Hollywood. Elton was invited to sit at the top table with the Queen, the Reagans and several other eminent Brits including Michael Caine and Julie Andrews. The cream of Hollywood was present too: Bette Davis, James Stewart, Gene Kelly and Fred Astaire. Elton was not impressed by the cabaret, featuring Dionne Warwick, Frank Sinatra and Perry Como, though, and he told the *Sun* that the event was so boring he had nearly fallen asleep. The *Sun*'s pun-writers spun into action and came up with ELTON RAPS QUEEN'S HOLLYWOOD PARTY, a *double entendre* with all the subtlety of a playground bully.

Meanwhile, Elton was becoming obsessive in his search for sexual escapism, another addiction to add to the list. He did not form relationships but would 'take hostages', using cocaine to enhance sex. He would refer to himself as Sharon Picket Fence because he would see someone and think, 'Oh, you're fabulous', and imagine himself in a scene of domestic bliss with them. Elton always got what he wanted. Once when a paramour threatened to leave he shaved off his eyebrows in protest. The boy stayed.

Throughout 1983 Elton was mainly off the road and in the air, flying from one party to the next, but the most significant journey he made that year was to China. This time it was not to bring rock and roll to the communist masses, but to promote his football team. Watford were booked to play two exhibition games in Beijing and one in Shanghai. To the Chinese Elton just looked like a western tourist, albeit a nattily dressed one. He was at ease as he walked around the streets, largely unrecognized, visiting the Great Wall and the Forbidden City, and doing a spot of light 'looting' at the Friendship Store. He bought $75,000 (£50,000) worth of Chinese antiques, including carved tiger and lion heads, each weighing six tons, for his garden. 'I've never seen Elton look so happy,' said Gerry Anderson, the Watford and Northern Ireland striker. 'It was a holiday for him.' He stopped at the tomb of Mao Tse Tung and removed his boater respectfully, only to give the media the scoop they wanted. The *Mail* reported: 'Six hair transplants, for which he had paid $27,000 (£18,000), had left him with only sparse wisps to cover his baldness.' The secret hidden for so long under an array of head gear was out in the open and under the scrutiny of the ever critical press once again.

Watford FC occupied an almost mystical place in Elton's life and to watch his team beat their hosts at Beijing's Workers' Stadium in front of a crowd of 70,000 and around 400 million on television, was as close to heaven as Elton could ever imagine. After the match he again paid tribute to people at the club for keeping his feet on the ground through their bluntness and honesty. 'In my business, it was luxury jets, the best hotels and shows in front of 20,000 people,' he said. 'Then I'd walk into Watford and the washing-up lady would toddle across and say, "I don't like your new record." I needed that.'

After China, Elton flew off again, this time to South Africa where he joined Rod Stewart on stage at Sun City. This occasion resumed the affectionate, *faux*-offensive banter between Sharon and Phyllis, and they planned a joint stadium tour featuring a battle of the bands, although they later called it off. Elton would later joke that they cancelled because Rod did not have enough hits.

In the early 1980s one of the most popular recording studios in the world was George Martin's AIR – Associated Independent Recording – on the Caribbean island of Montserrat. A state-of-the-art studio with an impressive list of clients including Paul McCartney, Stevie Wonder and Eric Clapton, it flourished until 1989 when the island was devastated by Hurricane Hugo. Like Château d'Hierhouville it was balmy and beautiful, and Elton recorded his next album, *Too Low For Zero*, there in the summer of 1983. Dispensing with his collaborators and part-timers, he went to the studio with his original band, exclusively using Bernie's lyrics, which he hadn't done since *Blue Moves* in 1976.

Elton and Bernie now demonstrated a new maturity in the way they worked together, instead of taking each other for granted. This time they were not afraid to step onto each other's territory. They discussed the songs and Bernie would comment on the melodies while Elton would make remarks about the lyrics, but otherwise it was just like the old days in Pinner. Elton was at his happiest performing on stage or in the ordered atmosphere of the studio. Discipline was encouraged, with the producer, Chris Thomas, as much a perfectionist as the star. Everyone worked to a strict timetable, and wives and girlfriends came to the studio for dinner, always a choice of Elton's English favourites – meat and two veg, followed by puddings and custard, complemented by a few local specialities. Elton cut the partying down to a minimum and out of respect to the rehabilitated Bernie, the whole team played it straight, which also benefited Elton.

Bernie was back on form and happily married to Toni, whom he thanked for pulling him from the abyss in the song, 'I Guess That's Why They Call It The Blues', on which Stevie Wonder played the harmonica. 'I'm Still Standing' was a brotherly tribute to his own and Elton's survival of the 1970s. The third single, which was less high profile, was ominously titled, 'Kiss The Bride'. Bernie may have written it for Toni, but it would soon take on significance for Elton.

He had hoped to produce an album worthy of the number-one spot but in fact *Too Low For Zero* only reached seven in Britain and twenty-five in America, although it spent more weeks in the charts than any of his other albums since *Captain Fantastic*.

Elton commissioned Russell Mulcahy, director of *The Fox* album video, to create a promo for 'I'm Still Standing', which they filmed on the beach in Nice. Elton met up with his new friends Duran Duran for a few vodka martinis at the Negresco Hotel on the promenade. During the shoot he downed eight in half an hour, and woke up in his hotel room to find that he had committed the ultimate rock-and-roll crime – the room was trashed, and he had beaten up John Reid, breaking his nose. Meanwhile Reid, still in his clown's outfit for the video shoot, and with blood pouring down his face, took Elton's car and drove back to London. During the journey he broke down, only to discover that his RAC membership had expired. For this, the diminutive clown sacked all the staff at Rocket. He returned to London to a deserted office and had to rehire everyone because he could not work the switchboard.

A love song called 'Crystal' was another track on the album that Elton had asked Bernie to write for his Australian friend Gary Clarke, who was at Elton's side during the recording sessions. The title alluded to Elton's nickname for Clarke, a camp reference to Crystal Gayle. Clarke had struck up a friendship with one of the tape operators in Montserrat, a German woman named Renate. She was quiet and unpretentious, and barely noticed by any of Elton's team, but she and Elton always shared a little joke at the sessions and to everyone's surprise there was a dedication on the album sleeve, 'Special Thanks to Renate Blauel'. He reluctantly recorded a special backing track for a *Top of the Pops* appearance and insisted that Renate was in the studio for the session.

The next album was scheduled for another recording session in Montserrat, and Elton refused to go unless Renate was there as tape operator. In the event, she was promoted to engineer. However this second trip to Montserrat was not the haven of tropical calm it had been less than a year ago. The writing and recording took place over five weeks at the end of 1983, including Christmas and new year, and the album was originally called 'Restless' – an allusion to Elton's life at the time. But it was ominously re-titled *Breaking Hearts*.

However demanding and short-tempered he might have been during the sessions, his mood was not helped by a few tempestuous days he suffered back in England before flying out to Montserrat on Boxing Day. His mother Sheila and stepfather Fred were staying in the Orangery for Christmas, and Elton was not at his best due to certain over-indulgences. When it came to looking after her son, Sheila was a meticulous housekeeper, making sure that every cushion was plumped to perfection, but this Christmas she had fallen out with the cleaner. Elton had a severe hangover and was in no mood for a kitchen-sink drama; he lost his temper with his mother, which proved to be a turning point in their relationship. Sheila realized that she had to cut the ties and let her son make his own mistakes. Sheila and Fred left the house. Not long afterwards, Elton swayed and fell into a dead faint. Luckily Bob Halley was in attendance and administered medication Elton kept for these attacks, brought on as a result of all the drugs he had taken over the years.

Once Elton arrived in Montserrat he was in a wild and crazy mood, sending flights to collect attractive young men who had caught his eye. He was on his best behaviour, however, when invited to dinner with George Martin who regaled him with stories of his times in the studio with The Beatles. Despite his off-duty excesses, he worked more closely with Renate, who kept a characteristically low profile, spending most evenings in the studio working on her own. Elton would join her after dinner, to listen to tapes. She was calm and reserved, and he warmed to her modesty and sense of fun. Renate also spent time with Gary Clarke on Jeep drives around the island; he was also very fond of her. Before the entourage flew from Montserrat to Sydney for the start of a major tour of Australia and New Zealand, Elton issued another ultimatum: he wasn't going unless Renate could come too.

Elton's entourage settled into their favourite Sydney retreat, the Sebel Town House Hotel, which catered for every rock star whim and turned a blind eye to most indiscretions. Within three weeks Elton announced that he was engaged to Renate.

The proposal took place in an Indian restaurant called the Mayur. According to Mr Benerjee, the assistant manager: 'It was very romantic. I could see they were in love. They seemed totally preoccupied with each other. He kept reaching over and touching her hand. Then when the meal was over they sat back and smiled at each other a lot over coffee.'

John Reid thought it was unbelievable, and most people thought it was a publicity stunt. While Elton was busy rehearsing for the forthcoming tour and listening to final edits for the album, Renate turned to Clarke for help with the wedding plans although he, like everyone else in the team, was still reeling with shock. Since Renate had no female friends in Sydney to assist her, she and Clarke drove around Sydney, gossiping in the back of a stretch limo like two best girlfriends, with a blank cheque from Elton to her buy a wedding dress, for what she hoped would be the happiest day of her life.

chapter ten

White Lady, White Powder

RENATE BLAUEL, the daughter of a successful German publisher, grew up in the suburbs of Munich. After leaving school, she rebelled against her middle-class family's wishes by taking a job as an air stewardess with Lufthansa before arriving in England when she was twenty-two. She dreamed of becoming a record producer, and for eight years before meeting Elton, had been progressing well in the recording studio, an environment traditionally dominated by men. When her engagement to Elton was announced, her life, including her sexuality, was mercilessly scrutinized. There was no apparent evidence of previous boyfriends, and it was observed that she only ever seemed to wear jeans and T-shirts. She was softly spoken, self-contained and modest, and did not appear to be the sort of girl who dreamed of a white wedding, at least not with a would-be knight in unusually shiny armour. She was also no gold-digger. What attracted Renate to a man whose sexual proclivities were so well known? It is perhaps easier to see what attracted Elton to Renate: she was meticulous and capable in his natural habitat, the recording studio, and they shared the same sense of humour. The power balance in the relationship would always be weighted in his favour – he was the boss.

On Valentine's Day 1984, one of the world's most eligible bachelors tied the knot at the tiny St Mark's Church in Darling Point, Australia. Under New South Wales law, marriage licences could only be issued after thirty days, but owing to the constraints of Elton's tour schedule, this legal requirement was waived by the state attorney-general, Paul Landa, who declared that, 'the couple were mature people who submitted good and sufficient reasons', and duly granted permission for Elton Hercules John to marry Renate Blauel. Absolutely nothing was going to stop Elton getting married when and where he wanted, and on first hearing about the thirty-day residency rule he threatened to hire a boat and hold the ceremony outside territorial waters rather than delay the happy occasion. This time he did not intend to wait for the disapproval of either his friends or his mother.

The groom wore a shimmering white morning coat with a New Zealand orchid on the lapel, a striped silk shirt and bow tie, a boater with purple ribbon, and teddy-boy-style, crêpe-soled shoes, which added a couple of inches to his height. He arrived twenty minutes early, alighting from a white stretch limousine from which fluttered a pink balloon, accompanied by a portentous clap of thunder. But when the bride arrived, five minutes late, the clouds parted and the sun shone. Renate was a head-to-toe soufflé of a bride in a white silk, high-necked dress, hastily and inexpensively bought in a Sydney department store, enhanced with a Swiss lace bodice encrusted with diamonds. She wore a heart-shaped, eighteen-carat gold pendant with sixty-three diamonds, her wedding gift from the groom. A veil and flowers in her hair completed the picture. Along with Bernie, John Reid was best man, and he denied allegations that this was a publicity stunt or 'lavender marriage', in the style of Hollywood stars such as Rock Hudson who married his agent's secretary. Reid confirmed: 'It's the real thing, that's for sure.' However, insinuation and speculation were never far away, and the *Express* printed an article with the headline, ELTON JOHN AND THE BOYS HE LEAVES BEHIND, on the eve of the wedding.

Despite the tiny venue, the wedding was a major event, broadcast all over the world. The service was relayed on loud speakers to the 2,000-plus crowd outside, cordoned off behind barricades, and Elton's 'Kiss The Bride' blared from portable stereos. Three people were trampled underfoot when the fans surged forward and pushed down a barrier to get a better view. A special police unit had to be called to control the crowd and clear a path for the newly weds.

More than eighty showbiz friends – but no family on either side – flew in for the day, including Olivia Newton John, and television interviewer Michael Parkinson and his wife Mary. A total of 3,000 white roses and orchids were flown in from New Zealand to decorate the church and the Sebel Town House Hotel, where the reception was held, and where guests marvelled when a wall disappeared into the floor to reveal a ballroom decked with white flowers. The menu was a lavish spread including oysters, lobster, crab, salmon, beef, venison, lamb, stuffed quail, accompanied by the best champagne and fine wines. The hotel chef had worked for more than twenty-four hours to create a five-tier wedding cake. A palm court orchestra transported Elton back to his childhood with old favourites such as 'Teddy Bears' Picnic', 'Washington Post' and 'Love Song', along with Strauss waltzes and Scott Joplin ragtime standards. The reception was more tea dance than Rock Around The Clock; more Great

Gatsby soirée than Keith Moon rave-up. Reid read out the telegrams, which included greetings from Watford FC, Cartier the jeweller, and Renate's employer, AIR studios. Sean Lennon's wire brought a tear to Elton's eye: 'My daddy would have loved to have been there.'

The only sour note was Reid's explosive reaction the next day when he saw the *Sun* newspaper. The headline on Nick Ferrari's feature came from a cat-call made by a member of the crowd outside the church: 'Good on yer sport, you old poof, you've finally made it!' Elton had been highly amused, calling back: 'It just goes to show how wrong you all were.' But the ferociously protective Reid, fired up after a few drinks, cornered the unfortunate journalist in the hotel lobby. The day after, a bruised and shaken Ferrari reported that Reid had hauled him from his seat, ripped his shirt, hit him in the face and slammed his head against the lift door.

Reid was not thought to be especially enamoured with Renate, naturally having had misgivings about anyone who might threaten his power over Elton. He was horrified that the couple did not sign a pre-nuptial agreement, an idea Elton had dismissed as cruel and unromantic. Elton put Reid firmly in his place by refusing to have his personal life manipulated by his manager.

The wedding was everything Elton had dreamed of. He told Nick Ferrari: 'This day is the most magical of my life. I'm in love and enjoying every minute of it. We will have another church blessing and party back in England after the tour. Now we can move out of our adjoining rooms and into the honeymoon suite – at last!' Renate added: 'I'm so happy, just like every bride on her wedding day. Elton's the nicest guy I have ever met.' On the steps of the church after the ceremony, Elton said: 'I know people have always thought I was gay, so this will surprise a lot of people, won't it?' The marriage surprised everyone in Elton's entourage, as well as his fans. Billy Gaff, Rod Stewart's manager and an old friend of Elton's, parodied one of his hits in a telegram which read: 'You may be still standing, but the rest of us are on the floor with shock.'

His mother was said to be delighted, despite her recent row with Elton. Sheila said she approved of Elton's choice of bride, and that she seemed as if she might keep him in his place. Sheila told *Daily Mail* reporter Baz Bamigboye that she would be buying a pram as a wedding present. She admitted that she had almost given up hope of becoming a grandmother, but thought Elton and Renate would soon start a family: 'He likes home life, and he loves children. And I don't think he'll waste any time making sure he gets some.'

In complete contrast, Stanley did not hear about his first-born son's marriage until journalists contacted him for his reaction, as Elton no longer kept in touch with his father.

Elton did not hide the fact that he wanted a family. He joked: 'Who knows, it could be the start of another Osmonds.' There is little doubt that Elton, like his Pinner peers, had been conditioned to get married, settle down and have children, like respectable suburban boys. Married, he might be more acceptable to society, not only to the Watford board and fans, but also to his newer friends, the royal family. After years of camping it up on and off stage, perhaps he wanted, in his mid-thirties, to build a new kind of life – with Renate he need never feel lonely and could even be a family man. Elton admitted later to Michael Parkinson, on BBC television: 'I thought it would change me if I got married. I would be happy. It would never change because I never gave up taking the drugs, so the marriage was doomed from the word go. You can't live a lie and I was a gay man.'

Everyone he knew was mystified by the wedding but Elton had great hopes at the time. 'I thought she was going to save me,' he would eventually say, 'which was a huge mistake.' Meanwhile, in public, Elton never hesitated to show his affection for Renate – she was 'wifey' to his 'hubby'. They were always exchanging loving glances, and he would touch her affectionately and pay her generous compliments.

The tabloids followed them on honeymoon to New Zealand, during which time Elton performed three sell-out concerts. The tour of Hong Kong, Australia and New Zealand was one of his most successful, and after the publicity surrounding the marriage, tickets sales broke all previous records in Australia.

A month later they were back in England, and Renate settled into her new role as Mrs John, in public. Elton was used to being able to call on Halley or Reid to ask his passing flings to leave when he was tired of them, but he couldn't do that with Renate. He had given no consideration to the emotional commitment any marriage needs to survive beyond the confetti and champagne. However much they loved each other, love would not be enough to save Elton from himself – he soon realized that if he did not remove cocaine from the equation, the marriage did not stand a chance.

Elton announced to the world that he was looking forward to settling down, cutting back on the parties and spending time with his family. While Renate looked every inch the dutiful wife, she had no intention of giving up her job as a recording engineer and playing hausfrau to 'hubby'. Elton wanted to do everything he could to ease Renate's transition into her new situation, and lavished gifts, flowers and clothes on her. Both Reid and Halley were informed that she was queen of his heart and her wish was their command, whatever their feelings on the subject. When Renate decided she needed a personal assistant to supervise her wardrobe, Reid balked – until Elton stamped his foot and got his way.

No sooner had Elton installed Renate at Woodside than he embarked on a European tour – without her. Surrounded by the abundant spoils of her husband's looting expeditions over the past fifteen years, she felt overwhelmed. It was like living in Harrods. He gave her a free hand to make improvements so she set about redesigning the kitchen and converting one of the master bedrooms into her own suite, in which she installed a computer system and her own telephone line. She also had a recording studio built in the grounds. Sheila and Fred visited Woodside less often after Renate moved in. Sheila, the devoted mother who had been so much part of Elton's life until their Christmas confrontation, was trying to come to terms with the fact that her boy had another woman in his life. She had been left out of the arrangements for the wedding, which begged the question, had Elton chosen to marry someone she had never met, on the other side of the world, as an act of defiance?

Elton not only left Renate behind on his European tour in spring 1984, he did not take Nigel Olsson or Dee Murray either. During the tour Elton made three appearances in Poland, where the banned Solidarity trade union continued its fight against Russian totalitarianism. He held an unlikely meeting with Lech Walesa, the Solidarity leader, in his Gdansk flat where they drank tea together. In his capacity as chairman of Watford FC, Elton was due to kick off a football match between the British Embassy and Polish journalists, but he cried off at the last moment because of an injury.

Days later, Renate flew to join Elton in Munich, where he had his first and last meeting with his parents-in-law, Joachim and Gisela. The *Daily Star* responded with a gratuitous *double entendre*, putting words in the mouths of Renate's parents: HE'S A NICE BOY. Elton, enjoyed the occasion, however, and got on well with his in-laws.

Then, in April 1984, in only Watford's second season in the first division it seemed possible that they might reach the FA Cup Final. They had been lucky to be drawn against inferior teams – Charlton, Brighton and Birmingham – and when they beat Plymouth 1–0 in the semi-final, the dream became reality: Watford were to meet Everton in the final at Wembley on 19 May. Elton was in Berlin at the time, but nothing would have stopped him from flying back from Germany to witness such a momentous occasion in Watford's history.

Seated in the royal box with Renate, an emotional Elton joined in the traditional pre-match rendition of 'Abide With Me'. During the match the teams' league positions soon showed. Everton were on the way up in 1984, rivalling Liverpool at the top of the old Division One. In contrast Watford had been trailing at eleventh position in the same division. Watford were outplayed and eventually beaten 2–0 by the Merseysiders, dashing Elton's

FA Cup dreams. After the match Elton ran on to the pitch to congratulate and commiserate with Graham Taylor and the team who had taken Watford to heights undreamed of just a few years before. In the early evening there was a welcome parade through the streets of Watford, followed by a lavish party for 230 guests at Reid's mansion in Rickmansworth, nearby, at which Elton and Kiki Dee sang 'Don't Go Breaking My Heart'. Despite the FA Cup defeat and an indifferent season, Taylor pledged his future to the club, signing a new six-year contract.

In summer 1984 Elton and Renate visited Reid in his St Tropez villa for a proper honeymoon, during which time Reid and Elton made a new agreement. They decided that Reid would be entitled to 20 per cent of all Elton's gross earnings in exchange for looking after everything in his business life. Nothing was written down and the precise nature of 'everything' for which manager or artist would be liable was neither discussed nor agreed. Reid would act on standard music business practice. Sixteen years later, the two men would admit in court that, crucially, they were both intoxicated at the time.

Then from August to November 1984 Elton was out of the country, and spending time away from his new wife, playing at fifty-three venues in America, on the Breaking Hearts Tour. He was so exhausted that in Charlotte, North Carolina, he collapsed in his dressing room with a 'virus infection' and was forced to cancel his sell-out concert.

Elton began 1985 in the recording studio, working on the album *Ice On Fire*. On a whim he had turned to his old producer, Gus Dudgeon, with whom he had not worked for seven years. Elton approached his new friend, George Michael, whom he had met while holidaying in St Tropez, to provide backing vocals on 'Wrap Her Up' and 'Nikita', an evocative love song to a lonely East European girl. The opportunity to work with Elton was a dream come true for Michael, and came at a perfect moment – he was on the point of splitting up with his former Wham! partner, Andrew Ridgeley, and wanted to progress as a solo, more mature performer.

By 1985 Elton's relationship with David Geffen had soured, and he blamed the lacklustre sales performance of *Ice On Fire* on indifferent promotion by Geffen Records. Consequently Elton was looking forward to completing just one more album for them. 'I'm sure that Geffen Records will be as glad to get rid of me as I will be to go,' he said.

Meanwhile, another of Elton's father-figures was facing a grim few months. After his quadruple heart bypass operation, Dick James, who had been told by his doctor to reduce his workload and avoid stress, found himself ignoring medical advice during his preparation to defend a case that would strike a mortal blow to both himself and his business. John Reid had spent nine years putting together his case concerning Elton and Bernie's involvement with DJM; their 1967 publishing agreement, the 1968 and 1970 recording deals and the foreign sub-publishing agreements. The outcome Reid aimed for was exactly the same as Gilbert O'Sullivan's victory against his publisher and record company two years previously. He argued that Elton and Bernie should take back copyright on 144 songs during the six-year period, that DJM should hand over to Elton the masters of his albums, as well as the thirty-six unpublished songs and twenty-four unreleased tracks still in its possession. Furthermore, that they should receive as damages the difference between what they had actually received and what it was alleged they should have received under the DJM contracts, plus interest.

It was estimated that a judgment against DJM would cost the Jameses $45 million (£30 million) and so it was no surprise that Dick James put aside his health concerns and devoted every waking hour to preparing his defence. He found it particularly painful that Elton's lawsuit named him personally along with his companies, DJM and This Record Co. Reflecting on the special relationship they had enjoyed when Elton first came to him, he could not make sense of Elton's behaviour. James's dearest wish was to meet Elton face-to-face and sort everything out without having to go to court. He was certain that if he could have a civilized discussion with Elton, they could come to an agreement, and he tried in vain to organize such a meeting.

The case eventually came to court on 4 June 1985. The suit was opposed by DJM on all counts and Dick James denied personal responsibility for the disagreement over the contracts. Such was the mass of paperwork brought to court that the oral evidence took thirty days to hear and the full hearing took nearly fifty days. Elton sat in court for much of the time, revealing his new hair which was drawn back in a scanty ponytail, and as he listened to the charges against his old mentor, he seemed unable to look him in the eye. Elton's QC described James as someone who had taken advantage of Elton and Bernie's lack of experience in their early career, and bound them to 'unduly onerous and one-sided contracts', while improperly channelling royalties on foreign releases into an elaborate web of sub-contracts.

Sheila was called as a witness to describe how she had supported Elton's ambition to become a musician, by giving him permission to leave school before taking his A levels, in order to start working at Mills Music. She had helped him reply to the crucial advertisement in *NME*, and signed his first agreement with DJM on his behalf because he was only twenty, although she was not completely sure of what she was signing. 'I didn't carefully consider it,' she said. 'I don't even understand them now.' Bernie was only seventeen when his contract was signed by his father, and neither the Dwights nor the Taupins had taken legal advice.

Muff Winwood, an A&R man for Island Records, who had known Elton and Bernie from their Pinner days was also called to the witness box. He explained how Chris Blackwell, Island's owner, had offered Elton and Bernie a $15,000 (£10,000) advance after looking over the DJM agreements, and had observed that the contracts had 'holes in them'. Elton turned down his offer because Dick James had agreed to let Elton and Bernie write songs of their own, and gave them the go-ahead to record *Empty Sky*, their first album.

Elton told the court that when Dick James made him and Bernie their first offer, that 'everything was done on trust', and neither of them had even thought of going to a solicitor. They had both felt like lottery winners with a $75 (£50) advance each, and wages of $22.50 (£15) a week for Elton and $15 (£10) for Bernie. The subsequent $10,500 (£7,000) to $12,000 (£8,000) costs that DJM paid to produce the *Elton John* album was like a dream come true for two unknowns. He never questioned the Jameses' belief in his prospects and their perseverance. In court, Elton was handed spreadsheets covered in figures showing his, Bernie's and DJM's earnings, but without any professional knowledge, he refused to be drawn on their content: 'I can't comment on them. I'm not a chartered accountant.' The figures showed that it had taken three years' investment to make Elton John a star, and five years to show a profit. Even after *Honky Château*, 'Daniel' and 'Crocodile Rock', there was a deficit of $295,500 (£197,000). It took until 1973, when *Goodbye Yellow Brick Road* was released, to show any profit from Elton and Bernie's work.

When it was alleged in court that the wrongly diverted royalties were estimated at $1.5 million (£1 million), Dick James laughed out loud. When he took the stand he was relaxed as he recalled how generous he had been when he took Elton and Bernie under his wing. His $150 (£100) advance had been perfectly acceptable, and the original 50-50 publishing split had been standard practice then, as it still was. Though Elton's royalty rate from This Record Company appeared less than adequate, there was no doubt it had been good at the time.

The court took a summer recess in July and, in complete contrast to the unpleasant atmosphere in the High Court, Elton became part of a ground-breaking charity-focused, musical project – Live Aid. Following the huge success of the 1984 Band Aid single 'Do They Know It's Christmas?', written by Bob Geldof and Midge Ure, and sung by a host of British popstars to raise money for the victims of the Ethiopian famine, Live Aid was a simultaneous eight-hour concert that took place in London and Philadelphia, which Geldof organized to continue raising money for the cause. On 13 July 1985, the concerts were broadcast live from Wembley Stadium in London and the JFK Stadium in Philadelphia.

Geldof had persuaded almost every major British and American star to appear, including Mick Jagger, Bob Dylan, Tina Turner, David Bowie, Madonna, U2 and Queen. 'It was everything rock and roll was supposed to be, ordinary blokes with long hair and denims playing a twelve-bar loud,' remembered Geldof.

It was the pop/rock event of the decade. Elton was given a thirty-minute spot towards the end of the Wembley event and, dressed in a striped lamé frock-coat and bonnet, he sang 'Rocket Man' and 'Bennie and the Jets'. The highlight was his duet with George Michael, an emotional rendition of 'Don't Let The Sun Go Down On Me'. Live Aid marked the beginning of Elton's charitable support in a higher league.

In November 1985, the case against DJM was brought to a close when Mr Justice Nicholls announced his judgment in a four-hour statement. Firstly he declared that Elton and Bernie had left their claim on the copyright of their early songs 'too late'. However, he found against DJM on virtually every count, but decided to award Elton and Bernie a mere fraction of the amount that they had claimed. Although Dick James was cleared of all personal blame or liability, he never recovered from the ordeal. The judgment would have major implications for the music industry when it stated that James should have acted as a trustee on behalf of the two youngsters, and acted in their best interests, rather than striking a deal that would benefit his company. Although James had acted within the law, and had not deliberately set out to take advantage of them, he should have realized that his dominant position in the industry would have exerted undue influence on them. Equally, Mr Justice Nicholls adjudged the 1968 recording agreement, with its fixed low royalty rate, to be unfair. The amended agreement in 1970 had increased the royalty rate, but it was still less than generous. As for the internal financial structure of DJM, a share in all proceeds from the licensing and use of his records should have been passed on to Elton.

It was announced that Elton was due damages on two levels: on his UK records royalty, the judge ruled that instead of 5.4 per cent of the retail price, Elton should have received 12 per cent, for which DJM would have to make up the difference with interest; on the foreign sub-publishing, a total of 35 per cent had been overlooked in the calculation of the partnership's overseas royalties.

The judge did not decree which side should pay the costs of up to $2.25 million (£1.5 million) and so both sides claimed to have won the case. In Reid's view, although copyrights were retained by DJM, Elton had won a 'moral victory' with regard to the UK royalty rate and sub-publishing. In contrast,

Dick James believed that he had 'lost a battle but won the war'. As far as both sides were concerned though, it was a pity that the action had been deemed necessary in the first place. Elton gained very little from the case – his early copyrights remained out of his control and the amount of damages awarded was much less than the hoped for $7.5 million (£5 million), being estimated to be less than $1.5 million (£1 million).

Case over, Elton was ready to camp it up again. He launched his next world tour to promote *Ice On Fire*. It planned to be his biggest ever, with twenty-two sold-out concerts throughout Britain in November and December 1985. It would be his glitziest since 1973–4 with a whole new wardrobe of outrageous costumes including an Eiffel Tower hat, a pink mohawk wig and a Tina Turner tea gown. His ten-piece band was energized with a sexy brass section called Onward International Horns.

After the court case, Dick James faced another, more serious struggle with his failing health. Less than three months later, he suffered a massive heart attack and died at home in St John's Wood. Elton was deeply shocked and immediately agreed to pay the court costs. He sent his condolences to Stephen James, via a phone call from someone at John Reid's office, but did not send flowers.

At the beginning of 1986, the British tabloids noticed something that had been obvious to Elton's inner circle for a long time. The marriage had been a threesome from the first night – Elton, Renate and cocaine – and the strain was beginning to tell. The evidence was there for all to see – the couple had not appeared in public together except for official functions, such as awards ceremonies or Watford football matches. There was a constant stream of derogatory comment in the tabloids about his gay past and now similar – unfounded – speculation that Renate might also have something of a sexual nature to hide.

Elton was to make yet another High Court appearance in the mid-1980s, this time as a witness at the Old Bailey, when his past bachelor lifestyle came under sordid scrutiny in a case against a man charged with stealing a $9,000 (£6,000) gold and diamond watch from Elton's bedroom at Woodside two years previously. The watch had been picked up in a dawn raid on the home of twenty-one-year-old Cornelius Culwick. When questioned about the provenance of the watch, his alleged response was: 'I'll give you a clue – the Pinball Wizard. Now work it out.' Culwick did not admit to taking the watch, and alleged that his bisexual friend, Tommy Williams, had given it to him, who in turn had received it from Elton himself. In court Elton revealed that on the night the watch vanished he returned to Woodside, accompanied by Tommy and two other men, changed into a bathrobe and removed his watch and a sapphire ring. After watching videos with his friends until 4 a.m. Elton fell asleep, and he did not wake up until about 9 a.m.

The case lasted for several months, during which time the charge was changed to 'dishonest handling'. Ultimately Culwick, who had alleged that he had had a gay fling with Elton, was acquitted, and because Elton did not try to reclaim the watch, the property was returned to Culwick.

The papers believed they had a story that would run and run, and Elton obligingly provided more copy. On his second wedding anniversary he appeared on a French television programme called *The Truth Game*, a show in which guests had to answer probing questions phoned in by the public. One questioner asked if his marriage was just a cover. Elton responded honestly, saying that he had truly wanted to marry Renate, not in an effort to hide his homosexuality, claiming that he had nothing to hide either then or now.

In April 1986, Renate made a rare appearance at her husband's side when he broke off his European tour to fly back to London to collect two Ivor Novello awards for outstanding services to British music and for 'Nikita', voted the best song of 1985. 'It's a real honour,' he said. 'I'm really lucky to be surrounded by such good songwriters.'

He was delighted to accept another accolade too – an invitation to appear on BBC Radio Four's *Desert Island Discs*, presented by one of his favourite interviewers and friends, Michael Parkinson. Originally devised by the late Roy Plomley, the 'castaway' of the week chooses eight favourite records, a book and a luxury item to take to a fantasy desert island. The programme has a wide audience and its timing was perfect for Elton while he was making every attempt to regain respectability. He spoke eloquently between records about his career, his concerts, John Lennon and Watford FC. He chose music ranging from Nina Simone's 'I Put A Spell On You' to the hymn 'Abide With Me', which he chose to remind him of Watford's Cup Final, a day which, aside from his wedding day, he described as the happiest day of his life.

In July 1986, five years after Charles and Diana, another royal wedding loomed. Elton was invited to join Prince Andrew on his stag night before his marriage to Sarah Ferguson, 'Fergie', the daughter of Prince Charles's polo manager. The bawdy boys' night out at the Guards Polo Club was best remembered for two gatecrashers, Princess Diana and Fergie dressed as policewomen. 'Song For Guy' was Fergie's favourite track by Elton, which he recorded specially as a solo piano piece for her wedding present. During the engagement, Elton and Renate became friends with Prince Andrew and his fiancée, and it was reported that the royal couple helped to save Elton's shaky marriage. Fergie would become one of Elton's most supportive counsellors in the years to follow.

All eyes were on Elton and Renate as they joined the royal guests at Westminster Abbey in July. Renate affectionately held her husband's arm while the public focused on his fly-away strands of hair, which were revealed as he took off his top hat to honour the royal couple. After the wedding Elton and Renate threw a party to thank the Duke and Duchess of York for their help and support. Elton chose Watford football ground as the venue because he also wanted to inaugurate the new West Stand.

Written in the summer of 1986, *Leather Jackets* was his last album for Geffen Records, who were probably wise not to put much effort into promoting it. It was a collection of remnants from *Ice On Fire*, re-mixed and re-dubbed, and no singles were released from it. It included a song written by 'Lady Choc Ice', a pseudonym adopted by Renate, and Elton had also added a sleeve note: 'Special thanks to Lady Choc Ice for being a continued source of inspiration'. A weak album that reflected not only an increasingly fragile marriage, but an increasingly distracted star, it is only remarkable for the fact that it was the only time Elton and Bernie have written songs together in the same room. *Leather Jackets* has since been described as 'copper-bottomed tosh from start to finish'. Although it reached twenty-four in Britain, it achieved his lowest American chart position, only just appearing in the Top 100 at ninety-one, marking a nadir in his career.

Elton continued his massive world tour in the autumn, giving thirty-eight concerts in America, but his performances were marred by continual bouts of what he thought was laryngitis. During four concerts at Madison Square Garden his voice deteriorated until the last night when he could hardly sing at all, and he had to rely on his faithful audience to sing the words for him.

In November he embarked on the Australian leg of the tour without Renate, which again provoked much comment in the tabloid press. He was dressed by Bob Mackie in a wardrobe that well and truly cast his sequinned 1970s outfits into the shade. They were bigger, more ludicrous, more outlandish and more weighty than anything seen before, ranging from a Mephistopheles costume complete with a four-foot-high scarlet ruff, to a Mozart suit complemented by a white wig and beauty spot.

The twenty-seven-date tour of Australia was not only large-scale in the wardrobe department, for as well as a thirteen-piece band, he was also accompanied by the entire Melbourne Symphony Orchestra. But when Gus Dudgeon arrived in Australia after the first week, he was greeted by a singer who had all but lost his voice. Elton found he could not speak before going on stage for his third Perth concert, and had to cancel the show at the last minute. The doctor's advice was to gargle with honey and lemon, and to keep completely silent for four days. Elton played the crazy patient to the hilt, trolling around with a small blackboard scribbling funny drawings and notes in order to communicate. The silent star still managed to make his entourage laugh. Fortunately, because the tour had been scheduled to coincide with the England cricketers' winter Test series, Elton was able to rest his voice while attending matches, thrilled to be watching England winning the Ashes.

At the end of the tour, in the Sydney Entertainment Centre, the scene was set for the recording of a live concert in front of 12,000 people by the US tv company ABC Television. Elton was supported by 101 musicians and Dudgeon was on hand to supervise the recording, for the purpose of producing a live album. No other pop musician had undertaken a major tour with a world-class orchestra before, and preparations and rehearsals had been taking place over two years. James Newton Howard conducted the orchestra, spending several months adapting Paul Buckmaster's orchestral arrangements. One of the highlights occurred during 'Candle In The Wind', when members of the entire orchestra held up lighted candles. The concerts received rave reviews, and despite his medical worries, Elton never lost his sense of humour. One night a stage light suddenly exploded and he grabbed his chest melodramatically, as if he had been shot, and fell to the floor smiling. As it was almost Christmas, Elton gave every musician in the Melbourne Symphony Orchestra a $750 (£500) Cartier watch. In turn, the orchestra made him their first honorary member.

At this stage Elton's voice was cutting out intermittently and the hot lemon and honey was giving no relief. Following the third night in Sydney, he visited a throat specialist. The closest members of his team were sitting in the lobby of the Sebel Town House Hotel waiting for him to return, when he entered the bar, his pudgy face ashen. He had terrible news. 'They think it might be throat cancer,' he said, and burst into tears. John Reid took control of the situation immediately and scuttled into action, closing the bar and shuffling all the other guests out. Elton had been advised to stop singing immediately, until further tests had been carried out, but he was determined to complete the recording, despite his coughing fits. The lighting technician frequently had to turn the spotlight away from him so that the audience could not see him coughing up blood. On the last night he was on the brink of cancelling, but when he thought of the audience, the filming and sound recording, he decided the show must go on. As it turned out, the last night in Sydney was one of his best ever performances. Most of the tracks Dudgeon selected for the live album came from that concert. Since leaving Geffen, Elton had returned to MCA, and their strong promotion of the live album made a top-ten single of 'Candle In The Wind' (live), his biggest British hit for two years since 'Nikita' in 1985.

Elton had hoped to return to England after the tour, to consult a Harley Street specialist, but he was advised that to go from the warmth of Australia to the cold December air of London might worsen his condition. He flew straight to Canberra to get the highly-recommended opinion of John Tonkin, Australia's leading ear, nose and throat specialist. The surgeon discovered several small nodules around Elton's vocal chords, which, if found to be malignant, would leave him with no choice but to remove Elton's larynx, rendering him unable to sing or speak properly again. Elton put on a brave face as he phoned his mother and told her not to worry – he told everyone not to worry, but of course, deep down, he was extremely frightened.

On 6 January 1987 at a private clinic in Sydney, Tonkin found the nodules to be non-malignant, and he removed them using laser surgery. Fond messages flooded in from all over the world, including tributes from the Prince and Princess of Wales, and the Duchess of York. But the messages of goodwill were soon overrun by speculation about his marriage, for throughout the entire health scare, his wife had stayed put in Los Angeles. The newspapers could excuse them not spending Christmas together, citing work and travel commitments, but the fact that Renate had been thousands of miles away in Los Angeles when her husband had a suspected terminal illness was rather different, and so the tabloids announced that the marriage was over. The *Sunday People* even made unattributed claims that the marriage had failed because of his bisexual lifestyle: 'Self-confessed bisexual Elton has been married nearly three years, but has always bluntly refused to give up his male friends.'

At the same time, Elton's name came up in news reports concerning an Australian sex trial. A former policeman, convicted of seducing teenage boys, was alleged to have boasted that he had been friends with Elton once, and used Elton's name to show off to his victims. There was no proof that they had ever met, but the news still helped to spice up the stories of claims that Elton's flings with other men were the reason for his failing marriage, because he had made little effort to change his lifestyle at all after his wedding day. According to Gary Clarke, Elton's Australian friend, he spent Christmas getting acquainted with more than one blond surfer-type whom he would place on the 'Elton John treadmill', showering them with Cartier watches and good times.

Rumours were rife. One claimed that Elton had asked Renate to come out to visit him for the sake of his image, but she refused because he had cut her out of his life. Indeed, they had only spent three days together in the previous four months. Another claimed that they had a heated argument and Elton decided to start divorce proceedings there and then. Yet another claimed that they were so in love that they were planning a second honeymoon on a luxury yacht complete with a mirrored ceiling in the master bedroom. Renate's spokesperson announced that she would be flying into Sydney on 22 January to join her husband on their love boat.

Renate actually flew back to Woodside, not Sydney, and was reported as saying: 'I just don't know where the rumours come from. We are very happily married.' She was said to be ever hopeful of having children. 'We are as close as we ever were, and the reason we are apart at the moment is that I must get on with my own career.' Renate announced that she had now become a record producer and was working on a song called 'Lonely Heart' by Elton and Osborne, with her friend Sylvia Griffin, a client of Reid and former lead singer with the band, Kissing The Pink.

The tabloids pursued Elton with renewed vigilance. To emphasize that Elton was not on a love cruise with his wife, the *Sun* printed a picture of him on a boat in Sydney Harbour during his convalescence, sitting next to a male companion – in an effort to prove all its insinuations were true. The friend was described as 'hunky bachelor Peter Iken', who was an old friend of Elton's and an executive of Warner Brothers Records – and, most importantly, straight. There was a new prurience in the air and the tabloids smelled blood. Their attitude towards cuddly Elton was about to change.

Elton began the fateful year of 1987 in low spirits. He was physically and mentally exhausted after a gruelling world tour. Depressed and still recovering from the cancer scare, he was advised to rest his voice and take a break from performing for a few months. He was at such a low ebb that he did not have the energy to face the future with Renate. Unbeknown to Elton, though, his strength of character and indomitable spirit were about to be put to a much more serious test.

chapter eleven

Conquer The Sun

SINCE THE START OF THE 1980s Elton had gradually become the focus for anti-gay slurs, in tandem with increasing fears about AIDS, a disease most associated with gay men in this decade. Discovered to be a major health threat in the early 1980s, human immunodeficiency virus, or HIV, is a virus transmitted through the transfer of infected blood, semen and vaginal fluids. If it develops into AIDS (acquired immunodeficiency syndrome), the body's immune system is irreparably damaged, and can no longer provide adequate defence against all forms of illness. Certain tabloids may have shown a tendency to print prurient or speculative stories about Elton but it was the *Sun*, in particular, whose reports started to turn its hero into a villain, targeting Elton as a scapegoat, and making 1987 the worst year of Elton's life.

At the start of the year the newspaper received some information that led it to a teenage male prostitute, Stephen Hardy, who had a story sleazy enough to make it the showbiz exposé of the decade. Hardy claimed that he could prove he acted as a pimp to provide teenage rent boys for Elton and Billy Gaff, Rod Stewart's manager, for drug-taking and homosexual orgies at Gaff's country mansion in Finchampstead, Berkshire. Because it corroborated their general anti-Elton theme, *Sun* journalists Neil Wallis and Craig MacKenzie (brother of Kelvin MacKenzie, the *Sun*'s editor) neither made the effort, nor saw the need, to investigate Hardy's convincing story, despite legal advice to be cautious and thoroughly check the facts. Kelvin MacKenzie, who always courted confrontation, was characteristically bullish and said, 'Fuck it, we'll run it . . . Elton never sues.' Hardy received $3,000 (£2,000) for his disclosures, as well as follow-up payments of $375 (£250) a time.

On 25 February 1987, flagged up as 'Another *Sun* Exclusive', the front page was given over to the headline ELTON IN VICE BOYS SCANDAL. Inside Stephen Hardy's supposed confession was printed under the alias Graham X. His story was that he had been paid to pick up teenage rent boys from seedy gay bars in London's West End for bizarre orgies at Billy Gaff's house, and he described how he would 'lure them to Elton's bed for a minimum of $150

(£100) plus all the cocaine they could stand'. The sex sessions were alleged to have begun eighteen months after Elton's marriage to Renate.

With this story, the *Sun* could be both the high priest of the moral high ground, while at the same time, the prurient tabloid, supplying its readers with gutter gossip. To reinforce the story, a confession by a thoroughly chastened and repentant Graham X appeared on the same spread as detailed descriptions of bondage sessions, drugs orgies and foursomes at Gaff's house. Graham X said he was now married and continued with a safety warning: 'I am speaking out to warn other gullible young kids to steer clear of people like these.'

According to Graham X, he decided to give up the rent-boy racket because he had fallen in love with a girl, for whom, with the proceeds of his last night's pimping, he planned to buy an engagement ring. He stated that, on 30 April 1986, he had taken two young men to Gaff's house and that was the last time he saw Elton. He said: 'He was stoned out of his mind on cocaine as usual. And he didn't say goodbye when we left the following day. As we were driven back to London I realized at last I had got out. Now looking back, I'm ashamed of my past, but I was desperate.'

On 30 April, the only specific date in the article, Elton had not even been in the country.

At the time of publication Elton was in Australia, still recovering from throat surgery. Mick Jagger was reported to have advised him not to sue after his own ill-fated libel case against the *News of the World* in 1967. Even with a cast-iron alibi, the newspaper could still dig up further salacious and damaging stories before a case could come to court. In Jagger's opinion, Elton should ignore the stories until the *Sun* gave up. Elton thought otherwise, however, and embarked upon a legal fight that would test even his robust spirit to the limit. His solicitor, Frank Presland, served a writ for libel immediately, and said his client would be seeking 'enormous damages' from the *Sun*. 'In view of Elton's reputation,' he said, 'plus the maliciousness and untruth of this report, I feel that $7.5 million (£5 million) will not be enough.' Next day the *Sun* confidently declared, 'The story they're all suing over,' and proudly explained that Elton's lawyers had failed to gain an injunction to prevent further revelations. On day two the *Sun* offered its readers ELTON's KINKY KICKS – more lurid details about cocaine-fuelled sex sessions. As if to emphasize that it was only carrying out its moral and civic duty, it added: 'Scotland Yard have begun an investigation into our allegations and want to quiz pimp Graham X.'

The *Sun*'s main competitor, the *Mirror*, placed itself firmly in Elton's corner, printing details of his movements on the date in question that could only have been provided by Elton's office. He could not possibly have been at Gaff's house on 30 April because he had been in New York. He was coming to the end of a trip to discuss new stage costumes with his designer, Bob Mackie, and was staying at the Carlyle Hotel. On that particular day he had lunched with his old friend Tony King. It was even noted that they were turned away from a smart restaurant because Elton had refused to take his hat off. After lunch he went to meet Mackie, who confirmed the meeting to the *Mirror*. British Airways also confirmed that he had flown back to England on Concorde with Bob Halley on 1 May, departing JFK at 9.30 a.m. The passenger list noted Mr E. John and Mr B. Halley.

Billy Gaff, although he decided not to sue, condemned the story as 'wicked lies' – on 30 April he was flying back to London from the Philippines. He revealed that Elton had never visited his Finchampstead home and that the two men had only seen each other once in the last two years, in Sydney.

Despite damning evidence to the contrary, the *Sun* stood by its story and quoted Graham X's reaction, under the headline – You're A Liar Elton!: 'Elton can say what he likes, but deep in his heart he knows I'm telling 100 per cent the truth. He wants to protect his image as the Royal favourite, loved by millions of fans, but he did have sex with the teenagers I brought to Gaff's home ...'

The *Sun*'s bosses presumably thought that if they kept up the pressure Elton would give up sooner or later. The story was headline news all over the world – even Elton's Australian friend Gary Clarke was tracked down in Melbourne for his reaction to the allegations, but he made no comment. Clarke later claimed that Elton paid $22,500 (£15,000) for him to take a fourteen-month pilot's course, an opportunity he had always wanted, during which time he would be kept out of reach from the press.

The risks of going to court for Elton were enormous, not least the prospect of having his lifestyle picked over in excruciating detail. The spotlight would not only fall on him but his whole family. It would affect his business associates, his football club, his friends and social life, and could also damage his precious association with the royal family. But most of all he was worried that it would hurt Renate. Elton persisted, however, and instructed his lawyers to issue a further writ after each scurrilous *Sun* headline. Frank Presland confirmed that while the Graham X saga continued, the issuing of writs would not cease. Elton was prepared to spend every penny he had to fight the *Sun*, though it would be a tough eighteen-month battle, during which he would reach the depths of mental and physical self-abuse – and the brink of suicide.

A total of 350 guests attended Elton's lavish fortieth birthday party at

Lockwood House, John Reid's new home, a ten-bedroomed Georgian mansion near Rickmansworth. Among the guests were Eric Clapton, Bob Geldof, Ringo Starr, George Harrison, film directors Ken Russell and Bryan Forbes, actor Sir John Mills, music mogul Richard Branson and the Watford football team. The Duke and Duchess of York made a late entrance just before midnight. It was an impressive roll-call of support for Elton during the first months of his fight, though one guest was missing; Elton had arrived without his wife, to the disappointment of many who had hoped to see the happy couple enjoying Elton's birthday together. He was still in high spirits as he cut his cake and removed the pink ribbons from Reid's birthday gift – an $120,000 (£80,000) Ferrari Testarossa sports car. During his speech Elton explained that Renate had flu, while proudly displaying her gift to him of an antique diamond and ruby watch.

The real reason for Renate's absence from Elton's party was revealed the following day when Reid's office issued a statement declaring that the couple had agreed to continue living separately, though they remained on 'very good personal terms' and they were not planning to divorce. It stated that they had taken the decision to live apart before the *Sun*'s unpleasant allegations had been printed. News of Elton's marital difficulties simply gave the *Sun* yet another opportunity to cast further doubts on his reputation. The headline trumpeted ELTON ENDS SHAM MARRIAGE with suggestions that the event was purely as a result of the rent-boy allegations, while assuring readers that it would print further stories about Elton and teenage boys from the previous decade.

The press soon discovered that Renate had moved out of Woodside already and was in the process of settling into a $450,000 (£300,000) flat in Kensington, paid for by Elton. Reports also disclosed that Renate was being comforted by her close friend and Kissing The Pink band member, Sylvia Griffin, openly suggesting a gay relationship, despite the fact that there had never been any evidence that they were anything more than friends.

Although the *Sun*'s campaign against Elton showed no sign of letting up, doubts had begun to creep in behind the scenes. Gradually it had dawned on the *Sun* that a rent boy who was desperate for money was probably not the most trustworthy informant, especially when the *Star* discovered Hardy's photograph in a three-year-old copy of a gay photo magazine called *Vulcan*. A man who had been present at the photo session was reported to have said, 'He [Hardy] is capable of doing anything for money.'

To keep up the story's momentum, it was crucial for the *Sun* to track down other rent boys who would support Hardy's story, but instead of employing a reliable investigative journalist to gather hard evidence, they hired the services of another former rent boy, John Boyce, who had a string of fraud convictions and one for attempted murder. The *Sun* promised him $2,625 (£1,750) for every signed affidavit he could procure, from any young man who could attest personally to Elton's allegedly depraved lifestyle. Each informant would receive $750 (£500), Boyce could keep the rest. He lived up to his reputation and produced not a single genuine informer, later admitting that he would take men to hotel rooms to hear their confessions even though he knew there was no truth in their admissions. The *Sun* kept up the pressure in earnest, evidently hoping that the more salacious material it could uncover, the more the original allegations would be obscured in the mire. Or perhaps Elton would be forced to give up the legal fight.

However, the further the *Sun* went, the more determined Elton became. In response to every new and unlikely claim against him, another libel writ would follow. Under the *sub judice* rule, both sides were legally obliged not to comment on the matter, but the *Sun* continued making its allegations. Elton was under pressure to make a public statement to defend himself and so he contacted his old friend and chat-show host, Michael Parkinson, and appeared on his television show *One to One*, which was recorded in front of a studio audience on 14 April, to be broadcast on 2 May.

At the time of his television interview events took an ominous turn. The headline ELTON PORN PHOTO SHAME featured on the *Sun*'s front page on 15 April, after someone claiming to be one of Elton's former lovers surfaced with three photographs, for which the *Sun* paid $15,000 (£10,000). There was one blurred nude shot of Elton in sunglasses (cropped above the waistline), a sharper one of him in a football shirt with his arm round the shoulders of a boy, and a third allegedly intimate shot of Elton with a young man, which the *Sun* said 'was too disgusting to be printed in a family newspaper'. It soon transpired that the photographs had been taken many years previously, judging by Elton's figure and his hairstyle, possibly in the mid-1970s. There was no suggestion of any sexual contact between Elton and the boy in the second picture, and the young man in the unpublished shot was considered old enough to be a consenting adult. In no way were the pictures linked to Graham X, or an orgy that had supposedly taken place the previous year. The same issue of the *Sun* featured yet another double-page spread, based on the story of another nineteen-year-old informant, Malcolm M, under the heading ELTON'S FIVE-DAY ORGY. A pompous editorial denounced Elton, and expounded in evangelical terms on its continuing campaign to unearth the 'truth': 'The *Sun* has no hard feelings towards Elton John. We wish him no ill. Certainly we shall never pursue him maliciously. But he must stop telling LIES about the *Sun*. In return we shall stop telling the TRUTH about him.'

On 16 April, the *Sun* piled on more rumours with I Ran Coke For Elton, quoting a showbiz executive, alias John D, who had once been an office boy at Rocket Records. He made claims about the high level of drug abuse and homosexual activity involving Elton and a number of young men, and alleged to have provided Elton with bags of cocaine.

In response to increased public interest, the Michael Parkinson interview was brought forward to 18 April. Staring into the camera through owlish glasses and wearing a red flying suit with a Watford FC baseball cap, Elton gave a fluent, if subdued performance. A downcast, deflated individual with several days' growth of stubble, he stated that the tabloid newspaper's allegations were nothing but lies and spoke of his will to prove it in court. He talked of the pressure on his family, especially his mother who was finding it difficult to cope, and because of the scandal and press harassment had moved to Minorca. The biggest disclosure in the interview was that he had spent the last week with Renate. 'We're known as the Odd Couple apparently,' he said. 'But we still get on very well with each other. I still love her and she still loves me.'

Afterwards, Parkinson gave Elton his full support saying: 'I enjoyed the show and so did Elton. In fact, I thought he was bloody marvellous, considering the pressure he is under. He's an old friend of mine, and a great mate. None of this nonsense is going to change that.'

During their separation, Renate had kept in regular contact with Elton, believing nothing that the *Sun* had printed, and for now she had returned to Woodside to give Elton the support he needed under such difficult conditions. 'It seemed stupid to face the pressures separately, when we could do so together and really help each other,' Elton said later. 'Renate was incredibly strong throughout it, she was wonderful and we became closer.'

As a result of his health problems and his battle with the tabloid press, in 1987, Elton's record releases were limited to the *Live in Australia* album and a live version single of 'Your Song'. Gus Dudgeon had performed a technical miracle on the production, considering the state of Elton's vocal chords, but despite his expertise Elton had decided he no longer required Dudgeon's services for his next album or tour, much to the producer's dismay.

In 1987 Renate appeared with her husband at Watford for the last matches of the 1986–7 football season. At the club, Elton had received many letters from ordinary supporters who said that as long as Elton's role as chairman of Watford was not compromised, his private life was no one's concern but his own. The adverse publicity had not damaged the club in any way, with the completion of the new west grandstand to celebrate (funded mainly by Elton), and high attendance figures on match days. On the pitch the team had

had a successful Cup run, almost reaching the FA Cup Final in April 1987, until they met Spurs in the semi-final and lost 4–1.

The unexpected resignation of Graham Taylor in May came at a difficult time for Elton, but even though he was losing a close associate, he showed his friend no ill will, and wished him well in his new role as manager of Aston Villa. During his ten years at the club, Taylor had transformed Watford, and the team's reputation seemed unassailable.

On a whim, and without heeding the wishes of the seven other board members, Elton appointed a new manager, Dave Bassett. The strain of the legal fight was beginning to tell and Elton was not giving the team the attention they deserved. To redress the balance, Elton threw himself into supporting the club by announcing that he would join Bassett and the team on their second tour of China in the summer. During the tour Elton revealed that although he had made a complete recovery following his throat surgery, he would be taking a break from singing for at least a year.

Sharing a home with Renate once again cheered Elton immensely, and he spent extravagantly on home improvements. He commissioned a new client of John Reid's, Viscount Linley, son of Princess Margaret and furniture-maker to the rich and famous, to build a new marital bed costing $112,500 (£75,000), with interlinking initials, E and R, engraved on the headboard. Also in October, Elton was presented with an award for twenty years of songwriting by the American Society of Composers, Authors and Publishers. The couple seemed as happy as they had ever been, which was clear from the photograph of Renate kissing him after the ceremony. As Elton had told Michael Parkinson, Sheila and Fred had gone to live in Minorca. He had failed to mention in the interview that the most important woman in his life had actually fled the country to escape his monstrous behaviour, fuelled by drink and drugs. He later confessed that he was a vicious and nasty drunk, who would often refuse to speak to his mother when she telephoned. Sheila had left for the Balearics, saying, 'I don't have a son any more.' All the Cartier rings and fabulous cars Elton had showered on her counted for nothing – all she wanted was his love. When his name was splashed all over the *Sun*, Sheila said she was too humiliated to live in England, but there was much more to it than that and he would eventually admit that she had disowned him because he had become 'disdainful, spiteful and totally selfish'.

Although he received over 500 letters of support from members of the public who were sympathetic to his plight, Elton's legal battle was gradually wearing him down. After the Malcolm M and John D claims, his lawyers served two more writs, bringing the total to twelve. Most upsetting to Elton was a *News of the World* story stating that, were it not for the stories about his alleged involvement with rent boys, he would have received an OBE in the Queen's birthday honours. It was rumoured that the Queen was not amused that the Yorks had attended Elton's fortieth party, and that they had been advised not to see him in the near future. If these suspicions were true, such drastic intervention by the Queen was a terrible blow to Elton's pride and honour.

Some in Elton's circle wondered if he could survive so many setbacks, given his two previous suicide attempts. 'I tried that before in my life and that isn't the answer,' he told David Wigg of the *Express* later. 'But what was happening did depress me. There was a danger of becoming very bitter but in the end it's not worth it. My true personality isn't like that anyway.' He was heartbroken by the accusations, and could not understand why the *Sun* was hounding him so aggressively.

There were days when he was optimistic, mindful that he would have to go to court and face cross-examination over his lifestyle which, like that of most rock-and-rollers, was far from pure. He tried to keep his resolve, though, and it became a matter of principle, not just for himself, but on behalf of ordinary people. 'The libel laws are such that it's too expensive for people to get involved in,' he said. 'I am one of the few people who can actually afford to keep this case going. It will cost a fortune.' In contrast, however, the bad days brought him close to a breakdown. At times he was unable to leave the house without weeping openly, which meant that he could not even attend matches at Watford for fear of making a spectacle of himself. He locked himself away, nursing his depression, unable to face the world yet fooling himself that he was in control. 'It was so bad that I actually considered going to a psychiatrist,' he said. 'Lots of my friends say it's wonderful to be able to unburden yourself, but I think I should overcome my own problems.'

At one stage at his lowest ebb, he locked himself inside the house for almost a week, steadfastly refusing to come out. Eventually Renate took a ladder and climbed up to his window. He emerged from his depression immediately – his spirits were so low that he was touched that anyone should care enough to save him, especially as Renate was afraid of heights.

During this difficult time, Elton became dependent on alcohol and cocaine. He would sit in his house for weeks at a time, watching pornographic videos, consuming packets of cocaine that were slipped under the door, and guzzling a bottle of Scotch every night. If he had to go out he would need to drink several vodka martinis to work up the courage to leave the house.

Then, on Remembrance Sunday in November 1987, an horrific event occurred that shook Elton from his depressive state. At a church ceremony in Enniskillen, Northern Ireland, the IRA detonated a bomb among the crowds, fatally injuring a nurse, Marie Wilson. Her father, Gordon Wilson, later described how, powerless to do anything to save his daughter, he had held her hand as she lay dying. Elton was deeply affected by Mr Wilson's brave words: 'That man was so forgiving, so gracious. I thought, this is what courage is all about. I said, come on Elton, enough's enough. You have to realize how lucky you are, what a privileged position you are in. Get out there, go back to work and be positive.'

Expectations of increased circulation figures following the stories about Elton had been high at the *Sun*'s offices, but it transpired that the anti-Elton stance had had the opposite effect. When the front page featured stories that didn't concern Elton, sales were at their usual high level, but on days when they printed allegations about the star, sales actually dropped, sometimes by as much as 200,000 copies. Perhaps this reflected the extent to which Elton had endeared himself to the public.

In the autumn the *Sun* made a serious miscalculation, when a story that emerged from Old Windsor described how the Rottweiler dogs at Woodside had had their voice boxes 'sliced through' to stop them from barking. A *Sun* reporter visited Elton's estate, found some dogs and made faces at them. They did not bark at him and the story he wrote was accompanied by a note stating that he could not be completely sure the allegation was true. Despite the doubts surrounding the story, the next day's front page had yet another 'exclusive': MYSTERY OF ELTON'S SILENT DOGS. The *Sun* had also encouraged a response from officials at the RSPCA, who were outraged that such an evil procedure had been inflicted upon the animals.

The *Sun* realized its mistake almost as soon as the first editions hit the streets. Elton's office announced that he had a donkey, a parrot and half a dozen ancient and not particularly deadly dogs, all of which barked. Not a Rottweiler among them. The only security at the perimeter of Woodside was a fence set deep into the ground to deter rabbits. Elton's solicitors issued their seventeenth libel writ. The final blow for the *Sun*'s campaign was struck when its original informant, Stephen Hardy, swapped sides and talked to the *Mirror*. On 6 November, the *Mirror* ran MY SEX LIES OVER ELTON, an interview with Hardy in which he revealed that his original story was a complete fabrication, that he only did it for the money and that he had never even met Elton.

Though the flaws in the *Sun*'s campaign against Elton were growing ever more visible, the newspaper was not about to give up, and stories would continue to be printed until early in 1988.

While Elton was battling against the tabloids, Rocket Records was experiencing similar bad fortune. Without a hit record for a number of years, in November 1987 it terminated its contracts with its few remaining acts, with the sole exception of Elton John. The decision to make this change signalled the first sign of a monumental clear-out in his life, not only of his possessions but of his dreams as well.

Days later Elton announced his resignation as Watford chairman; he would be selling his 95 per cent stake in the club for an estimated $3 million (£2 million). He explained he would have less available cash to invest in the club, and he wanted the club to have someone who would guarantee it a more stable future, financially. He would remain a director and life president, saying: 'I'm not leaving, I've just been kicked upstairs.' At first, the likeliest buyer was the business, and later press, mogul Robert Maxwell. A month later, however, Elton decided not to sell his share of the club to the tycoon, and he called off the deal.

In the new year, another unlikely Watford buyer surfaced in the shape of Paul Raymond, of strip-club fame. Elton's resignation as chairman left his manager, Dave Bassett, vulnerable during a poor season, and he resigned mid-season. Promoted from the Watford ranks, new manager, Steve Harrison, had made demands for the club before agreeing to the job, and as a result Elton promised to spend up to half a million pounds to boost the chances of Watford's return to top-division football. He also assured Harrison that Watford would remain a family club and therefore he would not be doing any deals with Paul Raymond. Watford's bad start to the season in 1987 continued in the following year, despite Harrison's efforts, and the club was eventually relegated to Division Two.

Throughout the turbulent times in Elton's life, the love-hate relationship between John Reid and Elton remained strong. There were constant rumours of rifts between them, with impasses that would last for weeks, finally broken by a gesture of generosity by one to the other. The diminutive, wily Scot always played protective big brother to his superstar charge, and certainly never shied away from confrontation on Elton's part. His first clash of 1988 occurred at an end-of-tour party for Whitney Houston, when Reid noticed Elton being hustled for a quote by a *Sun* reporter, Rick Sky. He was immediately on hand to sort things out, but used more force than was strictly necessary to remove the journalist from the venue. The paper reported the scene in the strongest possible terms: 'Reid shouted abuse as he GRABBED our man and shook him. The he BASHED Rick's head against a pillar five times and PUSHED him out of the club while punching him on the chest.' Reid, who blamed his actions on his drunkenness, was charged with assault and fined £150 after appearing at Bow Street Magistrates Court. After a lengthy recuperation it was time for Elton to put his voice to the test in March 1988, when he returned to the studio for the first time since his throat surgery. His spirits were still low due to the *Sun* allegations, but he was drawing on his deepest inner reserves and still determined to fight the case with more and more writs. Years later he admitted to thinking: 'Christ, I hope I don't do a Marianne Faithful – her last album was slit-your-wrists time.' But the sessions at AIR studios in Montserrat succeeded in taking his mind off his problems and, to his great relief, his voice was back in working order, perhaps even showing an improvement. Producer Chris Thomas rounded up a host of superstar support, with Beach Boys' Carl Wilson and Bruce Johnston, on backing vocals and Pete Townshend on acoustic guitar. He also enlisted the talents of the ever amenable Dee Murray and Nigel Olsson on one track.

The resulting album was cheerful and spirited, and defiantly entitled, *Reg Strikes Back.* Elton would say later that he and Bernie found a renewed creativity on this album, and that he had believed it had two or three really nice tracks. Despite its general inconsistency the album went gold five days after its release and spent five months in the charts, reaching number eighteen in Britain and sixteen in America. Elton would not be satisfied with mediocrity, however; he wanted to be free from commercial considerations on the next album.

Now aged forty-one, Elton was ripe for a review of his life; a mid-life crisis, in fact. First, his identity: should he carry on as fantasy Elton or go back to being real Reg? Then, his possessions: what should he do with the abundant fruits of his labours? His sexuality: should he be a married man or not? Lastly, his ambitions: should he diversify in his career? He spun off in every direction. He agreed to play a cameo role in a film adaptation of D. H. Lawrence's *The Rainbow,* planned by Ken Russell, but withdrew at the last minute. He was also rumoured to be cast as Liberace in a television biopic, but nothing came of it. He also contributed vocals and played piano on Olivia Newton-John's 1988 album *The Rumour.*

Reg was not only striking back, he was having a good clear-out at home, a highly significant and symbolic event for an obsessive collector. In August, Sotheby's, the auctioneer, revealed that Elton's vast collection of antiques and art was to be put up for auction. He intended to sell Woodside and start again in a more private house in the country with his wife. 'It's time, artistically and mentally, for a change of thought,' he said. 'You cannot stagger through life with all these possessions. This is kind of watching your own death. Hopefully I'll still be alive when the sale comes up in September.' It would be the first time a living superstar had sold all his possessions at public auction.

Elton's sale would consist of 2,000 lots over four days and would make almost \$22.5 million (£15 million). Sotheby's launched a spectacular worldwide marketing jamboree and certain items went on tour with champagne receptions held in Tokyo, Los Angeles, New York and Sydney before the sale in London. The Victoria and Albert Museum selected 500 pieces for a public sale preview – the first time relics from the glitter-rock era had been thought fit to grace the hallowed halls of the V&A.

Elton claimed that he had lost his passion for collecting and did not feel he needed to rely on possessions for happiness any more. He felt suffocated and thought it was time to stop before he became too much a caricature of himself. 'It sounds weird,' he said. 'But I want to get rid of a little bit of Elton in my life, and everything it had become.' Six weeks after he returned from each tour a lorry-load of crates would arrive at Woodside. 'My home had begun to resemble a high-class junk store,' he said. 'There was stuff sitting unopened in crates. Literally everything was covered. Every wall, every surface. It was suffocating me. Now I want to get back to basics.'

Elton was determined that everything had to go: every collectible, every reminder of his past, from priceless antiques to cheap trinkets, fine art to monumental tat, expensive treasures to sentimental souvenirs. It took three days for Sotheby's to pack and transport the consignment to London. The house was left bare apart from his grand piano, his favourite paintings by Francis Bacon and Magritte, fourteen cars, his record library, his marital bed and his prized collection of *Goon Show* scripts.

The 2,000 lots were crammed into every corner of Sotheby's showroom for viewing: among them were 150 Art Nouveau lamps, 200 Art Deco nymphs, pieces of Bugatti furniture, platinum and gold discs, piles of Cartier brooches and necklaces, jukeboxes, pinball machines, luggage, a life-size cardboard cut-out of Elton, his stuffed satin bananas, a guitar case full of novelty specs, a camisole Judy Garland had worn in *Meet Me In St Louis*. Even items of sentimental value went, including a programme autographed by Elvis Presley and a set of lithographs by John Lennon.

The sale was a gift to the press and Elton was on hand to promote it with his usual repartee. He talked about his costumes, and the ideas behind them, some of which were his but mostly he let the designers get on with it: 'That's why I ended up looking like a demented drag queen, because half the people who were designing for me were demented drag queens.'

Despite the *Sun*'s recent campaign, Elton's record sales were unaffected as *Reg Strikes Back* sold well. He had already had a surprise hit single in January 1988 with the live version of 'Candle In The Wind' on both sides of the Atlantic. Most gratifying was his invitation to perform at a Prince's Trust concert in June 1988, thereby proving that he was still very much in favour among his royal associates.

Elton wanted to test his voice on a short six-week, thirty-one-show tour before going worldwide. For the Reg Strikes Back Tour he abandoned his flamboyant costumes in favour of hat-and-suit combos, and relied on lighting and pacing for dramatic effect. His first tour without a piano, instead he played an electric keyboard with a giant screen showing close-ups of his hands. Numerous artists made guest appearances, including Eric Clapton, Bruce Hornsby, Jon Bon Jovi and Billy Joel. Elton still got a high from the adrenalin buzz of live shows. A diligent schoolboy at heart he said: 'Doing an album is like doing an A level, if you get it wrong you can do it again. On stage you get one chance.'

He was missing his mother and nostalgic for the whiff of HP sauce, Hovis and the homemade cakes of his childhood, which perhaps explains why he gave his next interview to *Woman's Own* magazine in August, in which he described how he intended to change his life and do different things. After a year in which he almost lost his voice, his marriage and his reputation, he felt as if he had been given a second chance, and said that the best thing to come out of his troubles with the *Sun* was that he and Renate were together again. 'Our marriage works very well for us,' he said. 'I'm on the road a lot and Renate's busy getting back into her sound engineering career. But we do spend a lot of time together these days.' He also admitted that he was terrified of AIDS. 'The AIDS problem worries me, it should worry everyone. People ask me if I have an AIDS test. Well, I have, I have blood tests all the time. I also do concerts to raise money to fight AIDS.'

As a self-confessed bisexual, Elton was in a high-risk category, but by the late 1980s every sexually active man and woman in the world was at risk. And sex was by no means the only way people could contract HIV. Elton talked for the first time about a young American teenager called Ryan White, a haemophiliac who had contracted the virus through contaminated blood. After hearing about the boy in 1986, he had contacted Ryan's mother and had kept in touch with the family. Elton was only too aware of the stigma attached to the disease. 'They took so long in America to get any action going,' he said. 'I think they hoped that it would go away and that the gay community would just kill themselves.' Elton's new mission was to raise awareness of the disease to stop the damage caused by ignorance.

By the time of the Sotheby's sale in early September, Elton was touring in America and could not attend. The atmosphere was more rock concert than dignified auction, with crash barriers erected and the police on hand to control the crowds outside Sotheby's. A total of 600 bidders reserved seats in advance and made their bids throughout six different halls, all controlled by closed-circuit television. Telephone lines from America, Japan, Australia and Europe were kept open and a computerized scoreboard over the auctioneer's head converted cash bids into the world's major currencies. Elton had not offered anything to his mother in her Minorcan exile, but she sent a friend along to bid for some mementos on her behalf. Gus Dudgeon couldn't resist either, paying $4,425 (£2,950) for a cushion depicting the sleeve of *Madman Across The Water*. The sale exceeded all expectations and raised almost $22.5 million (£15 million), minus 20 per cent buyers' and sellers' premium. Stephen Griegs from the bootmakers Doc Martens paid $16,500 (£11,000) for the giant boots Elton had worn in *Tommy*. Fifty pairs of specs fetched $90,000 (£60,000), four times the estimate. The sale demonstrated the extraordinarily high level of interest in rock and pop memorabilia.

Now that Woodside had been emptied, the stage was set for refurbishment. This time he left the job to Robert Key who ran Rocket Records. His task was to go through a range of different catalogues and mark off furniture and art that appealed to him and present it to Elton for approval.

Despite their continued closeness Elton wouldn't be sharing Woodside with Renate any longer. On 18 November 1988 it was formally announced that the couple were to divorce 'by mutual consent and with no fault attached to either party'. The dignified declaration of their separation was accompanied by a statement from Renate announced through John Reid's office: 'We are parting on the most amicable of terms and genuinely intend to remain best friends. I am obviously saddened to see our marriage end, and I wish Elton all the happiness in the world and I know that he wishes me the same.' Among the inevitable feast of headlines the *Sun* reported the event without any reference to rent boys or cocaine, calling them the BRIDE 'N' DOOM.

Renate's dignity and restraint during their long-drawn-out and much gossiped-about separation, reflected her love and admiration for Elton. She indicated that she was prepared to go to court to support him against the *Sun*. Renate has never again spoken about her marriage.

Following the statement, Elton spoke frankly to his friend Nina Myskow, of the *Mail on Sunday*. He explained that Renate had always been wonderful, and had done nothing wrong during the course of their marriage. He talked of the good times they had together, their shared sense of humour and love of chocolate, and spoke of his relief about the fact that they did not have children. 'Kids should be raised in a stable home,' he said, 'and rock and roll is not a stable business. I don't think you will ever see a little Elton Johnette running around.' He would later describe Renate as 'one of the classiest human beings on earth', and has since only mentioned his ex-wife in the most glowing terms.

Elton later admitted that getting married was a huge gamble and it was, as many suspected, an ill-judged charade. He was trying desperately to be someone he could never be. He told American gay magazine *10 PerCent*, that he had turned to Renate at the height of his confusion over his own sexuality, believing that a heterosexual relationship would cure him of men: 'I wasn't honest with her. I thought, this will change me. This will change who I am.'

Although the *Sun* knew it could never win the case against Elton after the lies of its chief witness, Graham X, had been revealed, it now ran the risk of humiliation by exposing its shoddy research methods. However, if its reputation was going to be ruined, it would make sure that Elton's would too. By going to court it could justify its own prejudice towards Elton specifically, and homosexuality in general, by bringing in character witnesses to damage him in court.

In the event, however, Elton's lawyers made a masterful legal move to ensure that Elton's name was not dragged through the mud. The first libel case to be presented in court would be the subject of the seventeenth and final writ, the ludicrous allegation that Elton owned mute Rottweilers. This would present the *Sun* with a case it could only lose, and for which no sordid evidence would be required. The case was to due to commence in the High Court on Monday 12 December, but the day before the proceedings began, the tabloid's lawyers had an all-day meeting with Elton's legal team. The *Sun*'s lawyers were only too aware of the fact that juries had been awarding celebrities increasingly large amounts in punitive damages in libel cases against newspapers. According to Kelvin MacKenzie, 'The 1980s saw particularly dim juries awarding ludicrous amounts.' If Elton were to match Koo Stark's damages of $450,000 (£300,000), and multiplied it by seventeen, it would amount to an epic pay-out. It did not take long to conclude that a $1.5 million (£1 million) deal would be cheaper in the long run.

Consequently the case never reached court. Instead on 12 December, as instructed by his lawyers, the *Sun*'s front page read: SORRY ELTON. Every word and every punctuation mark within the report had Elton's approval. It was the first time that a British newspaper had made such a prominent apology: 'The *Sun* last night agreed to pay megastar Elton John £1 million libel damages. The settlement followed allegations published in the *Sun* last year about his private life. . . A *Sun* spokesman apologized to Elton for running the stories which they acknowledge to be completely untrue.'

The *Sun* further trumpeted, 'We are delighted the *Sun* and Elton have become friends again. And we are sorry that we were lied to by a teenager living in a world of fantasy.' By pointing the finger at Graham X, the rent boy, the newspaper removed most of its own blame without any acknowledgement of the prime role it played in actually printing the lies about him, or its hounding of Elton with further unsubstantiated allegations over many

Elton wows the audience dressed in a pink Mohawk wig and star-studded suit.

Elton the showman: dressed as a cockerel in 1977 (**top**), and sporting one of his many outrageous wigs, along with matching specs (**top right**); in a glittery, feathery number at the Prince's Trust benefit concert in 1976 (**right**), and on stage in an early 'cat-suit' creation in 1973 (**far right**).

Left: An enthusiastic supporter of charity since his early days as a performer, Elton was involved in the Live Aid concert in July 1985, organized by Bob Geldof.

Below: The tragic story of Ryan White, a haemophiliac AIDS victim, had a profound effect on Elton. On the day of Ryan's funeral, Elton is pictured by his coffin with Ryan's mother.

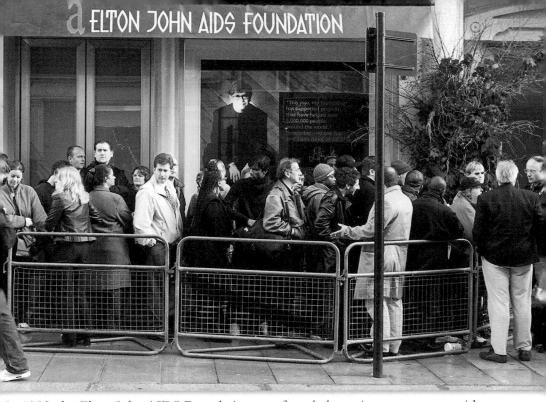

In 1992, the Elton John AIDS Foundation was founded to raise money to provide services for HIV-positive or AIDS victims, as well as funding for educational programmes to promote the prevention of AIDS. Queues await the opening of an EJAF clothes sale in London.

Elton and David Furnish open the 'Out of the Closet III' shop on New Bond Street, London, November 2000. All proceeds from the shop's sales go to the EJAF.

Friend to the royals: Elton could count Diana, Princess of Wales as one of his close friends, sharing in common their parental break-ups, ill-fated marriages, eating disorders, and deep involvement in charity work.

Fuck Panny
owe $10.00
Fuck
Ron & Sue

The late Princess Margaret (pictured with her son, Viscount Linley, in 1997) became an ardent admirer of Elton after attending his charity concert for the Invalid Aid Association in 1972.

Achievements and accolades:
winner of countless music industry
prizes, Elton is pictured with his
2000 Grammy Legend Award (**left**), and
1998 Ivor Novello Awards (**below**).

Though wigs and
outrageous costumes
remain in the distant past,
Elton still continues to
thrill and entertain as one
of the world's top-class
performers.

After a turbulent past
and private life, Elton
has found commitment
and calm with partner
David Furnish.

months. Nevertheless, MacKenzie said, 'It was not one of my happiest moments at the *Sun*. It cost the *Sun* a million pounds and Rupert Murdoch was bloody angry with me.'

Sun readers were now faced with the unlikely scenario of the former enemies kissing and making up. In a sycophantic centre spread the *Sun* explained how its erstwhile enemy had lost almost thirty pounds in less than eight weeks. Describing how he had had a terrible time in 1987, the worst year of his life, Elton told his former tormentors of his positive steps to regain his health and fitness. That evening he attended an AIDS benefit concert in the Strand Theatre with comedian Billy Connolly and afterwards burst into tears of relief.

After the $1.5 million (£1 million) settlement, and costs which were also paid for by the *Sun*, Mr Justice Michael Davies, the judge who would have presided over the Rottweiler case, made a complaint about the circumstances of the out-of-court settlement, pointing out that the courts were not, 'a supine adjunct to a publicity machine for pop stars and newspapers'.

Elton's management had stressed throughout the case that he saw it as a wider issue than merely clearing his name. He wanted it to improve journalistic standards and promised that, after the case was over, he would apply to the Press Council to make sure such a thing could never happen again, to him or anyone else.

By the end of the battle to clear his name, Elton had totally deconstructed his life: the possessions had been sold or removed, his wife and his mother had gone. Woodside was a mere shell, purged of all its rococo trappings and party atmosphere, and now in the process of being renovated and completely refurbished. The only remaining occupants were his grandmother, Ivy, in the Orangery, a skeleton staff, the donkey and a few friendly mutts.

Clearing surfaces, repainting the walls in muted colours and installing tasteful furniture seemed an altogether simpler prospect than cleaning up Elton himself. He was still in the grip of multiple addictions, but at pains to prove that he was in control and that he was up to the job of putting himself back together again. In short, he was in denial. In the process, Elton would push himself to ever further physical extremes on stage, which he described as 'the only place where I feel safe'. In the spring of 1989 he set out on a punishing world tour that would take him to more than thirty countries, playing to more than 2,300,000 people. It began in Europe, and during an energetic dance number at the Bercy stadium, near Paris, he collapsed on stage from heat exhaustion. A doctor revived him with damp towels and water, and within minutes he was back on his feet to complete the set. A couple of days later he threw a party for his forty-second birthday, hiring a château and spending an estimated $300,000 (£200,000). He flew 200 guests to France including Tina Turner and Viscount Linley. Hotels and limousines were laid on for everyone and the guests were served food and drink by footmen dressed in powdered wigs and tails. After cutting his birthday cake – a replica of the Eiffel Tower measuring nine feet – he sat down at the piano to play his guests a marathon session of his best numbers.

In the summer he embarked on the forty-five-date American leg of the tour. He was physically and mentally drained, and had to cancel several shows and radio interviews, which provoked much speculation about his health. At different times during the tour he was reported to be suffering from influenza, exhaustion, and there were even reports that he had 'yuppie flu', myalgic encephalitis. But the show had to go on. He felt safe in the company of his pop friends, and especially his audience. He took part in a huge all-star charity performance of *Tommy* at the Universal Amphitheatre in Los Angeles, joining The Who to sing 'Pinball Wizard' with Phil Collins, Patti LaBelle and Billy Idol. He performed a surprise forty-minute set in the China Club in Los Angeles when Michael Bolton joined him on stage and Michael J. Fox played guitar. Eric Clapton performed 'Rocket Man' with him at Madison Square Garden in New York, although it was reported that he had collapsed hours before the concert. Eleven days later he suffered a fit on stage and declared it was his last ever concert. He checked into the Ritz Hotel in Paris under strict doctor's orders to take complete rest for a month before continuing the tour in the Far East. Elton tried to reassure his fans: 'To say I collapsed is absolutely ridiculous. I am not seriously ill – I'm just plain tired. It's been a great tour, but it all caught up with me.' He had been due to headline at a Belgian music festival in Antwerp, in November, and be presented with a Diamond Career Award for services to music, but he was forced to pull out again for health reasons.

Wherever Elton was in the world, and no matter what his state of mind, he still maintained an avid interest in his global record sales. Every day his office would contact record companies all over the world for sales figures which he would have telexed through to him, enabling him to update his own charts with his coloured pens.

Halfway through the American tour, he returned to England to pour his heart out once again to his favourite counsellor, the television camera, on a special August bank holiday edition of the *Wogan* show. He wore an understated dark blue Versace suit, his platinum-blond wisps of hair covered with a purple, beaded Nehru hat. The studio audience greeted him with affectionate applause, and he remained good-natured and articulate throughout the interview, despite having to endure a montage of news clips concerning his recent troubles. On the show he played 'Healing Hands', a track from his new album *Sleeping With The Past*. Written to express thanks for a woman's love, it was of special significance to Elton, following his break-up with Renate, and would become poignant testimony to Bernie's marriage, which was also coming to an end.

'Healing Hands' failed to become a hit single, as did the follow-up, 'Sacrifice'. With a solo British number one becoming increasingly elusive, Wogan asked Elton whether he minded that this goal had still to be achieved. 'Not really,' he replied. 'It would have been nice, but it doesn't bother me, I don't suppose I will ever have one now.'

The album title, *Sleeping With The Past*, may have been an ironic nod to the scandal, but it was a chance for Bernie and Elton to collaborate to a greater degree than on any album since *Captain Fantastic*. On it, the two musical magpies paid tribute to R&B artists including Sam Cooke, Aretha Franklin, Otis Redding, Stevie Wonder, Percy Sledge, Ray Charles, the Four Tops and the Drifters, which gave the album a cohesive theme. Bernie suggested which artist he had in mind for each song when he gave the lyrics to Elton. They wrote eighteen tracks in the Puk studio in Denmark in just four days. There were questions about MCA's handling of the album, however, as the release date was delayed and the promotional campaign was unimpressive. On 18 October 1989 in New Haven, Connecticut, Elton rushed through his performance, hardly connecting with the audience at all, except to tell them that he would not be performing anything from the new album because MCA was not promoting it. All was not lost, however, because on the subsequent strength of the re-released singles, 'Healing Hands' and 'Sacrifice', in 1990, *Sleeping With The Past* would become his best-selling album of the 1980s, reaching number one in the British charts and number twenty-three in America.

No longer Watford FC's benefactor, in December 1989 Elton attempted to sell his 92 per cent holdings in the club once again. On this occasion the proposed buyer was Wrighton Enterprises, a leisure company with offices in London. He still intended to remain as life president, but without any financial responsibility for the club. Once again the deal was not completed, but in 1990 he eventually sold Watford FC to former West Ham director and time-share magnate, Jack Petchey, for $5.25 million (£3.5 million).

The non-American leg of the gruelling world tour continued in Australia. An exhausted Elton was unable to summon the energy for his usual keyboard gymnastics and either forgot his lyrics, or repeated the same verse over and over. 'Philadelphia Freedom' sometimes ran as long as fifteen minutes. During the tour Elton was again in the grip of drink, plus sex, drugs and food addictions. He was becoming as bloated as Elvis Presley, whose appearance had so appalled him in 1976. One ounce of cocaine was never enough, and he would stay up for three days and nights at a time, suffering nose bleeds and seizures. He used cocaine as an aphrodisiac. He lived out every one of his fantasies, but did not know when to stop. No one knew how to cope with him – he was determined to prove he was fit, yet he seemed completely withdrawn and isolated. According to those around him at the time, the 1989 tour was the worst period of his life. His production people felt as if they were the parents of a naughty child and, at the same time, nurses of a terminally ill patient. Connie Hillman, his American representative and tour manager, remembered: 'There are good days and you get encouraged and you hope for the best, but it was the worst during that tour. There were times when I walked out of his room and you felt like you had just left someone who was dying.' His increasing desolation and despair, and, on some occasions, apparent death wish, horrified his closest associates. Bob Halley remembers one incident when Elton got out of the car drunk, walked along the hard shoulder and lay down on the motorway repeating, 'I wanna die, I wanna die.'

Elton was spiralling into a vortex of self-destruction and self-pity. In private, when he could let the emotional barriers down, he was feeling so sorry for himself that he would sit and listen to records and burst into tears. He would imagine that Bruce Hornsby's 'Lost Soul', was about him. When he played 'Don't Give Up' by Peter Gabriel and Kate Bush, he would take the words to heart and think to himself, 'You'll be OK, don't give up.' The songs became a lifeline at a time when no one else could get through to his damaged spirit.

chapter twelve

Skyline Pigeon

A S THE NEW DECADE DAWNED, Elton had plummeted to a point at which his manners, dignity and humility had deserted him. If he recalled witnessing the sad demise of Elvis, he knew that if he did not act quickly he would be facing a similar future. He was marooned in a mansion undergoing refurbishment, cocooned by an ever present staff of carers, who catered to all his special needs. He had become bitter, withdrawn, self-abusive and deeply troubled. 'Clinically I should be dead,' he told David Frost in an interview.

Elton's unlikely saviour was the American teenager, Ryan White, whom Elton had befriended in 1986, and who became a potent worldwide symbol of prejudice against AIDS. Even at the beginning of the 1990s AIDS was still known as the 'gay plague', such was the fear and contempt associated with the disease. A haemophiliac, Ryan was accidentally infected with the HIV virus after a blood transfusion in December 1984. He first came to public attention in America when he fought a long battle to be readmitted to his Indiana high school after he was diagnosed with the virus. During his terminal illness, while being shunned by classmates, their parents and neighbours, Ryan campaigned for the rights of other people with AIDS through television and public appearances, in an effort to educate a largely ignorant country about the disease and to dispel the fears associated with it.

Elton read about Ryan White in *Newsweek* magazine and was affected deeply by the teenager's courage. He went to visit Ryan and paid public tribute to his enormous strength. Elton took a brave stand in a prevailing climate that was prejudiced and ignorant enough to think that, as a gay man himself, Elton might be more likely to spread the disease than prevent it. This made him all the more determined to raise awareness and dispel bigotry, even though he was criticized by some members of the gay community for taking a 'safe' option in supporting a non-gay carrier of the disease. As he became more open about his own sexuality he devoted more energy to supporting AIDS charities.

Elton spent the last few weeks of Ryan's life with the boy's mother, Jeanne, visiting him in hospital in Indianapolis. Before Ryan's death in April 1990,

Jeanne encouraged Elton to take part in a charity concert, Farm Aid IV, where he dedicated 'Candle In The Wind' to Ryan, and later broke down in tears during 'I'm Still Standing'. During the last week of Ryan's life, Elton kept a compassionate vigil at his bedside, and joined the family as a pall-bearer at the funeral, for which he paid all the expenses.

The funeral was broadcast to the nation and Elton, wearing a black sequinned hat, sat at the piano and solemnly placed Ryan's photograph on it before leading the 1,000-strong congregation. He sang his own tribute to Ryan, 'Skyline Pigeon', one of his earliest songs. Elton remained at Jeanne White's side when she said her last farewell to her eighteen-year-old son as he lay in his open coffin.

This episode made Elton stand back and reflect on his own life. If Ryan's mother could forgive all the people who had been so offensive towards her and her family, when she faced the tragic death of her own son, then he could stop complaining about the colour of his private jet, the flowers, the weather or anything other minor thing that happened to offend.

He was also shocked by the television pictures of himself at Ryan's funeral and vowed to change his habits. He told an American journalist: 'I had to change because I was frightened. I didn't want to die angry, bitter and sad, and that's what I had become – physically ugly, spiritually ugly . . . a slob, a pig.'

Elton was one of the first public figures to support research into AIDS and HIV, and to help charities set up to counsel and care for people who had the virus or the disease. He appeared in public service commercials in America and took part in numerous charity events, including the Atlanta AIDS walk.

In June 1990 he re-released 'Sacrifice/Healing Hands', as a double A-sided single, pledging all British royalties to four AIDS charities – the Terrence Higgins Trust, Body Positive, Jeffries Research Wing Trust and London Lighthouse. 'Sacrifice' was a slow, sentimental melody about failed relationships from the viewpoint of a middle-aged man, but its potential was picked up by DJ Steve Wright in May 1990 while on holiday in Florida, where he heard it on the radio. Back home, he played it on his BBC radio show, unaware that it had already been released. After forty-seven hit singles, 380 weeks in the charts and twenty-two years of disappointment at never having had a solo number one in his own country, 'Sacrifice' took the top spot and stayed there for five weeks, eventually selling more than 600,000 copies. To show his appreciation to Steve Wright, Elton played it live on his show on 26 June 1990. Along with the proceeds from the next single, 'Club At The End Of The Street', Elton presented cheques totalling $492,000 (£328,000) to the four AIDS charities. Furthermore, he declared his intention to donate all royalties from his British singles to AIDS charities.

Towards the end of the year, *Sleeping With The Past* became his first British number-one album since *Caribou,* sixteen years before. Elton's musical achievements had been largely eclipsed by his public persona for a decade and a half. Could he redress the balance so that his music became more important than his lifestyle?

In December 1990, on a Channel Four chat show, Jonathan Ross played host to a new-style Elton. He was considerably slimmer and dressed in a loose-fitting Versace suit and wide-brimmed felt hat. As always in front of the camera confessor, he was good-humoured and eloquent, unburdening himself about his new start, his weight loss, and his new diet. He described how he had put a stop to his excessive eating and drinking, and learned to be more satisfied with what he achieved in life, instead of always wanting more: 'I never gave myself time to stop and smell the roses. Well, now I can stop and I'm going to. I just want to smell a few roses.'

In addition to his new look and new attitude, Elton had also embarked on a new relationship. Hugh Williams was in his early thirties, a stocky, dark-haired man from Atlanta, where he owned the franchise to a Baskin-Robbins ice-cream parlour, who was quite different from the types to whom Elton was usually attracted. After his long-term pursuit of pleasure, he had finally met someone who had a life of his own – and, for the first time, someone with whom he wished to be monogamous. 'He's the love of my life. I'm so in love, it's wonderful,' Elton declared. Hugh had a settling influence and encouraged him to do the sort of ordinary, enjoyable things he had never done before. Elton had been to Paris many times to perform and to recuperate; he had worn the Eiffel Tower on his head and eaten it as a cake for his birthday, but when he went to Paris with Hugh he visited the landmark for the first time, purely for pleasure.

While the couple shared genuine happiness together, they also indulged in artificial stimulants. Before long, Hugh decided it was time to clean himself up, and he checked into a detoxification clinic in Arizona, which Elton interpreted as a sign of weakness. He was devastated and angry with Hugh for not being able to cope with his problems by himself. After a fiery visit to the hospital to see Hugh, he was so distraught that when he returned to their apartment, he wrecked it, tearing up all his precious photographs of Hugh. Convinced that the relationship was finished, Elton returned to London, where he stayed in his room and cried. 'Then I realized it was him I loved, there was no one else,' he said. It also occurred to him how much he admired Hugh for being courageous and honest enough to choose rehabilitation. Drugs had always influenced Elton badly, causing him to make irrational choices and decisions about his lovers, and so Elton decided that if he and Hugh were to have a future, he had to sort himself out.

Of his situation, Elton observed: 'He's tried to do something for himself, while here you are, fat, haven't washed for two weeks, vomit all over your dressing gown.' Indeed Elton had become a lazy and slovenly mess, living a typical addict's life, spinning webs of lies and deceit. Elton was in such a state of denial that he did not even think of himself as an addict. 'I thought addicts were people who stuck needles in their arms,' he said.

Having admitted to himself that he had major problems to overcome, Elton joined Hugh in some detox therapy sessions in Arizona. One of the tasks they faced together was to compile a list of what they believed to be the other's worst faults. Hugh was brutal: 'Elton does drugs, he's alcoholic, he's bulimic, he's a liar, he has terrible fits of rage.' Elton was stunned. His comparatively feeble offering referred to Hugh's inability to stack his CDs neatly.

The effect of Elton's dissipation had been to drive away all of those close to him, the ones who really cared. Elton said: 'The worst thing is that you isolate all your real friends.' His mother and stepfather had left the country, and his close friends had tried to warn him, but no one could get through. After his old friend Mike Hewitson (who is still part of the team) wrote to him saying, 'For Christ's sake, stop putting that stuff up your nose,' Elton was so enraged that he did not speak to him for a year. He did not want to hear the truth.

Once Elton had decided to seek proper help, it was almost impossible to find a clinic suitable to treat a patient with such a multiplicity of addictions. 'It was either clean up or die,' he said. 'Even though the dark side of me was thinking, well, you might as well die, I was saved by being all mouth and no trousers. I wanted to live.' He suddenly saw what his life had become and that the real Elton was intolerable.

Eventually he entered the Parkside Lutheran Hospital in Chicago on 29 July 1990, for a six-week course, checking in under one of his pseudonyms, George King. The conditions were far from luxurious – patients lived two to a room and had to do their own laundry. The new regime was a shocking confrontation with reality. All his wealth and fame could not shield him from the truths he had to face. It was an almost unbearable ordeal, so much so that he tried to run away twice because he hated being told what to do. When he started his treatment he had to describe how he felt, but found it difficult to express his feelings: 'I didn't have feelings. I was like an iceberg. All I felt was fear.'

One of his first tasks in therapy was to write an apology to all the people he had mistreated. He also wrote his history of drug and alcohol abuse, and a farewell letter to cocaine, a eulogy to his white mistress. 'In the lonely hours of pre-dawn light Mistress Cocaine calls you back – without me you are alone — and before the sun rises she has you again.' Bernie was moved to tears when

Elton read the letter to him, and responded with, 'You can write something like this, and you can't write lyrics?'

It was while Elton was being treated in Chicago that he renewed contact with his mother by letter. The bond was restored, resulting in Sheila and Fred's eventual return to England. They settled in Datchet, near Windsor, where, after a period of illness in Minorca, Sheila made a full recovery.

Elton was not the only one on whom the years of excess had taken a toll. It was reported that he had given John Reid an ultimatum: 'Get clean or I'll find myself another manager.' Reid checked into a detoxification clinic at the Cedars Sinai Medical Center, Los Angeles, in April 1990.

After drying out in Chicago, Elton returned to London to rent a modest house in the Holland Park area of west London, to try and give himself a taste of real life instead of living in splendid isolation in Windsor. He subsequently bought the house, known as Queensdale, which was renovated over a few months. Elton began doing things for himself – making his own breakfast, answering the phone and packing his own suitcases. He shared his home with an abandoned dog he adopted from Battersea Dogs' Home, a terrier called Thomas, who proved to be one of his best therapies. 'He helped me through a very bad time in my life,' he said. 'While I was at such a low ebb, Thomas was always there. He kept me company while giving me my own space.' During this transition period, to avoid stress and worry Elton's doctors advised him to take eighteen months rest from recording and performing.

He gave a frank interview to Radio One DJ Simon Bates, saying 'I've just got to get back to basics in my life . . . just noticing the sunset, sunrises, little things like that I lost touch with. I lost touch completely and it feels good to be back in contact with those sort of things.'

Through therapy Elton had begun to understand that his anger and resentment had not come from his upbringing or his relationship with his father, but from his work, which was so all-consuming that it left no time for anything else: 'It's going to take a long time to slow down but I've got to, because all I had was my career. I had no personal time and after a while you get bored with that and you get so self-centred. You don't realize it, but you do, and I was very unhappy with myself the way I was.'

Elton devoted himself to recovery and the process of throwing off his past meant that he was soon addicted to, or certainly dependant upon, therapy itself. He went to Alcoholics Anonymous meetings in west London to conquer his drink problem and would eventually attend more than 1,300 AA, Narcotics Anonymous and similar group meetings over the next three years. Like the others, he had to introduce himself and admit his problem: 'I'm Elton. I'm an alcoholic.' No one cared who he was. He would be there every morning at

7.30 a.m. taking the pledge with everyone else. He knew he had everything to lose if he was not committed to beating his addiction, and spoke to his AA sponsor every day to make sure he was.

Neither Elton nor Reid were quite so fiery after rehabilitation. All those around Elton observed the change. He had a new lightness of step, a fresh flurry of energy, a new radiance. He would come to the Rocket office frequently, often in fetching T-shirts and shorts that showed off his short Queen Anne legs, straight from the tennis court. He openly discussed his recovery with the girls in the office, and always had time to listen to stories of their lives and boyfriend problems. He might go up and play a few tunes on the piano, and if he was out of town he would ring every day for his record sales figures, introducing himself to the receptionist with a different pseudonym every time.

To celebrate Elton's twenty-five years as a recording artist, MCA released a four-CD boxed set, *To Be Continued,* as a greatest hits package in October 1990, although die-hard fans were hoping for a complete collection of rarities and out-takes. To satisfy the trainspotters there is a demo of 'Your Song', and the 1965 Bluesology single, 'Come Back, Baby', and the cds provide an extensive overview of his whole career. To add to the compilation Elton and Bernie recorded twelve new songs with producer Don Was, who was amazed at Elton's speed in the studio; he laid down four songs in one take. There was a minor moment over the American sleeve design, which was a colourful photo-montage that reminded Elton of his earlier excesses. Such was the transformation since embarking on his treatment, he demanded a more sophisticated, distinguished look, so that when the album was released in Britain the cover was much more subtle with large, tasteful photographs. He dedicated the boxed set to Hugh Williams, to acknowledge the significant role he had played in Elton's new sobriety.

Under doctor's orders, Elton devoted most of 1991 to his personal recovery and made only rare public appearances in the safe company of his mates. He supported his great friend Sting with a performance at his rainforest benefit concert in Carnegie Hall, New York, where they sang a duet of 'The Girl From Ipanema'. He celebrated his own birthday on stage with George Michael, and had some fun with his old sparring partner, Rod Stewart, on April Fool's Day. Together with Rod's management, he planned a trick right down to the last detail. Bob Halley was instructed to go out and buy a costume with all the trimmings, returning with a blonde wig, strapless gold gown with frills, and strappy shoes. On the first night of Rod's Wembley gigs, he was expecting his wife to appear, but it was quite another blond who tottered on stage and whispered, 'It's Sharon!' Although he had lost weight Elton still managed to look more like a middleweight boxer than a slimline babe. After Rod had regained his composure, the two sang a duet of 'You're In My Heart', while Elton sat on Rod's knee serving him brandy from a silver tray. Elton also performed light duties on the piano at a joint birthday party for Prince Andrew and Barry Humphries: he accompanied a trio of mermaids – Fergie, Pamela Stephenson and John Reid – who jumped out of a sardine box to serenade the birthday boys.

Elton had stripped away everything in his life and he began putting down new roots, imposing order on all his new possessions. All his trinkets were painstakingly positioned and had to be set down in exactly the same place after the precisely angled waft of a feather duster. There was a place and a time for everything; his birthday cards were only displayed on 25 March – by 26 March they had been cleared. He was on a strict diet and proved to be extremely self-sufficient. The kitchen was the hub of the new house – Elton liked to spend time there cracking jokes with his driver and unofficial bodyguard, Derek – also known as Deirdre, who had been with him for years – and Bob Halley, who no longer lived with Elton but drove over from his home in Sonning-on-Thames.

He also acquired an apartment in Atlanta in 1991, on the thirty-sixth floor of the exclusive Atlanta Condo in Park Place, West Peach Tree Street. Over the years, he would extend over five adjoining apartments, all knocked together to create a huge palace in the sky, complete with balconies landscaped with 16,000 plants and breathtaking views of the city. Elton briefed his interior designer, Fred Dilger, by handing him a pink rose and saying: 'Work from this. I want it to be scrumptious.' He wanted Dilger to take decorative cues from the Ritz Hotel in Paris and Gianni Versace's bathroom in Milan. It took a year to complete the work; the walls were scraped and repainted thirteen times to achieve the precise finish Elton required. According to one of Dilger's assistants, the colour of the walls was based around the colour of Elton's skin, in order to flatter him, so that he would look good everywhere in the apartment. It took four months to complete the 'shell room' alone, decorated with thousands of shells collected from Cornish beaches.

During this first year of restraint and sobriety, Elton took a holiday in the South of France while he was buying the Atlanta apartment. While visiting friends in Cahors during the annual photography festival there, he met David Fahey, a photography dealer, and for the first time became entranced by the power of photography. Since beginning to view the world with a new clarity, the directness of photography in some way reflected Elton's sober new vision of life. Although Elton had been photographed by world-class photographers in the past, he had never considered photography as an art form with intellectual depth, or something worth looking at. He thought of it merely as a publicity tool, a necessary evil, a threat, a critical eye, a weapon that could lay bare all his shortcomings. However, he was captivated by this new discovery and bought a dozen pictures from Fahey on the spot. As soon as he returned to Atlanta he found a photography dealer, and then another, and quickly learned how to buy works at auction. His new passion made him a dedicated student of photography and its history. From modern prints he graduated to vintage works by old masters such as Cartier-Bresson, Andre Kertesz and Man Ray. Elton sought out dealers in New York and London. He has built up a significant collection of more than 2,500 photographs and, as with pop music and football, now has an encyclopaedic knowledge of the subject. More than 900 prints hang on the walls of his Atlanta apartment, close together, floor to ceiling, all immaculately framed in white 22-carat gold. Elton likes to live with his pictures on display, not filed away in drawers. 'I've hated having my things shut away since I was a kid,' he said. He would become acknowledged by scholars, collectors and curators as the owner of one of the most important collections of twentieth-century photographs in the world. As well as his other accomplishments, Elton would become a grandee of the art world and in 1995 joined the Atlanta High Museum of Art's Director's Circle.

The misunderstandings and contradictions that had blighted Elton's adult relationship with his father all resurfaced when Stanley Dwight died on 15 December 1991, at his home in Hoylake, Cheshire, aged just sixty-six, after a long battle with chronic heart disease. Elton had last seen his father nine years previously, when proudly escorting him to the director's box for the Watford-Liverpool match at Anfield in 1982. In January 1983 his quadruple heart bypass operation had not been a complete success, and he had been forced to retire early from his job at Unilever. He had been in and out of hospital on numerous occasions, and aside from his heart problems, he had developed a duodenal ulcer and osteoarthritis, which confined him to a wheelchair.

Throughout Elton's *annus horribilis* in 1987, his father had been pestered by journalists for an inside story. Stanley refused to talk and gave Elton his total support, albeit from a distance, at one time writing to offer his son refuge should he need to get away, especially as Sheila had left the country. When his wife, Edna, once mentioned that people were saying that the *Sun*'s allegations might be true, she never saw Stanley react to anything so angrily. 'Don't ever let me hear you say that again,' he said. 'He's not guilty. He is my son.'

During his last days, his wife Edna and their four sons were at his bedside. Geoff Dwight remembered: 'He knew he didn't have long left, but someone comforted him, saying that he was leaving behind four great sons.' Stanley was quick to correct them, replying, 'No, you're wrong, I have *five* great sons.'

Stanley's health took a turn for the worse at the beginning of 1991, and Edna contacted Elton through John Reid's office. Elton called her from France to arrange a meeting because he would shortly be returning to England. However, not long afterwards, he appeared in an interview with David Frost on Sky Television, in which he discussed how he had feared his father during childhood, and yet what a good father Stanley had been to the four sons he had in his next marriage. Again tabloid journalists plagued the Dwight family home, and one reporter managed to charm Stanley into giving a brief interview. Splashed across the following week's *Sunday People* was: DYING DAD'S LOVE FOR ELTON. HE SENDS HEARTBREAK MESSAGE TO STAR THROUGH THE PEOPLE. In response to this and other embarrassing headlines, a furious Elton phoned Edna to say, 'Of course, I won't be meeting you now,' and he slammed the phone down. Stanley read the papers at breakfast and laughed out loud, imagining Sheila taking the Sunday papers up to Elton's bedroom, saying, 'Look at these, Elton!' mimicking his ex-wife to perfection.

After Stanley's death, Elton received word of the funeral arrangements from his half-brother, Geoff, who revealed, 'He was quite distant and offhand about it. He told me he had never really connected with our father, then he just thanked me for calling.' Elton decided not to attend the funeral, saying that he had made his peace with his father and that it would be hypocritical of him to be present at the ceremony. While the police were called in to escort the procession at the quiet family funeral, Elton, Stanley's beloved first-born, purveyor of sad songs and fan of funeral music, grieved for his father in his own way.

Elton did attend the funeral of his friend Freddie Mercury, who died of an AIDS-related disease aged forty-five on 24 November 1991. He introduced a BBC television tribute programme, describing Mercury as 'one of the most important figures in rock and roll in the last twenty years'. Another long-time associate, Dee Murray, his original bassist, also died following a stroke while suffering from cancer. In March 1992, Elton performed two emotional solo concerts in Murray's memory to raise money for his widow and children.

Weeks later Elton topped the bill at another memorial, the Freddie Mercury tribute 'Concert for Life' – a four-hour, five-star farewell to one of pop's greatest entertainers on 20 April 1992. The line-up included David Bowie, George Michael, Guns N' Roses, Annie Lennox and Seal, and every star who came on stage delivered a health warning – safe sex. The show was watched by an estimated half a billion television viewers in seventy countries. The organizers aimed to raise $15 million (£10 million) with a live video and album of the event. Elizabeth Taylor attended a pre-show party and was moved to tears when Elton presented her with a surprise gift of a $150,000 (£100,000) diamond ring in appreciation of her work for AIDS victims.

Elton sang Freddie's song 'The Show Must Go On' and duetted with Axl Rose, the controversial Guns N' Roses singer, in an emotional rendition of Queen's biggest hit, 'Bohemian Rhapsody', the song that Elton had been so dismissive of when it was first released. Their appearance together was intriguing, for in 1988 Elton had spoken out publicly against Guns N' Roses for their allegedly homophobic lyrics at an industry gathering. The London branch of ACT UP, the AIDS activist group, urged fans to boo Rose if he did not apologize for his alleged anti-gay lyrics and sentiments. When Rose came on stage would Elton keep his distance? The polite boy from Pinner had matured into a rock statesman and he reached out his arm in greeting, giving Rose the benefit of the doubt. 'We all say and do things we regret,' he said. 'I met him before the show and he seemed quite gentle, and I very much like some of his music.' Axl Rose would later credit Elton and Bernie for the inspiration they had given him, calling their work his 'classical music'.

The One was the album that celebrated Elton's return to the studio, sober; the first time he had recorded without the influence of drugs or alcohol since the early 1970s. On the first day of recording the pressure got too much and he had to go home after twenty minutes, but he kept his nerve and returned next day. The result was a collection of serious songs that were both touching and introspective, dealing with 'unpoppy' issues such as date rape, the disintegration of the family and overcoming adversity. Bernie submitted his lyrics mostly by fax, including 'The Last Song' about a father's reunion with his son who has AIDS. Elton received the lyrics in Paris, shortly after Freddie Mercury died, and was in tears as he wrote the melody. 'Simple Life' plainly alludes to Elton's new lifestyle. 'This album is like a new osmosis [*sic*] for me,' he said. 'It's kind of like I go in a caterpillar and come out a butterfly again.' Elton made up for the serious subject matter of the songs with his costume for the video for 'The Last Song'. Looking more like the Mayor of Munchkin City than a chastened addict, he showed off his waxed legs in skin-tight, zebra-patterned Lycra shorts, black, lacquered, square-toed slippers and a black frock coat.

Could *The One* compare with his classic early albums? Pop genres had come and gone in the intervening years. How would it stand against the music of a new generation of indie groups, growing up with rave and house music, in competition with bands like The Farm, Jesus Jones, EMF, Happy Mondays, the Stereo MCs, or boy bands such as Take That? Elton's fans bought enough copies to take it to number two in the British album charts and eight in America, and it was hailed a success.

After a three-year rest, he was ready to prove that he was fit enough to go back on the road, and launched what would become a 150-date world tour that would last until the end of 1993, joining up with Eric Clapton for a number of concerts. To make sure he kept fit, he took a full-time tennis coach as part of his entourage. Donald Watt, a former Scottish champion, said: 'Elton is not only a much improved tennis player, but in excellent shape and fitter than he has ever been.'

Elton began the tour in Oslo. On some occasions the gigs were AIDS benefits, at which he was joined by stars such as Sylvester Stallone and Sting. His great friend Gianni Versace, self-appointed emperor of fashion and master of the grand entrance, designed the set and Elton's costumes. During this tour he was calmer, less volatile; he would lock himself in his dressing room just before going on stage much less often. The atmosphere was more chamber orchestra than rock group, with nothing stronger than Earl Grey and Diet Coke on offer in the green room. When the American photographer Herb Ritts came to one of the gigs, he asked, 'Where's all the chaos?'

The new evangelistic Elton was a man with a message, winning praise for his sincerity and enthusiasm. However, fans and commentators alike were just as interested in the fashion statement Elton would make in his Versace outfit. He did not disappoint, wearing a yellow jacket with gold trimmings, low-cut red waistcoat, black trousers and motorcycle boots, plus pink-framed sunglasses and a new page-boy-style hair-weave. Between songs he mentioned his recovery and thanked his fans for being the one constant in his tumultuous life. He talked about losing many loved ones from AIDS, and performed 'The Last Song' and 'The Show Must Go On', in memory of Freddie Mercury. After six months on the road, Elton became exhausted once again, and so his doctors advised him to cancel three shows in Chile and Brazil, disappointing 20,000 fans. In contrast to the old days, Elton's music was upstaged by his wardrobe, but the reviews did not sparkle. Cliff Radel wrote in the *Cincinnati Enquirer*: 'The good news is he's healthy. The bad news is his show should see a doctor.'

Instead of a programme he produced a souvenir video, which was yet another camera confessional. A fit and slimmer Elton, sporting an auburn Beatles-esque mop, declares that he is over the dark days, offering a personal message to his fans after the break-up of his marriage and successfully overcoming his addictions.

After numerous vain attempts to disguise his baldness Elton had returned to his trichologist in Paris for a weave, which involved matting together the existing hairs and pulling them horizontally across the scalp, then twisting or sewing in fine human hair. It was said to have cost $22,500 (£15,000). 'I was tired of being bald and wearing hats,' he said with a smile. 'I knew I'd have to put up with all the "squirrel on your head" jokes in England, but it makes me feel better.'

Before the tour he granted an audience to an old supporter, Robert Hilburn, from *Rolling Stone*. He talked a great deal about the balance between his private life and the demands of his career. He could not afford to suffer a relapse into his former way of life and was concerned that habits associated with touring would set in again. Two days before rehearsals he ran away in a panic. His tendency to run away and hide in his room, or to block out reality with drugs, was still there, but he had begun to learn how to deal with it. He thought, 'I must not do this. This is going to take me away again.' Elton was looking forward to the American tour, not least because without booze and drugs he would be able to remember it afterwards.

Most public figures who were at any risk at all were keeping quiet about AIDS, but Elton was a loud and proud supporter of research, counselling and care of victims. He had donated $750,000 (£500,000) to British AIDS charities, from royalties. He donated all the royalties from his single, a live duet with George Michael of 'Don't Let The Sun Go Down On Me', which went to number one all over the world, to the Terrence Higgins Trust. In November 1992, he launched his own charity in order to have a bigger say in how the money was spent to help people with AIDS. He said: 'This is a terrible disease. I have lost many friends and know of many people who are either HIV-positive or have full-blown AIDS – not only men, but also women and children. I want to do whatever I can to help the fight against this disease.'

The Elton John AIDS Foundation was established with Elton as its chairman; its mission was to promote the welfare of people with HIV and AIDS by helping with medical and nursing care, providing facilities and equipment, and providing support for physical, mental and financial hardship of sufferers. The scope of the foundation was originally to fund British organizations, but with the rapid spread of the epidemic its remit became global, with funds being sent to support projects all over the world. The spread of the disease has remained unpredictable. Fewer people in Europe and America have been infected than were originally forecast, but AIDS has spread through Africa and Asia at an unforeseen, terrifying rate.

The foundation established international agencies in countries with high HIV prevalence, with the aim of teaching local people how to run their own support organizations so that the work will continue when the international teams move out. Funds go towards training doctors, nurses and volunteers in primary healthcare so that help can be given locally where it is needed. The foundation also works with the most prominent international AIDS agencies, including the United Nations, and government agencies from Britain, America, Australia, Thailand and South Africa, as well as many international charities.

Elton appointed his right-hand man, Robert Key, as executive director of EJAF. Nicola Greening, the receptionist, remembers 'young, gorgeous guys' coming to meet Robert to ask for grants for housing, because obtaining a mortgage is impossible with an AIDS diagnosis.

Elton promised to donate the proceeds from all his singles released anywhere in the world to the foundation, although this did not altogether suit his accounts department, who had responsibility for paying his vast credit card bills every month.

Some of the tabloids had not learned from the *Sun*'s failure to check its facts in 1987. In December 1992, Elton received a panicked phone call from his mother who read him the *Sunday Mirror*'s front page: ELTON'S DIET OF DEATH. As his mother's words sank in he felt incensed and completely outraged. The article described how Elton was allegedly seen at a Hollywood party hosted by John Reid, chewing shrimp and crab canapés and then spitting them out into a napkin. Elton was alleged to have said that it was a way of keeping his weight down, but the article went on to suggest that he had faltered in his battle to conquer bulimia. The paper helpfully quoted a medical expert who said that the diet was potentially fatal, and that Elton was killing himself with a diet that compelled him to behave in a 'disgusting and shocking way'. The story came from three women who had gatecrashed the party and been thrown out. Elton was understandably angry and dismayed, and immediately issued a writ against the *Sunday Mirror* for exemplary damages for the paper's recklessness in publishing a completely inaccurate story without making adequate checks. At the time of Reid's party he was thousands of miles away in Atlanta. With Elton recovering from near addiction to therapy itself, having attended well over a thousand meetings with Alcoholics Anonymous, Narcotics Anonymous and Over-Eaters Anonymous, it was a cruel blow that might have tipped a weaker man back into the abyss. The newspaper offered to apologize but denied libel, admitting that its sources had made a mistake. Elton's paper boy would have one less title to deliver for the time being.

Elton was thought to be unhappy with MCA's marketing of his music since the débâcle over *Sleeping With The Past*, and he was tempted to sign to Polygram for $13.5 million (£9 million). But in November 1992, Elton and Bernie signed a record-breaking deal with Warner Chappell, giving them the biggest advance in music history – $39 million (£26 million) was twice the amount given to Prince two months before. The agreement allowed the pair to retain ownership of their catalogue since 1974 and gave the music publishing arm, Warner Chappell Music, the largest music publishing company in the world, sole right to market their catalogue since 1974, plus material from the next six albums. Les Bider, chairman of Warner Chappell, called Elton 'one of the last of the great superstars' and compared him and Bernie to George and Ira Gershwin. He said: 'They are among the finest writers of popular songs ever, including The Beatles. Elton's music crosses universal boundaries of taste.'

After earning $6 million (£4 million) appearing in a series of television commercials for his new favourite drink, Diet Coke, it was widely thought that Elton was securing his financial future for retirement. The campaign emphasized his new clean image, as much as his massive consumption of Coke rather than coke.

Elton began 1993 with another camera confessional on the UK breakfast programme *GMTV*, in which he talked about his former self. 'I was practically insane,' he said. 'Basically, I played God and I was God. What I said was gospel.' He described how once, when staying at a London hotel, he was annoyed about the blustery weather, and turning to the faithful Bob Halley, asked, 'Can't you do something about the wind?'

In January 1993, he finally severed his professional connection with his beloved Watford, resigning as director of the club because his international commitments were getting in the way of his director's duties. He had only been able to attend Vicarage Road once in the previous four months, although he kept up with their results through Clubcall by telephone, at a cost of $150 (£100) a week. Chairman Jack Petchey said, 'We want to see him back at Vicarage Road as soon as his commitments allow. His part in the development of the club will always be treasured.'

As well as taking legal action against the *Sunday Mirror*, Elton took steps to prevent revelations by his former Australian friend, Gary Clarke, being played on an 0898 telephone line. However, he could not prevent the publication of a revealing book about their time together. While he completed the final leg of his world tour in Australia, he was forced to cut short a concert in Clarke's home city of Melbourne, when a plague of grasshoppers invaded the stage, attracted by the warm weather and bright lights. They got in his hair, his clothes and his mouth, and as Elton stamped on one of the insects, he muttered, 'I've just killed a dirty little bug. I think his name was Gary.' Later Elton confronted the camera and his past saying that he should shoulder everything that was written about him, but he would allow himself to make the odd slur, in jest, of course. The concert was restaged after a visit from the pest controllers.

Elton was becoming more and more relaxed and open about his sexuality after much brow-beating since 1976. He appeared on stage in May dancing back-to-back with a statuesque black singer and quipped, 'That was what you call safe sex – she's certainly safe from me.' Humour gave way to compassion when he gave one of his greatest fans, Diana, Princess of Wales, a hug while she visited him back-stage. The Princess was putting a brave face on her troubles when coming to terms with being alone and struggling to find herself a public role, just after her separation from Prince Charles and the publication of the Camilla-gate tapes. She knew exactly who to turn to for a sympathetic cuddle and a joke.

Although Elton had completed his world tour, he went back on the road again in the spring for twenty more shows in America, which he performed solo at a grand piano, accompanied by his favourite percussionist Ray Cooper. The shows featured many of his old 1970s hits, and in a rare moment of doubt about his memory, he sang with the help of an inconspicuous teleprompter. The shows did not suffer and he impressed the critics. 'The elder statesman of rock isn't resting on his laurels. John played his instrument with passion and agility,' wrote Sarah Rodman in the *Boston Herald*. He took the show on to South Africa for four further dates with Ray Cooper.

Elton's new laidback persona was severely tested in June when he caused a minor international incident in Israel. His visit to the Holy Land for an open-air concert lasted just two hours before he turned tail and headed home. Security arrangements appeared to be non-existent at Tel Aviv's Ben-Gurion airport and Elton was anxious about his safety, as he had to sign autographs while he waited with other passengers at passport control. After a scuffle broke out at his hotel between photographers and Elton's bodyguards, who tried to stop them from taking pictures, he ordered his limousine back to the airport. Meanwhile, he leaped over a sofa in the lobby of the Tel Aviv Hilton Hotel to avoid a stampede of people surging towards him. 'You should have seen us,' he told the girls in his office. 'We jumped over the seats waving our handbags, darlings!' Elton claimed that his safety had been threatened by a lack of VIP treatment at both the airport and the hotel, and over-zealous media attention. It took the intervention of the British ambassador to restore harmony and persuade him to return to Israel to restage the concert next day, on condition that security was stepped up. Israel was keen to end years in the rock-and-roll wilderness, and there was relief all round when Elton agreed. Before the ambassador's announcement four out of forty thousand disappointed fans had gone to court demanding $20,000 (£13,300) in damages for the cost of their tickets, loss of enjoyment and mental suffering. Twenty-four hours later Elton finally made it on stage, where he graciously apologized to his fans.

Elton returned to his television counselling couch on the American show *Entertainment Tonight*. He told the world about his new companion, estate agent John Scott, through whom he had bought his Atlanta apartment. A monogamous relationship, he had found happiness with Scott, but confessed that he had been lucky to escape AIDS after a string of gay lovers over a seventeen-year period, and blamed his dangerous behaviour on drugs and drink. 'You don't stay up three days at a time doing drugs, then sleep for two, eat for three and not be lucky to be alive,' he said. 'I'd be on my hands and knees searching the carpet for cocaine. I became like an animal, a pig.' He also described his bulimia in painful detail: 'I was paranoid about my weight, so I would pig out and make myself sick. I wouldn't wash and I'd vomit on my dressing gown. I was living a hell on earth.'

Still in confessional mode, he poured out his heart to gay magazine *10 PerCent*, confirming that the years of torment when he had tried to be straight were long behind him. He had overcome the fear that his sexuality might affect his popularity and described himself as a committed gay activist, saying, 'We're everywhere folks!'

When Elton's libel case against the *Sunday Mirror* came to court in November 1993, the jury awarded him $525,000 (£350,000), another record sum in damages. Elton had not gone to court for the money, but in the hope that this award would curb the excesses of the tabloid press once and for all. He had wanted to punish the paper and would donate most of the money to charity.

The *Sunday Mirror* was also faced with a bill of up to $300,000 (£200,000) in costs. Claiming that the article was written in good faith and that it was a clear case of mistaken identity, the paper refused to apologize. The jury agreed that the article was libellous because Elton had publicly stated that he had overcome his addictions, including bulimia in particular, and the paper in effect accused him of being a hypocrite and a failure. He was setting an example to others in trying to beat their addictions and the article accused him of relapsing. It was somewhat preposterous to suggest mistaken identity when the subject was one of the best known faces in the world.

Now that he was sober and living a more balanced lifestyle, it was time for another clear-out. In July 1993, he sold off his entire record collection of 25,000 albums and 23,000 singles which, if laid out flat, would cover twelve tennis courts. The auction raised $271,500 (£181,000), which he donated to the Terrence Higgins Trust. Among the records were rare demos by The Beatles, David Bowie, Marc Bolan and the Rolling Stones. The anonymous bidder from St Louis, Missouri, said: 'There are records in here by artists I have never even heard of.' They were a bargain at $5.63 (£3.75) each. Elton certainly hadn't lost interest in his collection – it was now on CD and he needed the space. In London he goes to the same shop every Monday. 'I like nothing better than to go to the CD shop and spend an hour there. I enjoy going rummaging about,' he told Jonathan Ross on BBC Radio Two. When he is away, the office orders five copies of the latest CDs every week, one for each home. If a particular new artist takes his fancy, the great pop educator and enthusiast will insist on buying even more copies to distribute to friends.

Elton had another low-key, pre-Christmas jewellery sale at Sotheby's – just the items he no longer used – to make way for a new passion, Staffordshire pottery and paintings by Gainsborough. The collection was a dazzling display of rings, watches, bracelets and brooches. The items he valued most were his hundreds of watches, many encrusted with gold and diamonds, and most of which he was not planning to part with. He said in the sale catalogue: 'Collecting is my passion. I love wearing jewellery, but I can't stop buying more.' Among the hundred pieces up for grabs were an onyx ruby and diamond brooch designed as a Watford FC rosette, a birthday present from his manager, Reid. It was inscribed, 'To EJ on your 38th birthday. Love JR.' The ultimate piece in the sale was a tortoise-shell walking cane topped with a gold and diamond encrusted bust of Napoleon, which had featured on the cover of his album *Ice On Fire*, but Elton withdrew it minutes before the sale for 'sentimental reasons'. The jewellery sale raised nearly $1.5 million (£1 million), $375,000 (£250,000) more than expected.

The AIDS Foundation is a perfect vehicle for Elton's flair as a party host and entertainer. His birthday, on 25 March, falls around the time of the Academy Awards and each year he celebrates in Hollywood by hosting a glittering Oscars' party at which he raises funds for the AIDS Foundation. Elton's Oscars' party has become one of the most prestigious events of the celebrity year. He hosts a glamorous evening at a Los Angeles restaurant and invites friends, celebrities and of course Oscar winners, to gossip, eat, drink and listen to him sing. Each guest takes away a goodie bag filled with CDs, perfume, cosmetics and chocolates.

At Christmas Elton's generous spirit also knows no bounds where friends and employees are concerned, or so everyone in the Rocket office thought. Expectations were high: people towards the top of the hierarchy usually received a little bauble from Theo Fennell, Elton's favourite jeweller; those lower down would be given a $300 (£200) Harrods voucher. But this year was different, and Elton would not be Lady Bountiful this time around. He knew people were expecting something nice but he felt hurt and used – last year, to his immense disappointment, no one had even said thank you.

chapter thirteen

Dreamboat

ELTON'S LIFE SO FAR resembled something of a rock-and-roll morality tale with more than a touch of pantomime. But on Halloween 1993 he met his Prince Charming, and together they would become the most famous gay couple in the world.

Elton returned home from Atlanta after splitting up with John Scott feeling defiant but deflated, and decided not to look for another relationship. 'I'm going to play the field, stay single, because obviously I'm not meant to be in a relationship,' he said. The prospect of the field was grim because all his gay friends in London had either died or moved away, and he was out of the social loop after his long world tour. To extend his circle, he asked a friend to round up some people for an informal dinner at Woodside.

When David Furnish arrived at the table it was love at first sight, but the meeting nearly did not happen at all. 'I got the call at 4 p.m. on my answering machine. I had other plans for that night and my first reaction was to say no,' recalls David. He was not in the habit of going to dinner with strangers, famous or not, and did not want to be picked up by Elton's chauffeur. However, he did think that it would be an opportunity to meet a unique man and so he drove to Windsor in his own car so that he could make a quick getaway if necessary. But David warmed to Elton immediately. 'He didn't behave like a star at all, he was so down to earth. I thought he'd be all showbizzy and want to talk about himself all the time. I wasn't really that big a fan. I loved his earlier albums when I was growing up, but that sort of drifted away,' he said.

There were no footmen or servants, just a housekeeper to serve spaghetti bolognese. Far from spending the evening regaling his guests with rock-and-roll tales, Elton was genuinely interested in all eight people around the table, asking about their lives, families and friends. David was the quietest of the party, his soft Canadian accent barely heard above the other guests. Elton talked to David about paintings and films, and he realized there was something special about him. 'I hadn't met anyone like him before,' said Elton. By the end of the evening something had clicked between them.

'I'm wary about using the phrase "love at first sight" but it was something close to it,' said David. 'There was a definite mutual attraction. I was at a stage when I was ready to meet someone and for him it was much the same.'

When the evening drew to a close they knew things could not end there. Elton phoned David next morning. He was up at the crack of dawn but waited until a civilized eleven o'clock before dialling David's number. 'Thank God I made that one call to him,' said Elton. 'Years ago I wouldn't have made that phone call. I would have sat there feeling sorry for myself, shut in a room, and pined.' Twenty-four hours later the relationship took off. Elton invited David to his Holland Park house the next evening for a Chinese takeaway, ordered from Mr Chow's in Knightsbridge. Elton took personal care of every detail. Lin Watson, Elton's housekeeper, remembers: 'Elton was grinning from ear to ear. He invited David to dinner and it was the only time I saw Elton hands-on. He got into the stock cupboard where all the different china is kept. He chose the china and the candlesticks, even though they were only having a takeaway.' When David arrived, Elton, unusually, gave his staff the night off. Lin recalls: 'The next day he couldn't stop talking about him, it was obviously love from the word go.' It was not long before Elton announced that David would be moving in.

It was a momentous and extraordinary time for David. Elton was in court every day during his libel case against the *Mirror*, while David was carrying on life as normal; he would go to work and read the newspapers only to see his new lover on all the front pages. From the beginning he was aware that his life would change: 'I knew that being involved with someone so famous would mean that things would never be the same again.' That first Christmas, just weeks after they had met, David not only had to tell his parents that he was moving in with Elton John, but also to drop the bombshell that he was gay.

Born in 1962, David grew up in a secure and happy family atmosphere in the comfortable middle-class suburb of Scarborough, Toronto, the middle son of a successful accountant, Jack, and his wife, Gladys. After school, he studied at the University of Western Ontario in London, Canada, where he gained his Bachelor of Arts degree. He was ambitious with a strong work ethic. Growing up, he had a paper round, worked in a video store and set up a successful poolside catering company at a local golf and tennis club.

A cinema fanatic, David had refined cultural tastes and would often visit the National Ballet in Toronto, sometimes on his own, though this handsome, easy-going young man with polished manners was always popular with girls. As much as he loved women, David could not make a real sexual connection, and came out in his second year at university. He owned up to his mother, but she assumed it was just a phase and that he would grow out of it. Naturally

David was bewildered, and during one attempt to find the right girl, he had a girlfriend and a boyfriend at the same time.

His colleagues at work had no idea. 'David and I worked quite closely together but I never dreamt he was gay,' remembers one workmate. 'He would come in on Monday morning and I would say, "How were the chicks over the weekend?" silly boyish banter. David would just smile and make some polite comment.'

His personal confusion drove him to leave Canada at the age of twenty-seven, to make a fresh start in London, a large, anonymous city. 'I ran away because I hadn't dealt with my sexuality. I didn't want to let my family down, so I put an ocean between us,' he said. It was not until his relationship with Elton was about to become public that he braced himself to tell his family – he did not want them to read about it in the press. When the time came, he said he was petrified. 'I was raised to believe it was a sin and there was no future in it. But my father and mother were brilliant. They have been incredibly supportive and are very fond of Elton.' Now David's family – his parents, brothers and their three children, whom Elton adores – are welcome visitors.

In London David went to work for the top advertising agency Ogilvy and Mather, where he spent nine years as an account executive and eventually became the youngest member of the board of directors. At first David kept his other life secret from his colleagues, but they must have suspected that something was up when David started dressing with a little more flair – Versace rather than Marks and Spencer, and the plain white shirt buttons turned to solid gold. When Elton phoned David at the office he would use one of his pseudonyms, such as George King, but their cover was blown when they were snapped getting out of a car together at a London film première. When David walked into the office next day all conversation suddenly stopped. After demure denials to his colleagues, David told the managing director, who said: 'David, I know how happy you've been lately. Where you get that happiness from is your business.'

The strain of keeping up with his superstar boyfriend was beginning to tell. David would leave work on Friday evenings, dash to the airport and fly to join Elton in Atlanta, if he was in America. He would be back at his desk on Monday morning distinctly jet-lagged. According to a colleague at Ogilvy and Mather, there was a redistribution of company cars at the time and David was keen on the BMW convertible that had been allocated to his boss. He was disappointed to have been overlooked, but the next week apologized to his boss for his bad humour. He added that he had sorted out his car problem and when the boss asked what he had in mind, David replied, 'It's a toss up between an Aston Martin or a Ferrari.'

Elton went to extraordinary lengths to keep the relationship secret and avoid being photographed with David. Above all, he wanted to protect David from the lurid glare of the limelight. Elton's recent partners had been hounded by the press, their faces plastered across the front pages of tabloids around the world, only for the relationship to end, but that was the last thing he wanted this time. At the beginning of the relationship David ignored rumour or innuendo that suggested that he was just another of Elton's little friends on the conveyor belt, headed for a Cartier watch and Versace suit kiss-off.

David was different. His uncamp charm and self-assurance were foils to Elton's theatrical tendencies and bouts of low self-esteem. David's level-headedness fortified the relationship and boosted Elton's self-confidence. 'He's had a crazy past, but I don't begrudge him that,' said David. 'It has helped shape him and he's learned from it. He wouldn't be the man he is today without it.' David does not bother himself with the salacious and sometimes bitter material written by Elton's aggrieved ex-lovers. 'I've never read a book about Elton,' he said, 'because he can't go into a bookshop and read a book about me.'

David was relieved when their cover was blown and the press found out about their relationship. Despite his impeccable manners and passive nature he would not have been content to lurk in the shadows. 'I found it humiliating to be snuck in and out of back doors to sit in a car behind Elton's car. It is not honest.' At first David hated being referred to as 'Elton John's boyfriend', but he learned to cope and soon asserted his identity.

Elton has credited David with saving his life, and admitted: 'David gives me a lot of love which I find very difficult – and yes, it is what I've always wanted. I've always wanted my relationships to go on forever. I always thought my relationships failed because I was impossible. I hope this one will last to the end.' David has had a remarkable effect on him, although David is equally generous to Elton saying that he has been good for him too: 'It has been wonderful to watch him learn to love and like himself after so long. Elton had a lot of demons to purge and it can't be done overnight. But he's getting there.'

Although David is not football-mad like Elton, they share a love of tennis and David keeps fit, going to the gym regularly, riding in Windsor Great Park and enjoying water sports. They are both incurable romantics and every Saturday, because it was the day they met, they send each other cards or flowers if they are apart. From time to time, they spend months apart and speak on the phone every day. Elton's energy sometimes wears David out. 'Living with Elton is totally exhausting,' said David. 'He may be fifteen years older than I am but he has far more energy. He lives life at an incredible pace. He is complex and driven, compassionate and passionate.' Soon after they met, Elton told him: 'One year with me is like ten years with someone else.'

Life is not all a bed of roses, however. 'We have our rows,' David has admitted. 'Both of us are strong characters and sometimes it boils over.'

Elton began the new year as one half of a happy couple and visibly more comfortable with himself, establishing a pattern of making new friends and collaborating with old ones, socially and professionally. He was inducted into the Rock and Roll Hall of Fame by his old sparring partner and admirer, Axl Rose, and he dedicated the award to Bernie. He recorded a dance version of 'Don't Go Breaking My Heart' as a duet with the statuesque drag queen and self-styled 'Queen of All Media', Ru Paul. The song was a worldwide smash and in an evening of wise-cracks and make-up tips, they co-hosted the 1994 BRIT Awards.

Work-wise, Elton was ready for something new. He had known the lyricist Tim Rice since 1970, when they were both MCA artists. They met at one of Elton's first gigs at the Fillmore East, New York, while Rice was promoting his musical *Jesus Christ Superstar*. Rice was impressed by Elton's musicianship, even though he was worried that MCA might be putting more energy into promoting their rock superstar than his biblical one. 'Elton established himself not through a wacky stage persona, but by a string of extraordinarily good songs,' remembered Rice, who wrote the lyrics for Elton's song 'The Legal Boys' in 1981. Best known for his collaborations with composer Andrew Lloyd Webber on the musicals *Jesus Christ Superstar* and *Evita*, Disney approached Rice to write the words for its new animated movie, *The Lion King*. They asked him to suggest composers and he put Elton's name forward for half a dozen numbers. Elton jumped at the chance, not only to create music for a different medium, but to work with Walt Disney. 'Those films are around forever and they are the best at it,' Elton said. Unusually for Disney, the story was written from scratch and Rice spent a little longer on the lyrics than Elton did on the music. Like Bernie, Rice would send lyrics off to Elton and, only two or three days later, a beautifully recorded CD would return.

Elton's collaboration with Rice has an entirely different signature from his work with Bernie – he was, after all, composing to a brief and not to complement his soulmate's raw, immediate lyrics. One of Rice's lines read, 'When I was a young warthog . . .' After all his years of undignified eating habits and scraping cocaine from the carpet, Elton thought to himself, as he cried with laughter, 'Has it come to this?'

Elton sang on three of the songs on the album, which sold over seven million copies in 1994. Three of his songs were nominated for Oscars and 'Can You Feel The Love Tonight?' won a Grammy and an Oscar for Best Original Song in 1995. 'Our songs were a vital reason the film was so big,' said Rice. 'It wasn't just big, it was mega.' It paved the way for Elton to work on *The Lion*

King stage show, which has been a huge success in New York, London and Los Angeles. He now has a new generation of six-year-old fans, who pester him at airports and tell him they love his Lion King songs. 'Can You Feel The Love Tonight?' also set a new record for Elton, making him the first artist to achieve a top-forty hit in America for twenty-five consecutive years.

Another of Elton's heroes is the American star, Billy Joel. The two met in the mid-1970s in Amsterdam through John Reid, and remained friends ever since. In early 1994 Joel suggested that they go on the road together – it became a twenty-one-date tour of America as a celebration of piano rock. The two singers played centre stage on two grand pianos and then performed a set, each with their own bands. The two bands jammed later in the concerts with storming performances of songs that had influenced both Elton and Joel, such as The Beatles' 'A Hard Day's Night', Little Richard's 'Lucille' and Jerry Lee Lewis's 'Great Balls of Fire'. As a finale they performed 'Piano Man' sung as 'Piano Men' with Elton on a Yamaha and Joel on his Steinway. The tour succeeded beyond all expectations, grossing $47 million (£31.3 million).

In November 1994, Elton inaugurated an event that would become a charity sale to outclass any thrift shop. His first 'Out of the Closet' sale, to raise funds for the Elton John AIDS Foundation, took place in a shop in Fulham Road, London, which he filled with his cast-offs from three decades of bulk-buying. While fans with only a few hundred pounds to spend might not have been able to afford anything at Sotheby's in 1988, his clothes (many in duplicate, various sizes) and shoes (size eight only) were now well within their reach. Elton's wardrobe master, Bob Stacey, was not worried that Elton would be left with nothing to wear: 'He's got roomfuls of gear at home in Windsor.' The sales became a regular way of making extra space for new clothes in his other homes. In June 1996 he held a sale in the Atlanta branch of Neiman Marcus, the department store. After opening the sale, he scuttled off and bought back one of his favourite jackets.

Bolstered by the enormous success of *The Lion King* and his Oscar nomination, Elton spent the end of 1994 and the beginning of the new year in the studio working on his album, *Made In England,* released during the Britpop era of Blur, Oasis and Pulp. The theme was a reflection on his roots with musical, if not lyrical, references to The Beatles on every track. He co-produced it with Greg Penny, who called on George Martin, The Beatles' producer, to arrange the track 'Latitude'. The title track is autobiographical and alludes to his early heroes Elvis and Little Richard. This time, Bernie wrote the lyrics at the studio. Elton asked him to write a set of words that he could relate to and Elton felt closer to this collection of songs than anything he had done in twenty years. Elton would usually record and then go shopping during post-production, but this time he was hands-on throughout the process. 'I wouldn't be there for half of it,' he said of past album recordings. 'I don't want to do that any more. An artist doesn't let someone else finish off his paintings, does he?'

Elton invited his guitarist, Davey Johnstone, to re-join the band and Paul Buckmaster returned as arranger. Elton really believed in his latest work: 'Since I've been sober I've made three albums and this is the best.' He made himself available for the worldwide publicity campaign, even signing autographs with Bernie at Tower Records in Los Angeles after midnight on the day of its release. It caused a family storm over the lyric, 'I had a quit-me father and a love-me mother'. His half-brother, Geoff, spoke out angrily saying, 'I don't think what he sings and what the truth is are necessarily the same thing. His father loved him to bits.' The reviews were generous; *Rolling Stone* described it as 'a startlingly fine album' and *The Times* called it 'a strong set from an enlightened survivor: pungent, coherent, brimming with good tunes'. It entered the American charts at number thirteen, the highest debut since *Blue Moves* in 1976, and peaked at number three in Britain.

Within a year of meeting Elton, David was confident enough in the relationship to leave his job and reinvent himself professionally. He launched his career as a film-maker, thus fulfilling of one of his earliest ambitions. With Elton, he set up Rocket Pictures. David's first activities as chief executive included assembling a slate of potential projects by optioning novels, reading scripts and meeting writers and directors. However, the project that would launch David's film-making career marked the end of his honeymoon period with Elton. There had never been a serious arts documentary about Elton John before, but that was not the intention of *Tantrums and Tiaras*.

A cinema buff since his teens, David had run the university film society, and he enrolled on various courses at the British Film Institute when he came to London. It was Elton's idea that David should make a fly-on-the-wall video diary of a year in his life, during his gruelling world tour of 1995. For an aspiring film-maker it was the offer of a lifetime – but was David brave enough to risk his precious relationship with Elton by pointing a camera at him for a year? Elton is not the camera's biggest fan, after all. David would have to know where to draw the line between reasonable and unreasonable invasion of Elton's psyche. But from Elton's perspective, offering himself up to David's camera was the consummate gift he could bestow upon his lover.

They agreed that it would not be a straight, tasteful and reverential arts documentary, which may have been why the BBC rejected it. In the event it was broadcast by Carlton, on the ITV network, well after the watershed hour. Elton said: 'As my Nan would have said, there's no room for bullshit.'

It seemed only natural that Elton should want to be the subject of his boyfriend's first film, which was effectively a narcissistic video diary in which he allowed a complete invasion of his privacy. The film was an unlikely marriage of kiss-and-tell confessional and home movie, which at times made the viewer feel like a voyeur. Due to the closeness of their relationship, David could ask the sort of questions which would have been impossible for an outsider to voice, and once Elton got used to being filmed, he gave honest responses. David knew Elton would give good screen value. 'He's learned that a happy and burden-free life comes out of being honest,' said David. 'So I think that was why he was willing to open himself up in the way that he did.' And David was uniquely able to capture the strange abnormalities of celebrity with objectivity because he was still a relative outsider – he had known Elton for two years but would never be his poodle. There was no outside backer for the project at first, and it is a measure of David's desire to be independent that he put all his own savings into getting the film off the ground.

It proved to be a bold move for both men. Elton wanted his fans to see him at work, rest and play, and the film reveals a range of delightfully contradictory Eltons: crazy but sane, the camp clown, the spoilt brat, the tireless charity worker, the shy extrovert, the devoted son, grandson and ex-husband, the reformed addict. He was nervous and confident, hateful and affectionate. David shouldered all the risks in the project and Elton allowed him editorial control, trusting that David would to make an honest, revealing and edgy film, warts and all. He said to David, 'I don't care how badly I come out of it, I just want people to see how I am and to know what actually goes on – the pressure, the bad behaviour, the good behaviour, the relationships, whatever happens on a year of touring.' Quite soon he became oblivious to David's small video-camera.

Charity benefits and collaborations were by now a regular part of Elton's work. He performed at an all-star concert at the Commitment to Life AIDS benefit for Bernie who was a co-producer, then went to Japan with Ray Cooper and to America with Billy Joel for another Piano Men show. He joined Bruce Springsteen, Paul Simon, Jon Bon Jovi, James Taylor and Jessye Norman at Sting's Rainforest benefit concert. He promoted *Made In England* on a US tour with his full band. In October he showed off his vaudevillian credentials and appeared on stage in drag as Elton Jane in a little black dress, blond wig and black stilettos, singing a duet of the old Andrews Sisters' song, 'Sisters' with Kylie Minogue at the Stonewall Equality Show at London's Royal Albert Hall, in aid of gay rights. One of the things he adores about England is that, straight or gay, Englishmen can't resist jumping into drag.

Elton and Gianni Versace threw a glittering party in the Versace gallery in London's Bond Street to launch Versace's new book *Men Without Ties,* in support of the Elton John AIDS Foundation. Wags at the party dubbed it 'Men Without Trousers'. Appearing with David, on only his second public outing since meeting, they wore 'his and his' co-ordinating pink and lilac suits with matching shoes; happy to demonstrate their closeness, they were reported to have fed each other oysters from a seafood tower and swapped kisses. Tickets were in short supply but 700 celebrities paid $150 (£100) each for entry, including Rod Stewart, Michael Caine, George Michael, Catherine Zeta Jones and Bob Geldof.

Elton caused a minor sensation on stage at his beloved Madison Square Garden in New York in October 1995 by wearing a gold band on the third finger of his left hand. During the concert he broke off to give an emotional tribute to his 'Mum, Dad and in-laws', when a woman from the crowd called out, 'Who's your wife, Elton?' Sitting at the piano, he looked at the audience across his right shoulder and smiled enigmatically. Such provocation tends to drive the tabloids wild, but the ring was explained by his publicist, Sarah McMullen, who pointed out for those who had not noticed, 'He wears all kinds of jewellery.' Elton later announced: 'I think it's the first time I've been happy living in this skin since I was born.'

The couple succeeded in keeping their relationship private for nearly two years. Life was settled but there is never a typical day in Elton's life; seven days a week there is something going on. His day would start with a rinse and style by his live-in hairdresser, followed by tennis before breakfast with his coach who was on permanent standby at Windsor. David spent more time at the London house when he first moved in, to be near friends and colleagues who would often visit the house for parties. Through David, Elton was meeting new people – actors, film-makers and media types.

As an energetic collector, Elton has played with many styles of interior decoration. His townhouse in London is an immaculate repository for Biedermeier furniture, an understated yet decorative style popular in Germany in the mid-nineteenth century. Examples fill almost every room – tables, sideboards, beds, pedestals. Every dust-free surface is covered with a profusion of opulently framed photographs, porcelain ornaments of cherubs and puppies, antique Lalique glass, equine statuettes, heart-shaped Limoges pill boxes, paperweights and endless trinkets. Everything, including the kitchen sink, must be pristine – he once left staff a note: 'The sink needs Ajaxing. Love, housewife of the year.'

There is a constant programme of home improvements with a flow of builders and decorators in all his houses. If there is so much as a scratch on a skirting board the whole thing has to be stripped down and redecorated. Everything in the house is immaculate, from woodwork to jasmine-scented candles. Flowers bring life to the houses, arranged by two florists who visit once or twice a week. He likes to have a succession of different displays because, according to his housekeeper, his threshold of boredom is so fine.

When he comes home he changes into a bathrobe and rolls around the floor with his dogs, telling them how much he has missed them and how he keeps their photographs with him when he is away. He has twenty, each with its own territory and individual Wedgwood bowl, in one or other of his houses. He prefers dogs that have been abandoned and rescued because he thinks they love him more for saving them. On one occasion Billie Jean King called Elton to tell him of a little dog she had seen in an underpass being pelted with stones by children. She took it to the police station but there was little they could do. Elton took the dog to join his gang at Windsor. The dogs are not allowed in the bedrooms but like sitting on the sofas.

Elton's new-found happiness with David was public knowledge by 1996, and for his lover's birthday he hosted a lunch at The Ivy in Soho and gave him a $117,000 (£78,000) Aston Martin. To crown a happy year, Elton achieved another step up in society in 1996 when he was awarded a CBE in the Queen's new-year honours list.

Birthdays are special to Elton and his parties have become something of a highlight in the social calendar – he is usually in Hollywood for his Oscars' party. That year he was unamused to be awoken by a 'Happy Birthday' serenade on bagpipes beneath the window of his suite at the Four Seasons Hotel in Los Angeles. His mood changed for the better when the piper informed him that he was playing with compliments and best wishes from Rod Stewart. He promised he would repay the compliment when Rod was least expecting it. He returned to London to host a fancy-dress party, with a ballroom theme, at which he arrived in a full-bottomed eighteenth-century wig, his round face adorned with round specs framed by curls. His squat frame was adorned with satin breeches and an elaborately embroidered satin jacket with lace collar and cuffs.

Tantrums and Tiaras was broadcast in July 1996 and Elton was so pleased with the final cut that he watched it twenty times on the trot. 'I've been amazed at the number of people that he's had round to the house for screenings,' said David.

The film opens with Elton in screaming camp form, opening the door to John Reid. With no inkling of the rift that was to come he greets him in his best Kenneth Williams voice: 'Bona to see you! This is my manager, the fabulous Beryl. I bet she's worth a few bob.' After a shot of Elton in relaxed mode, wearing a Versace bathrobe, chatting in the kitchen with Bob Halley, the mood quickly changes in the next scene, which shows Elton in full tantrum mode, displaying all the insecurities and spoilt-brat defiance of a pampered star. He had arrived at a studio to shoot the video for 'Believe' but the costume had disappeared – a wardrobe assistant had driven off with it in error. He has a fit of extraordinary petulance and intensity, storming about in his full-length, fake leopard-skin coat like a deranged soap-opera fishwife, swearing so furiously that the profusion of F-words ensured the programme would be placed firmly in the post-watershed category. The tension in the confined space of the dressing room is excruciating, to the point that David, behind the camera, feared that the footage would be unusable because he was shaking so much.

Making the film brought to the surface all Reid's jealousy of David's position at Elton's court. Reid, who, with David, was a director of Rocket Pictures, was unhappy that David had editorial control – he was not only jealous, but so concerned that the film would show Elton in a bad light, that relations became strained. Meanwhile, David felt threatened by the politics going on behind the scenes, and not least by Reid's efforts to undermine his project. 'I'm not making a film about Adolf Hitler,' David kept telling him, 'I'm making a film about a wonderful man.'

The viewing public were not privy to another tantrum that was edited out of the final programme. Princess Margaret was invited for an audience with Elton in his dressing room after a grand finale of fourteen gigs at the Royal Albert Hall. Elton had been presented with a plaque for the sell-out concerts, but because he was so disappointed with his performance, he proceeded to smash the award against the table. As her Royal Highness was coming down in the lift, Elton was leaving the building.

In a lighter moment, while scenes of the flower arrangements, four-poster beds, porcelain cherubs and indoor swimming pool inside Woodside adorn the screen, Elton recalls that it used to be a rampant party house where he did a lot of drugs, but now he reveals: 'I love coming home. There's a lot of love in this house.' Elton reads a card as if sent in by a curious fan. 'Are you a mummy's boy?' he reads. 'I think I've always been a mummy's boy.'

The next scene features Elton on the sofa with his mother who, in her seventies, is as on the ball as ever. She breaks down in tears as she recalls the time when she thought he was going to die during Elton John Week in Los Angeles in 1975. It is a moment of surprising intimacy as Sheila describes the pain of not being able to get close to her son during his drug-crazed years. 'And that was just the beginning,' he reminds her, while reassuring her that this emotional outpouring is what the filming is for. The viewer sees how Elton has been constantly reminded of his mother's feelings towards his father, and how she has kept him on her side: 'I don't think he ever really liked you,' she says. 'If ever he could have a little dig at you in things like table manners . . . You were frightened of him weren't you?' How could her boy disagree?

In another scene Elton is interviewed by journalist Tony Parsons, to promote *Made In England*. He talks of how he can give love, but how difficult he finds it to receive love, which David gives him. Although it is what he has always wanted, part of him always pushes it away.

Elton the list-maker appears on screen later, busily colouring in an immaculately colour-coded spreadsheet of his record sales. Then, in an extraordinarily intimate moment, his lover behind the camera asks what a balanced life would be for him. 'Spending enough time with you probably,' and he whispers to the camera, 'Shhh'.

The interior of the Orangery, his Nan's home for fifteen years, is the focus of the next scene. Here Elton is a dutiful and loving grandson, affectionately calling Ivy, 'A silly old sausage.' He makes sure she has received his postcard from Japan and that she is still getting flowers from him weekly.

Cut to Elton in Hollywood for the Oscars' ceremony, exercising his penchant for schoolboy humour. He wants to check into the hotel as Fanny Beaver Snatch Clit, but the hotel management disapproves of the pseudonym because they deem it degrading to women. 'Which is a shame,' he says, 'because I've always been a bit of a c**t.' This naughty schoolboy has a valet to organize his uniform and in this scene also approves a pair of socks for later.

With lyricist Tim Rice he is presented with the Oscar for best original song, 'Can You Feel The Love Tonight?' for *The Lion King*, and makes a speech dedicating the award to his grandmother Ivy, who had died a few days earlier. David caused a stir at the ceremony when he kissed Elton on the cheek. This was the mystery David whom Elton had thanked in his acceptance speech.

After a montage of travelling shots, the viewer is taken behind the scenes at the Stonewall concert, where Elton is tottering on black stilettos. He is heaving himself into a black sheath dress and blond wig to pose first with the *Absolutely Fabulous* team, Jennifer Saunders and Joanna Lumley, then with Kylie Minogue, and lastly revealing his smooth waxed chest to Madonna.

At the Grand Hotel at Cap Ferrat, in the South of France, David gives the audience an insight into a typical Elton holiday, and all that it entails. He asks Elton whether he would ever consider going away without his driver, valet and tennis coach. 'Probably not,' Elton replies, and continues, 'No, I wouldn't enjoy it very much.' Then David asks whether he would consider doing any traditional holiday activities, such as water-skiing, driving through the countryside or lying by the pool, or perhaps taking a walk round the Cap together: 'I think that's a very special thing that two people can do together. Wouldn't you do that?' 'Not really,' Elton responds. 'I *might* consider that one, but the other three are absolute no-nos.'

A tour of his suite follows, notably concentrating on the contents of the kitchen and wardrobe. Elton explains that travelling is so boring that, wherever he goes, he takes his Marks and Spencer's muffins, a bottle of HP sauce and his closet to remind him of home. 'People think you're crazy, and it is crazy, but it does keep me sane,' he says. Then the camera pans over row upon row of meticulously arranged suits, jackets, shirts and shoes to rival the collections of Imelda Marcos or the Great Gatsby. There are drawers and drawers full of spectacles, all colour-coded, and two tiaras, 'Because,' Elton says, 'you never know when you are going to be invited to something really formal.' David asks whether owning so many clothes is obscene. 'I suppose it is,' Elton replies meekly. 'I can't defend myself in that respect, but for some reason I find it comforting.'

In a later shot Elton is found on a tennis court in the South of France, revealing precisely why he feels he must avoid public displays of physical activity on holiday. He suddenly throws his racket at the net and storms off court. The action then moves to the claustrophobic interior of a mirrored lift, where, trapped in the small space, he sweats and huffs with anger while, reflected in the mirror, David dispassionately records every moment of this Little Moment on camera. 'I'm on fucking holiday,' he pouts. Later in the day Elton is on the phone ordering a plane to take him home that very evening. 'I'm never coming to the South of France again,' he hisses, and leaves the room. Three days later he is still in France and explains contritely that a woman had called out, 'Coo-ee,' to him while he was playing tennis and he simply lost his temper. 'I take my tennis seriously,' he says, submissively. 'I couldn't handle it.'

In an uncomfortable scene Elton lounges on his bed, watching a video recording of David and his analyst, Beechy Colclough, discussing their mutual subject. David asks Colclough whether he thinks Elton buys people, to which Colclough replies that Elton buys them with his personality and with gifts. The therapist thinks a lot of people feed off Elton and that he is only happy when he is playing, but that he never believes the audience's reaction. 'He hates himself. He's a totally addictive, compulsive person,' says Colclough, as he counts off the check list on his fingers. 'If it hadn't been the alcohol, it would have been the drugs. If it hadn't been the drugs it would have been the food. If it hadn't been the food it would have been the relationships. If it hadn't been the relationships it would have been the shopping. And do you know? He's got all five.'

Understandably, Elton remarks that watching the two of them discussing him was like watching a couple of vultures picking over a carcass. It is hard not to disagree, however accurate it might be. What most riles him is how David and Colclough talk about people feeding off him and how concerned they are that he works too hard. 'Why are people always telling me to slow down?' he demands. 'I am responsible for other people's livelihoods apart from my own. And I like working.' He acknowledges that he thinks more highly of himself now, but admits, 'It's hard to start loving yourself.'

The next scene reveals the interior of a Mercedes, with Elton driving himself around Atlanta. According to David driving his own car makes Elton feel normal: 'It relaxes him in a way. It's like stepping off the machine. There's a side of his life in Atlanta which feeds his soul. It kind of balances him.'

At a concert performance, where Elton sneaks a kiss with David behind the camera before he walks on stage, the audience catches a glimpse of the physical pressures of his marathon tours. Elton loses his voice and later, on his 108th show of the year in Rio de Janeiro, nearly collapses on stage. He staggers off in a daze to be resuscitated but, like a punch-drunk boxer, he rallies and returns from his corner. The show must go on – he cannot let his audience down.

The film ends with Elton explaining how his records are never going to stop selling. Determined that Elton should never get too big for his bootees, Bob Halley has the last word: 'They're a load of old crap.'

David did not show any of the footage to Elton until it was finished. When Elton viewed the programme for the first time, he said, 'Is it over? I wish I could see more.' He said he knew it was the truth – he was not acting out a part. Elton thought he came across as moody, unreasonable and miserable – 'Some of my behaviour in it is totally atrocious' – but it still made him laugh.

Meanwhile, Watford FC were in the doldrums and the life-time president decided to take matters into his own hands. He could not bear to watch them any more. He had not seen them score a goal in three years and he decided there was only one way to stop the rot. Elton approached his old friend Graham Taylor, the architect of Watford's golden years in the late 1970s and early 1980s. Over the last nine years the club had had a miserable time on the pitch and the crowds were dwindling. Could Taylor work his magic again?

Elton put all his energy into luring Taylor back. After a couple of unsatisfactory phone calls, Elton flew from Atlanta to try to convince him face to face. Over fish pie and mineral water at Woodside, the two old friends remembered the good times, recalling the wonderful garden parties Elton had thrown at the house, with every member of the team present, and sing-songs with Elton at the piano customizing his songs for general amusement. Until then, they had kept to their agreement that Taylor would not advise

Elton on music, if Elton did not advise Taylor on football – it was time for Elton to be frank.

After the 1990 World Cup Final, Taylor had been chosen to succeed Bobby Robson as England manager. This was the crowning glory to his career, or so he had thought. It turned out to be a doomladen sojourn. Taylor took the national team into the European Championship in the summer of 1992 with just one defeat in twenty-one games, confident of success. Following two goalless draws against Denmark and France, however, Taylor's team suffered a catastrophic 2–1 defeat against Sweden. Having failed to win a single game, England's European campaign came to a disappointing end, finishing bottom of their group.

Despite this setback, Taylor believed that England would have no problems qualifying for the World Cup between October 1992 and November 1993, and he allowed the cameras to follow himself and the England team during qualification, pre-empting Elton's warts-and-all television documentary by four years. The cameras covered a disastrous game against Holland which included some questionable refereeing. The abiding memory of the programme was of a foul-mouthed manager stalking the touchlines, expressing himself in a string of F-words, which was worthy of comparison with Elton's opening scene in *Tantrums and Tiaras*. After enjoying a promising start, England lost three vital games and failed to progress to the finals. In November 1993 Taylor realized his reign as England manager was drawing to a close after hearing on his car radio that a press conference had been called to discuss his future. He later returned to club management with Wolver-hampton Wanderers in 1994.

Thanks to Elton's powers of persuasion, Taylor agreed to come home to the club he had nurtured from the sidelines of the fourth division to the top of the first. He was taking on an uphill task, with the team languishing at the bottom of the Endsleigh Insurance League Division One and facing relegation if he was unable to make a success of the eighteen matches remaining in the season. Elton made it clear that he would give Taylor full moral support. Appearing at the manager's side to announce his reappointment, Elton promised to attend more matches and get involved in the community side of the club. He also warned that he could not put more of his own money into the club for the moment because he did not want to tread on Jack Petchey's toes. One of Taylor's first moves was to appoint the ex-England striker Luther Blissett, one of the club's golden-era protégés, as first-team coach.

Only three months later, rumours abounded that Elton was preparing to buy back the club, but he kept everyone guessing, and later in the year denied that he was thinking of buying it back for a reported $9 million (£6 million).

The rumours began again in October 1996, as stories circulated that Elton was head of a consortium bidding to purchase the club for $6.9 million (£4.6 million). Jack Petchey dropped his price when he resigned in September after angry fan demonstrations, and Elton headed the consortium takeover to become chairman for the second time in April 1997.

In December 1996 Elton made legal history again. The $525,000 (£350,000) libel award he had received from the *Sunday Mirror* in 1993 was reduced to $112,500 (£75,000) by the Court of Appeal, which declared that libel actions would not, in future, be 'a road to untaxed riches'. In capping the legal jackpot, juries would be given a benchmark against which to measure libel compensation for personal injury claims; the bruised celebrity ego would henceforth be on a par with the broken leg of the common man. The Master of the Rolls, Sir Thomas Bingham, declared that it was unfair that libel plaintiffs walked off with more than the tragic victims of accidents. It may have been a victory for common sense but it raised concern, especially after Elton's experiences, that newspapers might be more inclined to print false or fantastic stories, without the fear of having to pay exemplary damages for defamation. However, as pointed out in a letter to *The Times*, the real losers might be newspapers, now deprived of the chance to report sensational column inches relating to libel circuses.

No sooner had he performed on the National Lottery television programme with Luciano Pavarotti than Elton applied for lottery funding. He was seeking $58.5 million (£39 million) from the $234 million (£156 million) fund to help Rocket Pictures produce films. Thanks to his Disney connection, Elton was offered a deal to make movies through Rocket Pictures if Disney was given first refusal on all projects. The company was formally launched in 1996 with Disney's backing.

chapter fourteen

The Flowers Will Never Die

THE SEVENTH YEAR OF EACH DECADE in Elton's life has had a certain significance for him. He was born in 1947; Elvis conquered the world in 1957; he met Bernie Taupin in 1967; he took temporary retirement in the wake of the punk revolution in 1977; he sued the *Sun* newspaper in 1987; and 1997 was his fiftieth birthday – and his most momentous year seven yet.

On 25 March, his fiftieth birthday, his gifts included honorary membership of his alma mater, the Royal Academy of Music, an accolade previously awarded to Mendelssohn, Liszt and Richard Strauss. But he had no intention of entering his sixth decade without making a splash. Bob Halley spent a whole year organizing his master's half-century birthday party in early April, which was reported to have cost $450,000 (£300,000). Purple and gold invitations, embossed with Elton's crest, went out to 600 friends and staff, summoning them to the Hammersmith Palais at 6.30 p.m. in fancy dress; carriages at 1 a.m. Timing was all – Elton wanted everyone there to witness his majestic arrival. It was to be the last word in fancy-dress parties and Elton's costume outdid them all. It took two hours to get into his handmade eighteenth-century-style outfit designed by Sandy Powell, the film costumier, whose credits include *Interview with the Vampire*, *Caravaggio*, and *Orlando*. His white, diamante-encrusted brocade coat with lacy ruffs and cuffs, breeches and court shoes, were topped off with a three-and-a-half-foot, white powdered wig, adorned with pearls and silver spangles, and crowned with a silver galleon under full sail, puffing steam. His 20-foot train lined with ostrich feathers was carried by two male models dressed as slaves clad in mini-togas. David played Buttons to Elton's pantomime dame, in an eighteenth-century lilac brocade outfit with a full-bottomed lilac wig and tiara.

The entourage set off from the Holland Park house for the short journey to Hammersmith in a furniture removal lorry, the only vehicle large enough to contain the vast bulk of Elton's wig. The cabin was ornately decorated in the style of an eighteenth-century drawing room, with two gold thrones, candles, red velvet drapes, oil paintings from the house and a fireplace containing a television screen that relayed images of a burning log fire.

Unfortunately, all the limousines and the crowds of onlookers caused traffic chaos on Shepherd's Bush Road so Elton's driver took an alternative route to avoid the crowds, only to succeed in getting gridlocked on Hammersmith Broadway. All the guests who were lined up to welcome His Fabulousness had to wait. The star made his grand entrance, fashionably (a little over an hour) late. He was eventually deposited at the Palais and lowered from the lorry by a pneumatic platform, grinning with pain from the weight of the wig. Once inside he swapped it for a more manageable smaller version.

Hammersmith Palais was decorated with an extravagance of flowers, palm trees, candles and ice sculptures. The birthday cake, a gift from the *Sun* newspaper, was a huge meringue swan decorated with flashing lights, which Elton cut with a full-size sword. Entertainment was provided by a gospel choir and the Ystrad Fawr Ballroom Formation Team from South Wales, who led the way in the foxtrot, tango and Viennese waltz.

Elton invited all the staff from his office and his Windsor and London homes, who mingled with the celebrity guests; most people were so well disguised that they were barely able to recognize each other. The designer Jean Paul Gaultier came as a French maid, and Sir Tim Rice came dressed as a teddy boy. Elton's mother and stepfather caused quite a stir, thanks to their uncanny resemblance to the Queen and the Duke of Edinburgh. Sheila asked everyone to address her as 'Your Majesty' all evening.

☆

Elton and Gianni Versace had become close friends during Elton's 1992 world tour and had much in common. Like Elton, Versace came from modest roots. He was born in southern Italy to a gas and electrical-fitter father, and was particularly close to his mother, who was a dress-maker. Versace had been honoured by his country with the Commendatore della Repubblica Italiana for services to the fashion industry in 1986, and was closely involved with AIDS campaigning. He was no slouch at shopping either, with a magpie eye to match Elton's. Boasting that he could spend $3 million (£2 million) in two hours, he told the *New Yorker* magazine: 'I go shopping one day in Paris buying things for my house in Miami. That night I come home and I see the figure I spent. Oh, I start to dance . . .'

Versace, like Elton, was a self-effacing man who liked to laugh and poke fun at himself. He was also an optimist with an enthusiasm for people and beautiful things. The two men inspired each other. Versace did not believe in the concept of good taste and he became Elton's mentor in many ways. He taught him to stop and observe beauty – a photograph, a fresco, a church, a painting or a garden – while Elton introduced Versace to the glories of Lalique glass. Elton has always loved flowers, but Versace inspired him with the design of his gardens and suggested that he should create a formal Italian garden at Windsor with pavilions and statues. Elton invited Sir Roy Strong, who had designed Versace's garden in Como, Italy, to transform part of his grounds, and he now has an Italianate vista from his bedroom of box hedges and statues, balustrades, pavilions, obelisks and red geraniums.

Elton loved Versace's 'prostitute meets princess' style, a provocative fusion of glamour and vulgarity. Versace designed for a media-obsessed age; his photogenic clothes radiated in the spotlight. He described himself as 'super-gay', and designed overtly sexy clothes for both men and women, because in his world you were yourself and proud of it. His candour and openness must have fascinated and delighted Elton who had been so painfully shy in his youth. The two would speak every day on the phone, sharing jokes and repartee. In conversation with Michael Parkinson in November 2000, Elton said: 'Gianni Versace, my dear friend, taught me that life is to be taken and you must take in things at every moment – you must look at things, you must explore things. You must go and see things and enjoy what life has to offer because there are so many abundantly good things. He would say, "I have ten minutes, you must come and see this church fresco, this museum, this mosaic, this building." Before that I never did things like that; I just shut the curtains and turned everything off.'

Elton sent his interior designers to Versace's Milan residence to see the bathroom, before doing up his own. Consequently, Elton's bath water is drawn from the mouth of a trademark Versace Medusa's head. Versace also encouraged Elton's love of photography, and together they collaborated on a sumptuous book of photographs called *Rock and Royalty*, with profits going to Elton's AIDS Foundation. In a foreword Elton wrote: 'I always have to dress for an audience. They expect it. It is an essential part of my performance. Great performers have always had a sense of the dramatic and what they choose to wear enhances that sense. It adds another dimension to their art. Fashion is like art to me. The creative process of fashion never ceases to impress me.'

The photographs were taken by Richard Avedon and, as it was in a good cause, Elton put his fear of the camera aside for the day. In his first pose he lay across a piano completely naked except for a Versace duvet. He waxed off and dragged up in a specially made black metal mesh fabric and lace off-the-shoulder dress. He completed his strident 'diva as lorry driver' look with lots of jewellery, strappy platforms and his weave of new hair gelled down flat. Bill

Bachmann, Richard Avedon's assistant, said: 'Richard came away with the feeling that Elton was a very comic actor.'

Versace dedicated the book to his friends Diana, Princess of Wales and Elton John: 'To the Princess of Wales who has glamorized royalty and to my dear friend Elton who has become the royalty of rock.'

Before seeing the book's content, Diana, a highly valued client and friend of Versace's, had agreed to write a foreword. She gushed: 'From the optimism which shines from the pages of this book one can tell that he loves mankind. All the successful artists who appear in this new book give tribute to art and beauty: with their work through the years they have touched people's feelings and emotions and made a difference in the lives of hundreds of human beings. This book is a contribution. It supports the efforts of Elton John's Foundation for AIDS because no battle has ever been won alone. Battles are won only by many joined hands and spirits aiming at the same goal.'

When Diana saw a preview copy of the finished book she realized, to her horror, that she had blessed a series of somewhat outré photographs of mostly male models juxtaposed with a collection of old royal portraits. She had been placed in an excruciatingly embarrassing position with the Royal Family. The book included a photograph of the Duke and Duchess of Windsor on their wedding day, uncomfortably close to a shot of a near-naked Ryan Giggs, the Manchester United footballer. The Queen is merely a few pages from a man with both hands stuffed in his underpants, along with other assorted homo-erotic beefcake. Elton himself is facing a photograph of the Queen Mother. He is reported to have said: 'Some people are born royal, others become queens on their own.' However, it was no joke when the princess demanded that her words were removed from the book and she announced that she would not be attending the publisher's launch party. According to Elton: 'She must have come under a lot of pressure to distance herself from it because it was kind of racy. But all Versace's books were racy. I think she panicked.'

In his quest to make this the most talked-about book of the year, Versace had invited a glittering array of 650 designers, models and showbiz hangers-on to the launch party, at $750 (£500) a seat, in a converted warehouse in Shepherds Bush. The guest of honour was to have been the *über* fashion-plate herself, Princess Diana, but Versace and Elton decided to cancel the event to save her further embarrassment. Having already sold all the tickets for the event, it turned into a public relations nightmare for the foundation. A few books had already been sold in Italy and Germany but rather than pulping the rest, the page containing Diana's foreword was cut out.

When Elton found out about her change of heart through the newspapers, he phoned her immediately to say that he wished that she had told him personally, and followed up the conversation in writing. Elton said: 'I wrote her a very to-the-point critical letter which she didn't like very much. I was just being honest with her. She found it hard to take. I wish she'd had a few more people to tell her the truth sometimes or to question her, because it would have made her a much stronger person.'

Diana replied frostily, her letter beginning ominously, 'Dear Mr John', which, a year later, Elton would find uproariously funny. At the time, however, when he tried to phone her at Kensington Palace, he could not get through and she did not return his calls. He said: 'I think she wanted me to write her a formal letter of apology saying "I'm sorry I made a mistake". But I didn't think I had made a mistake so I wasn't going to do it.'

Diana's behaviour was textbook Elton: the anger, the obstinacy, the refusal to be intimidated by anyone. She was a worthy adversary for him – in Diana he had found a personality which matched his own in many ways. They both harboured deep wells of unhappiness going back to childhood. Both came from broken homes, had sham marriages, run-ins with the media, a stubborn streak, low self-esteem, both were public confessors, both suffered from eating disorders and depression. They liked shopping for clothes. They both arrived on their own public stages as ingénues, fairy-tale successes in their own way. Both became spectacular stars, crazy neurotics, victims, narcissists, survivors, glamorous celebrities and, latterly, reformed characters and charity supporters. They appeared to labour under the illusion that in order to care they had to be victims themselves, so that the more they suffered the more virtuous they seemed. Both loved being on the public stage, feeding off reassurance from an audience – Elton the entertainer, Diana the princess – but offstage neither found it easy to be themselves. They offered themselves up as canvases on to which anyone could project; they were multi-purpose personalities, offering something for everyone. Elton said: 'When I admitted to being bulimic she wrote me little notes, something like, from one bulimic to another.' Like Elton, Diana could give, but she found it much harder to cope with any kindness or generosity towards her. Her reaction to Elton's letter was exactly the same as Elton's response to his close friends when they advised him to stop taking drugs. He froze them out for up to a year, much as Diana put up the barricades and avoided Elton.

Elton's royal row did nothing to spoil his friendship with Versace. They kept in daily contact by phone, holidayed together in the Mediterranean with their respective partners and were planning further collaborations, in particular, a new ballet to premiere at the Chaillot Theatre in Paris. Then one day, Elton had a shock unlike anything he had experienced since John Lennon's death nearly seventeen years before. On 15 July 1997, Gianni Versace was gunned down on the steps of his Miami Beach mansion as he walked home with the morning newspapers. All the high priests of the fashion world and their fabulous clients, style gurus, supermodels, superstars, VIPs and royalty, in head-to-toe black Versace, later attended a memorial mass in Milan Cathedral. Among the 10,000 mourners were a hundred workers from the Versace factory, and the shops in the fashion district closed as a mark of respect. Versace had become a household name all over the world and was a hero in Italy. Before the service Elton paid a visit to the Versace villa where the casket containing the ashes lay. It was surrounded by Versace's favourite flowers, white roses and freesias, and ornate, cherub-adorned candelabra.

The image on all the front pages of a distraught Elton being comforted by Diana was to become all the more poignant because she herself had little more than six weeks to live – the memorial service was the last time Elton saw her. He could not contain his tears and it was a slightly disconcerted Diana who placed a comforting hand on his arm. There is another image of a distraught Elton leaning towards her but, according to Elton, he is actually offering her a Polo mint. The occasion marked a public reconciliation for the rock star and the princess who were united in their grief. They had, in fact, settled their differences by phone a few days earlier when Diana contacted Elton to talk about the shock and distress she felt over Versace's death. They also discussed their estrangement and their mutual stubbornness over the other matter. She asked Elton if she could sit with him and David in the congregation.

During the service Elton was also comforted by David, and regained his composure sufficiently to sing the twenty-third psalm with Sting. In his sermon, Monsignor Angelo Majo said: 'We are not here to put on a show but to mourn the loss of a friend, a brother in the eyes of God. A man who spread goodness throughout his life is not afraid of death.'

Elton still grieves for Versace: 'I don't think I'll ever get over losing him. Every day, whether I'm spraying his perfume on, whether I'm wearing his clothes, whether I'm using his towels, I'm always in touch. I've only got to hear *Cavalleria Rusticana* and I'm off.'

Since its $7.5 million (£5 million) refurbishment, Woodside is decorated in the best possible taste and Versace's influence is plain to see. The sweeping driveway is lined with neoclassical sculptures of Adonis-style male figures. Gone are the juke boxes, the pinball machines, the neon signs, the Art Deco nymphs, the Tiffany lamps and kitsch cuddly toys. They have been replaced by Meissen and Staffordshire figurines, prompting Mick Jagger to remark: 'I've never seen so much fucking porcelain.' Woodside is no longer an unhappy rock-star's house, but the tranquil home of a country squire, albeit one who has a corridor, floor and ceiling lined with gold and platinum discs. The mirrored-ball disco is now the drawing room, the flashy cinema is now an elegant video screening room. The squash court is now a well-stocked library with a Francis Bacon self-portrait and a harp, two horses heads and an ivory dildo decorated with the Royal crest. The five-a-side football pitch lined with Watford logos became a flower garden. Now Elton describes it as a house full of love and peace where people can come and stay. Along with his appetites, everything is under control from the silent panic alarms to the precise humidity and the temperature. 'Woodside is the hub of my soul, probably. It is the centre of my life,' said Elton.

Late in 1996 he agreed to have his love of flowers celebrated in a book, *Elton John's Flower Fantasies*, written by Caroline Cass and photographed by Andrew Twort, on condition that it would be 'beautiful and not gimmicky' and that a large proportion of the royalties should go to EJAF. Up to 1,000 flowers a week are used in his country house and about 650 in the town house. His florists use only the best blooms. For the shoot, Elton left the florists and the photographer pretty much to it, making only a couple of appearances while they were taking pictures. The team worked at both Woodside and Queensdale, the Holland Park house, under the watchful eye of Elton and David's butler, George, a trusty professional who had only been in residence for about six months, but who had an innate understanding of what would be acceptable to his masters. George prepared all the props for the photographs, supervising arrangements of Elton's clothes and shoes to complement the flowers. An obvious foil for the flowers would have been Elton's trademark spectacles. George was not sure about this idea, but one of the maids thought she knew exactly the right way to ask Elton. The planning for this photographic shoot highlights the reverse psychology that keeps the momentum ticking over in Elton's households. He likes to have the final choice and needs someone to disagree with.

Elton was in Atlanta when the photographs were being taken and the maid spoke to him during the daily phone call, lighting the touch paper to a transatlantic Little Moment. Spectacles were most definitely a no-go area. Photography had to come to a halt immediately and before the job could proceed any further Elton insisted that all the pictures taken so far should be shown to Robert Key, his taste guru. In Key's opinion, Elton would hate everything. Susan Hill, one of the florists, decided to show Elton all the work to date when he came back from Atlanta. She was well prepared. The transparencies were displayed in pristine card mounts and arranged in order of acceptability – safe, mildly questionable and borderline. She put them in the pocket of her florist's apron and chose her moment carefully. Elton had just finished a game of tennis with David and was in a relaxed mood when he returned to the house, so she whipped out the pictures there and then. He did not reject a single one. The team had been particularly worried about their visual jokes, such as the picture of Elton's ripe purple plums adorned with cobwebs, or the statue of a male dancer with castanets in one hand and a daisy chain dangling from the fist of the other.

The photographic team were at Woodside while the florists were decking the house for Christmas – the fairy on top of Elton's tree is a Ken doll (as in Ken and Barbie) in drag, with pearl necklace, halo and gossamer wings.

Woodside was also a haven for a surprise visitor while the photographic project was taking place. Twort said: 'There was a fat bloke wandering around in what looked like an inside-out tracksuit, talking to the staff. He was staying in one of the main bedrooms.' No one recognized him at first – but it was Robbie Williams, in recovery from the excesses of his recent lifestyle. Elton had generously invited him to make himself at home at Woodside, use the gym, stay off the booze and sort himself out with Beechy Colclough.

Elton's houses are humming hives of building work, French polishing, carpentry and restoration, whether he is in residence or not. Every detail is perfect and he only hires the best craftsmen. So many alterations have now been made at Woodside that, in 1998, the government removed the neo-Georgian mansion's Grade II listing. A local historian, Margaret Gilson, said: 'It was never a particularly elegant building and Elton John has completely redone it. He has taken it apart and put it back together again.'

While his Atlanta apartment is a repository for his collection of twentieth-century photography, Woodside houses a significant number of oil paintings, including one of the largest private collections in the art world by the artist Henry Scott Tuke (1859–1929), a member of the Cornish Newlyn School, along with Gainsboroughs, and many important Victorian landscapes.

The Orangery has been converted into a chapel in memory of Elton's beloved grandmother. Elton was unable to attend her funeral because it took place while he was in Hollywood at the Oscars' ceremony. When he returned, however, the family gathered at the Orangery, said prayers and scattered Ivy's ashes among the flowers. The chapel is a serene white-and-gold room with a small altar containing two rare seventeenth-century giltwood chairs, which originally resided in the private apartments of King William III at Hampton Court. Religion is not a strong element in Elton's life, although he was brought up as a Protestant. 'I'm someone who believes in a god, or in a higher power, but I'm extremely distrustful of the way religion divides people,' he says.

When Elton is at home he rarely plays the piano. The only time George, the butler, ever heard him play was to serenade Versace when he came down to breakfast one morning. Elton relaxes by reading magazines and loves books, especially biographies. 'I like to find out about people and I like anything that is well written,' he said. One of his great pleasures and a favourite way to unwind at home is to watch football or tennis on television.

Elton had been looking for a permanent place in the sun and since November 1996 had been viewing properties in the South of France. In July 1997, for an estimated $7.5 million (£5 million), he acquired a three-storey pink villa in a secluded position on a wooded hill overlooking the Bay of Nice. This is home to his collection of modern artists: Warhol, Basquiat, Schnabel and Eric Fischl. Just like his dogs, his cars and his closest friends he has pet names for his two glass-topped coffee tables by pop artist Allen Jones, the bases of which are formed by sculptures of two women on their hands and knees – the one in a brief green costume is 'Nice Janet' and the other in black bondage gear is 'Nasty Janet'.

While Elton was settling into his homes-and-garden lifestyle, he recorded a collection of lush middle-of-the-road ballads with sweeping orchestral arrangements to match. His album *The Big Picture* reached number three in Britain and number nine in America, but it did not compare with the classics of his early years. It is not a great album and its sales were probably buoyed by Elton's contribution to an event that shook the world.

Elton's life is packed with record highs, record lows and record records, superlatives and achievements, but it reached its zenith on Saturday, 6 September 1997. Watched by an estimated two billion people all over the world, Elton John sat down at the piano in Westminster Abbey to sing the reworked 'Candle In The Wind' at the funeral of Diana, Princess of Wales. Elton took centre stage for three and a half minutes for the biggest moment of his life on one of the saddest days generations would witness, and then made a joke about it afterwards. When Elton watched the video playback of Princess Diana's funeral service and his moving rendition of 'Candle In The Wind', he had only one thing to say: 'Look at my eyebrow, it's working independently.' Then he let go of his suppressed emotions – and was inconsolable.

Although Elton had established himself almost as royal minstrel by appointment, his inclusion in the funeral arrangements was not confirmed until two days beforehand and it represented an edgy compromise between populists and royalists. In a week when the royal family looked decidedly uncertain of their grasp of the national mood, there were many debates about whether or not it would be appropriate for a pop star to sing at the funeral. There were four conflicting criteria for the arrangements: dignity, informality to reflect public opinion and Diana's personality, the views of both families, and tradition. Friends of Diana, who sat on the committee, wanted a modern element woven into the service to echo something of her spirit. How best to commemorate a non-royal princess whose marriage into the Windsor family had transformed it from tweedy dynasty into glossy soap opera?

Elton was asked whether he would be prepared to sing at the funeral, but the committee had not yet agreed whether he would set the right tone. Should he sing a hymn or one of his own songs? He considered writing something new, but noticed on the news that many of the people who signed the book of condolences at St James's Palace revealed that they were using the words 'Candle In The Wind'. He phoned Bernie Taupin in America and asked him to rework the lyrics of the original 1974 song. After only a couple of hours he faxed the new lyrics to Elton, who in turn faxed them to the Prime Minister and Diana's family for approval.

After many fraught committee meetings, the populists won through, and he provided the perfect note of mournful glitz – the people's pop star sang at the funeral of the people's princess, representing the democratic choice. Any fears that Elton's contribution might be unbecoming to such a solemn occasion proved unfounded. Elton provided the perfect theme to Diana's last episode in the royal soap opera. His customized Yamaha grand piano was installed in Westminster Abbey and the words were approved by all concerned. The original song is an emotional ballad, a bitter-sweet elegy to Marilyn Monroe who died in her prime; a fragile character, a flawed star, who had suffered the pressures of the media throughout her working life. During the days after Diana's death the song seemed to catch the public mood and was chosen to accompany television montages of Diana's life.

Bernie Taupin removed the more caustic, but all too appropriate lines from the original song, 'Even when you died, The press still hounded you.' These words were far too apt after the controversial role of the paparazzi in Diana's death. To avoid offending the royal family he also removed the lines, 'You had the grace to hold yourself, While those around you crawled . . . They set you on a treadmill, And made you change your name.'

Elton's calm professionalism enabled him to remain unruffled in the hours before the funeral. On the day, Elton was supported by David Furnish and George Michael who came to the London house so that they could all travel to Westminster Abbey together. This was no time for an outpouring of emotion. 'You are providing the emotion, you can't afford to let go,' he said, but he was so fearful of making a mistake or breaking down that he described the experience as being like hanging on to a cliff top with his fingertips. It was not only the knowledge that his close friends were seated in the front pews that helped Elton hold his nerve, but also that he was singing for his country in the eyes of the world, for a friend he loved and respected. At the beginning of the song Elton was composed, but he admitted later that he had felt himself faltering at the beginning of the last verse, so he closed his eyes and stoically completed the song. Doubtless it was all the more emotional for him, knowing he had not let the princess down. He had helped to heal the rift between the traditionalists and the masses, and everyone knew it was exactly what Diana would have wanted.

While the princess's coffin was driven northwards out of London to her final resting place at Althorp, the Spencer family home, Elton went to Townhouse Studios in west London where Sir George Martin was waiting for him to record the track live, with just piano and voice. They did two takes and the second was released, with some vocal harmonies, strings and woodwind mixed in. The production process sped into full gear and the final tape was delivered to Elton at his London home at 11 p.m. that night. The staff at Polygram's Blackburn pressing plant worked round the clock to produce the CD for distribution to the shops.

The day after the funeral Elton received a hero's welcome when he attended a football match at Vicarage Road. The 12,000-strong crowd gave him a standing ovation when he took his seat in the director's box, the first time he had attended since returning as Watford FC chairman in April. They chanted, 'Elton, Elton,' at the end of the match as 'Candle In The Wind' was played over the loud-speakers. Here was public affirmation where it mattered most. Watford beat Wycombe Wanderers 2–1 – Graham Taylor was beginning to work his magic again.

In the days following the funeral Elton seemed elevated in stature and the shy boy from Pinner seemed to gain an extraordinarily mature self-assurance and gravitas as he assumed the mantle of secular spokesman for the grieving British nation. In the absence of royal pronouncements and spiritual guidance, he praised the Great British Public for the way they had conducted themselves in their emotional response to the princess's death, which would be his enduring memory of such a sad week. He reflected on Diana's sense of humour, her wicked laugh, her teasing and flattering, but most of all her compassion and sincerity. He told David Frost on BBC One: 'It's up to everybody now not just to grieve publicly for a week and then to forget about it, but to try to carry on what she was all about.' Then, less than two weeks after Diana's death, Elton pronounced that the nation should bring its grieving for Diana to an end. 'Life should go on,' he proclaimed from Florida. 'Princess Diana would not want this sadness to continue.'

Elton seemed to be continually in mourning, as later in September he flew to New York for a memorial service for Versace. Elton became the subject of an urban myth in Italy – every time people saw him in the street they would cross themselves and walk to the other side of the road, or turn off the radio whenever one his songs came on. A year later, Elton told *Daily Telegraph* journalist John Preston that as he sat down at the piano at Diana's funeral a wicked thought had entered his mind: what if he had walked to the piano and announced, 'I'd like to do something from my new album'?

Elton refused to allow the BBC and ITN to include the song in charity videos of the funeral. He was unhappy that a mere $5.25 (£3.50) from the sale of each $19.49 (£12.99) video was going to the princess's memorial fund; he thought the channels should have donated more by reducing their production costs, as he had done on his CD. Elton remained determined, and as a result none of the funeral videos included his moving homage to Diana.

People queued at record shops all over the country on the morning 'Candle In The Wind '97' was released. Tower Records in London's Piccadilly opened at midnight and sold 1,000 copies in an hour to 300 customers. Buyers wanted fifty or a hundred copies at a time and were rationed to no more than ten copies each; they wanted discs for all their friends and families. Many shops opened an hour early, selling out of huge stocks of up to a quarter of a million within hours, such was the phenomenal demand. That night, one million more copies were ordered, to be distributed all over the country. Shops in America ordered 3.4 million copies in advance, and during the first week, 20,833 copies were bought, that is 5.8 copies per second.

Richard Branson, the Virgin chief, who was also a friend of Diana's, had been a key figure in the organization of the funeral, and after the ceremony he produced an all-star charity tribute album. Elton had decided that he did not want 'Candle In The Wind '97' included on the album because he thought it would raise more money for the princess's memorial fund if it were released as a single. He did not want the public to have to buy it twice effectively. Branson accused Elton of donating the song to the album initially, then changing his mind, but Elton was not to be swayed and an undignified row between the two men ensued. In November 1997 he wrote to tell Elton how he feared that Elton's decision would cost the fund millions of pounds in lost revenue, and that he was beginning to 'see a different side' to Elton and hoped he would not 'let down' his admirers. For Branson to question Elton's integrity and motives, and his behaviour throughout this time, caused such offence that John Reid fired off a strong reply to Branson, telling him that his 'implied threats' were 'distasteful'. Mysteriously, details of the exchange of letters appeared in the *Mirror* on 14 January 1998, but the paper would not reveal its source. 'It was very odd at the time,' remembers Reid, 'I didn't know where it had come from. I wasn't sure whether Branson had leaked it.' Reid could not have known then that the revelation of these letters was just the tip of an altogether more sinister iceberg and marked the beginning of the end of his long relationship with Elton.

Elton's instincts were vindicated and both his and Branson's CDs raised millions for the princess's charity. Both men knew the potential damage their public row could do their reputations given the sensitivity of the issue, and they did not delay in patching up their differences. The day after the revelations in the *Mirror*, in a flamboyant display of mateyness, Elton and Branson talked to each other on the popular BBC Radio One Breakfast Show, hosted by Chris Evans, and on air Elton invited Branson to dinner.

'Candle In The Wind '97' remained at number one in Britain only to be toppled by the all-conquering Spice Girls, who delayed the release of their single 'Spice Up Your Life' by a week so that Elton's record could stay at the top for longer. Even the government agreed to pay the VAT of 70 pence on each disc into the memorial fund.

All the royalties of the $5.99 (£3.99) 'double A-side' CD were donated to the Diana, Princess of Wales Memorial Fund and by 21 October Elton was able to hand over a cheque for $30 million (£20 million). His song would eventually raise more than $150 million (£100 million). On 22 October it was declared the world's biggest-selling single of all time, achieving the number one spot in twenty-two countries. According to the *Guinness Book of Records*, 31.7 million copies of 'Candle In The Wind '97' have been sold all over the world. The previous record holder, 'White Christmas' by Bing Crosby, sold 30 million copies over fifty-five years. Elton's record beat this figure in just five weeks. How satisfying it must have been for the fastidious book-keeper and listmaker that his song was the fastest-selling British number one, the best-selling British single and the top-selling single by a British artist – ever.

Elton's fundraising zeal was limitless, almost an addiction. He performed in a charity concert in aid of the victims of the devastating volcanic eruption in Montserrat, home of George Martin's AIR studios. He launched a $73.50 (£49) scented candle in America, perfumed with hyacinth, freesia, jasmine and rose, in a frosted glass holder embellished with the EJ monogram, with 10 per cent of the profits going to his AIDS foundation. Bernie also decided to sell his handwritten lyrics of 'Candle In The Wind '97' in aid of the Los Angeles Children's Hospital and auctioned the papers at Christie's in Los Angeles. Diana's brother, Earl Spencer, bought them for $38,000 (£25,300) for the Althorp Museum.

In November Elton revealed the extent of his other remaining addiction, shopping. Three years after his clear-out of 2,000 items for his AIDS foundation, he staged another, bigger affair. He opened a temporary charity shop in Dover Street in London's West End, calling it 'Out of the Closet 2'. This time he selected about 10,000 unwanted items from his homes in Britain and America, for sale at knock-down prices. Considering that he kept back vast quantities of clothes, a quick calculation reveals that he must have bought, on average, ten items of clothing every day for three years. His shopping sprees may seem random, but the great planner has it all worked out in his mind, thinking ahead about what to wear to events, parties, performances, interviews and tennis matches. He may have paid $3,000 (£2,000) for a Versace suit and worn it once, if at all, but he seemed quite happy to sell it for $300 (£200), the money going to his charity. Like the first sale, the shop contained wall-to-wall bargains with designer suits and overcoats from $262.50 (£175) to $450 (£300), hundreds of shirts at $75 (£50), silk scarves, ties, shoes and baseball caps. The sale raised $75,000 (£50,000) on its first day, and after five days the total was more than $494,000 (£329,000).

At the end of the year he embarked on his first British tour for six years to promote his new album, *The Big Picture*. His first performance took place in December in Glasgow in front of 10,000 fans, for whom he performed an astonishing three-hour set. Even at the age of fifty he could not resist a few piano acrobatics and during 'Bennie and the Jets', kicked his stool away, fell to the floor and played the piano from there for a full two minutes. He told the crowd that it had been a difficult few months and thanked everyone for their support. An emotional night, the purveyor of sad songs knew exactly how to pull the audience's heart strings and during 'Don't Let The Sun Go Down On Me', an image of Gianni Versace was projected on to the crowd. He dedicated 'Last Song' to the men, women and children living with HIV and AIDS.

The crowning achievement of Elton's historic year was the announcement that the Queen was to honour him with a knighthood at New Year, not only for services to music but for his work for AIDS charities. His joy was said to be 'immeasurable'.

With statesmanlike flair, Elton again spoke to the nation six months after Diana's death, to plead with people to end their mourning. He criticized Earl Spencer's plan for a charity pop concert in the grounds of her family home, Althorp, where she was buried on an island in the middle of a lake, and said he did not want to be bouncing on stage doing concerts in her memory. In the end, Sir Paul McCartney, Luciano Pavarotti, George Michael and Elton himself, all of whom had been suggested as artistes, had prior engagements.

Sir Elton now had the confidence to speak up and no subject escaped an Eltonian tongue-lashing. He pronounced his displeasure at some of the tackiness produced in Diana's name, such as special packs of Flora margarine, and criticized her brother's plans to charge visitors to the museum he had set up at Althorp in her memory. In Sir Elton's opinion it was thoughtless to have buried her on an island – he would have preferred her to have been laid to rest in Westminster Abbey so that her sons could visit her more easily and people would not have to pay to see her grave.

For Elton, the strain was beginning to tell once again. He admitted on GMTV that losing two close friends during the summer of 1997 had taken a terrible toll. Seven years after giving up the chemical support of alcohol and drugs, he said: 'If someone's doing coke I can still taste it in the back of my throat. I do miss a glass of red wine, but I just rule it out. I'm not complacent about my recovery.'

On the day of his investiture Elton was in the middle of a tour and flew in to London from Los Angeles the day before. His green turbo-charged Bentley swept through the gates of Buckingham Palace on the morning of 24 February 1998 carrying David, Sheila and Fred. It was the proudest day of his life, even though the Lord Chamberlain, Lord Camoys, announced his name back to front – 'Arise, Sir John Elton'. It is a measure of the Queen's admiration for Elton that she asked if he wanted the blunder edited out of the souvenir video. But he laughed it off. 'It's unique. Let's leave it the way it is,' he said. The Knight Bachelor was Elton's supreme achievement: 'I'm extremely proud. I love my country and to be recognized in such a way, I just can't think of anything better.' He posed briefly for photographs with his mother, stepfather and David, and made a swift getaway for a celebration lunch. Significantly, John Reid, the man who had been with him since 1970, was nowhere to be seen. 'He didn't invite me to go with him, which upset me,' Reid would tell the High Court in 2000. The strain in the relationship was beginning to tell and to the keen observer Reid's absence was obvious, although rumours would not become headlines for another three months.

Sir Elton flew to Australia to continue touring with Billy Joel. Two days after receiving the most prestigious honour his country could bestow, Elton won a Grammy award, the American music world's equivalent to an Oscar, for best male pop vocal performance of the year on 'Candle In The Wind '97'. Then, in May 1998, he received two Ivor Novello Awards, one for sales of the record and the other, a special award for the message in the song.

Later that month Elton agreed to add a special concert to his touring schedule. As the singer now most closely associated with landmark international events after Princess Diana's funeral, he was persuaded by the then Ulster Secretary, Mo Mowlam, to appear at a vast open-air peace concert in the grounds of Stormont Castle in front of a crowd of 15,000 – his first appearance in Northern Ireland for ten years. The venue for the all-party peace talks, this would be the first open-air concert at the castle. To set the stage in time, more than 350 staff worked round the clock unloading forty-eight trucks of equipment, including Versace-style drapery with gold escutcheons on a royal blue background, to set off Elton's lime green suit. Elton drew a crowd of Unionists, Nationalists, Protestants and Catholics, and the only sour note was sounded by the Reverend Ian Paisley, who protested: 'Sodomite plays Stormont'. Clearly overwhelmed by the occasion, Mo Mowlam must have been more nervous than Elton – she introduced him as Mr Elton John, forgetting his new title. She continued: 'Tonight is not a night for politics, tonight is for music. This is a truly historic occasion for Belfast. Everyone is really positive and eager to move on into the future.'

Rather than getting himself entangled in Northern Irish politics, less was more on this occasion and Elton did not say a word to the audience, he just gave them a peace sign and settled down to an energetic three-hour set, one of his longest ever. Elton's tour manager was completely carried away with the emotion of the day and told the *Daily Mirror*: 'Elton wants to be ambassador for Northern Ireland to tell every international artist that Belfast is a date they have to put in their tour calendar.'

At the end of the year, Sir Elton, as national spokesman and moral counsellor, widened his scope to play agony aunt to his footballing friends. Clearly unjaded by a punishing world tour of 130 concerts in 180 days, he took the stage for a press conference at Watford FC, his first for three years. He revealed how, in Paul Gascoigne's lowest months of depression and self-destruction, he sent an encouraging get-well message to the footballer. Elton said: 'I wrote to Gazza when he was in treatment and told him he was a genius.' Like an elderly relation, he also mentioned how proud he was of two other reformed footballers, Tony Adams and Paul Merson.

When Sir Elton gives the world his opinion on football the world listens. He accused Premiership players of being lazy and overpaid, and bemoaned huge transfer fees. This new-found confidence meant that he could publicly criticize heroic figures such as the former England captain Alan Shearer, and former England coach Glenn Hoddle, but he heaped praise on his young heroes, such as David Beckham. 'I like sexy football,' said Elton.

chapter fifteen

She Sings Rock And Roll

THE PARTNERSHIP between Sir Elton John and John Reid, as artist and manager, was the longest and most lucrative the British music business had ever seen, and so in May 1998 the news that the Odd Couple of pop were to split after twenty-eight years was as sensational as it was unexpected. Elton's talent and charisma combined with Reid's aggression and sharp eye for detail, had made them one of the most potent and richest forces in entertainment. Over the years the ferocious Highland terrier had defended the honour of his prize suburban poodle, fought his fights and protected his territory. But both hounds also fought tooth and claw between themselves, and this was to be their final battle.

Under Reid's guidance and financial administration both men had prospered – Reid's fortune was estimated at $18 million (£12 million) and Elton's at $225–$300 million (£150–£200 million). Reid had set up a network of companies that traded with each other, through which Elton and Bernie withdrew their earnings. After twenty-seven years Elton still relied on Reid to steer his empire and protect his corner, and he was perhaps the only person who could bring common sense to bear when Elton got out of control. Such was Elton's love for his manager that Reid had been guest of honour at his fiftieth birthday party, less than twelve months previously. Together they had grown up, learned about sex, taken cocaine and alcohol in addictive quantities, and scaled the highs and lows of rock and roll. Eventually, in 1991, Reid checked into the same Chicago hospital that Elton had attended, to kick his addictions to cocaine and alcohol. Elton was a true friend and tower of strength, calling him regularly during his four-week stay. When he came home Elton encouraged 'the fabulous Beryl' to seek help with his therapist, Beechy Colclough, and Reid has remained clean ever since. Their rows were notorious, and when the split was announced some commentators predicted that they would kiss and make up. But not this time, and no one in their circle expected it to be an amicable separation.

Reid's nemesis was an extraordinary man called Benjamin Pell, a failed law student and professional muckraker who claims to have tipped off national newspapers with several big stories over the past few years. He goes through people's rubbish looking for evidence which he collates, and argues, by this method, to have exposed corruption and malpractice throughout the worlds of celebrity, journalism, the law, politics and even royalty. Pell's discoveries in the bins outside Reid's office would lead ultimately to the final split between Reid and his prize client.

Pell was no cyber-terrorist or computer-hacker, as initially suspected. The only tools of his trade were a clapped-out van, a pair of sturdy rubber gloves, a fluorescent waterproof jacket and a fistful of bin liners. This urban fox stalked the streets in the dead of night, scavenging for confidential scraps in bins outside the offices of lawyers, accountants, showbiz agents, PRs, politicians and anyone else with whom he had a particular obsession. He had discovered that most security-conscious people did not normally bother to shred unwanted paperwork, preferring instead to throw it in the wastepaper basket. Pell's motives were not strictly fiscal – he found that recycling rubbish in this way brought him the notoriety he craved, by creating chaos and leaving mayhem in its wake. He suffered from a severe form of obsessive-compulsive disorder, hoarding binbags stuffed with hundreds of thousands of confidential papers in his back garden. Once he had discovered the location of Reid's office, the bins became his night-time workplace, and within two weeks he had found copies of Richard Branson's letters to Reid about the Princess of Wales charity tribute CD.

When Pell realized he had a hot story in his hands he turned to Max Clifford, the public relations guru, and arrived at Clifford's New Bond Street offices with thirty bags full of papers. His story made front-page news in the *Mirror* on 14 January 1998 – Branson's letter was printed in full and thus a private disagreement about how to commemorate the Princess developed into an undignified public spat. But further inspection of Pell's papers at Clifford's office yielded a much hotter story – correspondence sent from Elton's accountants to his management company about the dubious state of his finances. This was Pell's biggest story yet.

'I have seen all of Elton John's bank statements for the last five years,' claimed Pell. 'I have seen masses of private documents relating to Elton John and other celebrities.' A letter from the accountants Price Waterhouse to Andrew Haydon, managing director of John Reid Enterprises Limited (JREL), dated 7 January 1998 was reproduced in the *Mirror* on 26 January 1998, outlining, in detail, concerns that 'available headroom' in Elton's cashflow would be running out by April 1998, and listing ways he could raise income. In short, a major cash injection was urgently required. Publication of that letter was the *coup de grâce* in Elton and Reid's relationship. The source of the letter was enigmatically described as 'an anxious senior member of his [Elton's] circle, so worried by Elton's extravagance that he provided an in-depth rundown on his expenditure'.

The source also pointed out helpfully that Elton liked to go shopping in one of his fleet of Bentleys because there was plenty of room in the boot for carrier bags. The detail, as well as the shopping lists, was incredible. Not only were the contents of the letter printed, but an inventory of Elton's cars, a typical week's spending and allowances made to his former wife and his mother. Suggested ways in which he could increase his income included adding profitable one-off shows into the already scheduled 1998 world tour, a private summer concert for the Sultan of Brunei, brokering a new publishing deal with a large cash advance and auctioning some of Elton's treasures.

Elton was livid to see his private financial affairs splashed across the *Mirror*, and blamed Reid for negligence. At seven o'clock in the morning, on the day the letter was printed, Elton rang Reid in New York. 'He was incandescent with rage,' said Reid (to the High Court in 2000), 'and he believed that someone from John Reid Enterprises had sold the information to the newspapers and told me in no uncertain terms to find out how it happened.' Very few people had been privy to the sort of details that had been revealed and Elton assumed it had been leaked by someone close to him.

Relations between Elton and Reid became hostile. 'It was not until afterwards that we discovered that it had been Benjamin Pell who claimed to have gotten the letter from the rubbish bins,' Reid said. 'I remember having a conversation with my lawyers and the people that work for me and saying that this kind of stuff could cost me my relationship with Elton, and ultimately it did.' The end was brutal. Elton John and John Reid have not spoken to each other since 18 March 1998. Elton had already blocked Reid out of his life, most visibly by not inviting him to Buckingham Place for the investiture. 'As far as I'm concerned, he doesn't exist any more, which is very sad,' Elton told David Frost in an interview in August 1999.

These revelations marked the beginning of a terrible year for Reid. His mother died in February 1998 and he was dropped by former client Michael Flatley following a legal wrangle. On the day the Flatley case ended, Reid's old friend, David Croker, died suddenly of a heart attack. Croker had been instrumental in Reid's meeting Elton at EMI in 1970, and had been part of the Rocket story ever since. At forty-eight he was the same age as Reid. A chastened Reid reflected on his life and his acquisitiveness, and he set about decluttering his affairs. He sold his New York apartment, his houses in St John's Wood and the South of France, and sold all his furniture at Christie's.

Reid lodged a writ at the High Court against Pell and took legal action against both the *Mirror* and Max Clifford over the removal, sale and publication of the private documents. Reid's people spent seven days searching Pell's house, but the material had been hidden. Pell, with Clifford's help, used several different aliases when he was dealing with the *Mirror*. 'I called myself Doris White as it abbreviates to D. White or Dwight, Elton's real surname,' Pell said.

When Reid finally got Pell to the High Court, the case did not develop as Reid had hoped. 'He played something between a simpleton and a lunatic,' Reid said. Pell appeared in court armed with all his Elton John merchandise, including an Elton John umbrella, carrying numerous bags brimming with Elton John magazines and tapes. The judge apparently decided that he was a harmless eccentric and no charges were brought, but the damage had been done to the most enduring association in rock and roll.

Elton took immediate steps to gag the *Mirror* in an attempt to prevent any further revelations, issuing a writ against the paper at a cost of $15,000 (£10,000). Elton turned to Frank Presland, his personal lawyer, who had masterminded his case against the *Sun* in 1987 and whom he had known for seventeen years, to take over his affairs. Elton instructed an audit of his business empire by his newly appointed accountants at KPMG, who calculated a shortfall of $30 million (£20 million).

At a concert in Wembley in summer 1998, Elton made his feelings clear when he told his fans that a friend had lost all his money to his wife, bitterly adding: 'Lately I've come to know how that feels.' Elton also went on the record to lambast Reid as a liar and a cheat. 'The treachery and betrayal of a man I counted on as a friend and confidant have caused me eighteen months of heartbreak,' he said. Clearly the separation would be far from cordial.

It was announced on 12 January 1999 that Elton would begin a legal battle against Andrew Haydon, former managing director of JREL, who had been on the team for seventeen years, and accountants Price Waterhouse Coopers, for the disputed $30 million (£20 million) plus alleged breach of trust, breach of contract and negligence. Haydon would defend the claims. Elton accepted a $5 million (£3.4 million) out-of-court settlement from Reid over his claims against him.

Elton's spirits were later lifted by another old friend. In June, Watford secured a place in the Premiership League with a 2–0 win against Bolton at Wembley. Elton watched the match 5,000 miles away in Atlanta and wept tears of joy when he spoke to Graham Taylor afterwards. 'I am so happy for the team, I am happy for the fans, all the staff and the board,' he gushed, 'but most of all I am happy for you.' Over the $15,000 (£10,000) Sky TV satellite link the two men expressed their friendship for each other. 'You know how much I think about you, Graham,' continued Elton. 'You are the best and you have been an incredible part of my life. I can't thank you enough.'

Though the relationship between the charismatic pop star chairman and the brilliant manager had given Watford renewed momentum, the team faced a battle to stay in the Premiership, in competition with clubs who could afford expensive, big-name players. Elton made it clear that he did not have bottomless pockets, however, and it was up to the club to raise funds. Taylor wanted to continue the policy of prudent management, especially in the developing youth team, and spending money on top players would ruin that.

Though Elton had parted with an old friend, he was acquiring new ones in Victoria Adams and David Beckham. Still understandably sensitive to tabloid intrusion, he made an official protest on their behalf to the Press Complaints Commission (which was upheld) when they were photographed sunbathing by the pool at his villa in the South of France and the pictures were published in the *Daily Star*. A highlight of the Beckham's wedding in Ireland in July 1999 was to have been Elton serenading the couple on the piano. However, they received one of his last-minute cancellations – this was no Little Moment, but a genuine heart scare. Elton was on the plane on his way to Ireland when he lost his balance and keeled over. His doctors thought it might be an ear infection, but the old family spectre of heart problems hovered as he was rushed to a private hospital in London with an irregular heartbeat. Elton had a routine two-hour operation to fit an electronic pacemaker to regulate the heartbeat with tiny electrical impulses. After an overnight stay he returned to Nice to recuperate. Elton was ordered to rest for at least two months and had to postpone a series of open-air concerts at Leeds Castle in Kent. He could not resist the lure of an audience for long, however, and just seven weeks after surgery he made his first appearance at Harewood House, near Leeds. It began to rain half an hour into the performance and, as he always does during a downpour, he belted out 'Singin' in the Rain' for a communal singsong. The drenched fans loved every moment.

In many ways, Elton's life was complete: he had achieved personal happiness and contentment with David, he had resolved his confusion about sex and relationships, and he had overcome his addictions – the harmful ones, at least. However, he can still switch from harlequin to harridan in a moment of uncontrollable temper. He admits that some of his behaviour has been atrocious, and knows his outbursts are unreasonable: 'When I lose my temper now, it's because I'm tired and it's over something really stupid.'

In April 1999, at a rehearsal in a New York television studio, the tension surrounding his legal battle may have provoked a severe bout of stage rage with Tina Turner. Plans for a joint world tour had to be scrapped after Elton threw what La Turner described as 'a little boy tantrum'. During rehearsals Turner tried to show him how to play 'Proud Mary' on the piano. 'There was a long silence before he suddenly exploded,' she recalled. 'YOU don't tell ME how to play the piano!' he cried as he stormed off.

After the worldwide success of their *Lion King* collaboration, Elton and Tim Rice tackled a classical opera, Verdi's *Aida*, as a musical. Again they were backed by Disney, which had already successfully transferred *Beauty and the Beast* and *The Lion King* to the stage. But why tackle a classical work with words and music already in place? 'The story appealed to me,' said Elton. 'I thought, we're on a hiding to nothing here, and if we do *Aida* we're going to get criticized anyway. That's dangerous, let's do it!' He wrote nineteen songs in as many days, earning himself $1 million (£666,600) each day. The show premiered in Elton's American home city of Atlanta in October 1998, but reaction to this version of *Aida*-made-easy was mixed. One critic denounced the production as 'trash' and another as, 'lowest common denominator camp'. Elton retorted: 'It's meant to be camp, very camp It's theatrical and for all the family.' Technical problems dogged the show from the start, however, and at the opening-night party Elton reportedly snapped: 'This is Disney and they should be able to get it right.' Disney closed the show, and started again with a new director and choreographer.

After countless revisions to the sets, and the addition of two new songs, the new show previewed in February 2000, but Elton was still not happy with the arrangement of two of the songs. He was so riled about the 'dated' sound, that just fifteen minutes into the performance, he and his entourage left their mid-row seats, and noisily clambered past members of the audience. A month later *Aida* opened in Chicago and New York. Despite the initial problems, Elton subsequently admitted his delight at the show: 'I'm so proud of it, I've seen it thirteen or fourteen times. It's been a huge success.' Elton and Tim Rice would win Best Musical Award at the Brits that year.

Elton's case against Andrew Haydon finally came to court in October 2000, and during a preliminary hearing in the High Court, Elton's QC, Gordon Pollock, set the scene. He described how Elton's impatience with the minutiae of financial administration had led him to lose track of some $30 million (£20 million), which he now wanted to reclaim. Pollock explained that Elton had completely trusted the 'men in suits' to whom he had a strong aversion, and paid them a lot of money to take care of boring details. The central dispute was whether or not the costs charged to Elton John's companies – William A. Bong Ltd, J. Bondi Ltd and Happenstance Ltd – should have been borne by JREL. Elton claimed that Haydon was negligent in letting JREL charge US tour expenses to Elton's companies, which Haydon denied, stating that this was normal practice in the entertainment industry. Haydon claimed that everything had been done in accordance with management contract terms and conditions. Price Waterhouse Coopers vehemently denied Elton's allegations and argued that its employees had acted according to the highest professional standards.

In the agreement made between Reid and Elton in 1984, Reid's income was increased in return for JREL looking after everything in his business life. When Elton discovered in 1998 that all his foreign tour expenses had been charged to his own companies, he interpreted this as Reid's betrayal. Reid said in court that he would never have agreed to pay touring costs at that meeting and, to complicate matters, there was nothing on paper.

Between 1984 and 1989 Elton's companies 'bore several million pounds worth of costs or fees which we say contractually should have fallen on JREL', Pollock explained. These costs were for foreign touring expenses such as payments to booking agents, accountants and producers. Elton argued that Price Waterhouse Coopers was negligent in not reporting that costs were charged to his companies, as they had been before the 1984 agreement with Reid. Pollock pointed out that Elton had been phenomenally successful and that others had enjoyed the fruits of his success, and that in one single year Reid had earned $22.5 million (£15 million) in commission, while JREL took $110.25 million (£73.5 million) between 1980 and 1988.

Elton's legal team were not in favour of the opposition bringing evidence of his spending habits to court, claiming that it was irrelevant to the case. They argued that if Elton had to endure cross-examination about his shopping habits and flamboyant lifestyle it would put pressure on him and the inevitable media frenzy would embarrass him, which was no doubt what the opposition had in mind. If putting his lifestyle on trial did not succeed in making him blush, it would certainly catch the public imagination, just as a cross-examination could have tarnished his reputation in his libel case against the *Sun*, had it gone to court. Whatever the risks, this time the strategy worked to Elton's advantage – he became the nation's favourite shopaholic.

On the day, he rolled up to the Royal Courts of Justice in his green Bentley, accompanied by David. This was to be a different kind of performance for Elton – he stepped into the witness box with his auburn hair weave, wearing a demure charcoal suit with a white shirt and spangly blue tie. In front of an audience of about fifty, he took the oath as Elton Hercules John. He was on his best behaviour and with divine understatement endeared himself to the nation. On his colossal expenditure on floral arrangements – $440,000 (£293,000) in twenty months – he admitted: 'I like flowers.'

It was calculated that Elton had spent more than $60 million (£40 million) in a twenty-month period during 1996 and 1997: £4 million on jewellery, £10 million on furniture, fine art and antiques, including a one-day spree totalling

£527,849 at Sotheby's and Christie's, and a £250,000 payment to his interior designers. He spent £400,000 on maintaining his fleet of cars and £9.6 million on extending his property portfolio – he has houses in London, Windsor, Atlanta and the French Riviera. For his lavish fiftieth birthday party, he paid £3,500 for his wig and £121,000 on catering alone. He was not averse to spending £250,000 at Versace on one visit. Revealing that his monthly spending could amount to £2 million on average, he defended his extravagant lifestyle: 'I don't have any people to leave money to. I am a single man. I like to spend money.'

If the opposition had hoped to cause him embarrassment by exposing his spending habits, the public were fascinated by every extravagant detail. In a week he might spend £50,000 at his favourite jewellers, Theo Fennell, £10,000 on flowers and sending up to 250 bouquets, £5,000 on vet's bills, £2,500 in petty cash, £15,000 on a piece of David Linley furniture, and perhaps £30,000 at an antiques auction. He once said: 'I could find a shop in the Sahara desert.'

Public condemnation of his excessive shopping tendencies was rare, because as generous as he was to himself, he was equally bountiful in his donation to charity and fundraising efforts.

Elton is an icon for the new consumer society at the dawn of the plentiful twenty-first century. Thrift is out, shopping is in, and as the anointed king of consumerism, Elton is courted by the new rich – a funky mix of footballers, film makers, pop stars, couturiers, models, and aristos. According to Victoria Beckham, no stranger to the delights of Sloane Street herself: 'He can totally shop me under the table any day, he's a great guy and he knows how to spend a lot of money.'

The philosopher Anthony Grayling defines two classes of people who spend on an Eltonian scale: 'There are some who have little sense of taste and buy lots of very expensive hit-and-miss objects. And there are some who do have an idea of who they are and what they want and who can, by chance or otherwise, create something good that can last.' Elton falls into both camps. Robert Key, director of Elton's AIDS foundation, a longstanding associate and fine art graduate, acts as his art scout and taste guru, and supervised the comprehensive refurbishment of Woodside ten years ago. Elton relies on Key's taste and knowledge, and when Key's former assistant, Gabrielle Hardy, was asked, 'Does Elton have any taste?' Her silence was revealing. Taste is not essential if one buys in bulk, and being a connoisseur isn't necessary when one can rely on an array of designer labels from Gucci to Versace.

Shopping is the perfect addiction. It carries none of the complexities of food or drugs bingeing, it brings immediate relief, comfort, adrenalin rushes, elation and satisfaction – if one can afford it. After a quick fix Elton can walk out of a shop, upright, sober, with an armful of divine carrier bags and no nasty side-effects: 'I'm like a magpie. If I see something beautiful, I have to have it. Anyway I could be run over by a bus tomorrow.'

Mr Hapgood QC, representing Price Waterhouse Coopers, began by asking Elton about his relationship with John Reid. Elton had ruthlessly cut Reid out of his world and as he faced his diminutive ex-friend and ex-manager, who was seated less than two metres away across the court, he ignored him completely, avoiding eye contact. He began: 'He would not be the first man in the world to get caught with his fingers in the till. I trusted him implicitly. I never thought he would betray me. But he did betray me.' Reid sat and listened to this vitriolic attack impassively.

When Elton and Reid were on holiday in St Tropez in 1984 they could not have known that the informal deal they were to broker would lead directly to their final row. Ultimately, after much haggling, Elton and Reid shook hands on an agreement which gave Reid 20 per cent of the singer's gross earnings with which to run the business side of the partnership, including a share of his songs. Elton would say in court: 'For an artist it is the most precious thing you can give, it is like giving away a piece of your soul. When I write a song, that is like a child to me. I was prepared to give him part of the songwriting to shut him up for all his whining. When I did a deal with him I didn't have to write anything down, or so I thought.'

It was surprising that either man could even remember the meeting, let alone the detail, given that both were in the grip of drug and alcohol addictions. Elton revealed: 'You were dealing with people who were not dealing with reality on a day-to-day basis. During the years when I was taking drugs and alcohol I could be irrational and unmanageable at times. My manager had a bigger problem than I did, so it was a miracle anything got done.' Competitiveness was a keynote of their relationship – their drinking, drug-taking, even their spending sprees. 'The more I bought something,' said Elton, 'the more he bought something.' Both had extravagant taste and Reid was able to keep up; he bought property, artworks, furniture and expensive clothes. Money was no object and the two men exchanged fabulous gifts, from luxury boats to jewellery, and racehorses to cars.

Although Elton had been advised in the past that his agreement with Reid was too generous, he had been happy with the arrangement. Hapgood pressed Elton on the reasons why he chose to ignore the advice being offered, suggesting that he could have been a great deal tougher. Elton replied, 'I never judged my relationship with Mr Reid in monetary terms at all. It was all based on trust.' Hapgood seemed surprised and Elton retorted: 'You've obviously never trusted someone as much as I trusted John Reid.' When Hapgood asked if he was seeking to get back from the deep pockets of Price Waterhouse Coopers some of his past generosity to Reid, Elton, to everyone's surprise said, 'Yes.'

In 1990 Andrew Haydon had flown to meet Elton in Los Angeles to discuss a 'serious financial crisis', but Elton had refused to meet with him. Elton didn't remember the occasion, but admitted that his memory of events and grasp of history was not exactly enhanced by his cocaine and alcohol dependence until later in 1990. Elton said plaintively that he had 'wanted an uncomplicated life' so he had left it all to his management team. He was now paying the price for ignoring the small print and for not ensuring that any existed in the first place.

In the more recent past, however, he saw no reason why he should have followed the advice of his financial team in any case. 'There was so much money coming in,' he said. 'I decided I could live a lavish lifestyle. I had a bigger idea of my talent than they did. I was still prepared to work and earn money,' he said. Indeed his 1999 American tour grossed $32.5 million (£21.6 million). He argued that it was his choice and that he owned quite a few assets in pension funds, publishing and *objets d'art*, should he need to raise cash. He laughed out loud in court when he heard how his accountants thought he might retire before he was fifty, commenting that it was the sort of advice his father might have given him. He did admit that he had *threatened* to retire on more than one occasion, but only when he was in a particularly bad mood. At fifty-three, touring and performing were still his *raisons d'être*; he enjoyed his work more than ever and had no intention of retiring. 'Why can't I drop dead on stage?' he asked. 'I have no interest in retiring.'

Haydon's counsel suggested that his spending sprees added considerably to the administrative burden of the management company. Elton didn't like this at all and responded: 'I just don't get this administrative burden thing. I was the only major artist they had. I have the pressure of going into the studio every year and writing fifteen songs. I have the burden of fulfilling concerts. I have to turn up on time and give a good show. They weren't out on the road with me. They weren't in the studios with me. What else were they doing?'

As if to prove his point, he flew to Belgium after his court appearance to give a concert in Antwerp and appeared in court again the following day.

The strain was beginning to tell, though, and Elton threw a couple of punches below the belt when he made reference to Reid's criminal record and his short spell in prison. When asked if he believed whether Reid had deliberately defrauded him out of millions of pounds, he answered: 'Why would someone with a criminal record be incapable of doing something like that?' He was alluding to an incident that occurred in New Zealand in 1974 when, in defence of Elton, Reid had punched a journalist and ended up in jail.

Elton regretted his hasty reply, however, and the next day offered an apology for his choice of words: 'It was a very passionate response and a very irresponsible remark . . . I do not think it has anything to do with his financial judgment. I would like to apologize for saying that.'

When Elton left the court after giving evidence he said: 'It has been very tiring, but I think I got very fair treatment from all the QCs . . . and I still like flowers.'

John Reid sat through Elton's acrimonious evidence and was later called to the witness box. He said that working for Elton for nearly thirty years had left him disenchanted and that the singer's extravagance and disregard for advice had meant that he was ready to put it all behind him. Reid had been distraught when Elton fired him: 'I was very concerned about the disregard personally and professionally for us, JREL, as his managers, and his disregard for his own personal responsibilities in the way he conducted his own personal expenditure, and his refusal to listen to some very important aspects of his career.'

A manager's function is to deal with the invisible matters, to provide the support mechanisms and organize the infrastructure. It is his responsibility to cocoon and pamper his star, so that all his needs, and more, are catered for. With Elton's energy, his prolific output and schedule it was a round-the-clock job for his management team. It was natural that Reid should have wanted to be fairly compensated for his efforts on Elton's behalf, but whenever Reid mentioned his own remuneration it never struck the right chord. Reid said in court: 'It's not a good practice between anyone and Elton to complain steadily.' Elton considered Reid's regular conversations about money tedious, and thought he had come to a fair agreement with Reid in 1984.

Outside the court, life went on. In November 2000 the pop number-cruncher was back at one of his favourite venues, Madison Square Garden in New York, for his fifty-first sell-out gig there; he was to make a live concert recording for his forty-first album, *One Night Only*, to be mixed and in the shops within three weeks. He had just completed 165 solo shows and was relishing the thought of playing again with Nigel Olsson on drums and Davey Johnstone on guitar. The stage was decked out in Romanesque Versace motifs, and old friends joined him to sing old favourites from his career – Kiki Dee, Billy Joel, Bryan Adams, Ronan Keating, Mary J. Blige and a new star, Anastacia, whom Elton had taken under his promotional wing.

Elton's third 'Out of the Closet' sale was the biggest and most ghetto-fabulous yet. The owners of the former Tommy Hilfiger shop in Bond Street let EJAF have the shop in December 2000 until all 16,000 cast-offs were sold, and he raised $645,000 (£430,000). The stock revealed the sheer scale of

Elton's ability to spend, and why he is the patron saint of retail therapy. Rail upon rail was tightly packed with suits, jackets, shirts, casual tops, knitwear, jumpsuits like giant babygros, baskets stacked with coloured tennis shorts – almost all Versace – and 2,000 pairs of shoes at a bargain $45 (£30) each. There was more in the basement. There were textures and trimmings to make a haberdasher's head spin. A polka-dot mini-kilt, a PVC shellsuit, zebra print and fake ponyskin jackets, cowboy boots and a fetching pair of slip-on shoes with fluffy pom-poms and leatherwork penises stitched on to each foot. Elton opened the sale with a champagne breakfast for celebrity friends, saying: 'It's the poshest charity shop I've ever been in.'

The legal proceedings ended in February 2001, after forty-three days in court, and when the verdict was eventually announced in April, Elton was in America, halfway through a twenty-seven-city tour of the United States, Europe and Scandinavia. He was relaxing at home in Atlanta between concert dates in Kansas City and Memphis, taking time out for a game of tennis when the call came through, but his financial advisers let him finish the game before telling him that he had lost the case. Elton, self-confessed financial dunce, shrugged it off as a minor setback, saying, 'It's just business.' Knowing his single-mindedness and determination to see things through, his new manager, Frank Presland, thought an appeal was likely. He added on behalf of his client: 'I don't think he will cut back on his flowers.'

Reid was in court to hear the verdict. Now fifty-one, he was dignified, saying, 'It is very sad that my very long relationship with Elton has ended in this way.' But, as a businessman with a reputation to protect, he was relieved that the question mark hanging over him for the last three years had been removed. The revelations in court meant that no one had come out of the case in a good light. He said he felt sorry for Elton, but did not admire his strategy. 'I was fired overnight from a job I had for twenty-eight years. This case was brought to try and justify that,' said Reid.

Elton was refused permission to appeal and faced a $12 million (£8 million) legal bill. The judge was not satisfied that an appeal 'would have any real prospect of success'. However, later in the year he won the right to challenge the result against his accountants, whom he still alleged were negligent in managing his affairs. In June 2002, the case reached the Court of Appeal. Three judges deliberated over the evidence, and came to the same conclusion as the High Court judge over a year previously, ruling against Elton by a majority. Elton's lawyers made no application to take the case to the House of Lords, and so now, it seems, Elton has had to accept defeat.

A month later Elton had to face another blow of a more tragic nature, when he received news that Gus Dudgeon, producer of some of his greatest hits, had been killed in a car accident. Describing Dudgeon as 'an incredibly talented producer and a dear friend', Elton said, 'I will miss him terribly.'

☆

To date, twenty years after the first report of the disease, there is no cure for AIDS and twenty-two million people have died of AIDS-related illnesses all over the world. Another forty-two million are affected by HIV. It is estimated that by 2020 HIV and AIDS will have caused more deaths than any disease outbreak in history. EJAF estimates that 16,000 people a day become infected with HIV. New drugs have helped bring the disease under a degree of control in Europe and America, but complacency is now the biggest threat. Africa bears the brunt of the disease and many experts think the worst is yet to come.

With headquarters in London and Los Angeles, EJAF has supported more than 200 projects in Britain, including helping to instigate the first National Hardship Fund for HIV, commissioning the first independent assessment of HIV needs in prison and helping to establish the only forum for AIDS charities. EJAF has contributed to organizations in thirty-two countries and Elton has lent his name as patron to many AIDS-related organizations including UNAIDS, Amnesty International and International AIDS Vaccine Initiative. Between 1992 and 2001, his foundation distributed more than $30 million (£20 million) and funded more than 2,000 grants in America. Elton subsidizes the overheads so that more than 90 per cent of the money goes directly to patient care grants, and EJAF is now one of the world's largest non-profit AIDS charities.

Elton's money-raising events continue to boost funds considerably for victims of AIDS. In March 2002 his Oscar night party raised over $500,000 (£333,000) for EJAF. He was also involved in planning an all-star fundraising tennis tournament with Billie Jean King and a host of tennis champions including Pete Sampras and Andre Agassi, which took place in October 2002, in Philadelphia, and raised over $700,000 (£467,000) for EJAF and other local charities.

David is passionate about supporting Elton in his fundraising efforts. As a film-maker, David visited Kenya and South Africa to record the horror of the epidemic in the heart of the continent, and while Elton took in a whirlwind seven-date concert tour of the Far East and a Royal Variety Performance, David marked World AIDS Day 2001 by making a sponsored eleven-day climb to the summit of Mount Kilimanjaro in Tanzania, the highest mountain in Africa.

In contrast to the old days, Woodside is now a refined home. Elton and David are gilt-edged, A-list hosts for their annual White Tie and Tiara Ball to raise funds for EJAF. (Neither Elton nor David wear their tiaras.) At $1,500 (£1,000) a ticket, everyone who is anyone is on the guest list – there are representatives of royalty, rock and roll, the media, the catwalk, the sports arena and the silver screen.

David divides his time between fundraising for EJAF and film production with Rocket Pictures. Following the success he had achieved with his independently financed first movie, *Women Talking Dirty*, starring British actress Helena Bonham-Carter, Rocket Pictures renewed its development deal with Disney in 2001. The company has five projects in development including a big-budget Disney animation with the working title *Gnomeo and Juliet*.

A consistent supporter of new talent throughout his career, Elton has dubbed the white rap star Eminem a genius, and nominated his album, *The Marshall Mathers LP*, one of the two most important albums of the last twenty years, the other being *Nevermind* by Nirvana. In a gesture of unabashed hero worship he performed a duet with Eminem at the Grammy Awards in February 2001, singing the rap star's hit 'Stan'. It was a curious sight – the doyenne of the rock establishment in a pink-and-yellow polka-dot suit and supporter of gay causes, embracing the bad boy in baggy trousers and writer of homophobic lyrics, however tongue in cheek, with 200 gay protesters outside and a standing ovation inside. A month later Elton was presenting his new friend with the award for Best International Male at the BRIT Awards in London.

The Gay and Lesbian Alliance Against Defamation (GLAAD), which had honoured Elton in 2000 for his efforts in fighting homophobia, described the rap star's songs as having 'the most blatantly offensive, homophobic lyrics we have ever heard'. And the formerly gay-baiting *Sun* observed that the album promotes 'drugs, gun-running, torture, incest, murder, rape and armed robbery'. Eminem claims that his lyrics should be taken with a grain of salt. Elton judged them 'intelligent hardcore stuff' and said: 'It appeals to my English black sense of humour. When I put this album on for the first time, I was in hysterics.' Eminem claimed that he did not realize that Elton was gay when the duet idea was first suggested to him.

It is flattering for the venerable pop fan to be fêted by his younger counter-parts. Moby has said that Elton is one of the greatest vocalists alive, Ross Robinson, the man behind the Nu Metal band Limp Bizkit has always been a fan, and Puff Daddy or P Diddy, aka Sean Combs, the world's most successful rap producer, intends to sample some riffs from Elton's early work. A new generation of cinema-goers have recently discovered the classic tracks, including 'Tiny Dancer' in Cameron Crowe's *Almost Famous* and 'Your Song' in Baz Luhrmann's *Moulin Rouge*. 'It's wonderful,' said Elton, 'especially because they are used so well and in such significant scenes.' And on US television, in the lead-up to Christmas 2002, some of Elton's best songs featured on the soundtracks of a number of top television shows, to promote sales of his triple CD, *Greatest Hits 1970–2002*.

Elton may have churned out middle-of-the-road lift music on his less than best albums, but he holds a unique place in the pop pantheon. He remains hip enough for the next generation of musicians to associate with him without embarrassment. He collaborated with the boy band, Blue, to cover his 1976 hit 'Sorry Seems To Be The Hardest Word'. In 1976 it reached number eleven in the charts, but in 2002 it knocked Eminem off the British number-one spot. He defended scathing criticism of the single in the *Daily Mirror* in a fax which snapped: 'Thanks for the nice review with Blue. "Sorry" happens to be a beautiful song sung by Frank Sinatra, among others. As a musician I know this. Have a nice day.' According to producer Felix Tod: 'He's a music nut and his knowledge and genuine enthusiasm makes him one of us.'

He is also a car nut. He decided to put up for auction twenty of his luxury cars, leaving him with just eight. Elton's enthusiasm for expensive vehicles goes back to when he bought his first Aston Martin in 1970. He indulges his passion for music while he is driving; there are CD autochangers in the boot of each car, filled with his current favourites. Among the Bentley, Jaguar, Rolls-Royce and Ferrari marques was a 1978 Aston Martin V8 Vantage which had once been painted in black and yellow with a red stripe, the Watford colours – it was later resprayed a tasteful blue. Prince Philip once said to Elton: 'Oh, it is you who owns that ghastly car is it? We often see it when we are driving into the back of Windsor Castle.' The sale at Christie's made nearly $3 million (£2 million). 'I'm sad about the collection going,' said Elton. 'I've really loved collecting it, but I have it here in the garage not being seen by anyone.'

Elton's association with Watford has perhaps given him the most pleasure over the years. Along with music, he has always been passionate about football and the people at the club have, to a certain extent, kept his feet on the ground in the unreal world in which he lives, but in May 2002, he announced that his twenty-five year association with Watford FC was over, and resigned as chairman and director. Elton no longer felt able to fulfil his duties, and wished to make way for 'a chairman who will be able to devote more time to the club'.

Earlier that same month, Elton, minstrel by appointment, became the first pop star to perform inside Buckingham Palace for the Queen's Golden Jubilee concert. He was due to be touring on 3 June, the day of the concert, and was invited to make his contribution to the prestigious event a month early, by recording a song in the palace which was to be played to the crowds on a giant video screen.

While *The Lion King* and *Aida* are running as number-one and number-two shows on Broadway, Elton is working with director Stephen Daldry on a stage version of the movie *Billy Elliot*. However much he has promised to cut back on his workload, he is still a frenetic globetrotter with fire in his belly, a troubadour doing what he loves best, playing live, giving his fans more than their money's worth. He toured throughout Europe and the United States between May and December 2002, and also played his first concert in India in early November to an enthusiastic crowd of more than 20,000. 'I'm doing solo shows all over Europe, Turkey and Morocco, places I've never been to before like Latvia, Estonia,' he said. 'I'm enjoying myself more than I ever have.'

Elton ended 2002 with two 'intimate' EJAF benefit concerts at the Shepherds Bush Empire, with a capacity for audiences of just 3,000, at which he entertained fans and celebrity friends alike. As ever, he summoned the spirit of Jerry Lee Lewis with virtuoso flourishes on the piano, and this time the spirit of John Lennon joined in as Elton called for world peace. He is planning new tours of America and the Far East and another tour with Billy Joel.

'If I don't start taking it easier,' he said, 'David will probably kill me. He misses me when I'm away. I'm so in love with the guy. The picture I keep beside my bed is one of my most treasured possessions.' Elton's favourite photo is one of David as a little boy. 'He's the first person I call in the morning and the last person I call at night,' said Elton. 'I'm away so much and it's hard, because David likes to be with me and I like to be with David.'

Elton continues to be garlanded with awards, including an honorary doctorate from the Royal Academy of Music. He inaugurated the Elton John Scholarship Fund, to give talented young musicians the opportunity that he enjoyed at Britain's senior music conservatoire. To raise funds for his alma mater he performed with the ninety-piece Royal Academy of Music Symphony Orchestra and Choir at London's Royal Opera House in December 2002, and still he smiles his wide, gap-toothed, little-boy smile, and his right, bushy eyebrow dances up and down in time to the music.

Time has mellowed the flamboyant superstar. Elton is now a man at ease with the world. 'My life has been a rollercoaster ride of ups and downs – fantastic times, really depressing times, incredibly irresponsible times,' said Elton. 'Apart from enjoying my happiness and helping those less fortunate, I just want to continue composing music which appeals to others, because that's what I really love doing.'

He is one of the world's number-one fundraisers and an international treasure, but he is without equal as the world's number-one piano showman: Sir Elton John – Made In England.

Elton John: Discography

1965 Come Back, Baby; Times Getting Tougher Than Tough: UK 7-inch single; (with Bluesology) reissued 1997

1966 Mr Frantic; Everyday (I Have The Blues): UK 7-inch single; (with Bluesology) reissued 1997

1967 Since I Found You Baby; Just A Little Bit: UK 7-inch single; (with Bluesology)

1968 I've Been Loving You; Here's To The Next Time: UK 7-inch single

1969 Lady Samantha; All Across The Havens: UK & US 7-inch single

1969 Breakdown Blues; Dick Barton Theme (The Devil's Gallop): UK 7-inch single; Bread & Beer Band

1969 It's Me That You Need; Just Like Strange Rain: UK 7-inch single; picture sleeve

1970 Lady Samantha; It's Me That You Need: US 7-inch single

1970 Border Song; Bad Side Of The Moon: UK & US 7-inch single

1970 From Denver To LA; Barbara Moore Singers solo – Warm Summer Rain: US 7-inch single

1970 Rock 'N' Roll Madonna; Grey Seal: UK 7-inch single

1970 Take Me To The Pilot; Your Song: US 7-inch single

1971 Come Down In Time; Country Comfort; Amoreena; Love Song: US 7-inch single; picture sleeve; jukebox

1971 Your Song; Into The Old Man's Shoes: UK 7-inch single; reissued 1977

1971 Friends; Honey Roll: UK & US 7-inch single

1971 Levon; Goodbye: US 7-inch single

1972 Tiny Dancer; Razor Face: US 7-inch single

1972 Rocket Man (I Think It's Going To Be A Long, Long Time); Holiday Inn; Goodbye: UK 7-inch single; picture sleeve & gatefold sleeve

1972 Rocket Man (I Think It's Going To Be A Long, Long Time); Susie (Dramas): US 7-inch single

1972 Honky Cat; Slave: US 7-inch single

1972 Honky Cat; Lady Samantha; It's Me That You Need: UK 7-inch single

1972 Crocodile Rock; Elderberry Wine: UK & US 7-inch single; reissued 1997

1973 Daniel; Teacher, I Need You; High Flying Bird; Crocodile Rock: US 7-inch single; picture sleeve; jukebox

1973 Daniel; Skyline Pigeon: UK & US 7-inch single; reissued 1977

1973 Saturday Night's Alright For Fighting; Jack Rabbit; Whenever You're Ready (We'll Go Steady Again): UK & US 7-inch single; UK version had picture sleeve

1973 Goodbye Yellow Brick Road; Screw You: UK & US 7-inch single; B-side entitled 'Young Man's Blues' in US; reissued 1977

1973 Step Into Christmas; Ho! Ho! Ho! (Who'd Be A Turkey At Christmas?): UK & US 7-inch single; 1992 US limited edition on green vinyl

1974 Candle In The Wind; Bennie And The Jets: UK 7-inch single; reissued 1977

1974 Bennie And The Jets; Harmony: US 7-inch single

1974 Don't Let The Sun Go Down On Me; Sick City: UK & US 7-inch single

1974 The Bitch Is Back; Cold Highway: UK & US 7-inch single

1974 Lucy In The Sky With Diamonds; One Day At A Time: UK & US 7-inch single; US version had picture sleeve; featuring John Lennon & The Muscle Shoals Horns

1975 Philadelphia Freedom (Live); I Saw Her Standing There (Live): UK & US 7-inch single; both with John Lennon; live at Madison Square Garden, New York, 28 November 1974; picture sleeve

1975 Someone Saved My Life Tonight; House Of Cards: UK & US 7-inch single; UK had picture label & limited edition with custom label

1975 Island Girl; Sugar On The Floor: UK & US 7-inch single; UK version had picture sleeve

1976 Grow Some Funk Of Your Own; I Feel Like A Bullet (In The Gun Of Robert Ford): UK & US 7-inch single; US edition had A & B sides reversed

1976 Pinball Wizard; Harmony: UK 7-inch single; reissued 1977

1976 Don't Go Breaking My Heart; Snow Queen: UK & US 7-inch single; with Kiki Dee; picture sleeve

1976 Bennie And The Jets; Rock 'N' Roll Madonna: UK 7-inch single

1976 Sorry Seems To Be The Hardest Word; Shoulder Holster: UK & US 7-inch single; UK version had picture sleeve

1977 Crazy Water; Chameleon: UK 7-inch single

1977 **Four From Four Eyes:** Your Song; Rocket Man (I Think It's Going To Be A Long, Long Time); Saturday Night's Alright For Fighting; Whenever You're Ready (We'll Go Steady Again): UK 7-inch EP; picture sleeve

1977 Bite Your Lip (Get Up And Dance!) (Tom Moulton Remix); Kiki Dee solo – Chicago: US 7-inch single

1977 Bite Your Lip (Get Up And Dance!) (Tom Moulton Remix); Kiki Dee solo – Chicago: UK 12-inch single; double A-side

1978 Ego; Flintstone Boy: UK & US 7-inch single; picture sleeve

1978 Funeral For A Friend – Love Lies Bleeding; We All Fall In Love Sometimes – Curtains: UK 12-inch single; picture sleeve

1978 **Elton John Special 12-Record Pack:** 1. Candle In The Wind; I Feel Like A Bullet (In The Gun Of Robert Ford); 2. Country Comfort; Crocodile Rock; 3. Don't Let The Sun Go Down On Me; Someone Saved My Life Tonight; 4. Honky Cat; Sixty Years On; 5. Island Girl; Saturday Night's Alright For Fighting; 6. Lady Samantha; Skyline Pigeon; 7. Philadelphia Freedom; Lucy In The Sky With Diamonds; 8. Pinball Wizard; Bennie And The Jets; 9. Rocket Man (I Think It's Going To Be A Long, Long Time); Daniel; 10. Sweet Painted Lady; Goodbye Yellow Brick Road; 11. The Bitch Is Back; Grow Some Funk Of Your Own; 12. Your Song; Border Song: UK boxed set of 7-inch singles

1978 Part-Time Love; I Cry At Night: UK & US 7-inch single; picture sleeve

1978 Song For Guy (Instrumental); Lovesick: UK 7-inch single; US edition in 1979 with picture sleeve

1979 Are You Ready For Love (Part 1); Are You Ready For Love (Part 2): UK 7-inch single; both with Philippe 'Soul' Wynne

1979 **The Thom Bell Sessions '77:** Are You Ready For Love; Mama Can't Buy You Love; Three-Way Love Affair: UK & US 12-inch single; picture sleeve

1979 Mama Can't Buy You Love; Three-Way Love Affair: US 7-inch single; picture sleeve

1979 Victim Of Love; Strangers: UK & US 7-inch single; UK version with picture sleeve

1979 Johnny B. Goode; Thunder In The Night: UK 7-inch & 12-inch single; picture sleeve

1979 Johnny B. Goode; Georgia: US 7-inch single

1980 Little Jeannie; Conquer The Sun: UK & US 7-inch single; picture sleeve; US limited edition with custom label

1980 Sartorial Eloquence; White Man Danger; Cartier Commercial: UK & US 7-inch single; A-side entitled 'Don't Ya Wanna Play This Game No More?' in US

1980 Harmony; Mona Lisas And Mad Hatters: UK 7-inch single; picture sleeve

1980 Dear God; Tactics (Instrumental): UK 7-inch single

1980 Dear God; Tactics (Instrumental): Steal Away Child; Love So Cold: UK double 7-inch single; picture sleeve

1981 I Saw Her Standing There (Live); Whatever Gets You Through The Night (Live); Lucy In The Sky With Diamonds (Live): UK 7-inch single; with John Lennon & The Muscle Shoals Horns; live at Madison Square Garden, New York, 28 November 1974; picture sleeve

1981 Nobody Wins; Fools In Fashion: UK & US 7-inch single; picture sleeve

1981 Just Like Belgium; Can't Get Over Getting Over Losing You: UK 7-inch single

1981 Chloe; Tortured: US 7-inch single

1981 Loving You Is Sweeter Than Ever (Single Edit) (with Kiki Dee); Kiki Dee solo – Twenty-Four Hours: UK 7-inch single; picture sleeve

1982 **Amnesty International:** press propaganda speeches: UK 7-inch single; pressed on random picture discs

1982 Blue Eyes; Hey Papa Legba: UK & US 7-inch single; picture sleeve

1982 Empty Garden (Hey Hey Johnny); Take Me Down To The Ocean: UK & US 7-inch single; picture sleeve; UK limited edition with picture disc

1982 Princess; The Retreat: UK 7-inch single; picture sleeve

1982 All Quiet On The Western Front; Where Have All The Good Times Gone? (Remix): UK 7-inch single; picture sleeve; limited edition with poster

1982 Ball And Chain; Where Have All The Good Times Gone? (Alternate Version): US 7-inch single

1982 When A Child Is Born (with Johnny Mathis); It's Gonna Be A Cold Cold Christmas (with Dana); Step Into Christmas; Winter Wonderland (with Linda Lewis): UK 7-inch single; picture sleeve

1983 I Guess That's Why They Call It The Blues; Choc Ice Goes Mental (Instrumental): UK & US 7-inch single; picture sleeve; limited edition with embossed sleeve & misprint

1983 I'm Still Standing; Love So Cold: US 7-inch single

1983 Kiss The Bride; Choc Ice Goes Mental (Instrumental): US 7-inch single; picture sleeve

1983 I'm Still Standing; Earn While You Learn (Instrumental): UK 7-inch single; picture sleeve; limited edition of piano-shaped picture disc

1983 I'm Still Standing (Extended Version); Earn While You Learn (Instrumental): UK 12-inch single; picture sleeve

1983 Kiss The Bride; Dreamboat (Edit): UK 7-inch single; picture sleeve

1983 I Guess That's Why They Call It The Blues; The Retreat: US 7-inch single

1983 Kiss The Bride; Dreamboat (Edit); Ego; Song For Guy (Instrumental): UK double 7-inch single; picture sleeve

1983 Kiss The Bride (Extended Version); Dreamboat (Extended Version): UK 12-inch single; picture sleeve

1983 Cold As Christmas (In The Middle Of The Year); Crystal: UK 7-inch single; picture sleeve

1983 Cold As Christmas (In The Middle Of The Year); Crystal; Don't Go Breaking My Heart (with Kiki Dee); Snow Queen (with Kiki Dee): UK double 7-inch single; picture sleeve

1983 Cold As Christmas (In The Middle Of The Year); Crystal; Je Veux De La Tendresse: UK 12-inch single; picture sleeve

1984 Empty Garden (Hey Hey Johnny); Blue Eyes: US 7-inch single; 'Back-to-Back Hits'

1984 I Guess That's Why They Call It The Blues; Too Low For Zero: US 7-inch single; 'Back-to-Back Hits'

1984 I'm Still Standing; Kiss The Bride: US 7-inch single; 'Back-to-Back Hits'

1984 Sad Songs (Say So Much); A Simple Man: UK & US 7-inch single; UK picture sleeve; UK 12-in single; UK limited edition of hat-shaped picture disc

1984 Sad Songs (Say So Much); Who Wears These Shoes?: US 7-inch single; 'Back-to-Back Hits'

1984 Who Wears These Shoes?; Lonely Boy: US 7-inch single; picture sleeve

1984 Passengers; Lonely Boy: UK 7-inch single; picture sleeve

1984 Passengers (Julian Mendelsohn's Extended Remix); Lonely Boy; Blue Eyes: UK 12-inch single; picture sleeve

1984 Who Wears These Shoes?; Tortured: UK 7-inch single; picture sleeve

1984 Who Wears These Shoes? (Extended Version); Tortured; I Heard It Through The Grapevine (Live): UK 12-inch single; live at Empire Pool, Wembley, London, 3 November 1977; picture sleeve

1985 In Neon; Tactics: US 7-inch single

1985 Breaking Hearts (Ain't What It Used To Be); In Neon: UK 7-inch single; picture sleeve

1985 Act Of War (Part 1); Act Of War (Part 2): UK & US 7-inch single; both with Millie Jackson; picture sleeve; limited edition in concertina pack

1985 Act Of War (Part 3); Act Of War (Part 4): UK & US 12-inch single; both with Millie Jackson; picture sleeve

1985 Act Of War (Part 5); Act Of War (Part 6): UK 12-inch single; both with Millie Jackson; picture sleeve

1985 Nikita; The Man Who Never Died (Instrumental): UK 7-inch single; picture sleeve

1985 Nikita; The Man Who Never Died (Instrumental); Sorry Seems To Be The Hardest Word (Live); I'm Still Standing (Live): UK double 7-inch single; gatefold sleeve; live at Wembley Stadium, London, 30 June 1984; also limited edition with pop-up sleeve

1985 Nikita; The Man Who Never Died (Instrumental); Sorry Seems To Be The Hardest Word (Live); I'm Still Standing (Live): UK 12-inch single; live at Wembley Stadium, as previous; picture sleeve

1985 Wrap Her Up (with George Michael); The Man Who Never Died (Instrumental): US 7-inch single; picture sleeve

1985 That's What Friends Are For (with Dionne Warwick, Stevie Wonder & Gladys Knight); Dionne Warwick solo – Two Ships Passing In The Night: UK & US 7-inch single; UK edition had picture sleeve

1985 **Dionne & Friends:** That's What Friends Are For; That's What Friends Are For (Instrumental); Dionne Warwick solo – Two Ships Passing In The Night: UK 12-inch single; as previous; picture sleeve

1985 Wrap Her Up (with George Michael); Too Low For Zero (Live): UK 7-inch single; picture sleeve with gift box

1985 Wrap Her Up (with George Michael); Restless (Live): UK 7-inch single; live at Wembley Stadium, London, 30 June 1984; picture sleeve; limited edition with rectangular picture disc; limited edition in folded-paper gift box

1985 Wrap Her Up (with George Michael); Restless (Live); Nikita; The Man Who Never Died: UK double 7-inch single; live at Wembley, as previous; picture sleeve

1985 Wrap Her Up (Extended Remix); Restless (Live); Nikita; Cold As Christmas (In The Middle Of The Year): UK double 12-inch single; live at Wembley, as previous; picture sleeve

1986 Crocodile Rock: US 6-inch single; cardboard record

1986 Nikita; Restless (Live): US 7-inch single; live at Wembley Stadium, London, 30 June 1984; picture sleeve

1986 Cry To Heaven; Candy By The Pound: UK 7-inch single; picture disc

1986 Cry To Heaven; Candy By The Pound; Rock & Roll Medley Live (Whole Lotta Shakin' Going On / I Saw Her Standing There / Twist And Shout); Your Song (Live): UK double 7-inch single, picture sleeve; UK 12-inch single; live at Wembley Stadium, London, 30 June 1984

1986 Heartache All Over The World; Highlander: UK & US 7-inch single, picture sleeve; US 12-in single

1986 Heartache All Over The World; Highlander; I'm Still Standing; Passengers: UK double 7-inch single; picture sleeve

1986 Heartache All Over The World (Mega-mix); Highlander; Heartache All Over The World (7-inch Version): US 12-inch single; picture sleeve

1986 Heartache All Over The World (Mega-mix); Highlander; Heartache All Over The World (Standard Cut): US cassette single

1986 Slow Rivers (with Cliff Richard); Billy And The Kids: UK 7-inch single; picture sleeve; limited edition with picture disc

1986 Slow Rivers (with Cliff Richard); Billy And The Kids; Lord Of The Flies: UK 12-inch single; picture sleeve

1986 Slow Rivers (with Cliff Richard); Nikita; Blue Eyes; I Guess That's Why They Call It The Blues: UK cassette single

1987 Flames Of Paradise (with Jennifer Rush); Jennifer Rush solo – Call My Name: UK & US 7-inch single; UK version had picture sleeve

1987 Flames Of Paradise (Extended Club Mix); Flames Of Paradise (Instrumental Remix) (both with Jennifer Rush; Jennifer Rush solo – Call My Name: US 12-inch single; picture sleeve

1987 Your Song (Live); Don't Let The Sun Go Down On Me (Live): UK 7-inch single; live at Sydney, 14 December 1986; picture sleeve

1987 Your Song (Live); Don't Let The Sun Go Down On Me (Live); The Greatest Discovery (Live); I Need You To Turn To (Live): UK 12-inch single, picture sleeve; cassette single (different running order); live as previous

1987 Candle In The Wind (Live); Sorry Seems To Be The Hardest Word (Live): US 7-inch single; UK edition 1988, picture sleeve; live at Sydney, 14 December 1986; UK limited edition with picture disc; US reissued with yellow & cream sleeves

1988 Mona Lisas And Mad Hatters (Part Two) (Renaissance Mix); Mona Lisas And Mad Hatters (Part Two) (Da Vinci Version); A Word In Spanish; Mona Lisas And Mad Hatters (Part Two) (Self-Portrait Instrumental); Don't Go Breaking My Heart (Album Version) (with Ru Paul): US 12-inch single; picture sleeve

1988 Candle In The Wind (Live); Sorry Seems To Be The Hardest Word (Live); Your Song (Live); Don't Let The Sun Go Down On Me (Live): UK 12-inch, cassette & CD singles; live as above; picture sleeve

1988 Candle In The Wind (Live); I Guess That's Why They Call It The Blues; I'm Still Standing; Nikita: UK PC-enhanced CD single; *Nikita* video

1988 Take Me To The Pilot (Live); Tonight (Live): US 7-inch single; live at Sydney, 14 December 1986; picture sleeve

1988 Don't Go Breaking My Heart; I Got The Music In Me: UK 7-inch single; both with Kiki Dee; picture sleeve

1988 I Don't Wanna Go On With You Like That; Rope Around A Fool: UK & US 7-inch single; US cassette single; picture sleeve

1988 I Don't Wanna Go On With You Like That (The Shep Pettibone Mix); I Don't Wanna Go On With You Like That (Single Version); Rope Around A Fool: UK 12-inch single; picture sleeve

1988 I Don't Wanna Go On With You Like That; Rope Around A Fool; I Don't Wanna Go On With You Like That (The Shep Pettibone Mix): UK CD single; card sleeve

1988 I Don't Wanna Go On With You Like That;

Rope Around A Fool; I Don't Wanna Go On With You Like That (The Shep Pettibone Mix): UK PC-enhanced CD single; *I Don't Wanna Go On With You Like That* video

1988 I Don't Wanna Go On With You Like That; Rope Around A Fool; Interview: UK 7-inch single; Elton interviewed by Simon Bates on BBC Radio One, 17–20 May 1988; picture sleeve; with poster

1988 I Don't Wanna Go On With You Like That (The Shep Pettibone Mix); I Don't Wanna Go On With You Like That (Pub Dub); I Don't Wanna Go On With You Like That (Just Elton And His Piano Mix); I Don't Wanna Go On With You Like That (Just For Radio Mix): US 12-inch single; picture sleeve

1988 I Don't Wanna Go On With You Like That; Rope Around A Fool; I Don't Wanna Go On With You Like That (Extended Mix): US CD single

1988 Town Of Plenty; Whipping Boy: UK 7-inch single; picture sleeve; limited edition with look-back pack and 4 photos

1988 Town Of Plenty; Whipping Boy; Saint: UK 12-inch single; picture sleeve

1988 Town Of Plenty; Whipping Boy; Saint; I Guess That's Why They Call It The Blues: UK & US CD single; card sleeve

1988 A Word In Spanish; Heavy Traffic: UK & US 7-inch single; US cassette single; picture sleeve

1988 A Word In Spanish; Daniel (Live); Song For You / Blue Eyes / I Guess That's Why They Call It The Blues (Live): UK 12-inch single; live at Sydney, 14 December 1986; picture sleeve

1988 A Word In Spanish; Heavy Traffic; Medley (Song For Guy [Instrumental] / Blue Eyes / I Guess That's Why They Call It The Blues); Daniel (Live): UK & US CD single; live at Sydney as previous; card sleeve

1988 Nikita; I'm Still Standing: UK 7-inch single; picture sleeve

1988 Song For Guy (Instrumental); Blue Eyes: UK 7-inch single; picture sleeve

1989 Through The Storm (with Aretha Franklin); Aretha Franklin solo – Come To Me: UK & US 7-inch & cassette single; UK picture disc; US picture sleeve

1989 Through The Storm (with Aretha Franklin); Aretha Franklin solos – Come To Me; Oh Happy Day (with Mavis Staples): UK 12-inch single; picture sleeve; CD in card sleeve

1989 Healing Hands; Dancing In The End Zone: UK & US 7-inch & cassette single; UK edition had picture sleeve

1989 Healing Hands (Extended Version); Healing Hands (Single Version); Dancing In The End Zone: UK 12-inch single; picture sleeve

1989 Healing Hands; Sad Songs (Say So Much) (Live); Dancing In The End Zone: UK & US CD single; live at Verona, Italy, 26 April 1989

1989 Sad Songs (Say So Much) (Live); Dancing In The End Zone; Healing Hands: UK PC-enhanced CD single; live at Verona, as previous; *Healing Hands* video

1989 Sacrifice; Love Is A Cannibal: UK & US 7-inch & cassette single; UK edition had picture sleeve; B-side from *Ghostbusters II* soundtrack

1989 Sacrifice; Love Is A Cannibal; Durban Deep: UK 12-inch single; UK & US CD single; picture sleeve; B-side as above

1989 A Word In Spanish; Heavy Traffic; Medley (Song For Guy [Instrumental] / Blue Eyes / I Guess That's Why They Call It The Blues); Daniel (Live): UK PC-enhanced CD single; *A Word In Spanish* video

1990 Sacrifice; Healing Hands: UK 7-inch & cassette single; picture sleeve

1990 Sacrifice; Healing Hands; Durban Deep: UK 12-inch & CD single; picture sleeve; profits donated to AIDS charities

1990 Club At The End Of The Street; Whispers: UK & US 7-inch single; UK version had picture sleeve

1990 Club At The End Of The Street; Sacrifice: US 7-inch single

1990 Club At The End Of The Street: US cassette single; no B-side

1990 Club At The End Of The Street; Give Peace A Chance: European CD single

1990 Club At The End Of The Street; Whispers; I Don't Wanna Go On With You Like That (Live): UK 12-inch & CD single; picture sleeve

1990 You Gotta Love Someone; Medicine Man: UK 7-inch single; gatefold picture sleeve

1990 You Gotta Love Someone; Sacrifice: UK 7-inch single

1990 You Gotta Love Someone; Medicine Man; Medicine Man (with Adamski): UK 12-inch single; picture sleeve

1990 You Gotta Love Someone: US cassette single; no B-side

1990 You Gotta Love Someone (Edit); Medicine Man; Medicine Man (with Adamski): UK CD single

1990 Easier To Walk Away; I Swear I Heard The Night Talking: UK 7-inch single; picture sleeve

1990 Easier To Walk Away; I Swear I Heard The Night Talking; Made For Me: UK 12-inch & CD single; picture sleeve

1990 **Elton John's Christmas EP:** Step Into Christmas; Cold As Christmas (In The Middle Of The Year); Easier To Walk Away; I Swear I Heard The Night Talking: UK 7-inch EP; picture sleeve

1991 Don't Let The Sun Go Down On Me (with George Michael); Song For Guy (Instrumental): UK & US 7-inch & cassette single; UK edition with picture sleeve

1991 Don't Let The Sun Go Down On Me (with George Michael); Song For Guy (Instrumental); Sorry Seems To Be The Hardest Word: UK 12-inch & CD single; picture sleeve

1991 Don't Let The Sun Go Down On Me (Live) (with George Michael); George Michael solos – I Believe (When I Fall In Love It Will Be Forever) (Live): UK & US 7-inch & cassette single; live at Wembley Arena, London, March 1991

1991 Don't Let The Sun Go Down On Me (with George Michael); George Michael solos – I Believe (When I Fall In Love It Will Be Forever); Last Christmas: UK 12-inch single; picture sleeve with poster

1991 Don't Let The Sun Go Down On Me (Live) (with George Michael); George Michael solos – I Believe (When I Fall In Love It Will Be Forever); If You Were My Woman; Fantasy: UK CD single; live as above

1991 Don't Let The Sun Go Down On Me (Live) (with George Michael); George Michael solos – I Believe (When I Fall In Love It Will Be Forever); Freedom (Back To Reality Mix); If You Were My Woman: US CD single; live as above

1992 Nikita; I'm Still Standing; I Guess That's Why They Call It The Blues: UK CD single

1992 Honky Cat; Harmony: US 7-inch single; limited edition on green vinyl

1992 I Don't Wanna Go On With You Like That; Nobody Wins: US 7-inch single; limited edition on green vinyl

1992 I Guess That's Why They Call It The Blues; Who Wears These Shoes?: US 7-inch single; limited edition on green vinyl

1992 I'm Still Standing; Blue Eyes: US 7-inch single; limited edition on green vinyl

1992 Island Girl; A Word In Spanish: US 7-inch single; limited edition on green vinyl

1992 Mama Can't Buy You Love; Are You Ready For Love: US 7-inch single; limited edition on green vinyl

1992 Rocket Man (I Think It's Going To Be A Long, Long Time); Kiss The Bride: US 7-inch single; limited edition on green vinyl

1992 Sad Songs (Say So Much); Club At The End Of The Street: US 7-inch single; limited edition on green vinyl

1992 Someone Saved My Life Tonight; Sacrifice: US 7-inch single; limited edition on green vinyl

1992 Sorry Seems To Be The Hardest Word; Healing Hands: US 7-inch single; limited edition on green vinyl

1992 The Bitch Is Back; Wrap Her Up: US 7-inch single; limited edition on green vinyl

1992 Your Song; Border Song: US 7-inch single; limited edition on green vinyl

1992 Bennie And The Jets; Saturday Night's Alright For Fighting: US 7-inch single; limited edition on red vinyl

1992 Candle In The Wind; Levon: US 7-inch single; limited edition on red vinyl

1992 Crocodile Rock; Friends: US 7-inch single; limited edition on red vinyl

1992 Daniel; Tiny Dancer: US 7-inch single; limited edition on red vinyl

1992 Don't Go Breaking My Heart (with Kiki Dee); Part-Time Love: US 7-inch single; limited edition on red vinyl

1992 Don't Let The Sun Go Down On Me (with George Michael); I Saw Her Standing There (Live) (with John Lennon): US 7-inch single; limited edition on red vinyl; live at Madison Square Garden, New York, 28 November 1974

1992 Goodbye Yellow Brick Road; Bite Your Lip (Get Up And Dance!): US 7-inch single; limited edition on red vinyl

1992 Little Jeannie; Grow Some Funk Of Your Own: US 7-inch single; limited edition on red vinyl

1992 Lucy In The Sky With Diamonds; Empty Garden (Hey Hey Johnny): US 7-inch single; limited edition on red vinyl

1992 Nikita; Take Me To The Pilot: US 7-inch single; limited edition on red vinyl

1992 Philadelphia Freedom; I Feel Like A Bullet (In The Gun Of Robert Ford): US 7-inch single; limited edition on red vinyl

1992 The One; Suit Of Wolves: UK & US 7-inch & cassette single; UK version had picture sleeve

1992 The One; Suit Of Wolves; Fat Boys And Ugly Girls: UK & US CD single; UK version in digipak sleeve

1992 The One; Your Song; Don't Let The Sun Go Down On Me; Sacrifice: UK CD single

1992 Runaway Train (with Eric Clapton);

Understanding Women: UK & US 7-inch & cassette single; UK version had picture sleeve

1992 Runaway Train (with Eric Clapton); Understanding Women (Extended Remix); Made For Me: UK CD single

1992 Runaway Train (with Eric Clapton); Through The Storm (with Aretha Franklin); Don't Let The Sun Go Down On Me (Live) (with George Michael); Slow Rivers (with Cliff Richard): UK CD single; live at Wembley Arena, London, March 1991; digipak sleeve

1992 Runaway Train (with Eric Clapton); Easier To Walk Away; Understanding Women (Remix): US CD single

1992 The Last Song; The Man Who Never Died (Instrumental, Remix): UK 7-inch single; UK & US cassette single; picture sleeve

1992 The Last Song; The Man Who Never Died (Instrumental, Remix); Song For Guy (Instrumental, Remix): UK & US CD single; double slimline case

1992 The Last Song; Are You Ready For Love; Three-Way Love Affair; Mama Can't Buy You Love: UK CD single

1993 Simple Life: US CD single

1993 Simple Life (Edit); The Last Song: UK 7-inch & cassette single; picture sleeve

1993 Simple Life (Hot Mix); The North: US 7-inch & cassette single

1993 Simple Life; The Last Song; The North: UK CD single

1993 True Love (with Kiki Dee); The Show Must Go On (Live): UK 7-inch single; live at Wembley Stadium, London, June 1992; picture sleeve

1993 True Love (with Kiki Dee); Runaway Train (with Eric Clapton): US 7-inch & cassette single

1993 True Love (with Kiki Dee): US CD single

1993 True Love (with Kiki Dee); The Show Must Go On (Live); Runaway Train (with Eric Clapton): UK CD single; live at Wembley, as above; digipak sleeve

1993 True Love (with Kiki Dee); Wrap Her Up; That's What Friends Are For (with Dionne Warwick and friends); Act Of War (with Millie Jackson): UK CD single

1994 Don't Go Breaking My Heart (with Ru Paul); Donner Pour Donner (with France Gall): UK 7-inch & cassette single; picture sleeve

1994 Don't Go Breaking My Heart; Don't Go Breaking My Heart (Edited 12-inch Remix): US cassette single; both with Ru Paul

1994 Don't Go Breaking My Heart (Remix); Don't Go Breaking My Heart (Don't Go Dubbing My Heart Mix); Don't Go Breaking My Heart (Album Version): US 12-inch & cassette single; picture sleeve

1994 Don't Go Breaking My Heart (with Ru Paul); Donner Pour Donner (with France Gall); A Woman's Needs (with Tammy Wynette): UK CD single

1994 Don't Go Breaking My Heart (Remix); Don't Go Breaking My Heart (MK Mix); Don't Go Breaking My Heart (Serious Rope 12-inch Version); Don't Go Breaking My Heart (Roger's Dub Mix): US CD single; with Ru Paul

1994 Don't Go Breaking My Heart (Moroder 7-inch Mix); Don't Go Breaking My Heart (Moroder 12-inch Mix); Don't Go Breaking My Heart (Serious Rope 7-inch Mix); Don't Go Breaking My Heart (Serious Rope 12-inch Mix); Don't Go Breaking My Heart (Serious Rope Instrumental); Don't Go Breaking My Heart (Serious Rope Dirty Dub): UK CD single; with Ru Paul

1994 Ain't Nothing Like The Real Thing (with Marcella Detroit); Marcella Detroit solo – Break The Chain: UK 7-inch single; picture sleeve

1994 Ain't Nothing Like The Real Thing (with Marcella Detroit); Marcella Detroit solos – Break The Chain; I Feel Free: UK & US CD single

1994 Ain't Nothing Like The Real Thing (Kenny Dope Extended Mix); Ain't Nothing Like The Real Thing (Troopa Mood Mix) (both with Marcella Detroit); Marcella Detroit solos – I Feel Free (Full Cream Mix); I Feel Free (Cry Out Loud Mix): UK CD single; Z-pack jewel case

1994 Can You Feel The Love Tonight?; Can You Feel The Love Tonight? (Instrumental): UK 7-inch & CD single; picture sleeve; CD in card sleeve

1994 Can You Feel The Love Tonight? (both sides): US cassette single

1994 Can You Feel The Love Tonight?; Can You Feel The Love Tonight? (Instrumental); Hakuna Matata (Cast Version); Under The Stars (Instrumental): UK CD single

1994 Circle Of Life; Circle Of Life (Cast Version): UK & US cassette & CD single, card sleeve

1994 Circle Of Life; Circle Of Life (with Carmen Twillie): UK 7-inch single; jukebox

1994 Circle Of Life; Circle Of Life (Cast Version); I Just Can't Wait To Be King (Cast Version); This Land (Instrumental): UK CD single

1995 United We Stand (1995 Remix, with Kay Garner); United We Stand (The Instrumental 1995 Remix); United We Stand (Original Mix, with Kay Garner); Neanderthal Man (Hotlegs): UK CD single

1995 Believe; The One (Live): UK & US 7-inch & cassette single; 7-inch for jukebox only; live at Greek Theater, LA, September 1994; US picture sleeve

1995 Believe; The One (Live); The Last Song (Live): UK CD single; live at Greek Theater, as previous

1995 Believe; The One (Live); Believe (Live): US CD single; live at Greek Theater, as previous

1995 Believe; The One (Live); The Last Song (Live); Sorry Seems To Be The Hardest Word (Live); Believe (Live): US CD single; live at Greek Theater, as previous

1995 Believe; Believe (Live); Sorry Seems To Be The Hardest Word (Live): UK CD single; digipak box

1995 Made In England; Can You Feel The Love Tonight?; Daniel (Live): Australian cassette single; live at Greek Theater, LA, September 1994

1995 Made In England; Made In England (Edited Version): US cassette single

1995 Made In England (Edit); Lucy In The Sky With Diamonds (Live) (with John Lennon): US 7-inch single; live at Madison Square Garden, New York, 28 November 1974

1995 Made In England (Junior's Sound Factory Mix); Made In England (Junior's Factory Dub); Made In England (Junior's Joyous Mix); Believe (Hardkiss Mix): US 12-inch single

1995 Made In England; Can You Feel The Love Tonight?; Your Song (Live); Don't Let The Sun Go Down On Me (Live): UK CD single; live at Madison Square Garden, as above

1995 Made In England; Whatever Gets You Through The Night (Live) (with John Lennon); Lucy In The Sky With Diamonds (Live) (with John Lennon); I Saw Her Standing There (Live) (with John Lennon): UK CD single; live at Madison Square Garden, as previous; digipak sleeve

1995 Made In England (Radio Edit); Made In England (Junior's Sound Factory Mix); Made In England (Junior's Factory Dub); Made In England (Junior's Joyous Mix): US CD single

1995 Made In England (Edit); Whatever Gets You Through The Night (Live) (with John Lennon); Lucy In The Sky With Diamonds (Live) (with John Lennon); I Saw Her Standing There (Live) (with John Lennon); Believe (Hardkiss Mix): US CD single; live at Madison Square Garden, New York, 28 November 1974

1995 **Bruce Roberts featuring Elton John:** When The Money's Gone (Radio Edit); When The Money's Gone (E-Smoove Club Remix Edit): US cassette & CD single

1995 Please; Latitude: US 7-inch & cassette single; UK editions in 1996

1995 Blessed (Edit); Honky Cat (Live); Take Me To The Pilot (Live); The Bitch Is Back (Live): UK & US CD single; live at Royal Festival Hall, London, 18 May 1974

1995 Blessed; Latitude: US 7-inch & cassette single

1996 Please; Honky Cat (Live); Take Me To The Pilot (Live); The Bitch Is Back (Live): UK CD single; live as above

1996 Please; Made In England (Junior's Sound Factory Mix); Made In England (Junior's Joyous Mix): UK CD single

1996 You Can Make History (Young Again); Song For Guy (Instrumental): US cassette single

1996 Live Like Horses; Live Like Horses (Live): UK 7-inch & cassette single; live in Modena, Italy, 20 June 1996; both with Luciano Pavarotti; 7-inch jukebox only

1996 Live Like Horses (with Luciano Pavarotti); Live Like Horses (Live) (with Luciano Pavarotti); Step Into Christmas; Blessed: UK CD single; live in Modena, as previous

1996 Live Like Horses (with Luciano Pavarotti); Live Like Horses (Live) (with Luciano Pavarotti); I Guess That's Why They Call It The Blues (Live); Live Like Horses (Solo): UK CD single; live in Modena, as previous

1997 Candle In The Wind '97; Something About The Way You Look Tonight (Edit): UK & US 7-inch, cassette & CD single; UK 7-inch for jukebox only

1997 Something About The Way You Look Tonight; I Know Why I'm In Love; No Valentines; Something About The Way You Look Tonight (Album Version): Canadian CD single

1997 Something About The Way You Look Tonight; Candle In The Wind '97; You Can Make History (Young Again): Canadian CD single

1998 Recover Your Soul (Single Remix); No Valentines: UK 7-inch single

1998 Recover Your Soul (Single Remix); I Know Why I'm In Love: UK cassette single

1998 Recover Your Soul (Radio Mix); I Know Why I'm In Love: US cassette single

1998 Recover Your Soul (Single Remix); Big Man In A Little Suit; I Know Why I'm In Love; Recover Your Soul (Album Version): UK CD single

1998 Recover Your Soul (Radio Mix); I Know Why I'm In Love; Big Man In A Little Suit: US CD single; card sleeve

1998 Recover Your Soul (Single Remix); No Valentines; Recover Your Soul (Album Version): UK PC-enhanced CD single; with *Recover Your Soul* video & 'Interactive Room'

1998 If The River Can Bend (Edit); Bennie And The Jets: UK cassette single

1998 If The River Can Bend (Edit); Bennie And The Jets; Saturday Night's Alright For Fighting; If The River Can Bend (Album Version): UK CD single

1998 If The River Can Bend (Edit); Don't Let The Sun Go Down On Me (Live); I Guess That's Why They Call It The Blues (Live); Sorry Seems To Be The Hardest Word (Live): UK & European CD single; live in Paris, France, 14 January 1998

1998 If The River Can Bend (Edit); Bennie And The Jets; Saturday Night's Alright For Fighting; Don't Let The Sun Go Down On Me (Live); I Guess That's Why They Call It The Blues (Live); Sorry Seems To Be The Hardest Word (Live): UK CD single

1999 *Sweet Suggestions of the Pink Moon*: When Day Is Done; Saturday Sun; Way to Blue: UK & US cassette & CD single

1999 Written In The Stars; Written In The Stars (Alternate Version): UK cassette single; both with LeAnn Rimes

1999 Written In The Stars (with LeAnn Rimes); Written In The Stars (Alternate) (with LeAnn Rimes); Aida Album Sampler (various); A Step Too Far (with Heather Headley & Sherie Scott): US cassette & CD single; card sleeve

1999 Written In The Stars (with LeAnn Rimes); Written In The Stars (Alternate) (with LeAnn Rimes); Recover Your Soul (Live): UK CD single; live in Paris, France, 14 January 1998

1999 Written In The Stars (with LeAnn Rimes); Aida Album Sampler – My Strongest Suit (The Spice Girls only) / Not Me (Boyz II Men only) / A Step Too Far (with Heather Headley & Sherie Scott); Your Song (Live): UK CD single; live in Paris, as previous

1999 Written In The Stars (with LeAnn Rimes); Your Song (Live); Recover Your Soul (Live); Aida Album Sampler – My Strongest Suit (The Spice Girls only) / Not Me (Boyz II Men only) / A Step Too Far (with Heather Headley & Sherie Scott): European CD single; live in Paris, as previous

1999 Written In The Stars (with LeAnn Rimes); Written In The Stars (Alternate) (with LeAnn Rimes); Aida Album Sampler – My Strongest Suit (The Spice Girls only) / Not Me (Boyz II Men only) / A Step Too Far (with Heather Headley & Sherie Scott): US & Canadian CD single; live in Paris, as previous

1999 Recover Your Soul (Live); Your Song (Live): US bonus CD single; live in Paris, as previous; only with *Aida* CD from Tower Records stores

2000 The Perfect Love / Hey Armadillo: US bonus CD single; only with *The Road To El Dorado* CD from Best Buy stores

2000 Someday Out Of The Blue; Cheldorado (Instrumental): US cassette & CD single

2001 *London Times*: Ballad Of The Boy In The Red Shoes; Snippets Taken from the New Album: *Songs From The West Coast* (I Want Love; Tiny Dancer [Original Studio Version]): US cassette & CD single

2001 I Want Love; North Star (Previously Unreleased); Tiny Dancer (Live); The One (Live): UK & US PC-enhanced CD single; live at Madison Square Garden, New York, October 2000

2001 I Want Love; God Never Came There; The One (Live): UK & US PC-enhanced CD single; live at Madison Square Garden, as previous; *I Want Love* video

2001 I Want Love; North Star; Tiny Dancer (Live): US cassette & CD single

2002 This Train Don't Stop There Anymore; Did Anybody Sleep With Joan Of Arc?; I Want Love (Live from BBC Radio Theatre): UK & US cassette & CD single

2002 This Train Don't Stop There Anymore; Did Anybody Sleep With Joan Of Arc? (Previously Unreleased); I Want Love (Live); Philadelphia Freedom (Live); American Triangle (Live): Australian PC-enhanced CD single; *This Train Don't Stop There Anymore* video

2002 This Train Don't Stop There Anymore; Did Anyone Sleep With Joan Of Arc?; I Want Love (Live); Philadelphia Freedom (Live): UK & US cassette & CD single; live at BBC Radio Theatre, London, 9 September 2001

2002 Original Sin; I'm Still Standing (Live); This

Train Don't Stop There Anymore (Live):
UK & US PC-enhanced CD single; recorded
at BBC Radio Theatre, as previous; *This
Train Don't Stop There Anymore* video
starring Justin Timberlake (N'Sync)

2002 Original Sin; Original Sin (Live); All The
Girls Love Alice (Live): UK & US
PC-enhanced CD single; recorded at BBC
Radio Theatre, as previous; *Original Sin*
video

2002 Your Song; Your Song (Instrumental); UK
PC-enhanced CD single with Alessandro
Safina for BBC charity, Sport Relief; *Your
Song* (video)

2002 Sorry Seems To Be The Hardest Word
(Radio Edit) (with Blue); Lonely This
Christmas; Sorry Seems To Be The Hardest
Word (Ruffin Ready Soul Mix) (with Blue);
Sorry Seems To Be The Hardest Word
(Album Version): UK & US cassette & CD
single

2002 Sorry Seems To Be The Hardest Word
(Radio Edit) (with Blue); Album Ballad
Medley; Sweet Thing: UK & US
PC-enhanced CD single; *Sorry Seems To Be
The Hardest Word* video

ALBUMS: vinyl, cassettes and CDs chronologically

1969 *Empty Sky*: UK LP
Empty Sky; Val-Hala; Western Ford Gateway;
Hymn 2000; Lady, What's Tomorrow?; Sails;
The Scaffold; Skyline Pigeon; Gulliver /
Hay-Chewed (Instrumental)

1970 *Elton John*: UK & US LP & cassette; 1992 US
reissue as digitally remastered cassette & CD
Your Song; I Need You To Turn To; Take Me
To The Pilot; No Shoe Strings On Louise;
First Episode At Hienton; Sixty Years On;
Border Song; The Greatest Discovery; The
Cage; The King Must Die

1970 *Tumbleweed Connection*: UK LP & cassette;
1971 US LP & cassette; 1992 US reissue as
digitally remastered cassette & CD
Ballad Of A Well-Known Gun; Come Down
In Time; Country Comfort; Son Of Your
Father; My Father's Gun; Where To Now,
St Peter?; Love Song (with Leslie Duncan);
Amoreena; Talking Old Soldiers; Burn Down
The Mission

1971 *Friends*: UK & US LP & cassette; from
soundtrack; * not played by Elton

Friends; Honey Roll; Variations On *Friends*
Theme (The First Kiss)*; Seasons; Variations
On Michelle's Song (A Day In The
Country)*; Can I Put You On?; Michelle's
Song; I Meant To Do My Work Today; Four
Moods*; Seasons Reprise

1971 *11-17-70*: UK LP & cassette; recorded for live
radio broadcast, New York, 17 November
1970
Take Me To The Pilot; Honky Tonk Women;
Sixty Years On; Can I Put You On?; Bad Side
Of The Moon; Burn Down The Mission /
My Baby Left Me / Get Back

1971 *11-17-70*: US LP & cassette; tracks as
previous; title uses American dating; 1992 US
reissue as digitally remastered cassette & CD

1971 *Madman Across The Water*: UK & US LP &
cassette; 1992 US reissue as digitally
remastered cassette & CD
Tiny Dancer; Levon; Razor Face; Madman
Across The Water; Indian Sunset; Holiday
Inn; Rotten Peaches; All The Nasties;
Goodbye

1972 *Honky Château*: UK & US LP & cassette;
1992 US reissue as digitally remastered
cassette & CD
Honky Cat; Mellow; I Think I'm Going To
Kill Myself; Susie (Dramas); Rocket Man
(I Think It's Going To Be A Long, Long
Time); Salvation; Slave; Amy; Mona Lisas
And Mad Hatters; Hercules

1973 *Don't Shoot Me, I'm Only The Piano Player*:
UK & US LP & cassette; 1992 US reissue as
digitally remastered cassette & CD
Daniel; Teacher, I Need You; Elderberry
Wine; Blues For Baby And Me; Midnight
Creeper; Have Mercy On The Criminal;
I'm Going To Be A Teenage Idol; Texan Love
Song; Crocodile Rock; High Flying Bird

1973 *Goodbye Yellow Brick Road*: UK & US
double LP & cassette; 1992 US reissue as
digitally remastered cassette & CD
Medley: Funeral For A Friend / Love Lies
Bleeding; Candle In The Wind; Bennie And
The Jets; Goodbye Yellow Brick Road; This
Song Has No Title; Grey Seal; Jamaica Jerk
Off; I've Seen That Movie Too; Sweet Painted
Lady; The Ballad Of Danny Bailey (1909–34);
Dirty Little Girl; All The Girls Love Alice;
Your Sister Can't Twist (But She Can Rock
'N' Roll); Saturday Night's Alright For
Fighting; Roy Rogers; Social Disease;
Harmony

1974 *Caribou*: UK & US LP & cassette; 1992 US
reissue as digitally remastered cassette & CD

The Bitch Is Back; Pinky; Grimsby; Dixie Lily; Solar Prestige A Gammon; You're So Static; I've Seen The Saucers; Stinker; Don't Let The Sun Go Down On Me; Ticking

1974 *Lady Samantha*: UK 8-track & cassette; 1980 UK reissue on LP & CD
Rock 'N' Roll Madonna; Whenever You're Ready (We'll Go Steady Again); Bad Side Of The Moon (B-side Version); Jack Rabbit; Into The Old Man's Shoes; It's Me That You Need; Ho! Ho! Ho! (Who'd Be A Turkey At Christmas?); Skyline Pigeon (1972 Version); Screw You; Just Like Strange Rain; Grey Seal (1970 Version); Honey Roll; Lady Samantha; Friends

1974 *Greatest Hits*: UK & US LP & cassette; US edition replaced 'Candle In The Wind' with 'Bennie And The Jets'; 1992 US reissue as digitally remastered cassette & CD
Your Song; Daniel; Honky Cat; Goodbye Yellow Brick Road; Saturday Night's Alright For Fighting; Rocket Man (I Think It's Going To Be A Long, Long Time); Candle In The Wind; Don't Let The Sun Go Down On Me; Border Song; Crocodile Rock

1975 *Empty Sky*: US LP & cassette; tracks as 1969

1975 *Captain Fantastic And The Brown Dirt Cowboy*: UK & US LP & cassette; UK limited edition on brown vinyl; 1978 UK reissue as picture disc; 1992 US reissue as digitally remastered cassette & CD
Captain Fantastic And The Brown Dirt Cowboy; Tower Of Babel; Bitter Fingers; Tell Me When The Whistle Blows; Someone Saved My Life Tonight; (Gotta Get A) Meal Ticket; Better Off Dead; Writing; We All Fall In Love Sometimes; Curtains

1975 *Rock Of The Westies*: UK & US LP & cassette; 1992 US reissue as digitally remastered cassette & CD
Medley: Yell Help / Wednesday Night / Ugly; Dan Dare (Pilot Of The Future); Island Girl; Grow Some Funk Of Your Own; I Feel Like A Bullet (In The Gun Of Robert Ford); Street Kids; Hard Luck Story; Feed Me; Billy Bones And The White Bird

1976 *Here And There*: UK & US LP & cassette; tracks 1–5 recorded live at Royal Festival Hall, London, 18 May 1974; tracks 6–9 recorded live at Madison Square Garden, New York, 28 November 1974; 1992 US reissue as digitally remastered cassette & CD
Here: Skyline Pigeon; Border Song; Honky Cat; Love Song (with Leslie Duncan); Crocodile Rock. *There*: Medley: Funeral For

A Friend / Love Lies Bleeding; Rocket Man (I Think It's Going To Be A Long, Long Time); Bennie And The Jets; Take Me To The Pilot

1976 *Blue Moves*: UK & US double LP & cassette
Your Starter For…; Tonight; One-Horse Town; Chameleon; Boogie Pilgrim; Cage The Songbird; Crazy Water; Shoulder Holster; Sorry Seems To Be The Hardest Word; Out Of The Blue (Instrumental); Between Seventeen And Twenty; The Wide-Eyed And Laughing; Someone's Final Song; Where's The Shoorah?; If There's A God In Heaven (What's He Waiting For?); Idol; Theme From A Non-Existent TV Series; Bite Your Lip (Get Up And Dance!)

1977 *Greatest Hits Vol. 2*: UK & US LP & cassette; US edition replaced 'Levon' with 'Bennie And The Jets'; some editions also replaced 'Sorry Seems To Be The Hardest Word' and 'Don't Go Breaking My Heart' with 'Tiny Dancer' and 'I Feel Like A Bullet (In The Gun Of Robert Ford)'; 1992 US reissue as digitally remastered cassette & CD
The Bitch Is Back; Lucy In The Sky With Diamonds; Sorry Seems To Be The Hardest Word; Don't Go Breaking My Heart (with Kiki Dee); Someone Saved My Life Tonight; Philadelphia Freedom; Island Girl; Grow Some Funk Of Your Own; Levon; Pinball Wizard

1978 *Candle In The Wind*: UK LP; only available from Marks & Spencer stores on the St Michael label
Skyline Pigeon (1969 Version); Take Me To The Pilot; Burn Down The Mission; Teacher, I Need You; Rocket Man (I Think It's Going To Be A Long, Long Time); Don't Let The Sun Go Down On Me; Elderberry Wine; Bennie And The Jets; Midnight Creeper; Dan Dare (Pilot Of The Future); Someone Saved My Life Tonight; Better Off Dead; Grey Seal (1971 Version); Candle In The Wind

1978 *Elton John Live 17-11-70*: UK reissue of 17-11-70 LP; also issued as *Best Live Rarities Of Elton John*

1978 *London & New York Live!*: UK LP; reissue of *Here And There*

1978 *A Single Man*: UK & US LP & cassette
Shine On Through; Return To Paradise; I Don't Care; Big Dipper; It Ain't Gonna Be Easy; Part-Time Love; Georgia; Shooting Star; Madness; Reverie (Instrumental); Song For Guy (Instrumental)

1979 *Goodbye Yellow Brick Road*: UK reissue on yellow vinyl LP

1979 *The Elton John Live Collection*: double LP in UK only; reissue of *17-11-70* and *Here And There*

1979 *Elton John*: UK five-LP boxed set, plus poster
1. EARLY YEARS: Lady Samantha; Skyline Pigeon; Empty Sky; Border Song; I Need You To Turn To; Sixty Years On; Take Me To The Pilot; Country Comfort; Burn Down The Mission; Where To Now, St Peter?; Levon; Madman Across The Water; Friends
2. ELTON ROCKS: Saturday Night's Alright For Fighting; (Gotta Get A) Meal Ticket; Screw You; Teacher, I Need You; Grow Some Funk Of Your Own; Grey Seal (1973 Version); The Bitch Is Back; Crocodile Rock; The Cage; Elderberry Wine; Whenever You're Ready (We'll Go Steady Again); Street Kids; Midnight Creeper; Pinball Wizard
3. MOODS: I Feel Like A Bullet (In The Gun Of Robert Ford); Mona Lisas And Mad Hatters; High Flying Bird; Tiny Dancer; The Greatest Discovery; Blues For Baby And Me; Harmony; I've Seen That Movie Too; Pinky; It's Me That You Need; Indian Sunset; Sweet Painted Lady; Love Song
4. SINGLES: Your Song; Rocket Man (I Think It's Going To Be A Long, Long Time); Honky Cat; Daniel; Goodbye Yellow Brick Road; Candle In The Wind; Don't Let The Sun Go Down On Me; Lucy In The Sky With Diamonds; Philadelphia Freedom; Someone Saved My Life Tonight; Island Girl; Bennie And The Jets
5. CLASSICS: Funeral For A Friend / Love Lies Bleeding; The Ballad Of Danny Bailey (1909–34); Ticking; Texan Love Song; Captain Fantastic And The Brown Dirt Cowboy; We All Fall In Love Sometimes; Curtains

1979 *Victim Of Love*: UK & US LP
Johnny B. Goode; Warm Love In A Cold World; Born Bad; Thunder In The Night; Spotlight; Street Boogie; Victim Of Love

1980 *21 At 33*: UK & US LP & cassette
Chasing The Crown; Little Jeannie; Sartorial Eloquence; Two Rooms At The End Of The World; White Lady, White Powder; Dear God; Never Gonna Fall In Love Again; Take Me Back; Give Me The Love

1980 *The Very Best Of Elton John*: UK LP
Your Song; Goodbye Yellow Brick Road; Daniel; Song For Guy (Instrumental); Candle In The Wind; Friends; Tiny Dancer; Rocket Man (I Think It's Going To Be A Long, Long Time); Don't Go Breaking My Heart; Sorry Seems To Be The Hardest

Word; Border Song; Someone Saved My Life Tonight; Mona Lisas And Mad Hatters; Harmony; High Flying Bird; Don't Let The Sun Go Down On Me

1980 *Milestones (1970–1980 A Decade Of Gold)*: US LP
Don't Go Breaking My Heart (with Kiki Dee); Island Girl; The Bitch Is Back; Honky Cat; Bennie And The Jets; Someone Saved My Life Tonight; Don't Let The Sun Go Down On Me; Sorry Seems To Be The Hardest Word; Mama Can't Buy You Love; Philadelphia Freedom; Crocodile Rock; Rocket Man (I Think It's Going To Be A Long, Long Time); Daniel; Lucy In The Sky With Diamonds; Your Song; Goodbye Yellow Brick Road

1981 *The Best of Elton John Vol.* 1: US LP & cassette
Border Song; Philadelphia Freedom; Lucy In The Sky With Diamonds; Honky Cat; Daniel; Pinball Wizard; Saturday Night's Alright For Fighting; The Bitch Is Back; Don't Let The Sun Go Down On Me; Bennie And The Jets

1981 *The Best of Elton John Vol.* 2: US LP & cassette
Your Song; Goodbye Yellow Brick Road; Rocket Man (I Think It's Going To Be A Long, Long Time); Candle In The Wind; Crocodile Rock; Someone Saved My Life Tonight; Island Girl; Grow Some Funk Of Your Own; Harmony; Tiny Dancer

1981 *The Fox*: UK & US LP & cassette
Breaking Down Barriers; Heart In The Right Place; Just Like Belgium; Nobody Wins; Fascist Faces; Medley (Carla-Étude/Fanfare/Chloe); Heels Of The Wind; Elton's Song; The Fox (Instrumental)

1981 *The Album*: UK LP & cassette
Pinball Wizard; Burn Down The Mission; Rock 'N' Roll Madonna; Sweet Painted Lady; Harmony; Crocodile Rock; Lucy In The Sky With Diamonds; Sixty Years On; Skyline Pigeon (1972 Version); Country Comfort; Lady Samantha; Goodbye Yellow Brick Road

1982 *Crocodile Rock*: UK LP
Honky Cat; Crocodile Rock; Border Song; Rock 'N' Roll Madonna; Skyline Pigeon; Bennie And The Jets; Candle In The Wind; Son Of Your Father; This Song Has No Title; Take Me To The Pilot; Empty Sky; The Scaffold

1982 *Jump Up*: UK & US LP & cassette
Dear John; Spiteful Child; Ball And Chain; Legal Boys; I Am Your Robot; Blue Eyes;

Empty Garden (Hey Hey Johnny); Princess; Where Have All The Good Times Gone?; All Quiet On The Western Front

1982 *Love Songs* (1982): UK LP & CD
Blue Eyes; Little Jeannie; Sartorial Eloquence; Shine On Through; Chloe; Elton's Song; Tonight; Song For Guy (Instrumental); Sorry Seems To Be The Hardest Word; Princess; Chameleon; Return To Paradise; Never Gonna Fall In Love Again; Strangers; Someone's Final Song; All Quiet On The Western Front

1983 *Elton John*: UK double cassette
CASSETTE 1: Your Song; Elderberry Wine; Friends; Grey Seal (1973 Version); Mona Lisas And Mad Hatters; Take Me To The Pilot; Skyline Pigeon; Daniel; Whenever You're Ready (We'll Go Steady Again); Harmony; I Think I'm Going To Kill Myself; The Greatest Discovery; Blues For Baby And Me; Lady Samantha
CASSETTE 2: Rocket Man (I Think It's Going To Be A Long, Long Time); Teacher, I Need You; Tiny Dancer; The Cage; I'm Going To Be A Teenage Idol; Border Song; Crocodile Rock; The Ballad Of Danny Bailey (1909–34); High Flying Bird; Burn Down The Mission; Love Song; Goodbye Yellow Brick Road

1983 *Too Low For Zero*: UK & US LP & cassette
Cold As Christmas (In The Middle Of The Year); I'm Still Standing; Too Low For Zero; Religion; I Guess That's Why They Call It The Blues; Crystal; Kiss The Bride; Whipping Boy; Saint; One More Arrow

1983 *The New Collection*: UK LP & cassette; recorded live at Madison Square Garden, New York, 28 November 1974
Crocodile Rock; Don't Let The Sun Go Down On Me; Saturday Night's Alright For Fighting; It's Me That You Need; Someone Saved My Life Tonight; Lucy In The Sky With Diamonds; Whatever Gets You Through The Night (Live) (with John Lennon); The Bitch Is Back; High Flying Bird; Elderberry Wine; Candle In The Wind; Your Sister Can't Twist (But She Can Rock 'N' Roll); Daniel

1983 *The New Collection Vol.* 2: UK LP & cassette
Your Song; Bennie And The Jets; Take Me To The Pilot; Island Girl; Rocket Man (I Think It's Going To Be A Long, Long Time); Goodbye Yellow Brick Road; Honky Cat; Philadelphia Freedom; Skyline Pigeon (1972 Version); Roy Rogers; I Think I'm Going To Kill Myself

1984 *The Superior Sound Of Elton John* (1970–75): UK LP & CD; all tracks remixed & digitally remastered
Your Song; Crocodile Rock; Rocket Man (I Think It's Going To Be A Long, Long Time); Daniel; Saturday Night's Alright For Fighting; Funeral For A Friend / Love Lies Bleeding; Goodbye Yellow Brick Road; Don't Let The Sun Go Down On Me; Philadelphia Freedom; Someone Saved My Life Tonight; We All Fall In Love Sometimes; Curtains

1984 *Breaking Hearts*: UK & US LP, cassette & CD
Restless; Slow Down Georgie (She's Poison); Who Wears These Shoes?; Breaking Hearts (Ain't What It Used To Be); Li'l 'Frigerator; Passengers; In Neon; Burning Buildings; Did He Shoot Her?; Sad Songs (Say So Much)

1985 *Ice On Fire*: UK & US LP, cassette & CD; cassette & CD with bonus track 'Act Of War' (with Millie Jackson)
This Town; Cry To Heaven; Soul Glove; Nikita; Too Young; Wrap Her Up; Satellite; Tell Me What The Papers Say; Candy By The Pound; Shoot Down The Moon

1986 *Your Songs*: US LP, cassette & CD
Your Song; Country Comfort; Tiny Dancer; Burn Down The Mission; Friends; Take Me To The Pilot; Candle In The Wind; Elderberry Wine; Razor Face; Harmony

1986 *Leather Jackets*: UK & US LP, cassette & CD
Leather Jackets; Hoop Of Fire; Don't Trust That Woman; Go It Alone; Gypsy Heart; Slow Rivers (with Cliff Richard); Heartache All Over The World; Angeline; Memory Of Love; Paris; I Fall Apart

1987 *Live In Australia (with the Melbourne Symphony Orchestra)*: UK & USA double LP, cassette & CD; recorded at Sydney Entertainment Centre, Australia, 14 December 1986
Sixty Years On; I Need You To Turn To; The Greatest Discovery; Tonight; Sorry Seems To Be The Hardest Word; The King Must Die; Take Me To The Pilot; Tiny Dancer; Have Mercy On The Criminal; Madman Across The Water; Candle In The Wind; Burn Down The Mission; Your Song; Don't Let The Sun Go Down On Me

1987 *Greatest Hits Vol. 3* (1979–1987): US LP, cassette & CD
I Guess That's Why They Call It The Blues; Mama Can't Buy You Love; Little Jeannie; Sad Songs (Say So Much); I'm Still Standing; Empty Garden (Hey Hey Johnny); Heartache All Over The World; Too Low For Zero; Kiss The Bride; Blue Eyes; Nikita; Wrap Her Up

1988 *Reg Strikes Back*: UK & US LP, cassette & CD
Town Of Plenty; A Word In Spanish; Mona
Lisas And Mad Hatters (Part Two); I Don't
Wanna Go On With You Like That; Japanese
Hands; Goodbye Marlon Brando; The
Camera Never Lies; Heavy Traffic; Poor
Cow; Since God Invented Girls

1989 *The Complete Thom Bell Sessions*: UK & US
LP, cassette & CD; recorded autumn 1977,
remixed January 1979
Nice And Slow; Country Love Song; Shine
On Through; Mama Can't Buy You Love;
Are You Ready For Love? (with Philippe
'Soul' Wynne); Three-Way Love Affair

1989 *Sleeping With The Past*: UK & US LP,
cassette & CD
Durban Deep; Healing Hands; Whispers;
Club At The End Of The Street; Sleeping
With The Past; Stone's Throw From Hurtin';
Sacrifice; I Never Knew Her Name; Amazes
Me; Blue Avenue

1989 *The Collection*: UK LP, cassette & CD
Funeral For A Friend / Love Lies Bleeding;
Sweet Painted Lady; Elderberry Wine; Come
Down In Time; I Need You To Turn To;
Border Song; Crocodile Rock; Mona Lisas
And Mad Hatters; The Greatest Discovery;
Country Comfort; Blues For Baby And Me;
Harmony; Teacher, I Need You; Ballad Of A
Well-Known Gun

1990 *To Be Continued ...*: US 4-cassette or 4-CD
boxed set; recorded live in Sydney, Australia,
14 December 1986; 2000 reissued as limited
edition
1. 1965–1972: Come Back Baby (Bluesology);
Lady Samantha; It's Me That You Need; Your
Song (Demo, 1969); Rock 'N' Roll Madonna;
Bad Side Of The Moon; Your Song (1970
Version); Take Me To The Pilot; Border
Song; Sixty Years On; Country Comfort;
Grey Seal (1971 Version); Friends; Levon;
Tiny Dancer; Madman Across The Water;
Honky Cat; Mona Lisas And Mad Hatters
(Part Two)
2. 1972–1974: Rocket Man (I Think It's Going
To Be A Long, Long Time); Daniel;
Crocodile Rock; Bennie And The Jets;
Goodbye Yellow Brick Road; All The Girls
Love Alice; Funeral For A Friend / Love Lies
Bleeding; Whenever You're Ready (We'll Go
Steady Again); Saturday Night's Alright For
Fighting; Jack Rabbit; Harmony; Young
Man's Blues; Step Into Christmas; The Bitch
Is Back; Pinball Wizard; Someone Saved My
Life Tonight

3. 1974–1982: Philadelphia Freedom; One Day
At A Time; Lucy In The Sky With Diamonds;
I Saw Her Standing There (Live) (with John
Lennon); Island Girl; Sorry Seems To Be The
Hardest Word; Don't Go Breaking My Heart;
I Feel Like A Bullet (In The Gun Of Robert
Ford) (Live – London, May 1977); Ego; Song
For Guy (Instrumental); Mama Can't Buy
You Love; Cartier Commercial; Little
Jeannie; Donner Pour Donner (with France
Gall); Fanfare (Instrumental); Chloe; The
Retreat; Blue Eyes
4. 1982–1990: Empty Garden (Hey Hey
Johnny); I Guess That's Why They Call It
The Blues; I'm Still Standing; Sad Songs
(Say So Much); Act Of War (Single Edit)
(with Millie Jackson); Nikita; Candle In
The Wind (Single Edit, Live); Carla-Étude
(Instrumental, Live); Don't Let The Sun Go
Down On Me (Single Edit, Live); I Don't
Wanna Go On With You Like That (12-inch
Shep Pettibone Remix); Give Peace A
Chance; Sacrifice; Made For Me; You Gotta
Love Someone; I Swear I Heard The Night
Talkin'; Easier To Walk Away

1990 *The Very Best Of Elton John*: UK LP, cassette
& CD; CD bonus tracks on Disc 1: Pinball
Wizard; The Bitch Is Back; CD bonus tracks
on Disc 2: I Don't Wanna Go On With You
Like That; Easier To Walk Away
Disc 1: Your Song; Rocket Man (I Think It's
Going To Be A Long, Long Time); Honky
Cat; Crocodile Rock; Daniel; Goodbye
Yellow Brick Road; Saturday Night's Alright
For Fighting; Candle In The Wind (1973
Version); Don't Let The Sun Go Down On
Me; Lucy In The Sky With Diamonds;
Philadelphia Freedom; Someone Saved My
Life Tonight
Disc 2: Don't Go Breaking My Heart (with
Kiki Dee); Bennie And The Jets; Sorry Seems
To Be The Hardest Word; Song For Guy
(Instrumental); Part-Time Love; Blue Eyes;
I Guess That's Why They Call It The Blues;
I'm Still Standing; Kiss The Bride; Sad Songs
(Say So Much); Passengers; Nikita; Sacrifice;
You Gotta Love Someone

1991 *To Be Continued ...*: UK 4-CD set; recorded
live in Sydney, Australia, 14 December 1986
Discs 1–3 As US Edition (see above)
Disc 4. 1982–1990: Empty Garden (Hey Hey
Johnny); I Guess That's Why They Call It
The Blues; I'm Still Standing; Sad Songs (Say
So Much); Act Of War (Single Remix, with
Millie Jackson); Nikita; Candle In The Wind

(Single Edit, Live); Carla-Étude (Instrumental, Live); Don't Let The Sun Go Down On Me (Live); I Don't Wanna Go On With You Like That (12-inch Shep Pettibone Remix); Give Peace A Chance; Sacrifice; Made For Me; Easier To Walk Away; Suit Of Wolves; Understanding Women

1992 *Love Songs* (1992): UK cassette & CD
Are You Ready For Love? (Clive Franks' Single Mix); Little Jeannie; I've Seen That Movie Too; High Flying Bird; Heartache All Over The World; Warm Love In A Cold World; Cry To Heaven; Sorry Seems To Be The Hardest Word; I Need You To Turn To; Harmony; Never Gonna Fall In Love Again; Candle In The Wind (1973 Version); It's Me That You Need; Give Me The Love; We All Fall In Love Sometimes; Curtains

1992 *The One*: UK LP, UK & US cassette & CD
Simple Life; The One; Sweat It Out; Runaway Train (with Eric Clapton); Whitewash County; The North; When A Woman Doesn't Want You; Emily; On Dark Street; Understanding Women; The Last Song

1992 *Greatest Hits 1976–1986*: US cassette & CD
I'm Still Standing; Mama Can't Buy You Love; Sorry Seems To Be The Hardest Word; Little Jeannie; Blue Eyes; Don't Go Breaking My Heart (with Kiki Dee); Empty Garden (Hey Hey Johnny); Kiss The Bride; I Guess That's Why They Call It The Blues; Who Wears These Shoes?; Sad Songs (Say So Much); Wrap Her Up; Nikita

1992 *Greatest Hits Vol. II*: US CD
The Bitch Is Back; Lucy In The Sky With Diamonds; Tiny Dancer; I Feel Like A Bullet (In The Gun Of Robert Ford); Someone Saved My Life Tonight; Philadelphia Freedom; Island Girl; Grow Some Funk Of Your Own; Levon; Pinball Wizard

1992 *Rare Masters*: UK & US 2-cassette or CD boxed set; *Friends* soundtrack is not available on CD elsewhere
DISC 1: I've Been Loving You; Here's To The Next Time; Lady Samantha; All Across The Havens; It's Me That You Need; Just Like Strange Rain; Bad Side Of The Moon; Rock 'N' Roll Madonna; Grey Seal (1970 Version); Friends; Michelle's Song; Seasons; Variations On Michelle's Song (A Day In The Country); Can I Put You On?; Honey Roll; Variation On Friends (Instrumental); I Meant To Do My Work Today (A Day In The Country) (Instrumental); Four Moods (Instrumental); Seasons (Reprise)

DISC 2: Madman Across The Water (1970 Demo); Into The Old Man's Shoes; Rock Me When He's Gone; Slave (Demo); Skyline Pigeon (1972 Version); Jack Rabbit; Whenever You're Ready (We'll Go Steady Again); Let Me Be Your Car (Demo); Screw You (Young Man's Blues); Step Into Christmas; Ho! Ho! Ho! (Who'd Be A Turkey At Christmas?); Sick City; Cold Highway; One Day At A Time; I Saw Her Standing There (Live) (with John Lennon, 28 November 1974); House Of Cards; Planes; Sugar On The Floor

1992 *Song Book*: UK cassette & CD
All Quiet On The Western Front; Tiny Dancer; Where To Now, St Peter?; Ego; Shooting Star; Wrap Her Up; Texan Love Song; Nobody Wins; Empty Garden (Hey Hey Johnny); Lady, What's Tomorrow?; Who Wears These Shoes?; Just Like Belgium; Empty Sky; Crazy Water; Island Girl; Friends

1993 *Duets*: UK & US cassette & CD
Tear Drops (with k.d. lang); When I Think About Love (I Think About You) (with P.M. Dawn); The Power (with Little Richard); Shakey Ground (with Don Henley); True Love (with Kiki Dee); If You Were Me (with Chris Rea); A Woman's Needs (with Tammy Wynette); Don't Let The Sun Go Down On Me (Live, with George Michael, Wembley Stadium, March 1991); Old Friend (with Nik Kershaw); Go On And On (with Gladys Knight); Don't Go Breaking My Heart (with Ru Paul); Ain't Nothing Like The Real Thing (with Marcella Detroit); I'm Your Puppet (with Paul Young); Love Letters (with Bonnie Raitt); Born To Lose (with Leonard Cohen); Duets For One

1994 *Greatest Hits*: reissue on 24-carat gold CD in USA only; all tracks digitally remastered; bonus track Candle In The Wind

1994 *The Lion King*: UK & US cassette & CD; from soundtrack; Elton performs on last three tracks only
Circle Of Life (Cast Version); I Just Can't Wait To Be King (Cast Version); Be Prepared (Cast Version); Hakuna Matata (Cast Version); Can You Feel The Love Tonight? (Cast Version); This Land (Instrumental Cast Version); ...To Die For (Instrumental Cast Version); Under The Stars (Instrumental Cast Version); King Of Pride Rock (Instrumental Cast Version); Circle Of Life; I Just Can't Wait To Be King; Can You Feel The Love Tonight?

1994 *Classic Elton John*: US CD; charity release only from McDonald's restaurants
Take Me To The Pilot; Burn Down The Mission; Friends; Saturday Night's Alright For Fighting; Madman Across The Water (1970 Version); Tiny Dancer; Honky Cat; Crocodile Rock; Mona Lisas And Mad Hatters; Levon

1994 *Reg Dwight's Piano Goes Pop*: UK & US CD; withdrawn; 1995 reissued as *Chartbusters Go Pop* (see below)

1995 *Empty Sky*: UK reissue on cassette & CD; 1996 US edition; all tracks digitally remastered; bonus tracks Lady Samantha; All Across The Havens; It's Me That You Need; Just Like Strange Rain

1995 *Elton John*: UK reissue on cassette & CD; 1996 US edition; all tracks digitally remastered; bonus tracks Bad Side Of The Moon; Grey Seal (1970 Version); Rock 'N' Roll Madonna

1995 *Tumbleweed Connection*: UK reissue on cassette & CD; 1996 US edition; all tracks digitally remastered; bonus tracks Into The Old Man's Shoes; Madman Across The Water (1970 Version)

1995 *17-11-70*: UK reissue on cassette & CD; *11-17-70* 1996 US edition; all tracks digitally remastered; bonus track Amoreena

1995 *Madman Across The Water*: UK reissue on cassette & CD; 1996 US edition; all tracks digitally remastered

1995 *Honky Château*: UK reissue on cassette & CD; 1996 US edition; all tracks digitally remastered; bonus track Slave (First Version)

1995 *Don't Shoot Me, I'm Only The Piano Player*: UK reissue on cassette & CD; 1996 US edition; all tracks digitally remastered; bonus tracks Screw You (Young Man's Blues); Jack Rabbit; Whenever You're Ready (We'll Go Steady Again); Skyline Pigeon (1972 Version)

1995 *Goodbye Yellow Brick Road*: UK reissue on cassette & CD; 1996 US edition; all tracks digitally remastered

1995 *Caribou*: UK reissue on cassette & CD; 1996 US edition; all tracks digitally remastered; bonus tracks Pinball Wizard; Sick City; Cold Highway; Step Into Christmas

1995 *Captain Fantastic And The Brown Dirt Cowboy*: UK reissue on cassette & CD; 1996 US edition; all tracks digitally remastered; bonus tracks Lucy In The Sky With Diamonds; One Day At A Time; Philadelphia Freedom

1995 *Rock Of The Westies*: UK reissue on cassette

& CD; 1996 US edition; all tracks digitally remastered; bonus track Don't Go Breaking My Heart (with Kiki Dee)

1995 *Made In England*: UK & US LP, cassette & CD
Believe; Made In England; House; Cold; Pain; Belfast; Latitude; Please; Man; Lies; Blessed

1995 *Chartbusters Go Pop*: UK CD; cover versions made in early 1970s; Elton sings and/or plays piano in studio bands
Don't Forget To Remember; I Can't Tell The Bottom From The Top; Young Gifted And Black; Signed, Sealed, Delivered (I'm Yours); Natural Sinner; She Sold Me Magic; Cottonfields; Spirit In The Sky; Good Morning Freedom; Travellin' Band; In The Summertime; Yellow River; United We Stand; My Baby Loves Lovin'; Love Of The Common People; Lady D'Arbanville; Snake In The Grass; Up Around The Bend

1995 *Visa Gold Presents Elton John's Gold*: US CD; only by phone order for Visa Gold cardholders
Your Song; Someone Saved My Life Tonight; Philadelphia Freedom; Come Down In Time; Rocket Man (I Think It's Going To Be A Long, Long Time); Honky Cat; I Guess That's Why They Call In The Blues; Sad Songs (Say So Much); Sorry Seems To Be The Hardest Word; I'm Still Standing; The Bitch Is Back; Saturday Night's Alright For Fighting

1995 *Love Songs* (1995): UK LP, cassette & CD; recorded live at Wembley Stadium, London, March 1991
Sacrifice; Candle In The Wind; I Guess That's Why They Call It The Blues; Don't Let The Sun Go Down On Me (Live) (with George Michael); Sorry Seems To Be The Hardest Word; Blue Eyes; Daniel; Nikita; Your Song; The One; Someone Saved My Life Tonight; True Love (with Kiki Dee); Can You Feel The Love Tonight?; Circle Of Life; Blessed; Please; Song For Guy (Instrumental)

1996 *Blue Moves*: UK CD; 1997 US edition; all tracks digitally remastered; four tracks restored (not on original CD release) Cage The Songbird; Shoulder Holster; The Wide-Eyed And Laughing; Out Of The Blue (Instrumental)

1996 *Love Songs* (1996): US cassette & CD; recorded live at Wembley Stadium, London, March 1991; 2001 reissued, all tracks digitally remastered

Can You Feel The Love Tonight?; The One; Sacrifice; Daniel; Someone Saved My Life Tonight; Your Song; Don't Let The Sun Go Down On Me (Live) (with George Michael); Believe; Blue Eyes; Sorry Seems To Be The Hardest Word; Blessed; Candle In The Wind (Live, Sydney, 14 December 1986); You Can Make History (Young Again); No Valentines; Circle Of Life

1997 *The Big Picture*: UK & US cassette & CD
Long Way From Happiness; Live Like Horses (Solo Version); The End Will Come; If The River Can Bend; Love's Got A Lot To Answer For; Something About The Way You Look Tonight; The Big Picture; Recover Your Soul; January; I Can't Steer My Heart Clear Of You; Wicked Dreams

1998 *16 Legendary Covers from 1969–70*: US CD; cover versions; Elton sings and/or plays piano with studio bands
Natural Sinner; United We Stand; Spirit In The Sky; Travellin' Band; I Can't Tell The Bottom From The Top; Good Morning Freedom; Up Around The Bend; She Sold Me Magic; Come And Get It; Love Of The Common People; Signed, Sealed, Delivered; It's All In The Game; Yellow River; My Baby Loves Lovin'; Cottonfields; Lady D'Arbanville

1998 *A Single Man*: UK reissue on CD; 2001 US edition; all tracks digitally remastered; bonus tracks Ego; Flintstone Boy; I Cry At Night; Lovesick; Strangers

1998 *Ice On Fire*: UK reissue on CD; 2001 US edition; all tracks digitally remastered; bonus tracks The Man Who Never Died (Instrumental); Restless (Live, Wembley Stadium, London, 30 June 1984); Sorry Seems To Be The Hardest Word (Live, London, May 1977); I'm Still Standing (Live, Wembley, as above)

1998 *Too Low For Zero*: UK reissue on CD; 2001 US edition; all tracks digitally remastered; bonus tracks Earn While You Learn (Instrumental); Dreamboat (Extended Version); The Retreat

1998 *Live in Australia*: UK reissue on CD; 2001 US edition; all tracks digitally remastered

1998 *Reg Strikes Back*: UK reissue on CD; 2001 US edition; all tracks digitally remastered; bonus tracks Rope Around A Fool (12-inch Shep Pettibone Mix); Rope Around A Fool (Just Elton & His Piano Mix); Mona Lisas and Mad Hatters (Part Two) (Renaissance Mix)

1998 *Sleeping With The Past*: UK reissue on CD; 2001 US edition; all tracks digitally

remastered; bonus tracks Dancing In The End Zone; Love Is A Cannibal

1998 *The One*: UK reissue on CD; 2001 US edition; all tracks digitally remastered; bonus tracks Suit Of Wolves; Fat Girls And Ugly Girls

1999 *Elton John and Tim Rice's Aida*: UK & US cassette & CD; Elton only performs on four tracks
Another Pyramid (Sting); Written In The Stars (Elton with LeAnn Rimes); Easy As Life (Tina Turner); My Strongest Suit (The Spice Girls); I Know The Truth (Elton with Janet Jackson); Not Me (Boyz II Men); Amneris' Letter (Shania Twain); A Step Too Far (Elton with Heather Headley & Sherrie Scott); Like Father, Like Son (Lenny Kravitz); Elaborate Lives (Heather Headley); How I Know You (James Taylor); The Messenger (Elton with Lulu); The Gods Love Nubia (Kelly Price); Enchantment Passing Through (Dru Hill); Orchestral Finale (Instrumental)

1999 *Live At The Ritz*: US CD; recorded live at Ritz Hotel, Paris, 15 January 1998; only from Target stores
Daniel; Don't Let The Sun Go Down On Me; Sorry Seems To Be The Hardest Word; Something About The Way You Look Tonight; Take Me To The Pilot; The Last Song

1999 *The Muse*: US CD; from soundtrack; all instrumental except last two tracks
Driving Home; Driving To Universal; Driving To Jack's; Walk Of Shame; Better Have A Gift; The Wrong Gift; The Aquarium; Are We Laughing?; Take A Walk With Me; What Should I Do?; Back To The Aquarium; Steven Redecorates; To The Guesthouse; The Cookie Factory; Multiple Personality; Sarah Escapes; Back To Paramount; Meet Christine; The Muse; The Muse (Remix by Jermaine Dupri)

2000 *The Road To El Dorado* (soundtrack): UK & US CD; US limited edition, only from Best Buy stores; bonus tracks The Perfect Love; Hey Armadillo
El Dorado; Someday Out Of The Blue; Without Question; Friends Never Say Goodbye; The Trail We Blaze; Sixteenth-Century Man; The Panic In Me; It's Tough To Be A God (with Randy Newman); Trust Me; My Heart Dances; Queen Of Cities; Cheldorado (Instrumental); The Brig (Instrumental); Wonders Of The New World (Instrumental)

2000 *Live at Madison Square Garden*: UK & US
CD; recorded in New York, 15–16 October
1999; only from Elton's official website as
part of membership deal
Your Song; Skyline Pigeon; The Greatest
Discovery; Harmony; Honky Cat; Rocket
Man (I Think It's Going To Be A Long, Long
Time); Philadelphia Freedom; Elton's Song;
Sweet Painted Lady; Ticking; Empty Garden
(Hey Hey Johnny); Crocodile Rock

2000 *One Night Only*: US cassette & CD; recorded
at Madison Square Garden, New York,
20–21 October 2000
Goodbye Yellow Brick Road; Philadelphia
Freedom; Don't Go Breaking My Heart (with
Kiki Dee); Rocket Man (I Think It's Going
To Be A Long, Long Time); Daniel;
Crocodile Rock; Sacrifice; Can You Feel The
Love Tonight?; Bennie And The Jets; Your
Song (with Ronan Keating); Sad Songs (Say
So Much) (with Bryan Adams); Candle In
The Wind; The Bitch Is Back; Saturday
Night's Alright For Fighting (with
Anastacia); I'm Still Standing; Don't Let The
Sun Go Down On Me; I Guess That's Why
They Call It The Blues (with Mary J. Blige)

2001 *First Visit 1971*: US CD
It's Me That You Need; Your Song; Rock Me
When He's Gone; Come Down In Time;
Skyline Pigeon; Rotten Peaches; Indian
Sunset; Ballad Of A Well-Known Gun;
Friends; The King Must Die; Holiday Inn;
Can I Put You On?; Country Comfort;
Honky Tonk Women; Border Song; Madman
Across The Water; Amoreena; Take Me To
The Pilot; My Baby Left Me; Whole Lotta
Shakin' Going On

2001 *Prologue*: US CD
Saturday Sun; Sweet Honesty; Stormbringer;
Way To Blue; Go Out And Get It; Day Is
Done; Time Has Told Me; You Get Brighter;
This Moment; I Don't Mind; Pied Pauper

2001 *The Superior Sound of Elton John 1970–75*:
US CD
Broken Bones; I Hate Tourists; Warped
Confessional; Refrigerator Heaven; Suicidal;
Guilty Face; Lexicon Devil; We're Not The
Abnormal Ones; I'm Too Good For Me;
Nothing Left; False Messiah; Halloween
Night; We Make Sanity; Idiots At Happy
Hour; Now Or Never; Die For Life; No One's
Ever Coming Home; Killing Me; Touched;
Violent Arrest; Sacrifice Not Suicide; It's Only
Alcohol; Loading Zone; Downtime; Trouble
If You Hide; Voices From My Window;

Timebomb; This Is Boston, Not LA;
American Town; Don't Forget Me Tommy

2001 *Live at Madison Square Garden Vol. 2*: UK &
US CD; recorded in New York, 15–16 October
1999; only from Elton's official website as
part of Year Two membership deal
Border Song; Tiny Dancer; Better Off Dead;
I Guess That's Why They Call It The Blues;
Carla-Étude (Instrumental); Tonight; Burn
Down The Mission; The One; Levon; Don't
Let The Sun Go Down On Me; Bennie And
The Jets

2001 *Songs From The West Coast*: UK & US
cassette & CD
The Emperor's New Clothes; Dark
Diamond; Look Ma, No Hands; American
Triangle; Original Sin; Birds; I Want Love;
The Wasteland; Ballad Of The Boy In The
Red Shoes; Love Her Like Me; Mansfield;
This Train Don't Stop There Anymore

2002 *Chartbusters Go Pop*: US CD
My Baby Loves Lovin'; Cottonfields; Lady
D'Arbanville; Natural Sinner; United We
Stand; Spirit In The Sky; Travellin' Band;
I Can't Tell The Bottom From The Top;
Good Morning Freedom; Young, Gifted And
Black; In The Summertime; Up Around The
Bend; She Sold Me Magic; Come And Get It;
Love Of The Common People; Signed,
Sealed, Delivered; Yellow River

2002 *Songs From The West Coast*: UK & US
double CD; limited edition; DISC 1 as above
DISC 2 (PC-enhanced): Your Song (with
Alessandro Safina); Teardrops (with Lulu);
Northstar (with Lulu); Original Sin (Junior's
Earth Mix); *I Want Love* video; *This Train
Don't Stop There Anymore* video; *Your Song*
video (with Alessandro Safina)

2002 *Live at the Ritz*: UK & US CD
Daniel; Don't Let The Sun Go Down On
Me; Sorry Seems To Be The Hardest Word;
Something About The Way You Look
Tonight; Take Me To The Pilot; Last Song

2002 *Elton John's Greatest Hits 1970–2002*: UK
CD boxed set
DISC 1: Your Song; Tiny Dancer; Honky
Cat; Rocket Man; Crocodile Rock; Daniel;
Saturday Night's Alright For Fighting;
Goodbye Yellow Brick Road; Candle In The
Wind; Bennie And The Jets; Don't Let The
Sun Go Down On Me; The Bitch Is Back;
Philadelphia Freedom; Someone Saved My
Life Tonight; Island Girl; Don't Go Breaking
My Heart (with Kiki Dee); Sorry Seems To
Be The Hardest Word

DISC 2: Blue Eyes; I'm Still Standing; I Guess That's Why They Call it the Blues; Sad Songs (Say So Much); Nikita; Sacrifice; The One; Kiss The Bride; Can You Feel The Love Tonight?; Circle of Life; Believe; Made In England; Something About the Way You Look Tonight; Written In The Stars (with LeAnn Rimes); I Want Love; This Train Don't Stop There Anymore; Song For Guy LIMITED EDITION BONUS CD: Levon; Border Song; Lucy In The Sky With Diamonds; Pinball Wizard; True Love (with Kiki Dee); Live Like Horses (with Luciano Pavarotti); I Don't Wanna Go On With You Like That; Don't Let The Sun Go Down On Me (with George Michael); Your Song (with Alessandro Safina)

2002 *Elton John's Greatest Hits 1970–2002*: US CD boxed set

DISC 1: as UK except 'Levon' is inserted before 'Tiny Dancer' and 'Don't Go Breaking My Heart' is omitted.
DISC 2: Don't Go Breaking My Heart (with Kiki Dee); Little Jeannie; I'm Still Standing; I Guess That's Why They Call It The Blues; Sad Songs (Say So Much); I Don't Wanna Go On With You Like That; Nikita; Sacrifice; The One; Can You Feel the Love Tonight?; Circle of Life; Believe; Blessed; Something About The Way You Look Tonight; Written In The Stars (with LeAnn Rimes); I Want Love; This Train Don't Stop There Anymore LIMITED EDITION BONUS CD: Candle In The Wind (Live); Don't Let The Sun Go Down On Me (with George Michael); Live Like Horses (with Luciano Pavarotti); Your Song (with Alessandro Safina)

Index